BC 37091

ETHICS, MORALITY AND INTERNATIONAL AFFAIRS

Willard D. Keim

University Press of America, ® Inc.
Lanham • New York • Oxford

Copyright © 2000 by
University Press of America,® Inc.
4720 Boston Way
Lanham, Maryland 20706

12 Hid's Copse Rd.
Cumnor Hill, Oxford OX2 9JJ

All rights reserved
Printed in the United States of America
British Library Cataloging in Publication Information Available

Library of Congress Cataloging-in-Publication Data

Keim, Willard D.
Ethics, morality, and international affairs / Willard D. Keim.
p. cm.
Includes bibliographical references.
1. Ethics. 2. World politics—Moral and ethical aspects. 3. Political ethics.
I. Title.
BJ55 .K45 2000   172'4—dc21   00-028663 CIP

ISBN 0-7618-1683-6 (cloth: alk. ppr.)

∞™ The paper used in this publication meets the minimum
requirements of American National Standard for Information
Sciences—Permanence of Paper for Printed Library Materials,
ANSI Z39.48—1984

Contents

Preface

Introduction

Chapter 1	Consciousness and Being Out-There	1
Chapter 2	Is There An Ultimate Purpose?	17
Chapter 3	Authenticity and Responsibility	39
Chapter 4	Facticity and Bad Faith	59
Chapter 5	Others	79
Chapter 6	The Problem of Morality: Why Ought We To Be Moral? Part I. Reasons for Adopting a Moral Stance	103
Chapter 7	The Problem of Morality: Why Ought We To Be Moral? Definitions and Distinctions Part II. Alternative Ethical Views	123
Chapter 8	The Political Situation	149
Chapter 9	Projects and Practice	179

Chapter 10	The Nation Part I. A Core of Values	199
Chapter 11	The Nation Part II. Nationalism and the Moral Community	221
Chapter 12	Implicating Others Unawares	247
Chapter 13	History	277
Chapter 14	The Diplomatic Role	291
Chapter 15	Pursuing the National Interest Part I. Security	315
Chapter 16	Pursuing the National Interest Part II. Interests Beyond Security	327
Chapter 17	A Commentary on Iraq	349
Appendix	Notes on Free Will	367

Preface

Willard D. Keim was born in Fairbury, Nebraska, on December 16, 1932. He received his baccalaureate degree from Northwestern University, and his M.A. and Ph.D. from the University of Hawaii at Manoa, the latter in 1969. His first teaching position was at the University of Pennsylvania and in 1976 he became a member of the Department of Political Science at the University of Hawaii at Hilo, where he taught until his untimely death in October, 1992. Those are the cold facts, but allow me to add some warmth to them.

Will and I were teaching assistants in political science in the mid-60s at the University of Hawaii at Manoa, where he had an East-West Center scholarship. There were only five of us, so we got to know each other rather well until I headed off to Northwestern, Will's alma mater, to work on my doctorate. After receiving our Ph.D.s Will taught in Pennsylvania and I in California. I left there in 1974 to take a position at the University of Hawaii at Hilo, and two years later Will applied for a position here as well. I was glad to see Will's application, as was my senior colleague, James Wang, who had known Will at the East-West Center. Shortly thereafter, Will was a member of the department.

Because our department was small, we each taught a variety of courses. Will's forte was political ideology and international relations, and although his previous published work dealt with Korea, he became intrigued with the relationship between political ethics and international affairs, and started a manuscript on the subject not long after returning to Hawaii. While he was writing, he was inspiring thousands of students in his classes. His love for the subjects he taught was quite evident to his students, and it was infectious. He always had groupies hanging around his office, discussing, debating, and just enjoying his company. But in the evenings he worked on his manuscript. He completed that manuscript in early 1992, shortly after he was diagnosed with a serious disease. He died a few months later. The manuscript existed only on floppy disks - it had never been edited nor printed in its entirety. His widow, Chiem, wanted his manuscript to be published, not only as a memorial to Will but as a way of making his wisdom available to those who never had the luck to meet him. Ann Usagawa labored for three years editing the manuscript while at the same time raising a family and finishing her college degree. It is because of Chiem and Ann that you are able to read the words of Will Keim.

This book was a labor of love: love for his students, his wife and two sons, and of scholarship. It took many years to write, and you will understand why as you read it. Although the international arena has changed considerably since he first started writing, and even since he completed his manuscript, the book is timeless because it deals with some very fundamental, but complex, issues. I hope you enjoy reading it as much as Will enjoyed writing it.

A. Didrick Castberg
University of Hawai`i at Hilo

Introduction

This is a book on international relations political theory which contends with the complex issue of the relation between morality and international politics. International politics is frequently regarded as a sphere of activity in which moral rules do not apply. The international realm is typically characterized as "anarchical" because no overriding authority exists to regulate the relations between states. In the absence of a central government to enforce global laws, states, it is supposed, are driven to pursue their own security and interests. One of the core principles of "realism," the dominant framework for understanding international relations, is that states must do what accords with their national interest and not be restrained by moral considerations.

In contrast to the dominant realist position, Willard Keim holds that moral principles can be applied in international relations. But his consideration of how morality applies to international politics does not neglect the insights and concerns of realism. It is understood that the international system is a complex and morally imperfect realm in which a number of projects are pursued and in which the results of pure intentions can be disastrous. Like the realists, Keim encourages consideration of consequences and a keen awareness of the conditions in which action is undertaken. He also upholds the idea that national security is the chief project of states which must be pursued even if this requires moral compromises. If we exhort strict adherence to moral lduties, Keim observes, we treat the world as if it were morally perfect and failure inevitably follows from such a formula. The position taken in this book is that morality is intended to apply to imperfect situations. "The moral problem," as Keim astutely observes "is to relate oneself morally to the imperfect world, in which compromises may be necessary, where duties really do clash with other duties" (ch. 7). "A morality too good for the world is an ineffective morality" (ch. 17).

The first part of the book delineates moral principles. The exposition takes as its starting point the existentialist philosophical view which focuses on the free human agent acting in the world and endeavoring to realize projects. Keim makes use of Jean-Paul Sartre's distinction, drawn from Hegel, of being-in-itself and being-for-itself. (Though he makes use of some of Sartre's philosophical categories and insights, Keim parts with Sartre on many of his political conclusions.) Being-in-itself represents the inert, unconscious matter of existence including completed human projects. Being-for-itself is consciousness; it is the agency which is both conscious of factual being and reflectively conscious of itself. This for-itself arises from and is supported by the in-itself, but is distinct from being in-itself. The for-itself is the origin and locus of freedom. Human beings as the for-itself direct themselves to actively creating and transforming the raw material of existence and implementing their projects in the world.

Keim, following Heidegger, conceives that human beings are "thrown" into this world. We unaccountably emerge into a world constituted by an arbitrary set of circumstances. The world, as we confront it, presents us with limiting conditions but contains no inherent ends which we are compelled to pursue. That is, although there are concrete obstacles to the realization of human plans, the choice of goals is not constrained by moral ends which are, as it were, sewn into the fabric of existence or engraved in heaven. Keim demonstrates that the idea that moral aims can be derived from nature or a transcendental, ultimate purpose is implausible. Human beings are absolutely free to select projects and ideals. Still our activities in the world can be guided by a couple of important considerations. As conscious for-selves, human beings are upsurges from the in-itself and constantly struggle against the inertia of the in-itself. In as much as we are engaged in this perpetual activity of self-creation and, more basically, are living things that strive to preserve our lives, we can be guided by aim of affirming existence. This affirmation of existence directs us to choosing goals which are life enhancing.

We can also be guided by what Keim refers to as "lucidity" which represents a clear appreciation of the human situation. Lucidity requires that we be acutely aware of our freedom to choose projects, make every effort to assess the situations in which we attempt to realize our projects, and to take full responsibility for the choices that we make. Lucidity also obliges us to recognize other human beings as independent sources of consciousness pursuing their own projects and take them into account. A lucid apprehension of the fact that other human beings are also for-themselves requires that we avoid treating others as objects or being-in-itself. This consideration of other human beings as fellow conscious persons capable of free projects is morality in Keim's view. Morality represents the "general principle of regard for the freedom of others" (ch. 6).

Keim makes a useful distinction between ethics and morality. Ethics is the larger category which refers to the broad range of ends and purposes pursued by human beings (see ch. 8). Ethics refers to the variety of goods we seek and these goods are necessarily different for different individuals and communities. Morality does not refer to the goals we pursue but is connected with the lucid manner in which we pursue these projects. We pursue our goals with a cognizance that other free beings are also pursuing their goals. In contrast the variegated possible ethical projects which one might choose, which are not universalizeable; morality is universally applicable. We can, and lucidity requires that we do, take others significantly into account while projecting our will into the world. This attitude does not require that we love humankind; it simply obliges us to recognize the freedom of other human beings. This "due recognition of others as independent origins of consciousness" is what has been understood as justice (chapter 10).

Morality is intrinsically connected with politics. Politics involves pursuing projects with others and thus taking these others significantly into account. When our ethical projects coincide and cohere with those of other human beings to a significant extent, we form a political community. Keim agrees with the social contract theorists that a human political community, in the first instance, rests on a tacit agreement by a group of people to establish a political authority. This political authority is established to maintain law and order and thus provide the mutual restraint necessary to prevent one person's free activity from impinging too egregiously on another's. But Keim also shares the view of more communitarian theorists that this rational, self-interested agreement to provide for mutual security is not sufficient to create a political or national community. Some perception of shared values–or a meeting of hearts and minds–among individuals is requisite for creating and maintaining a political community.

A full cognizance of our freedom to choose, however, precludes us from being totally immersed in the shared value structure of the community or blindly adhering to its norms. A thoughtless conformity with prevailing ethical codes is the essence of what Keim, following Sartre, refers to as "bad faith." Lucidity requires that we assess, question and challenge the dominant values of our community. Consciousness, Keim maintains, has its source in the individual and is not a characteristic of abstract entities such as nations. Insofar as ethical goals are individual and as long as individuals are authentically aware of their freedom to choose goals, there will be a (salutary) tendency for the individual to pull against, challenge or rise above the shared ethical goals of the community. Politics, though connected with some coherence of projects, also necessarily involves the conflict and the clash of competing projects.

Human beings are free agents who seek to realize their ends. It is through power that human beings endeavor to implement their aims in the world. Power enables us to make our way in the world and reach our goals. But our endeavors to exercise power and achieve our individual projects clash with other free persons pursuing their own projects. Political society is the arena for the manifestation of competing projects and the struggle for power. This persistent struggle and conflict is inevitable in Keim's view since human beings, as for-itself, consistently strive to realize ideals and create meaning in their struggle against the inertia of brute existence. Keim opposes the view that some future condition of material abundance will eliminate conflict. "Human society will most likely always be defined by scarcity, whether of tangible or intangible goods, and conflicts among ethical projects" (ch. 10).

Keim's philosophical excursion arrives at liberal democracy as the political form best suited to maximize the free pursuit of individual projects and balance the centripetal and centrifugal forces in human societies. The choice for a moderate democratic society is enjoined by lucidity or the cognizance that the individual human beings composing the political community are loci of consciousness who must be taken importantly into account. In less abstruse language, lucidity induces the choice for liberal democracy because this form of political organization is based on the recognition of the fundamental freedom and equality of human beings. The idea that each individual ought to enjoy the maximum exercise of freedom consistent with the same opportunity afforded to others is the basic premise of liberal democracy. In this connection, liberal democracy, with varying degrees of success, seeks to maximize the opportunity for citizens to freely pursue their interests and goals. In effect, liberal democracies institutionalize the regard for persons as free agents.

The jurisdiction which currently encompasses our common life and shared goals is the nation. The nation derives from individual human wills coming together through the "social contract" and coalescing around shared values. There is no social contract, however, between nations. The nation, again, is an abstract entity with no will of its own; it is a creation of individuals in whom will and consciousness reside. The nation then cannot act as an agent and enter into a social contract or agreement with other nations; social contracts can only be formed by individual consciousnesses. Consequently, it is meaningless to conceive of or hope for a global social contract between nations. It is conceivable that *individuals* will at some future time enter into a social contract binding on all human kind and create a global political community, but this is not the case at present. The international system, as we currently experience it is, indeed, an anarchical system composed of a great number of separate national jurisdictions all competing with one another on the global stage. Though there are some customs and treaties which regulate relations between states, there is no final authority to arbitrate disputes.

One of the shared interests of members of a national community is the survival of that particular community within the context of this anarchical global system. The diplomat or political leader is entrusted with the well-being of the nation by fellow citizens and, in conformity with the norm of taking others into account, is expected to discharge this duty by striving to advance the security interests of the nation. Indeed, it must be the first priority of national policy makers to secure the existence of the nation. But what about the human beings in other nations who must be taken into account? How do we balance the goal of national survival and the moral requirement of duly regarding the life and liberty of other human beings? This is the thorny moral problem which Keim trenchantly contends with in the last part of the book.

Keim shares the realist view that national security is necessarily the state's priority and that securing this goal involves one in inevitable moral paradoxes. While acting in the international realm, individuals who are authorized to act on the nation's behalf must consider the consequences to the nation and the broader ramifications of a course of action. Lucidity requires that policy makers be fully cognizant of the nature of the international system and the possible outcomes of activities in that realm. Very often it is clear that rigorous adherence to the principle of taking others into account will result in calamitous consequences for the nation or for peoples in other nations. Consequently, resolute conformity to moral principle must be suspended to avoid disastrous consequences and protect the security interests of one's own nation. But, unlike the realists, Keim does not think that, because morality must be held in abeyance in certain circumstances, morality is irrelevant or inapplicable in the realm if international affairs. His position is that, while morality cannot always be rigorously adhered to, it must be kept in view. Keim details a number of ways that this delicate weighing of ideals and reality might be accomplished and interweaves his discussion with concrete historical examples. His exposition is intricate and rich and I can only offer a few indications of some of his general points.

It has been established that basic national security and well-being are the first priorities of the representatives of a nation in international politics. We have also seen that the project of securing the nation's interests often requires sacrificing the moral principle of taking others significantly into account. But the way the national interest is defined and pursued is shaped by the constant acknowledgment of the validity (if not practicability) of honoring moral principle. According to Keim, keeping morality in view would restrain policy makers from pursuing the national interest in an unbounded or excessive manner. Since the international system is anarchical, there is a particular tendency for unbounded self-aggrandizement and grandiose designs to make an appearance in this realm. Lacking the restraints of a central political authority, the international system arouses the urge to exercise the will to power to the greatest possible extent. Consideration of the humanity of peoples in other nations curbs the tendency to unnecessary state expansion and focuses policy makers on the nation's genuine interests "defined as interests conducive to mutual pursuits enhancing existence" (ch. 15). The acknowledgment of other persons as equal presences in this world induces us to forego and disavow "glory" as a goal of our states and restricts our activities to maintaining basic security interests.

The anarchy of the international system not only calls forth the passions of megalomaniacs and territorial aggrandizers, but also summons the will to dominate on the part of those who wish to do good to others (whether the others want this good done to them or not). The will to bring about good in the world is especially aroused in response to violations of human rights. In conformity with the idea that all human beings are due equal regard, it is right to decry the atrocities committed against our fellow beings. But as has been indicated previously, moral actions must be weighed by their possible consequences and sometimes a policy of actively forcing conformity to morality leads to unexpected and unfavorable outcomes. A lucid understanding of the possible results of attempting to actively change the world restrains ideological zeal. Still, we need not abandon all moral concerns. Keeping morality in view induces us to recognize and denounce moral outrages where they occur. A country should take a stand on human rights and confront violations of human rights as "witnesses" to the truth. Witnessing is not the same as intervention or belligerent posturing. Witnessing affords moral regard to persons while recognizing the limitations to imposing our will. Lucidity obliges us to be a mirror to others and confront the others with a reflection of their own activities. It is bad faith to retreat into voluntary ignorance and disregard the fates of our fellow beings, though our power to change their fate may be limited.

Keim points to a number of specific incidents and policies which elucidate the points he makes about the relationship between morality and international affairs. He concludes with an illuminating chapter on Iraq and the Persian Gulf war which shows how the various aspects of the view developed in this book play out in a particular historical engagement.

This book is couched in the language and categories of existentialism, a philosophical view which currently is out of intellectual vogue. It would be a great loss if the prevailing slavishness to intellectual fashion influenced potential readers to forego the opportunity to engage with what is a perceptive, richly textured and highly relevant consideration of domestic and international politics. Among the many valuable aspects of this book is the philosophical defense of liberal democracy which the author provides in the course of developing his view of international politics. The debate between liberalism and its critics is as lively and acrimonious as ever. The philosophical grounding for liberal democracy which Keim offers represents a significant contribution to this on-going dialogue. Keim provides a compelling restatement of liberalism which will challenge and profit both the opponents and proponents of liberalism.

Keim offers a penetrating analysis of the fundamental and complex issue of morality and international politics and proves to be a sensible and astute guide to the messy realm of contemporary international relations. He enjoins the integrity to face the world in all of its intractable reality and imperfection, while showing how we might simultaneously keep the moral heights in view. This is a rare and admirable achievement.

Regina F. Titunik
University of Hawai`i at Hilo
January 2000

Chapter 1

Consciousness and Being Out-There

It will be the purpose of this book to propose moral principles related to the international behavior of nations. To do this, morality and ethical principles must be given a source or foundation, and the first chapters of the book will attempt to provide this. Some foundation is necessary so that principles are not plucked out of nowhere, willy-nilly, and haphazardly applied to international events. The purpose of these first chapters, therefore, will be to present a reasonable case in support of certain ethical and moral considerations that might apply to decisions made in the arena of international interaction. The ultimate question, of course, is whether morality ought to play any role at all in international affairs.

Morality is a topic that relates in the first instance to the behavior of individual people. Thus, in the early part of this presentation, principles will be derived that apply to the individual. Since individuals comprise societies, the moral principles will be applied to the relationships of people to their society, and to societies in their relation to other societies. Generally, this means the relationships among nations.

It ought to be mentioned at the outset, and it will be elaborated in a later chapter, that ethics can be taken to be a broad concept embracing two subcategories: one of these are values or goals, which are set out as the ends of individual existence; the second subcategory is morality, or relations with others. Such a division will make future discussions much more straightforward than they might otherwise be. It will be contended, for example, that goals or values are not necessarily intended to be universally accepted, while morality may regarded as universally applicable. For the time being, ethics will be used as a term that embraces morality.

At the beginning, it must be regarded as moot whether or not moral principles related to individuals can play an appropriate role when the problems of nations are at issue. It is also open to question whether ethics ought to play *any* role at the level of nation-to-nation interaction. Both Machiavelli (in *The Prince*) and Hobbes disassociate their political strictures from morals and theology. It seems, indeed, to be Machiavelli's tacit assumption that politics may be better off, or more effective, without morality, although he certainly proposes a political ethics: Machiavelli's Prince pursues very clear goals.

This question ought not to be prejudged, but the possibility that morality may not be appropriate, for whatever reason, at the level of the nation will be left open. There is always the possibility that an ethical approach to international affairs may lead to consequences that are undesirable. And it is also possible that some moral principles that are appropriate at the individual level of interaction might survive at the international level, or that entirely new principles may exist at that level underivable from the principles that provide an ethical and moral plan for individual action. Such conclusions at this stage will be held to be problematic.

However, there ought to be something of a *prima facie* assumption that a morality must apply to whatever roles people might be expected to assume in the normal course of their lives, including the roles of diplomat and decisionmaker in the international arena. If it does not, then perhaps the morality is inadequate or the roles themselves could be inherently immoral. In any case, any morality inappropriate to the roles people reasonably may be expected to play in the interactions of life is an inadequate or incomplete one at best.

On laying the foundation for an ethical system, some crucial and plausible choices must be made that make this endeavor somewhat unique. Other ethical systems might arise from different assumptions, just as other geometries will arise from altered axioms. Yet, one must approach ethical problems with some well-thought-out structure or other, with the possibility in mind that the result may not be too far removed from alternative structures that might rest on different basic assumptions.

Thus, there are a number of possibilities open to anyone who may disagree with the original basis for the ethical system that will be developed here: one might accept some of the ethical propositions as themselves valid, although they may be thought to be derivable from an alternative basis. Or it is conceivable that the reader might find some of these ethical principles unsupportable, but find the reasoning concerning the consequences of their application enlightening.

This chapter will concern an interpretation of how the human consciousness resides within its environment. The nature of that consciousness will be discussed. Oddly enough, it is at this basic level where politics really begin, as thinkers like Plato and Hobbes were well aware. This presentation on the nature of human consciousness will lead to conclusions regarding free will, which would appear to be necessary if the questions asked in this book are to have any significance. If history were predestined toward an end over which humans had no control, there would be no problems for moral choice. With these few reservations stated, the first questions that appear on the Long March toward moral applications in international relations must be how humans fit into the world. Anyone essaying the problems of ethics must decide which philosophies elucidate most clearly the world that we seem to experience.

Existentialism, resting on a basis of phenomenology (much of the methodology of which will not be incorporated here), has a number of recommendations. It calls us back to the human agent; biography is important for it, and it exemplifies the humanness of history.[1] In its treatment of a number of themes, the existentialist position more than some other philosophies strikes one as apt and on the mark. Whereas existentialism seems to focus on human situations that appear realistic, the expositions of some other philosophical approaches may appear formalistic and inapplicable by comparison; some comparisons among systems will be made later.

Some critics will aver that no morality can be generated from an existentialist basis, and this position is held despite the fact that the existentialist standpoint as adopted in the fictional work, for instance, of Jean-Paul Sartre or Albert Camus is strikingly concerned with ethical problems of value and morality. This is no facile criticism, however, for while existentialism may generate a myriad value systems and moralities, it may not, because of the nature of the existentialist philosophy, generate *a particular, single* morality.

This problem will have to be resolved in the course of this presentation. Our main route, therefore, will be that marked out by existentialism, with some appropriate detours along the way. Such detours will be often the result of certain reservations regarding the assumptions of certain existentialist authors.

Kant demarcated the phenomenon, the appearance that reality makes to consciousness, from the noumenon, the reality itself that must lie beyond the phenomenon.[2] Edmund Husserl accepted this approach in some part, while disavowing the hidden reality of the noumenon. He would have us rather look to the phenomenon itself to locate essence. While Husserl believed that knowledge and meaning must be based on the phenomenon, he was agnostic about any actual existence in the world of these phenomena. His efforts, therefore, were directed toward penetrating to the essence of phenomena, a project that he called a "return to things," a return to the world as it is actually experienced by humans.[3]

Through an intellectual stance called reduction or epoche (bracketing), phenomenology endeavors to derive the essences of things as they exist in consciousness transcendentally as phenomena. Thus, Husserl shows a possible path through which human consciousness enters into the world and comprehends it. The appearance leads us to the thing itself.[4] We are led for a distance, that is, but we do not thereby arrive-- phenomenology does not attempt to answer questions of ontology.

For the phenomenologist there is no purpose served by positing the noumenon; indeed, Kant himself, who posits the "thing-in-itself," assumed that it was not possible for the human mind to grasp it. The materialist, therefore, is the thinker who is the true metaphysician, penetrating beyond anything that the human mind can know. This is Kant's nice and effective answer to the materialists, such as the later Marxists, who liked to regard themselves as tough and realistic thinkers. Things are as they appear to consciousness, with all of the uncertainties that that entails.

A tentative hypothesis, one that is perhaps ultimately unprovable, that there is also a real world of things "out there," might be accepted as the origin of things as they appear to us, that is, as phenomenon. But what we can know of the real world, sometimes with the help of scientific instruments, are the phenomena and to assume that they may be anything more would be pointless, or at least, beyond comprehension. The methodology of existentialism (originally derived from the methods of phenomenology) is to use the concrete as a way of approaching the abstract or the general.[5] This standpoint does not seem to be a bad starting point in working our way in due course to the problems of international affairs.

Jeanson shows that there is an important shift from the phenomenology of Husserl to the ontology of Sartre, for, although beginning with the phenomenon in both philosophies, we must finally conclude with Sartre that the phenomenon does not "support itself as such," that the world not only is the world for us, but that it *is*, in fact, a so-called in-itself beyond what it appears to us.[6]

There are three important distinctions that grow from the existential interpretation of phenomenology, namely "being," "existence," and "essence." Olafson defines these as follows: "Being" is the term most frequently used in speaking of things in their "extra-phenomenal" and ontological status; "existence" depicts "conscious human existence"; and "essence" applies to both phenomenal qualities and concepts.[7]

This is the point at which the existentialist interpretation of Husserlian phenomenology departs from the original teaching, for Husserl finds being only in consciousness; absolute being exists only as constituted, and this constitution is an intentional constitution, so that what exists is only as a result of the proper operation of consciousness.

Husserl's method, therefore, is to probe the subjectivity where being has its source.[8] The difference in approaches between Husserl and Sartre, for example, is the reason that the latter's *Being and Nothingness* is subtitled "An Essay in Phenomenological Ontology," the "ontology" indicating Sartre's departure from Husserl, for Sartre posits a being-in-itself, out there in the world.[9]

Sartre's radical modification of phenomenology will furnish the most useful and appropriate entry for us into the political world. Thus, in *Being and Nothingness*, there is a division into the for-itself and the in-itself, terms borrowed, it is obvious, from Hegel. It is the in-itself that does not know, that cannot be other than what it is, that is known. That which knows is the for-itself, and it is this aspect of reality that engenders free will, without which there would be little or no point to any essay on ethical problems.[10]

On the one hand, there is unconscious being, which is massive being-there, "undifferentiated plenitude," the being-in-itself, while on the other hand, there is for-itself, separated out from the in-itself, an existence that is wholly dependent on being and that exists at a distance from it.[11] Since it is not being in-itself, the for-itself is nothingness, in Sartre's interpretation. So, as will appear later, freedom may be interpreted in one way as a lack of being.[12]

The concept of humanness that this interpretation suggests recalls Heidegger's cranky formula that "man is not just a thing among things but a subject, a person, . . . a being for whom, in his being, this being itself is at issue."[13] The human has a "relationship to being." The human being, therefore, differs from the being of a thing. For the in-itself, being is not an issue; for the for-itself, being *is* the major issue. Only a for-itself, only a human can ask questions, can be anxious, can hope or despair.[14] If there is to be a point-of-view or an evaluation of being-in-itself, this, too, is the province of the for-itself. In short, values are generated by human subjects.

The in-itself is the location of "blind happenings." Humans, of course, also contribute to the in-itself through producing the practico-inert, institutions that embody human projects, which eventually may come to have some of the character of the in-itself. Rituals, to take one example, may lose the viable loyalties of their adherents and become rote, slipping from human *praxis* into the practico-inert, the humanly produced in-itself. The idea of the practico-inert is the development Sartre provided the concept of being-in-itself as he elaborated upon it in his *Critique of Dialectical Reason*; this extended concept of the in-itself is a genuine contribution to sociology and political thought. The practico-inert is to human processes as being-in-itself is to nature's processes; both, of course, are essentially being-in-itself.[15]

Freedom would consist of the ability to transcend the in-itself.[16] Sartre in his "Reply to Lefort" argues that Marx, too, did not simply oppose materialism (with its emphasis on the in-itself) in favor of idealism (with its emphasis on for-itself), because the dialectic is a constant struggle on the part of mankind to overcome the constant tendency of the world to fall completely into the in-itself, to come to nothing, to turn into the inertia of a thing. "It is the hard labour of man to insert himself in a world which rejects him." The for-itself differs from the in-itself, so that it differs from the world which is fully determined. Consciousness is free and separated from the blind necessity that rules in the in-itself.[17] Sartre's conception of the in-itself is the in-itself of Plato and Parmenides, the awful and holy, the devoid of mind, fixed and immovable.[18] The for-itself does not in the manner of the in-itself coincide with itself--consciousness is impossible for an object, or that which coincides with itself.

Since the in-itself is being that is more than its actual appearing to the for-itself (standing out there beyond the phenomenon), the radical position of the idealists such as Berkeley can be avoided; and, for this reason, Sartre breaks with Husserl by "arguing for a being that cannot be identified with the *percipi*."[19] That which the for-itself is conscious of, therefore, is a concrete and full presence that is not itself consciousness. Consciousness is distinct from its object, although consciousness is supported by this being which is not consciousness.[20] Thus, Sartre's ontology is concerned with being, while the subject of phenomenology is appearance.

Since in-itself is the fullness of being, the for-itself seems to have emerged somehow and at some time from the compact density of this groundless in-itself. Thus, the for-itself is nothing; it is in need of the in-itself to be able to be for itself.[21] Although Sartre does not allude to the theory of evolution, it is obvious, given that process through time, that at some point in the changes occurring in the in-itself, consciousness made a sort of gradual intrusion into the world, dependent upon the in-itself but at the same time increasingly distinct. It would also seem to follow, if evolutionary principles are applicable to the gradual appearance of consciousness, that there is a continuum of consciousness, of consciousness expressed as for-itself shading by degrees toward in-itself among the living creatures of this world, although it is only mankind that is capable of supporting full for-itself.[22] Thus, although taking on somewhat the appearance of idealism, existentialism really espouses realism, for that of which we are conscious, namely the in-itself, is taken to be real and independent.[23]

Hegel's effort, of course, was to reconcile the *subject* and the *object*, to show that the world and the mind were one; this is idealism. For Sartre, however, the in-itself and the for-itself are forever separated and irreconcilable, even though it may be accepted that the for-itself at some juncture of evolutionary history emerged out of the in-itself. So, while finding Sartre's interpretation acceptable, in the main, we may also wonder whether the emergence is total at this point in human evolution, whether the for-itself is equally separated from the in-itself in all thinking beings.

Indeed, there may be a multitude of consciousnesses at various levels among the species that inhabit the world, from the slug to the dog. Reservations may be in order; the schism between in-itself and for-itself may not be absolute. By positing an absolute dichotomy between the for-itself and the in-itself, of course, Sartre avoids a host of philosophical complications, in particular in the problem of free will. However, it is not certain that these philosophical complications ought to be so easily put to rest.

In the course of the present work, a number of problems will be raised that cannot here be fully explicated, for the goal is to push on to the realm of international politics from as firm a foundation as can be laid within an acceptable compass. Therefore, while the import of the existentialist analysis of being-in-itself and being-for-itself will be accepted, an analysis that affords an argument in favor of free will, the philosophical problems of this standpoint will not be solved here.

Since the intention of this work is to provide a ground for the ethical propositions that will be used in analyzing international relations, some interpretation of the nature of consciousness will be set forth briefly. Mind will be regarded as ontologically independent of matter, although it is obviously dependent in some sense on matter; without the matter comprising the brain, mind ceases to function.[24]

Were an extraterrestrial to have surveyed the world as it must have existed prior to the emergence of life, it would have seemed unlikely that something with the attributes of life would emerge from the in-itself. Given nothing but in-itself, consciousness as an upsurge from being, also would have seemed quite improbable. It is also improbable, assuming primitive life forms enmeshed in the world of determination, that freedom eventually would make its appearance. Thus, an appealing rhetorical defense of the existence of freedom results: It is preposterous, given our knowledge of the in-itself that freedom would make its appearance in the world; but, given the nature of the primordial earth, it is equally preposterous that life would make an appearance. But preposterous as it seems, life did make an appearance into the world, ergo, freedom is no less possible. In Heidegger's succinct formulation, Why is there being rather than nothing?[25]

Consciousness, the for-itself, following its upsurge from being-in-itself, is separated from being (the in-itself). This separation has rendered the for-itself completely void. Desan suggests it is this lack of even a "granule of being" that provides consciousness the freedom that will be depicted later: there is nothing for "deterministic influence to take hold of."[26] Yet, while this is a compelling argument in the case of the human reality at some point in its development, considering the evolution of for-itself, an evolution that is apparent all around us, some reservations concerning Sartre's absolute formulation of the concept of for-itself, an absolute formulation that admittedly saves Sartre from innumerable problems in arguing the freedom of the will, may well be warranted.

The standpoint of consciousness, insofar as it is aware, is in nothing--whatever it is aware of is not *in* it but beyond it. The object of consciousness, the image, *is understood as other*. All entities, natural, social, and self are separate from consciousness, or from consciousness as prereflective cogito.[27] (This aspect of ontology, the separation of consciousness from the origins of its representations has an additional result that will be examined in some detail later, for it provides the basis for committing ethics to such values as lucidity, honesty, and logic, and to the avoidance of self-deception and bad faith. An ontology such as this accepts that there is a reality of which our images are appearances or representations.)

So Sartre regards subject and object as two types of being, as contrasted with the ontological non-commitment of Husserl's phenomenology. Indeed, Natanson shows that the "validity, consistency, and the significance of Sartre's ontology require the unresolvable dualism" of in-itself and for-itself.[28] We have hinted at some possible reservations regarding such an absolute position as Sartre's, however, and a less extreme position that seems acceptable is provided by Merleau-Ponty.[29] It is Merleau-Ponty's interpretation, based on his extensive consideration of psychological studies, that the schism between the in-itself (for instance, the in-itself of the human body) and the for-itself is ambiguous, and that only some human decisions qualify as free.

While the in-itself exists in complete positivity, without (conscious) possibilities and without negativity, consciousness structures the in-itself, positing it as both being and nothingness, for any part of the imagery of consciousness may be brought into focus or annihilated.[30] In ordinary and immediate, non-reflective knowledge, we have what Sartre refers to as the prereflective cogito, consciousness *of* something, consciousness that is egoless and impersonal.[31] (Here, consciousness is a pointing-towards, which takes consciousness beyond itself to the object, consciousness as intentionality. Such consciousness exists only through its objects.)[32]

As nothing by itself, consciousness is aware of its own lack of being and is possessed by values and possibilities. Thus, consciousness is that through which values are revealed. The fate of consciousness to be nothing, but to be oriented toward being, therefore, provides a basis for an urge toward ends or goals; hence, the existentialist position shows why humans have the urge to evaluate. Humans are the beings through which values come into the world.[33]

As Desan explains the problem of the for-itself as a lack of being, consciousness in its prereflective form points to that which it lacks, namely being, a lack that could only be remedied by the for-itself becoming a for-itself-in-itself, a consolidation of nothingness into being, and an impossibility for mankind, for for-itself-in-itself is just that definition that Thomists propose for the Supreme Being.[34] The prereflective cogito is always, however, out of itself and committed to something, to some future project. This is the nature of humans, to be committed to the future--always.[35]

But to be engaged fully with activity, as an animal, is to be "fully at one with its activity." Humans acting on this level in the face of worldly demands and immediate urgencies would be simply pulled along and would avoid asking about values and meanings. But unlike the lower animals, man can adopt in addition a reflective state, whereby values can be questioned--hence, anguish arises, for anguish is the concomitant of questioning, of the recognition of alternative possibilities. Animals are without anguish. Animals are stagnant beings, while humans can distance themselves from their activity, making it an object of knowing. This is the state of the reflective cogito.[36]

Thus, while all consciousness is consciousness of an object, it can be also consciousness of itself as well. Sartre refers to the reflective consciousness as a moral consciousness, for it cannot avoid the disclosure of values. The reflective consciousness may be directed to disclose or to ignore values.[37] In a sense, as animals act within the prereflective consciousness, paying no heed to values, humans might assume such a stance, which they do, certainly, from time to time, and would certainly do were they to totally absorb theory into *praxis*. But in reflective consciousness there is a source in humans for values.

Kant, too, attempted to wed free choice to the determined world that exists in time through his distinction between the noumenon that is me and the phenomenon that is me as constructed in the determined world by the free choices of the noumenon, which was free to have constituted an empirical me quite differently. Kant can here be observed to have struggled to reconcile determinism, which we certainly must admit in being-in-itself, with the freedom of ethical choice, a struggle that Broad feels that Kant lost.[38] But for Sartre, as a self one may also be an object for oneself when the consciousness is appealed to as reflective.[39] Such a standpoint of consciousness can never grasp the reflecting consciousness except through "retrospection."

The only unity of prereflective cogito is provided through its self-appropriation of its just-completed intentional acts, which it claims as its own and designates in the process of reflection as "me."[40] Thus, consciousness designates, on the one hand, the prepersonal operating intentionality that plunges through the world gradually acquiring an ego[41], and on the other hand, the reflexive awareness that this consciousness is indeed "my path" in the world.[42] And the "I am" may designate a state of facticity, my body as it is immersed in the world (in the in-itself) or the "being that I am in the mode of not-being what I am." This latter "I am" is a nothingness in the sense that it is the objective correlate, the whole range of cognitive, affective, and moral experiences, which is sustained by a consciousness that is impersonal and nihilating.[43] The existence of the ego outside consciousness, as it were, leaves it thrust into the world, in the city, in the nation, on the highway, beyond the interior life--as individuals, as egos, we are "outside in the world among others."[44]

Consciousness, this lack of being, this nothing, has one irreducible desire, to be being, to appropriate being but not simply to appropriate dense and massive in-itself, but conscious in-itself. In Sartre's formulation, it is the fundamental project of all for-itselves to become God in the Thomistic sense of combined essense and existence, or being-for-itself-in-itself, to be, that is, self-created.

Sartre, ever dramatic, has possibly exaggerated this as the universal fundamental project. However, there is evidence of such a fundamental project in people's urge to situations of total security, or of their urge to attain total well-being. And, more to the point, the inevitable frustration of such an impossible fundamental project leads to the urge toward total destructiveness among certain individuals, for if we may be unable at long last to become being-in-itself-for-itself, we can still destroy the world that stands against this culmination. While the prereflexive cogito is an empty for-itself, authentic reflection, the knowledge of myself knowing this table assumes the presence of the ego. Sartre's emphasis on the prereflexive cogito is an effort to emphasize the emptiness of for-itself.[45]

Later, we will return to some of this discussion in order to determine the nature of identity, for ethics and morality would seem to require a continuity of experience, some connecting theme. Identity in the sense of the ability to forsee and create a chain of cause and effect would seem to be a requisite for a morality.

In this introductory chapter, we have demarcated the human experience into the in-itself that is perceived and the for-itself that develops each individual identity. The standpoint of existentialism, largely as developed by Sartre, has established, albeit with reservations that will be noted from time to time, an appropriate standpoint on which to found an ethics. The consciousness that has the power to reflect on itself is the origin of the values and moral propositions that will be expounded upon in later chapters. The existence of freedom and the establishment of ego or identity have also been adumbrated. Indeed, freedom is the vital prerequisite to any system of morality; while we have proposed it, and while it is the very crux of Sartre's philosophical system, its existence will have to be accepted; it is not the task of this work to prove certain of the assumptions that condition morality as they apply to international policies; but it is also not appropriate to take too much simply for granted, for which reason, some effort will be expended to make propositions plausible.

This chapter leads logically to a discussion of what values, if any, or what destiny is contained in the in-itself, for some philosophies of history affecting international relations would have it that mankind is a secondary actor in the world, and that the world itself contains the causal engine of events. If this is true, it remains only to find what this destiny might be, so that we can understand it, even if we cannot direct it, and that will be an end to our discussion. But perhaps it will be the case that our destiny is not guided by the world working itself out within the in-itself, which would seem to be the appropriate conclusion on the basis of existentialism. Even supposing that the in-itself provides no clue as to our destiny, however, there is still the additional problem of the appropriate position to adopt with respect to in-itself, or the world at large. There also may be some basic choice of value that we may make in accordance with our recognition of the mutual independence of the destinies of the in-itself and the for-itself. For if we are free, we are free to adopt an attitude toward the in-itself and toward the basic human condition in the world.

Notes

1. Thomas R. Flynn, *Sartre and Marxist Existentialism* (Chicago: University of Chicago Press, 1984), p. 159.
2. Thomas M. King, *Sartre and the Sacred* (Chicago: The University of Chicago Press, 1974), p. 22. This book affords an excellent introduction to Sartre's philosophy.
3. Joseph S. Catalano, *A Commentary on Jean-Paul Sartre's Critique of Dialectical Reason, Volume 1, Theory of Practical Ensembles* (Chicago and London: The University of Chicago Press, 1986), pp. 50-51.
4. Samuel B. Mallin, *Merleau-Ponty's Philosophy* (New Haven: Yale University Press, 1979), p. 160-161.
5. Mary Warnock, *Existentialism* (New York: Oxford University Press, 1970), p. 133.
6. Francis Jeanson, *Sartre and the Problem of Morality* (Transl. from the French by Robert V. Stone. Bloomington, Ind., Indiana University Press, 1980), pp. 116-117.
7. Frederick A. Olafson, "A Central Theme of Merleau-Ponty's Philosophy," in Edward N. and Maurice Mandelbaum, eds., *Phenomenology and Existentialism* (Baltimore: The Johns Hopkins Press, 1967), p. 191, fn. 19.
8. Quentin Lauer, *Phenomenology: Its Genesis and Prospect* (New York: Harper and Row, Publishers, 1965), p. 79.
9. Frederick A. Olafson, *Principles and Persons: An Ethical Interpretation of Existentialism* (Baltimore: The Johns Hopkins Press, 1967), pp. 66-67, provides a clear statement of the transition from the phenomenological outlook of Husserl to the "ontological turn" given by, first, Heidegger, then Sartre. Klaus Hartmann's *Sartre's Ontology: A Study of Being and Nothingness in the Light of Hegel's Logic* (Evanston: Northwestern University Press, 1966), p. 17, points to an interesting parallel between Sartre's argument from the phenomenon to the in-itself, sheer being, and St. Anselm's projection from the idea of God in the mind to the existence of God.
10. There is an additional problem that should be noted, although it would be best dealt with in a more specific philosophical analysis, namely, the problem of the body. Sartre suggests that man "exists" the body, and he deals with this aspect of experience in a chapter of *Being and Nothingness*. But the most penetrating consideration of this whole problem is Merleau-Ponty's *The Phenomenology of Perception*.
11. Hazel E. Barnes, *The Literature of Possibility: A Study in Humanistic Existentialism* (Lincoln: University of Nebraska Press, 1959), 42.
12. *Ibid.*, p. 41.
13. William A. Luijpen, *Existential Phenomenology* (Pittsburgh: Duquesne University Press, 1969), p. 196-197.

14. In the Critique, according to King, the formulae of in-itself and for-itself give way to another nomenclature, namely that of dialectical reason, which is a withdrawal from what is, and the analytical reason, which acts on the inert. See King, *Sartre and the Sacred*, p. 173.

15. Joseph H. McMahon, *Humans Being: The World of Jean-Paul Sartre* (Chicago and London: The University of Chicago Press, 1971), p. 296, footnote.

16. Nicolai Hartmann, *Ethics* (Vol III; *Moral Freedom*) (Atlantic Highlands, N.J.: Humanities Press, 1974), p. 144.

17. King, *Sartre and the Sacred*, p. 29.

18. *Ibid.* pp. 25-26. Hartmann, *Sartre's Ontology*, p. 35, also notes this affinity of Sartre's idea of the in-itself and Parmenides' account of being.

19. *Ibid.*, p. 24.

20. See also the explanation in Luijpen, *Existential Phenomenology*, pp. 376-377.

21. *Ibid.*, p. 375.

22. An intelligent exposition of the possible impact of evolution on ethics and international relations is provided by Mary Maxwell, *Morality Among Nations, An Evolutionary View* (Albany: State University of New York).

23. Arthur C. Danto, *Jean-Paul Sartre* (New York: The Viking Press, 1975), p. 47, and Lucien Goldmann, *Lukacs and Heidegger* (London: Routledge and Kegan Paul, 1977), trans. by William Q. Boelhower, p. 102.

24. For the materialists, this interpretation smacks of a position called *epiphenomenalism*. But a more valid interpretation, in my opinion, is provided in Karl R. Popper and John C. Eccles, *The Self and Its Brain* (New York: Springer International, 1977), who provide good evidence for interaction with being from the side of consciousness. In Sartre's ontology, consciousness is not an epiphenomenon of being, for it has been severed from being. See Hartmann, *Sartre's Ontology*, p. 29, Francis Jeanson, *Sartre and the Problem of Morality*, pp. 115-116, Hazel E. Barnes, *An Existential Ethics* (New York: Alfred A. Knopf, 1969), pp. 243-244, and Peter Caws, *Sartre* (London: Routledge and Kegan Paul, 1979), p. 48. As Caws puts it, for Sartre consciousness is "absolutely given without presupposition." Consciousness, according to Barnes' interpretation, while a function of the body or being, transcends its base of support. It is not a thing, but since it is dependent on the body, it is always a localized point of view; it is always individual consciousness.

25. Sartre expresses this unlikely event as follows: "All happens *as if* the In-itself in a project of grounding itself has given itself the modification of the For-itself." But this is not possible, for being-in-itself simply is and cannot intend to become the For-itself. Such a contradiction, says Desan, is flagrant. See Wilfrid Desan, *The Tragic Finale: An Essay on the Philosophy of Jean-Paul Sartre* (New York: Harper Torchbooks, 1960), pp. 181-184. Marvin Farber, *The Aims of Phenomenology* (New York: Harper and Row, 1966), p. 223, is quite right to suggest that reading the literature of evolution and anthropology would have

aided Sartre in mitigating his somewhat extreme image of man.

26. Desan, *The Tragic Finale*, p. 158.

27. Joseph P. Fell, *Heidegger and Sartre: An Essay on Being and Place* (New York: Columbia University Press, 1979), p. 258. Fell's book, by the way, is a brilliant exposition.

28. Maurice Natanson, *A Critique of Jean-Paul Sartre's Ontology* (The Hague: Martinus Nijhoff, 1973; reprint of the original 1951 publication), p. 92.

29. Maurice Merleau-Ponty, *The Structure of Behavior* (Boston: Beacon Press, 1963). See in particular Wild's comments on this topic in the foreword to Merleau-Ponty's book, pp xiv-xv; and see also Lauer, *Phenomenology*, pp. 179-181.

30. James M. Edie, "Sartre as Phenomenologist and as Existential Psychoanalyst," in Lee and Mandelbaum, eds., *Phenomenology and Existentialism*, p. 158.

31. Desan, *The Tragic Finale*, p. 9, p. 27.

32. *Ibid.*, pp. 30-31.

33. *Ibid.*, p. 34.

34. Etienne Gilson, *The Philosophy of St. Thomas Aquinas* (Trans. by Edward Bullough. New York: Dorset Press, no date), p. 64, states the Thomist position: "It is indeed incontestable that in God essence and existence are identical."

35. Desan, *The Tragic Finale*, p. 103.

36. Luijpen, *Existential Phenomenology*, p. 246.

37. Jean-Paul Sartre, *Being and Nothingness: An Essay on Phenomenological Ontology* (Trans. by Hazel E. Barnes. New York: Philosophical Library, 1956), p. 95. Kierkegaard differed from Sartre on this point. For him, there is no transcendental consciousness for which the empirical ego can be a phenomenon. As Stack expresses it, the problem is that of "postulating a transcendental ego that knows the empirical ego as object," George J. Stack, *Kierkegaard's Existential Ethics* (University, Alabama: The University of Alabama Press, 1977), pp. 160-161. However, for Sartre, unlike Husserl, there is no transcendental ego as a condition of the reflective consciousness.

38. C. D. Broad, *Five Types of Ethical Theory* (London: Routledge and Kegan Paul, 1971), pp. 137-138. This very well-written work was first published in 1930. To revert somewhat to a previous topic, it is pertinent to note the comment of Julian Huxley, that ". . . at a certain point in time, once and for all in the evolution of the species, but repeated afresh in the evolution of each of its individuals, morality appears," Thomas E. and Julian Huxley, *Touchstone for Ethics* (Plainview, NY: Books for Libraries Press, 1971; original copyright, 1947), p. 228.

39. Danto, *Jean-Paul Sartre*, pp. 58-59.

40. Edie, "Sartre as Phenomenologist," p. 150.

41. King, *Sartre and the Sacred*, pp. 97-98, points to the interesting parallel between Sartre's theory of consciousness and the Buddhist doctrine of *anatta*, of the no ultimate self.

42. Edie, "Sartre as Phenomenologist," p. 161.

43. *Ibid*, p. 161.

44. King, *Sartre and the Sacred*, p. 27, and Barnes, *An Existentialist Ethics*, p. 13.

45. Desan, *The Tragic Finale*, p. 150. There are two forms of reflection, the pure, which is an instantaneous knowing that does not adopt a point of view with regard to what is known, and the impure. The consciousness that reflects is the consciousness that is reflected on. Impure reflection reveals the acts, states of mind, qualities, and ego. This is the psyche, the inner world that is the object of the science of psychology. See King, *Sartre and the Sacred*, pp. 70-72.

Chapter 2

Is There an Ultimate Political Purpose?

The designation of being into being-in-itself and being-for-itself offers a basis for an individualist position concerning morality. But, preliminary to establishing any principles of morality as such, it will be useful to inquire whether the nature of being-in-itself offers an end point, a culmination of which it may be asserted, this is the movement of history, this constitutes the wave of the future, it is to this end that we have been created?

If there is, then many problems will be answered, and any ethical theory will be instructed by this supreme purpose. To acknowledge some ultimate purposes is not to establish that there may be projects the individual can devise in the world, but rather to determine that there may be an overarching project, a built-in purpose in things that all individuals ought to heed. For if such there is, by not paying appropriate attention to such an overarching purpose, the individual may well render his or her projects irrelevant.

At the end of the *Tractatus*, Wittgenstein strikes this depressing note:

> The sense of the world must be outside the world. In the world everything is as it is, and everything happens as it does happen: in it no value exists–and if it did exist, it would have no value. If there is any value that does have value, it must be outside the whole sphere of what happens and is the case. For all that happens and is the case is accidental.[1]

What this means is that if life were to be obliterated on this planet through a bombardment of meteors, it would be purely fortuitous and not some judgment upon mankind. Perhaps, although luckily not, life on earth might have been obliterated in the aftermath of the hypothesized meteor that contributed, so some scientists hold, to the extinction of the dinosaurs. All forms of consciousness having disappeared on earth, all forms reduced to pure in-itself, an objective consciousness from another galaxy might, in such a case, have hypothesized that the ultimate purpose of earth forms was the dinosaur, now, alas, extinct. The obliteration of earth would not have mattered in any cosmic scheme-of-things. But, accidentally, life was not obliterated by the hypothetical meteor and instead, continued to evolve. The ultimate goal of the earth, so far as can be ascertained through scientific knowledge, is to eventually become a dead planet, on which all conscious forms will have fallen back entirely into the in-itself. Whether mankind learns to transport itself to further reaches of the solar system, or even further into the galaxy, is immaterial. Most likely, extinction is the final end for mankind and other species, sooner or later. This is at least as far as secular thought can reach.

The being of mankind is, therefore, contingent and meaningless in the sense that there is a destiny for mankind within the processes of the world. Mankind has, in Heidegger's apt phrase, been thrown into the world. Mankind is alienated from the source of its being.[2]

There are at least four lines of argument that seek to overcome this sense of alienation, and a fifth position that tries to make something out of the presumed failure of these solutions. First, there is the theological argument that mankind has been created by a deity. This is an argument, according to St. Thomas and Soren Kierkegaard, that can be supported by rational arguments but that rests ultimately on faith. Therefore, it would be unconvincing to attempt a refutation of such an argument.

It might, however, be suggested that the existence or non-existence of a deity will not affect arguments to found values in the world, for if values are established by God, it may still remain the difficult task of human individuals to determine what these are.[3] What is God's stand on human conflict, and how might this be determined? If God exists, how can one decide whether for this particular conflict to be a pacifist or a warrior? Perhaps, an authoritative statement has been set out somewhere? But where? As the historical account of Joshua shows, it is clear that belief in a deity might vindicate all kinds of political strife. Mohammed quite forthrightly accepted the role of warrior. From a theological view, therefore, the search for a ground for morality and values need not be affected by beliefs regarding Creation; in any case, theology does not ameliorate that search. Of course, if it is a matter of locating the basis for values in a text or the pronouncements of a particular sect or person, the problem of deriving a basis for values is thereby solved, but the individual may also risk choosing values in bad faith, an argument that will be elucidated later.

To rest the argument for values on sources like these is to remove responsibility from the individual, to fall into all kinds of hypocrisies, to engender bland beliefs that have little passion. Indeed, a plausible position from a theological standpoints might be that values and morality ought to be the result of intellectual struggle rather than learned by rote, for it is this effort that provides a morality with substance. It is a position like this that makes Berdaeyev so interesting a religious writer.

A second line of argument leads to Being. Since in the real world that we perceive, "we have been given no purpose, we are unneeded, unjustified, and superfluous,"[4] we might be inclined to seek somehow beyond the real world of perception for the foundation of our being. Thus, we encounter within this second type of argument, as in the later writings of Heidegger, the proposition that there is abstract and absolute Being. Persons come to be transformed in Heidegger's view to a sort of strict passivity, engaged in the task of bringing Being to light, letting things reveal themselves as what they are.[5]

There is an affinity in some of Heidegger's later writings to the spiritual mysticism of the East, and the passive Buddhist relationship to the world, which is not prominent at all in the earlier *Being and Time*. "How does it stand with being," is the question posed by the later Heidegger.[6] Heidegger finds that mankind has been a negligent shepherd of Being. Technology has ravaged the earth and degraded natural forms to mere utility.[7] Yet, one might ask, how can the all-embracing Being be in any sense degraded?

There is some clue to this view in statements by Heidegger such as that "matter keeps itself hidden in the still unthought nature of the way in which anything that is under the dominion of technology has any being at all."[8] Without further elaboration, this is a puzzling statement indeed, although a possible interpretation will be provided later in this chapter. For now, whatever distinctions there are in how the in-itself presents itself to us, it would still seem to be undifferentiated Being which is present, regardless.[9] But perhaps more telling, the positivists, the language philosophers, who are so often attacked for their focus on minutiae, probably are correct in the case of this aspect of Heidegger's philosophy: The term Being is so contentless as to lack linguistic meaning. Does Being cease when it is transformed from forests to newspapers? There is no possible way this question can be answered satisfactorily. Even Hegel found the concepts of Being and Nothing the most abstract in the philosophical vocabulary, which is, he opines, probably why Parmenides began his ruminations with the concept Being.[10]

But ought we to return to the supposed beginnings of philosophy with Heidegger in a search for the authentic meaning of Being? Nietzsche, too, was a phenomenological ontologist, regarding the phenomenon as a disclosure of Being, but for him, in contrast with Heidegger, Being was relative, while the apparent world was the true one.[11] The crux of the problem for Heidegger's later philosophy lies in whether "distinctions of thought (concepts, universals) really belong to things, rather than being conventional ways of dividing up a seamless matter."[12]

In all likelihood, Heidegger was following a chimera. The same criticism applies to Jaspers' Encompassing, of which may be argued adds nothing to phenomena. Both positions succumb to the simple and effective criticism by Aristotle, who asks, what do Plato's Forms possibly contribute to our understanding of the world and of events? In Jaspers' case, however, his will-o'-the-wisp may not vitally injure his interpretation of human events. Let us agree here with the positivists that there is no ultimate purpose to be discovered in the "pursuit of Being."

A third direction of search for ultimate purpose dispenses with the supraphenomenal, and finds goals immanent in being-in-itself or in the practico-inert of society. Hegel's Spirit progressing through history is one model here. The problem with this position is revealed by our notorious inability to predict the course of human events based on a supposed understanding of the motive power of history or society. An understanding of the ultimate purpose and course of history ought to allow the forecast of major events. Retrospectively, sense seems to be made of history as a somehow conscious goal when it is posited as revelatory of Spirit, but prospectively, insights into the future resting on such supposed historical goals seem to be dim at best. The question arises, of what use, then, is this supposed knowledge of Spirit?

Karl Popper's astute critique of historicism provides a summary of these views and their definitive refutation. The Marxian system partakes to a significant degree of the Hegelian historical view, but Marx and Engels moved the motive power of history from Spirit to human economic relationships. A class, the proletariat, was charged with the imposing task of moving society into the next level of history, the dictatorship of the proletariat. The dialectical relationship between the class-conscious activity of the proletariat and the mode of production under capitalism was to eventuate in the classless society, the end of history, and, indeed, the termination of philosophy, when exploitation and private property were to be abolished and all forms of alienation ended.

It is hard to comprehend that a creatorless world would have such a built-in utopian culmination. But, be that as it may, and not to explore the possible flaws in Marxism, which would take us too far beyond the scope of this coverage, it may be concluded that the chief problem with the system is that the predictions generated by the application of the dialectic failed of fulfillment. Only in Russia--where the system displaced was hardly a highly developed capitalist one, and indeed, was close to an "oriental despotism" in Karl Wittvogel's challenging analysis--did a proletarian revolution of sorts occur.

But the collapse of the Soviet Union in 1991 did not vindicate the Marxist view of history. Other ultimate historical projects have included that of race, although the Aryan mythology of the Nazis remained on a much lower intellectual level than Marxism. The racial doctrine was a sort of anemic intellectual offspring of Hegel's Spirit. Of course, none of these themes can be accepted as appropriate worldviews except in bad faith, Nazism least of all.

In the *Critique*, Sartre has provided high praise for Marxism, fortifying it with his own not inconsiderable socio-psychological insights on social movements, but he has signally failed to resuscitate the "philosophy of the 20th century," as he calls Marxism in *Search for a Method*.[13] Indeed, Sartre's acceptance of the Marxist philosophy has always appeared singularly unsubstantiated. As an explanation of a major project in history, Marxism as a full-blown intellectual system has collapsed, although the original system still presents some philosophical challenge.[14]

There is a corollary of importance to be made here concerning these historical or social projects, all of which partake of historicism. Those who hold millenial or utopian views frequently believe that ethics are a topic that must await the endpoint, the final arrival, of the Spirit moving through time. An ethical system, in this view, cannot be framed in an extant and imperfect human condition. Sartre himself supports this view. In a similar case, Sidgwick criticizes Herbert Spenser, who in his *Social*

Statistics claims that ". . . a system of morals which shall recognize man's present imperfections and allow for them cannot be devised. . . ."[15]

But this is the very purpose of a morality, to apply to an imperfect world--the idea of human perfection is a fundamentally totalitarian idea, fraught with danger, for, since morals must await human perfection occurring in some ideal culmination of history, all means hastening such a desirable end may be admissible, and in the meantime, anything goes. In denouncing just this position in Herbert Marcuse, Vivas says, ". . . I am not interested in what man can become in the future . . . *if* my future involves the denial of my humanity at this moment in this place. But that is what placing man's essence in the future entails: the denying of man's humanity here and now."[16]

If we speak of ultimate goals in history, it is obvious that such ends usually justify all means to attain them. If not, if some means effective in gaining our ultimate end, for instance, the exiling of all persons over the age of twelve from our Republic-to-be, are to be ruled out, then it follows that there is a controlling principle superior to the ultimate goal, which is not possible by definition. Hobbes argues the case for ultimate sovereignty according to this logic, holding that if there is some controlling factor over, say, the monarch, then the monarch cannot, after all, be sovereign. Thus, if our ultimate goal be truly ultimate, there is no moral principle that ought to override its realization. Therein lies the danger inherent in the belief in ultimate historical goals.

The same warning may be made in international relations, where the goals of states ought to be subordinate ends and not directed toward millenial goals. One such millenial goal, of course, might be absolute security. Finally, it may be suggested on the basis of the argument against ultimate historical goals that because international relations may be a particularly imperfect arena of human activity, this does not preclude the application of moral principles to international problems. Moral principles are intended to apply in imperfect situations.

A fourth line of argument proposing ultimate purpose locates purpose in the efforts of individuals, but finds values and goals somehow outside the individual, or ready-made in the individual psyche. Such ready-mades are often groundless prescriptions that do not fit plausible assumptions on ontology and freedom. There will be no attempt to critique the whole host of personal goals individuals might project for themselves, but a few of these prescriptive agruments merit mention.

To Kant, and some of the Stoics, virtue was regarded as the

appropriate end for man.[17] Virtue, however, is contentless in so far as it constitutes a valid human project. The human upsurge from being-in-itself could be taken, certainly, to herald a more substantial goal than virtue, whatever other goals people might choose to freely pursue. Virtue is like peace in international affairs, a desirable condition in itself in most cases, but not a positive end that stimulates human activity.

Kant's ethical principles, as virtue as an end-in-itself would indicate, are too formalistic, probably because they rest on such a passive grounding. This is the reason Kant could argue, against all practical reason, that one ought never to lie under any condition. This is a sterile principle for anyone who has to choose within political situations, particularly in those situations of agonizing choices so frequent in the totatitarian regimes of the 20th century. As a result of the shortcomings of the Kantian ethical system, a distinction will be offered later between values, ends and goals, and morality, which is also a value but one that relates more narrowly to how one is to value other people.

There are some superficial resemblances between existentialism and situation ethics. But situation ethics shares some of the shortcomings of Kantian virtue as an end, for the chief end of situation ethics is love. The foremost exponent, Joseph Fletcher, states this ultimate purpose as follows, "There is only one end, one goal, one purpose which is not relative and contingent, always an end in itself. Love."[18] The prescribed task for situation ethics in the world is to seek an optimum of loving-kindness. But like happiness, this goal does not posit anything. It presents an attitude toward something. It is dubious as a project for the same reason that happiness is a moot goal, for a person may will to be lucid but may find it hard to will to be happy; similarly, it is not easy, indeed, it may not be possible, to will to love. Yet, while we may not be able to love our fellows, we may still will to treat them humanely.

As a political stance, love of our fellows is dubious, for while we may love those intimate to us, it is an emotion that is not easily extended universally; it does not appear spontaneously during political projects that call for negotiating with enemies, distant from us by geography, culture, and ideology. Politics is not properly fueled by motivations of love; the qualities it can properly call up are those concerned with justice. We may treat our fellows with justice, regardless of our feelings concerning them, but this is as far as politics calls upon us to go.[19] Considering the artificiality, the forced quality, of many professions of love for political persons, for mankind, a question for ethical analysis might be whether the havoc wrought by the lovers of mankind outweighs the good they have done. It is commonly remarked that the great lovers of mankind have often treated their immediate friends and intimates rather shabbily.[20]

The utilitarian principle of pleasure as the highest end fares little better than virtue and love, and Kant himself had a well-justified contempt for it.[21] More will be said of this position in a later chapter. For now, an extreme argument might be considered that takes the pleasure principle to its logical conclusion. In laboratories, it is possible to provide animals, as in experiments with cats, brain stimulation that provides constant pleasure. It would be possible, one supposes, to hook humans to laboratory apparatus and provide them a lifetime of pleasurable stimulation, while feeding them intravenously. While this vision might be terrifying to some, it would provide the seekers of pleasure with the attainment of their goal beyond any possibilities previously imagined.

This vision of such permanent pleasure, however, carries with it its own refutation. Sexuality and the will to power, advocated by Freud and Adler, have been criticized by Sartre, for these are projects that should remain relative rather than being made the essence of human existence.[22] Such ends might possibly be valid as means among other means for some more fundamental projects, such as being an artist or a diplomat. In fact, the will to power is suggestive as an initial choice, viewed as the will to life.

Sartre himself, in one of his penetrating insights into human for-itself, discusses as the fundamental human project the desire to attain the condition of for-itself-in-itself, the condition of providing the foundation for our own free existence. That is, remaining free to be while at the same time fixed in the mold of what we are. Ontologically, this is a futile and impossible project, as Sartre shows. It is part of the human condition, another aspect, as it were, of the human nature that Sartre accepts in the form of a common human situation. The person who would solidify himself once and for all in the form of a soldier, or an athlete (as a weightlifter might construct a living statue of himself), or the young man who tries to embody himself for all time, like a physical force, in the image of the anti-Semite in Sartre's brilliant portrayal in *The Childhood of a Leader*, or the leaders of a state motivated toward the goal of permanent and total security-- all pursue an impossible end. All these endeavors are those of the for-itself in its futile flight to become simultaneously in-itself, to become God, as Sartre puts it. For were the in-itself-for-itself possible, it would be godlike.[23]

Goals might also appear to us from the world of things, being embedded for us to discover in being-in-itself. This may be an appropriate juncture for dealing with this problem in moral foundations, which usually goes by the name of the naturalistic fallacy. An associated problem, the impossibility of deriving morals from reason in the sense of the derivation of an "ought" from an "is," is famously discussed by Hume.[24] From time to time such an argument re-emerges in the form of another ingenious proof of deriving "ought" from "is," such as that of Searles, who argued that it is possible to do so logically, a position effectively refuted by Stroh.[25]

The naturalistic fallacy, stated by Hare is to "so characterize the *meanings* of the key moral terms that given certain factual premises, not themselves moral judgements, moral conclusions can be deduced from this." As Foot phrases it, ". . .words with emotive or commendatory force, such as 'good,' were not to be defined by the use of words whose meaning was merely 'descriptive'."[26] The problems concerning deriving 'ought' from 'is' and the naturalistic fallacy center on the notion that values are not ready-made, out there in the world, embedded in some way in the in-itself, awaiting discovery.[27]

Santayana is sometimes accused of committing the naturalistic fallacy, but Stroh defends him from this accusation and at the same time clarifies the naturalistic position by showing that Santayana affirms that things are good because they are desired, rather than being desired because they are good. The value, that is, is generated out of the act of interest taken in objects, but the objects are not good before anyone desires them. So Santayana escapes. One could also fall into the fallacy by identifying good with pleasure or desire, or any other naturalistic phenomenon, thereby confusing two entirely different properties by making them identical.[28]

Moore may go beyond his original argument by further asserting not only that moral judgments may not be deduced directly from natural properties but that "no relevant evidence can be adduced at all in support of moral judgements." But here he goes too far, and we agree with Kupperman that he is clearly wrong in this extended argument..[29] It will be found necessary, for example, in the course of evaluating good acts to weigh their consequences, as will be shown later.

Briefly, on the basis of the foregoing discussion, some comment should be made concerning natural law and natural rights. The question, as Hare puts it, seems patently to be to decide what the law, say, the law of nations, ought to be, rather than trying to search out "what the natural law really is."[30] It seems probable that such a search for a basis of natural law and rights somewhere in the in-itself is clearly futile. It is just as clear that we do not reach the same inevitable conclusions regarding natural law by searching our mental contents through reason. This does not obviate the need to fit other people, other cultures, and other nations into a moral scheme, but it will have to be done unaided by a doctrine of natural law. This is probably too short shrift for a doctrine so rich in historical and moral importance, but natural law would seem to be unsupportable from the viewpoint taken in this work.

Finally, among theories of morality that enlighten us from without, there is the behavioral doctrine of B. F. Skinner, for whom "the ultimate improvement comes from the environment, which makes [people] wise and compassionate." Looking toward an eventual world without moral struggle, Skinner rests good and bad behavior on contingencies, reinforcers that control the good and bad behavior of people.[31] In his *About Behaviorism* (p. 244), he solves the problem of moral behavior quite economically by explaining it as a "product of special kinds of social contingencies arranged by governments, religions, economic systems, and ethical groups." Indeed, this is quite a sound attitude to convention, and a fine description of Heidegger's "They." But, like the naturalistic fallacy, this explanation, sound within its limitations, ignores the fact that people nonetheless continue to express moral opinions at variance with received ones. Moral innovation and reform would be difficult to explain in Skinner's deterministic setting.[32]

With these few thoughts on competing views on the grounding of values and morals, an attempt will be made to provide a possible solution to the dilemma of mankind as a useless passion. Aside from the fundamental and futile goal of founding one's own free existence as for-itself-in-itself, there remain more plausible human projects. However, as had been suggested, there may turn out to be no ultimate goal, the same for everyone, but, instead, a number of commendable projects. Despite Sartre's contempt for liberal society, it deserves a better repute, for liberalism does not provide a single goal for all individuals; rather, it offers the arena for a pluralism of paths.

For Sartre, there are two different levels of choice: there is the fundamental project, which is the founding choice of who we are to become, a choice made, apparently, at the prereflective level without deliberation. Indeed, it is not certain how a choice could be freely made without deliberation. In any case, for Sartre, at the second level of choice, voluntary deliberation takes place in the framework of the fundamental project, so that there are subsidiary projects that rest on this prior decision.[33]

The fundamental choice operates to shape later projects into a coherent pattern. It means the establishment of an identity. It constitutes the person as a totality, albeit, the totality is always open, subject to radical (and uncommon) conversions. Thus, mankind is a free and creative project. A person creates himself or herself, in a sense, in the image of the human that they believe a human ought to be.[34] Thus, people are responsible for others, because in their free choices, they are presenting the general criterion of what humans ought to be, or perhaps a better phrasing might be a general criterion of what humans can be if they so choose. There are no standards that govern such a choice, of course, since we make this choice freely, in the face of the contingencies of the society and the in-itself.[35]

While accepting some of Sartre's position, reservations must be voiced concerning the so-called fundamental project, this choosing oneself all at once, as Genet presumably chose to be a thief.[36] Merleau-Ponty (and Olafson; see the previous Note) finds the argument for the fundamental choice unconvincing for the reason that all choices presuppose a previous choice, and some one fundamental choice is self-contradictory.[37]

It may be concluded, tentatively, that any ultimate choice, or fundamental choice, if there are such, rests on a decision to found one's projects in freedom, a decision that on the one hand is inescapable ontologically, but that may be denied in bad faith. The fundamental choice, as we understand it, is not that of Sartre's, for we have expressed reservations about his interpretation, but a choice fundamental enough that it provides a way, nonetheless, of making the myriad additional projects of the individual coherent.

Having discarded a number of possibilties that found values in in-itself, beyond the for-itself and other ready-made ultimate values, it still does not seem appropriate to discount entirely the possibility that there might be some foundation choices open to--not enforced upon--us. We will survey a possible position that rests on the common human condition and our acknowledgement of it.

Having discounted a number of sources of values and ultimate values, it is apparent that the argument has already provided an assumption for the method of choosing values, namely, that no values ought to be admitted without reason. Lucidity ought to be a quality of how values ought to be selected. A choice may be made in other ways, of course, or, as argued later, made in bad faith. In bad faith, a choice might be excused as that choice which is enforced upon us, as that ultimate value that is inescapable--but there is no such choice. Therefore, values become the chooser's own.

Lucidity is the effort to establish, so far as reason may take us, the condition of humanity from which our choices will be made. Thus, any fundamental choices must be based on as accurate an understanding of the human condition as we can command. Of course, such a choice is also free: a lucid choice is not an enforced choice, for it is sometimes advantageous to violate lucidity; but generally lucidity may be recommended for the reason that to ignore it would be intellectually and emotionally disappointing. It would be disappointing in the same way that to win a chess game by undetected cheating would be disappointing. Existentialism often conveys the impression that irrationality, or perhaps, rather, arbitrariness, is the mark of free choice: this is incorrect, and a close interpretation of Sartre's discussions of the relationshiop of for-itself to being-in-itself and the practico-inert provides a firm basis for the choice of lucidity, reason, and logic.

Thus, it has been established that out there is being-in-itself and that there are no ultimate values conveyed to us from that source. But there are potential choices open to us. While being is homogeneous as being, its manifestations are nonetheless myriad. These manifestations range from water, stones, and earth to trees, eagles, and humans. Within being-in-itself, being lacking consciousness of itself, we see the second law of thermodynamics at work.

There is in being-in-itself the tendency toward entropy; a system containing movement, for instance, will gradually wind down and all its elements will come to rest. There is a kind of eternal conflict apparent in the world between movement and rest and between complexity and primordial simplicity. On one level of this conflict are life-forms, at their various levels of consciousness, exerting control against the tendency toward entropy. Thus, life contests entropy and in general seems to provide an urge toward greater complexity as against simplicity.

Life is this effort and burden, a struggle against the restful condition of non-life. All of this may occur within the in-itself without the complicity of the in-itself. However, this condition leads to the first and most basic choice for any conscious being, the choice to strive against entropy, or, to express this another way, the choice of life. This choice is not enforced upon us, for we might choose otherwise, or, more likely, we might simply neglect any choice at all. Indeed, such a choice is rather like Locke's social contract: most people are not aware that they have made any such choice. But the choice, even if made implicitly, is a critical one; it is, for the human, the fundamental choice.

The fundamental choice of life is manifested in many different ways. Nietzsche notes that one of the amazing things about the ancient Greeks was the enormous abundance of gratitude their religiosity seemed to exude. "It is a very noble type of man that confronts nature and life in this way," Nietzsche writes.[38] This is certainly one meaning of Nietzsche's notorious "will to power"; taken in some of its senses, it is quite simply the choice of life.

Freud presents another case by formulating the concepts of Eros and Thanatos, ". . . as well as Eros there was an instinct of death. . . A more fruitful idea was that a portion of the instinct is diverted towards the external world and comes to light as an instinct of aggressiveness and destructiveness."[39] And this is an important point, for the choice against life does not reveal itself directly in a choice to die, but it reveals itself in some persons as the choice to destroy the world and other persons. A basic distinction between political leaders may rest in this basic choice of life or death: it is a choice that distinguishes a Jawaharlal Nehru from an Adolph Hitler.

Although the great religions frequently take a negative view of earthly existence, they are not without affirmations either, as in Aquinas' idea that "good" is the perfection of the individual nature, or Augustine's exclamation in his *Confessions*, "You, therefore, O Lord, who are beautiful, made these things, for they are beautiful; you who are good made them, for they are good . . . ."[40] Thus, lucidity reveals two possible fundamental choices in the world into which we are thrust, namely, life or death. It would appear that to accept the former is to accept certain other rational demands, provided that we choose to act rationally.

Camus emphasizes the concept of "throwness," which he interprets as "absurdity." There is no rhyme nor reason to our being here and now in this place, at this time, in this world. We are fortuitous upsurges from being-in-itself, arising out of the inert into consciousness. In his *Myth of Sisyphus*, Camus suggests that we can choose to function in spite of a lucid understanding of the absurd condition of our existence. This choice constitutes a rebellion against the knowledge of our "throwness," a rebellion that might take a bitter and destructive path, on the one hand, or, by way of a more courageous decision, a constructive path.

This courage, provided that lucidity is its basis, is evidenced not only by projects of great import in the world, as in Machiavelli's Prince of *virtu*, but also by an affirmative and constructive attitude toward a workaday existence in the everyday world. Thus, while one may understand the shortcomings of "the They" and the mundane world, one also has to make his way in it; it requires courage to do this.

Camus' *The Rebel* traces through Western literature the possibilities of destructive rebellion in the face of absurdity, a rebellion founded on contempt for life. He does not commend this. There was a faddish form of existentialism that chose unpredictability and unconventionality to signify its rebellion against society, and Sartre himself did much to encourage this position; but free choice need not opt for rebellion in this form. Civil roles may not be despicable. On the other hand, frenetic nonconformity and the attempt to perpetrate great deeds of "sound and fury" may be manifestations of despair.

Thus, it has been shown that there is no fundamental choice enforced upon us, but that a fundamental choice, such as life, may be freely made. Having affirmed life in the face of absurdity, in contrast to choosing death and aggressive destruction, does such a choice imply any logical relationship toward the in-itself from which human consciousness has emerged? (Of course, it ought to imply certain relationships toward others, but that important topic will be deferred to a later chapter.)

The illusory "pursuit of Being" has already been eschewed. But the fact of our origin in the evolutionary process has left some mark on us in the sense we have of awe and of beauty, a certain curiosity and even admiration for other sentient creatures in which consciousness is present but not yet consciousness as for-itself. In this view, there is for-itself and in-itself, and in our throwness, we are plunged into nature and society to make our way, where there is no transcendent Being, no encompassing, so far as can rationally be known, and no certain clues for meanings out there in the world. Indeed, there is a theological counterpart to this throwness, the idea of the fall from grace, so well presented in a literary form in Milton's *Paradise Lost*.

Existentialism has been characterized hitherto by its narrow humanistic outlook, which is in some ways a shortcoming, for it is interested only in human activity, in persons as the measure of all things, an outlook distinctively appropriate, of course, to the political arena. Indeed, Macquerrie cites Roger Shinn's distinction between a "closed humanism," in which responsibilities attach to man alone, and in which the in-itself, the nonhuman world is open to unmitigated conquest (and existentialism would seem to be such a closed humanism), and "open humanism," which accepts the possibility of responsibilities affecting the nonhuman world as well.[41]

But existentialism has lacked a philosophy of nature, nor has it taken much interest in the natural sciences.[42] By contrast, Camus from time to time evinces an awareness of the effect of nature on people, but Sartre holds the common view of nature as "an instrumental hierarchy of possibilities."[43] One would like to know what interested Sartre on those long bicycle trips he often took with Simone de Beauvoir. Perhaps there are aspects of his own experience that he neglected to treat in his philosophy. In any case, the existentialist viewpoint, unmitigated by a philosophy of nature, gives rise to a possibly destructive attitude of mankind toward the environment, an attitude predominant in both the former eastern bloc countries and the West, and evident, despite contrary myth, in the Third World.

One expected better from eastern Europe, if only for the reason that Marxism denounced capitalism for, among other things, its alienation of man from nature. But the horrifying revelations of pollution in Czechoslovakia, Poland, Romania, and the former Soviet Union after *glasnost* set those expectations at rest. One can characterize the common human attitude as "kill it if it moves; chop it down if it doesn't move." The rhinoceros will therefore be exterminated shortly for the supposed aphrodisiac quality of its horn; the rain forests will be obliterated by the urge for short term profits; and bays and shores will become increasingly polluted.

While the full implications of Heidegger's later philosophy were unacceptable, there is nevertheless something compelling in his depiction of humans as shepherds of being. The for-itself may no longer be rooted as incipient consciousness must have been at one time in nature, but nature is still the originating medium for humans and contains the source of other emergents. Sartre's depiction of the world, the in-itself, as "soft," "dull," "tepid," "viscous," suggests a profound alienation from the world, which could also alternatively be regarded as a home.[44]

Humanity will not likely escape the final demise of the earth and the neighboring planets, even given gains in space technology. But the fatalistic view is the cowardly one, the choice against life, the choice that we have not recommended. Our period of existence may be more intriguing given a world of myriad fellow creatures and abundant flora, rather than a future sojourn in a sterile and overpopulated desert or an unending urban sprawl. The world mankind inhabits is the world that will have been a free choice. To have chosen for life in the first instance, the evidence of this choice will be the kind of dwelling we prepare for ourselves. We may even choose to accept some responsibilities toward future inhabitants of the globe. What is it we want to leave them, or do we want to obliterate their possibilities for the future? This is the significance that can be derived from Heidegger's incorrect depiction of the different forms of being: everything is being, but the technological products of the human mind can be reproduced and replaced; the products of the natural environment, however, are, beyond certain limits, irreplaceable.

The fundamental choice, therefore, seems to prescribe an attitude of concern toward the environment, a concern that accepts that the world is our dwelling, even if it is a temporary one. The world we produce and leave behind is a testimony to our values. The acceptance of life has also been the acceptance of the struggle against entropy, and this implies an effort to preserve the possibilities within ourselves and within the natural world. As will happen many times, by reasoning from a very different standpoint, a conclusion has been reached that might have resulted from alternative routes. Consider the comment of Berdyaev:

> My salvation is bound up with that not only of other men but also of animals, plants, minerals; of every blade of grass—all must be transfigured and brought into the Kingdom of God. And this depends upon my creative efforts. Thus, the province of ethics is the whole world.[45]

As a rule, a destructive and thoughtless attitude toward the environment probably translates into a similar attitude toward society. Perhaps that is one reason Sartre's politics tend always toward violence. It is a sign of a for-itself unable to overcome the gap of nothingness that divides it from others and from the in-itself.[46] The preceding Note aptly shows how Sartre's view follows understandably from his ontology and the human problems this position raises. But lucidity could also open to us less alienated views of nature. It is not that we ought to immerse ourselves in the all-embracing in-itself and lose our identities; mysticism is not the only available stance. Indeed, the notion of "being-one-with-nature," whatever that can possibly mean, has already been discarded as a goal of human values. But it ought at least to be recognized that humans are an upsurge together with countless (but rapidly disappearing) other creatures, other upsurges that have not achieved full separation from the in-itself as for-themselves.

While Olson states that "all existentialists agree . . . that knowledge of the laws of nature has no human value," this does not necessarily follow from the philosophy.[47] What the statement means is that there are no values enforced upon humans by the laws of nature, not that values cannot be freely extended to include nature within free choices. There is, for one thing, the purely pragmatic case of science as the technological project that cannot be ignored in any progressive human society: even science for its own sake, as curiosity about our surroundings, has generated knowledge useful for any number of human projects.

It is curious that some members of the countercultural and antipositivist communes of America's 1960s still owned stereos. The computer, on which this text was written, is a remarkable achievement of technology that makes human communication much easier. Biology has made remarkable strides, thanks to the science of genetics, in developing strains of more productive rice and wheat. Biology in its subbranch of genetic engineering is also a field for the application of values, and a source of new achievements or new horrors. It is puerile to deny our reliance on and valid interest in science. But there is a further argument in favor of pursuing scientific knowledge that rests on the concept of lucidity, on an increasing knowledge of the human position and the potential projects and roles this unveils in the world.

The most useless science of all may be astronomy, and yet its fascinating revelations in the last few decades are a contribution to the lucid comprehension of humankind's place in the universe and, for that matter, to awe. Lucidity is not solely a concern with the ontological condition; it must also be applied to understanding the human condition in the world and the relation of for-itself to in-itself. The existentialist view was intended to open up the vast possibilities for human projects, and among these possible projects, curiosity and the search for scientific knowledge are no mean pursuits.

In the sum total of possible human projects, who is to judge that scientific endeavors for their own sake are more futile than the pursuit of the proletarian revolution (which did not turn out all too well). Is Archimedes' project or that of Euclid any less interesting than the building of the Roman Empire, at least from the distance of time? It has been the unfortunate case that for some existentialists only revolution, only Machiavelli's kind of *virtu*, holds interest for them, but this is not a necessary conclusion from the existentialist philosophy. In this respect, the Marxist position, with its consuming interest in the dialectic of natural science, of evolution and technology, is potentially more fertile than Sartre's. It is queer that Sartre for whom it was all one whether a person became drunk at the bar or conquered the world should so denigrate the projects of science.

As Barnes expresses it in relation to Camus' outlook, ". . . the absurd man is stubbornly honest, and he seeks the fullest possible awareness of all that is involved in whatever he experiences."[48] Thus, the scope of lucidity can be expanded, which, in part, is what Heidegger appears to have done in his later writings, although his interpretation of man's role in the universe is an unacceptable choice for most of us. The expanded sense of lucidity will be brought prominently into play later when the problems of political situations and the consequences of projects are considered. In that discussion, science, including social science, will not be neglected.

A final comment is in order. The choice of lucidity and life has made it apparent that we must also accept the ethical responsibility of a duty to ourselves. Lucidity and a dedication to life over death and destruction implies a certain responsibility of self-cultivation, of the preservation of mental and physical health. Without assuming the unexistential position of an inflexible human nature to be realized, it is appropriate to expand this duty to self to a concept of self-realization.[49]

All humans face the choice of affirmation or negation of the world. This choice is certainly basic, although it is not quite the fundamental choice in the Sartrean sense. A person can select a project of self-destruction in the world through drinking himself to death. Affirmation can be evidenced in the enthusiasm of a teacher explaining algebra to her pupils. But it is in the political realm that people can act out this basic choice on a much larger stage, and it is here that acts have a wide-ranging effect on others. It is here that the destructive projects of the seekers of death cut their bloody swath through the world, as have the Tamerlanes, Stalins, Pol Pots, Saddam Husseins, and Hitlers. Viewed in this light, the choices open to mankind that have been discussed in this chapter are crucial. It is a fundamental assessment to make of a political leader, whether that person is directed toward an affirmation of life or death.

Lucidity reveals to us the possibility of selecting a number of basic projects in the world, a choice that we are free to make. That all projects are possible, however, does not mean that all projects are desirable. The choice of construction over destruction appears to be a preferable choice, and arguments that will be presented later ought to give that preference additional support. And, yes, this preference seems to have placed us within the embattled camp of the so-called environmentalists.

Notes

1. Ludwig Wittgenstein, *Tractatus Logico-Philosophicus* (London: Routledge and Kegan Paul, 1961; trans. by D.F. Pears and B.F. McGuinness), p. 71.

2. Robert G. Olson, *An Introduction to Existentialism* (New York: Dover Publications, 1962) p. 37.

3. There is a pertinent argument by Kai Nielsen in *Ethics Without God* (New York: Prometheus Books, 1973), pp. 7-10, that goes as follows: If we call God good, it is because of the goodness of his acts. But to know the goodness of these acts we must have a prior moral criterion to use in making such a judgment. If God is good whatever his attributes, then the case rests on definition. But if God is good for substantive reasons (that is, if it makes sense to say that God might be evil), then moral judgment has to rest on a basis outside the existence of God. We must ascertain our moral principles independently of a belief in a deity. It ought to be noted, too, that for some theologians, the existence of God solves the problem of ultimate purpose, but for others, such as Nikolai Berdyaev, it does not.

4. Thomas M. King, *Sartre and the Sacred*, p. 142.

5. Gerald N. Izenberg, *The Existentialist Critique of Freud: The Crisis of Autonomy* (Princeton: Princeton University Press, 1976) p. 264.

6. Martin Heidegger, "What is Metaphysics?" in Werner Brock, ed., *Existence and Being* (South Bend: Regnery/Gateway, Inc., 1979), pp. 325-361; the translation is by B. F. C. Hull and Alan Crick.

7. George Steiner, *Martin Heidegger*, p. 136.

8. Martin Heidegger, *What Is Called Thinking?* trans. by J. Glenn Gray (New York: Harper and Row, Publishers, 1968), pp. 24-25.

9. Reinhardt Grossmann, *Phenomenology and Existentialism: An Introduction* (Boston: Routledge and Kegan Paul, 1984), pp. 192-195, provides a logical argument on this very point, using the term *existence* rather than *being*: The upshot of his presentation is that there can be no modes of existence, no different ways of existing. I prefer to accept this argument as concerning being rather than existence. Being is being, and an entity is an entity, regardless of whether we are speaking of a tree or a motorcycle.

10. Walter Kaufmann, *Hegel: A Reinterpretation* (Notre Dame, Indiana: University of Notre Dame Press, 1978), p. 205. Kaufmann's analysis of Hegel and Nietzsche are solid, reasonable, and readable.

11. Fell, *Heidegger and Sartre*, p. 16. The coverage by Fell of Heidegger's philosophy is very perceptive. It ought to be mentioned that Fell exonerates Heidegger from the accusation of mysticism.

12. *Ibid.*, pp. 382-383.

13. New York: Vintage Books, 1968; trans. by Hazel Barnes.

14. Leszek Kolakowski has a succinct essay on the lasting contribution of Marxism in his book of essays, *Toward a Marxist Humanism* (New York: Grove, 1968).

15. Henry Sidgwick, *The Methods of Ethics* (Indianapolis: Hackett Publishing Company, 1981; a printing taken from the 7th edition of 1907).

16. Eliseo Vivas, *Contra Marcuse* (New Rochelle: Arlington House, 1971), p. 111.

17. Bertrand Russell, *Human Society in Ethics and Politics* (London: George Allen and Unwin, Ltd., 1954), pp. 48-49.

18. Joseph Fletcher, *Situation Ethics: The New Morality* (Philadelphia: The Westminster Press, 1966), p. 129.

19. Some interesting contributions to this position appear in James Nuechterlein, "The Feminization of the American Left," *Commentary*, Vol. 84, No. 5 (November 1987), 43-48.

20. Paul Johnson, *Intellectuals* (New York: Harper and Row, 1988), does this convincingly in the cases of Rousseau, Tolstoi, Ibsen and others, but the phenomenon has been remarked by many others.

21. Kierkegaard agreed with Kant that ". . . unfortunately, the notion of happiness is so indefinite that although every man wishes to attain it, yet he can never say definitely and consistently what it is that he really wishes and wills." George J. Stack, *Kierkegaard's Existential Ethics* (University, Alabama: The University of Alabama Press, 1977), p. 177.

22. Charles E. Scott, "The Role of Ontology in Sartre and Heidegger," in Paul Arthur Schilpp, ed., *The Philosophy of Jean-Paul Sartre* (SaSalle, Illinois: Open Court Publishing Company, 1981), p. 294.

23. On this aspect of Sartrean thought, see Phyllis Sutton Morris, *Sartre's Concept of a Person: An Analytic Approach* (Amherst: University of Massachusetts Press, 1976), p. 108, fn 8, and *Being and Nothingness*, pp. 566-567, where Sartre specifically rejects this project.

24. See David Hume, Book III, "Of Morals," Part I, Section I, "Moral Distinctions not Derived from Reason," in *A Treatise of Human Nature, Vol. II* (London: J.M. Dent and Sons, Ltd., 1953), pp. 165-178.

25. John R. Searle's argument, "How to Derive 'Ought' from 'Is'," may be found in Pahel and Schiller, *Readings in Contemporary Ethical Theory*, pp. 156-168. The same source contains R. M. Hare's "The Promising Game," pp. 168-179, which purports to refute Searle. Searle's reply to Hare's criticism, pp. 180-182, makes some strong points, but in the end seems to fail. Guy W. Stroh's argument may be found in *American Ethical Thought* (Chicago: Nelson-Hall, 1979), pp. 250-251.

26. R. M. Hare, *Freedom and Reason* (Oxford: At the Clarendon Press, 1963), p. 86; Philippa Foot, *Virtues and Vices* (Berkeley: University of California Press, 1978), p. 100. The most famous refutation of the naturalistic fallacy, of course, is that of George Edward Moore, *Principia Ethica* (Cambridge: At the University Press, 1959), p. 114. In his *The Language of*

Morals, pp. 92-93, Hare presents a refutation of naturalism that is based on Moore's.

27. Bernard Williams, *Ethics and the Limits of Philosophy* (Cambridge, Mass.: 1985), p. 128.

28. Stroh, *American Ethical Thought*, pp. 177-179.

29. Joel J. Kupperman, *Ethical Knowledge* (New York: Humanities Press, 1970), p. 31.

30. R. M. Hare, *Moral Thinking* (Oxford: Clarendon Press, 1981), p. 151.

31. See his *Beyond Freedom and Dignity* (New York: Alfred A. Knopf, 1971), p. 113, p. 171.

32. Some of this argument is based on Hare's *Moral Thinking*, p. 69, and refers to the naturalistic fallacy. As Hare in a fine argument in *The Language of Morals* (Oxford: At the Clarendon Press, 1952), pp. 148-149, suggests, Skinner's arguments would seem to leave people with a ritualistic view of morality, a Pharaseeism, in which morality literally means to do what it says in the Ten Commandments. On natural rights, Skinner has this to say: "Life, liberty, and the pursuit of happiness are basic rights. But they are the rights of the individual and were listed as such at the time when the literature of freedom and dignity were concerned with the aggrandizement of the individual. They have only a minor bearing on the survival of a culture." This is a gem from his *Beyond Freedom and Dignity*, p. 180. I cannot derive any rational argument whatever from Skinner's presentation.

33. Morris, *Sartre's Concept of a Person*, pp. 115-119. See Sartre's presentation in *Being and Nothingness*, pp. 480-481.

34. "Existentialism is a Humanism," trans. by Philip Mairet in Walter Kaufmann, ed., *Existentialism from Dostoevsky to Sartre* (Cleveland: The World Publishing Company, 1956), pp. 291-292.

35. Gentile agrees that ". . . the aim of all volition is the creation of a self." Giovanni Gentile, *Genesis and Structure of Society* (Urbana: University of Illinois Press, 1966; trans. by H. S. Harris), p. 94. Stressing the factor of contingency, Ortega y Gasset states, "I must achieve myself in the world, among things, among other men, with a body which has fallen to me by chance and which suffers illnesses, with a soul that perhaps is not very well-endowed with will or memory or intelligence," Jose Ortega y Gasset, *Some Lessons in Metaphysics* (New York: Norton, 1970; trans. by Mildred Adams), p. 70.

36. Sartre's analysis of Genet (*Saint Genet: Actor and Martyr*, New York: George Braziller, 1963; trans. by Bernard Frechman) is a literary *tour de force*, but it is not very convincing. Why is to be a thief the central choice? Why not homosexuality? Or literature? And was the choice made freely? In fact, Olafson, *Principles and Persons*, pp. 171-172, holds that the idea of the "original" choice is unnecessary to existential viewpoints. Becoming is a process not set in any fixed starting point as a single and fundamental choice. This is my view.

37. This is from Merleau-Ponty's *Phenomenology of Perception* and is cited by Jeanson, *Sartre and the Problem of Morality*, p. 187.

38. Friedrich Nietzche, *Beyond Good and Evil* (New York: Random House, 1966; trans. by Walter Kaufmann), p. 64.

39. Sigmund Freud, *Civilization and Its Discontents* (New York: W. W. Norton and Company, 1961; trans. by James Strachey), p. 66.

40. Augustine, *Confessions*, (New York: Image Books, 1960; trans. by John K. Ryan), p. 280, in Chapter 4 of Book 11.

41. John Macquarrie, *3 Issues in Ethics* (New York: Harper and Row, 1970), p. 77.

42. John Macquarrie, *Existentialism* (New York: Penguin Books, 1973), p. 281.

43. Barnes, *The Literature of Possibility*, p. 189.

44. Maurice Cranston, "Sartre and Violence," *Encounter*, Vol XXIX, No. 1 (July 1967), p. 24, is the source of Sartre's depictions.

45. Nicolas Berdyaev, *The Destiny of Man* (London: Geoffrey Bles, 1937), p. 294.

46. Fell, *Heidegger and Sartre*, p. 179, states, "Sartre's disaffection with nature and rural settings, and his preference for the artifactual and for cities, is the personal analogue of his philosophical view that 'we are on a plane where there are only men [and women].' Sartre's personal fear of contingency (the *merely* natural) and his consequent effort to surpass it literarily in making himself a destiny and a permanence has its philosophical analogues in the [*Being and Nothingness*] description of the project to conceal contingency through synthesis and in purifying reflection's rectification of one's fall into self-deceptive complicity with one's past and with nature. I have called this the religion of humanism. In short, Sartre's personal drive to maintain whatever transcendental purity and lucidity are possible in the face of his ambiguous relation to an alien primeval slime--nature--that constantly threatens to pull him down is the counterpart of his central philosophic view of consciousness as split from actuality by an impassable negation that in principle precludes synthesis." Fell's is a splendid summary of Sartre's position. There is a poem by Baudelaire among the Flowers of Evil that puts the case exactly, an imaginary scene with all that is natural obliterated by human works--Sartre, who has written an existentialist psychoanalysis of Baudelaire's original choice must have been familiar with it.

47. Olson, *An Introduction to Existentialism*, p. 88.

48. Barnes, *The Literature of Possibility*, p. 170.

49. We agree, then, with David Hume, *Enquiries Concerning Human Understanding and Concerning the Principles of Morals* (ed. by L. A. Selby-Bigge, Oxford: Clarendon Press, 1975), pp. 322-323. See also Kerry H. Whiteside, *Merleau-Ponty and the Foundation of an Existential Politics* (Princeton: Princeton University Press, 1988), p. 140.

Chapter 3

Authenticity and Responsibility

The existentialists, who have assured us that we exist in freedom, also recommend for our souls that we exist this freedom in an authentic way. In the first place, since there is in the Sartrean formulation no apparent escape from freedom, it is not possible to make decisions that have been forced upon us, as by genetics, by the gods, by our own past. Whether we are willing to recognize it or not, our decisions will have been freely adopted, for freedom rests on an ontological foundation. Both the authentic person and the inauthentic person will have chosen their position in freedom. Without proposing at this time the reasons why we ought to be authentic rather than inauthentic in our stance toward our path through being, we first will endeavor to adumbrate the differences.

Sartre had promised to deliver a work on ethics following his first major statement of his philosophy, *Being and Nothingness*, but like the second volume of Heidegger's *Being and Time*, this never appeared. Yet, Sartre has not ignored ethical problems, for they are certainly inherent in his concept of authenticity, elaborated from Kierkegaard and Heidegger.

Wild rightly regards the twin concepts of authenticity and inauthenticity as an "ontologically grounded ethics" and the "crowning phases of this metaphysical doctrine," in all, "an illuminated approach to the moral problems of our time."[1] While the utilitarian pursues the happiness of the individual, while religious individuals must be concerned with the doctrinal rightness of their acts, authenticity is the measure of existentialist ethics.[2]

The idea of authenticity proposed by Martin Heidegger is that of the "genuine" existence that does not fear to face death. While the inauthentic may fear death, their fear must always be that fear based on the death of others. The inauthentic stance toward death is that of immortality, which, were it possible, would reduce each act to insignificance. Thus, authentic time is finite, while inauthentic time is infinite.

No doubt the realization that Dasein can come to an end points up the importance of acts within finite time.[3] To dread death, on the other hand, admits the ultimate possibility of nonbeing. This serves as an incentive to escape the distractions of the everyday, of the trivial, of the indifferent "they."[4] Since the sphere of the trivial, the nonauthentic, the *Verfallen* (the fallenness) is always with us, it is difficult to distinguish the authentic person from those immersed always in the everyday.[5,6]

Heidegger appears to omit from his concept of authenticity any mention of the dignity of all individuals, a stance that ranks high in the hierarchy of Kantian values. And the concept of being-together (Mitsein), which can result only in a diminution of experience, a trivialization, seems to be an incomplete conceptualization of authenticity.[7] Nonetheless, it would seem to follow from a concept such as authenticity, that it is relevant to one's relationship toward others and refers to a moral relation to the world.[8] Heidegger does not wholly ignore our relatedness to others; he suggests that in the resolute stand toward death, Dasein becomes the "conscience" of others. An authentic choice of Being-themselves is a precondition to being authentically with others.[9]

In light of the difficulties of existing authentically in the world of Das Man, of the everyday and trivial, it could be argued that the political is the epitome of everydayness. The political life is mainly concerned with the resolution of metaphysically unimportant conflicts. This attitude deserves consideration, both at this juncture and later when society is discussed.

In the first place, everydayness need not be treated with contempt, because it is the realm in which our mundane necessities are provided. We need to adjust to society and to conform to some degree in order to survive and to avoid unnecessary, that is, unconstructive, conflicts with others. We must choose our conflicts wisely; the authentic person will conform to some degree and dissent to some degree, the latter where significant matters are at stake. Of course, the consequences of dissent differ in various societies; in some polities it is easier to dissent than in others.

Politics are certainly trivial at some levels; one need only follow current political campaigns in the United States to understand this. But underlying many current issues, however shallow the debates concerning them appear, are profound differences in attitudes toward equality, liberty, authority, and the dignity of others. Inauthentic minds may well trivialize the political arena, but it is no surprise that great philosophical minds--Plato, Aquinas, Hobbes, Rousseau, Arendt--have found the conflicts occurring there to be of profound interest and significance.

The search for authentic existence is not original with the existentialists, nor does it appear only in modern philosophy following Descartes. The great religions have stressed the distinction between an authentic and an inauthentic life. Reading Sartre, one cannot help but taste the flavor of some austere Protestant theologian. Sartre sounds sometimes the atheistic equivalent of Jonathan Edwards.

Among the oldest religious writings extant are the Upanishads, and throughout these spiritual essays runs the theme of seeking an authentic existence. Indeed, Jasper's Transcendence and Heidegger's search for Being are profoundly anticipated in the Upanishads. It might even be suggested that since the Upanishads, little intellectual progress has really been made in explicating concepts such as Transcendence.[10]

Sartre seems to expand Heidegger's concept of authenticity somewhat.[11] With him it has become not a viewpoint taken with regard to the possibility of one's own death, but a correct recognition of our freedom to choose. There may be no incompatibility in the basic nature of these seemingly different views, but their reconciliation would be beyond the scope of this discussion.[12] Let us suggest, however, that recognition of the end of one's being also would enhance the significance of each free choice, for each choice signifies as well the possible choices that were not made and that, given a finite life, can never ever be made.

Because choices are made freely, no matter what these choices may be, they are ontologically free, and the perpetrator must be held responsible for them. It is not destiny, it is not the evolution of the in-itself that is responsible for choices, it is the for-itself that makes free choices. If the basic foundation of this free choice is understood, if the actor accepts this freedom with all its implications, then the choice is an authentic one. Indeed, an authentic choice cannot really be morally wrong.[13] To choose authentically, one must in the first instance choose with lucidity, which can only mean that a choice begins with a clear view of the world; the individual's place in that world, considering goals, aims, and projects;

and an insight into the condition of human existence.

While authenticity may appear to be divorced from reason and logic, this cannot be an adequate conception of free choice--free choice cannot be simply a spontaneous and irrelevant upsurge, a fortuitous and ungrounded act, or else the very concept of freedom would be rendered meaningless. By positing freedom as the attribute of the prereflective consciousness, however, Sartre runs into the danger of making choice meaningless. This is why lucidity, in an extended version, would seem to be a requirement for the exercise of freedom. Choice must be exercised on the basis of a full understanding of the environment of choice. Of course, reason and the knowledge of how culture or science or ethics or theology interpret the world does not determine a person's decision in the world unless the actor chooses to be so guided. But lucidity is a basic requirement for authentic, free choice. A choice is not authentic if it is made in an intellectual void.

Facticity, the disposition of being-in-itself out there as well as one's body, does, of course, matter. In cases of brain-damage (see note 6), an authentic decision may be impossible. This contingency, recognized and analyzed at length by Merleau-Ponty, is not taken adequately into account by Sartre. This may suggest a difficulty in Sartre's account of the for-itself, because there may be the possibility of a diminished for-itself. But it does not necessarily detract from the interpretation of freedom to admit that the capacity for freedom may be diminished by material factors, for it has been assumed that freedom, like life, made a gradual appearance in the world. Brain damage would represent a sort of reversed evolution.[14]

We do not assume that animals act freely but attribute much of their behavior to instinct or conditioning. We know, on the other hand, that animals are conscious. It is the prereflective consciousness that they possess. But if this is so, then freedom does not rest on the prereflective cogito, which is pulled spontaneously by the world (a world that includes our own body), but on the reflective cogito, which can view and judge our acts. So lucidity and a taking into account of the environment for decision is the true situation, even if we also are inclined to agree with Jeanson that "it is only by starting with himself that [one] can attempt to endow his acts with value."[15]

It would seem to be a common misconception of existentialism to assume off-handedly that a choice of those values that are provided by the surrounding culture or society cannot be freely chosen. Unfortunately, a lot of existentialist writing supports Bronowski's mistaken view that existentialism requires the gratuitous act. This is wrong; a person need not be in eternal contradiction to Das Man in order to be authentic. In fact, an individual can hardly attain to a human status, as Rousseau would have it, lacking a social and political culture. Hence, we disagree with Sartre, as he avers in *L'Idiot de la Famile*, the impossibility of obedience as a choice of authentic action. For Sartre, the free act "comprises an inexplicit negation of obedience".[16]

This is a foolish position, unless it is taken in the mitigated meaning that one ought never to agree to obey an authority, a culture, a state, a movement, "once and for all." In politics, there is a distinction between Hobbes' Leviathan, which demands a permanent choice of rule, not to be changed, and Locke's polity, which is obeyed provided it adheres to limitations; Locke's polity is always on trial. Even accepting the notion of the free sovereignty of the act, Sartre's conclusion need not follow. It is more an expression of Sartre's inherent anarchism than a sound philosophical conclusion on his part.

When existentialism was a fad, we enjoyed pictures of youths engaged in various acts of patent nonconformity, banqueting on a raft in the Seine, and so forth; Sartre, of course, encouraged such shenanigans. But authentic choices need not always be nonconformist, in particular, because we ought to be aware of the consequences of our activities. Liberty and an expanded scope for human choice are not the inevitable outcome of every revolt, of every revolution. By the end of the twentieth century, we know better. Nonconformity can too easily sink uncomprehendingly into conformity. Sartre may frequently be taken to task for the too facile belief in revolt for its own sake. One can also become the conformist of the anarchistic stance.

But if we may underwrite some of the values that are ready-made in a lucid understanding of the world, this must be done authentically, with the acceptance of full responsibility for all that these values bring in their wake. We acquire, according to Merleau-Ponty, cognitive-linguistic structures that limit speech and thought to meanings that are known (sedimented) by our culture.[17] In inauthentic speech, we make use of such means of communication in the belief that they are somehow natural, somehow all that there is or can be--this is the inauthentic stance. Authentic communication is the recognition that these meanings can also be freely accepted or changed; they are not carved in granite.

In politics, conflicts rage over the meaning for society of such terms as "political prisoner," "murder," "tradition," and so forth. Indeed, this was the discovery and originality of Socrates, to challenge the current meanings of the moral concepts of his day, a very exciting and, as it turned out, dangerous vocation.[18] But whereas Merleau-Ponty is interested in a balance between the self and the world (a balance in one's being-in-the-world), an overemphasis on the need for authenticity might lead to a lack of balance, to a choice of fortuitous nihilism and aimless rebellion.

Hence, Merleau-Ponty views the mediating function of public "meaning" as an indispensable element in the dialectic between the individual and the moral community to which the person belongs.[19] Merleau-Ponty's view makes better ethical sense than that of Heidegger and Sartre, to whom, seemingly, any reliance upon collectively-held standards of evaluation and action defeats authenticity. Such a view is extreme and unfounded. The freedom to choose implies the freedom to conform if circumstances warrant. This possibility would appear to be at the basis of any reasonable politics.

In brief, we may depict authentic individuals as persons who (1) act for freedom, (2) have "a true and lucid consciousness of the situation," and (3) accept responsibility for their decisions. To act inauthentically, is to act in bad faith, a cognate term that will be elucidated later.[20] Given the description of the for-itself, it follows necessarily that all complete (physically unimpaired) persons will chose freely in any case. But the authentic choice is a choice in which the chooser recognizes the freedom to choose. Hence, there are no excuses for this choice, although one might admit that he may have been mistaken in the understanding of the situation. One will accept full responsibility for the act he or she introduces into the situation and the predictable consequences that flow from that act.

Sartre goes further than this, however, in depicting the authentic person as the one who values freedom above all else. The moral implications of this stance are not clear, but they cannot be neutral. We will attempt in the course of the argument to delineate some of the differences that this outlook might make. Whether freedom will emerge as a kind of ultimate value, however, must still remain open to question. In any case, the principle of authenticity stands as the prime existentialist virtue.

Sartre is clear that inauthenticity is the main obstacle to human relationships based on reciprocal recognition of one another as fully responsible moral agents.[21] And it is the attribution of responsibility to others for their acts that constitute them in our eyes as moral persons. To regard unimpaired persons as not responsible for their acts is to diminish their status as humans. As Hartmann states, "If anyone deprives me of the responsibility which I take upon myself, he sins against my essential nature as a person."[22]

Sartre never quite accomplishes an ethical thesis with his doctrine of authenticity. In the first place, as Manser admits[23], Sartre never makes clear whether authenticity is a means to a freely chosen morality or an ultimate end itself; at times he seems to intend the latter interpretation. It is also not clear why authenticity should be so highly regarded as either a means or an end, if all our acts are ontologically free in any case. In Sartre's view, we cannot escape freedom. It would appear that one ought to be authentic rather than inauthentic for the reason that inauthenticity is dishonest. It is as though honesty to self has been raised to the highest level of morality, but why should this be so? And why ought we to accept responsibility for acts? Where is the moral imperative that supports this?

Hazel Barnes states that once the decision to be ethical has been made, which must be a free choice (obviously, as choosing to not be ethical, in Sartre's view, must also be a free choice), then the inauthentic life is ruled out. The chief problem with the inauthentic choice, which may be made out of the fear of sustaining values by oneself all alone, is that it is based on self-deception; it is dishonest.[24]

It follows, according to Sartre, that authenticity entails respect for other people. Manser points to the clear resemblance of this aspect of Sartrean authenticity to Kant's categorical imperative in its formula of treating other people as ends rather than as means only.[25] There are some compelling reasons why such a corollary might follow from a concept like authenticity. As free and rational persons, we can only desire relations with other free persons. This important result will be pursued in more detail when the discussion turns to the topic of others.

But there are ambiguities in existentialist discussions of authenticity. De Beauvoir makes statements such as ". . . the oppressed can fulfill his freedom as a man only in revolt . . . ."[26] But freedom seems to exist in Sartre's view no matter what choice one makes. We can choose to acknowledge this honestly and choose a way of life accordingly, or we can choose not to acknowledge this and be inauthentic; both are, however, free choices for which we are responsible.

De Beauvoir appears to have chosen a project. She has set about to recommend this project to everyone--commit yourself to this project, and you will have used your freedom well. But she has not shown any evident reason why we must do so. Once again, we seem to have come upon two different meanings of freedom. De Beauvoir recognizes this problem, for she defends the "willing of freedom" against the charge that it is a hollow formula. Freedom, she avers, realizes itself only by engaging itself in the world.[27]

But has she really shown us the connection between the existence of freedom and engagement? Indeed, in *Being and Nothingness*, freedom does appear as ethically hollow, for Sartre claims to see no apparent difference between the drunk at the bar and the ruler of worlds. (Actually, Sartre really does make distinctions in the uses of freedom; he is guilty here of shocking the reader with a startling exaggeration.)

There are substantial problems with authenticity as a starting point for a morality. It must be acknowledged that authenticity is not a *state* attainable by persons. We never succeed in "situating" ourselves in authenticity. There is never a once-and-for-all choice, because one of the insights from a position of authenticity is that a person is never completed. Liberation is never total. One can never be delivered from the incessant problem of new situations, and authenticity is not a final attainment but requires renewed effort in each choice. If one does succeed in an authentic choice, this provides no permanent solution but only a "point of departure for new problems."[28]

Additional criticism of the concept of authenticity holds that it may not do justice to the hard facticities of human existence, realities that must be taken into account, else we fall into fantasy or pretense.[29] While at the time of *Being and Nothingness*, such a criticism was well merited, by the time of writing the *Critique*, Sartre had taken this problem to heart and had made efforts, successfully, to rectify it. His view, it is important to acknowledge, is that of a free for-itself within a world, an in-itself, that harbors determinism.

Marcuse criticizes Heidegger for his lack of historicity and his attempt to locate destiny in the individual. Marx had introduced the concept of *historical existence* whereby an "authentic" existence would be correlated with "the science of history."[30] Without accepting a science of history, it is true that existentialism offers and may even overemphsize an individual focus. We will be concerned with mitigating this criticism and will try to relate the individual, with his or her freedom, to history, to society, and to the nation. Without doubt, the emphasis of existential authenticity is antithetical to the Marxian placement, following Hegel, of historical meaning within the society. The concept expounded by Heidegger and Sartre resembles the concept of inwardness, or subjectivity, associated with Kierkegaard. It is in the *Critique* that Sartre attempted, with a measure of success, to reconcile these views. But it also should go without saying that the particular historicity that Marcuse had in mind is defunct. In this respect, existentialism is on firmer ground.

The doctrinally conservative Pope John Paul II naturally disagreed with the Sartrean presentation of the authentic individual, who possesses, according to this august critic, no mooring for the exercise of freedom. This criticism conjures up a vision of the totally permissive society, which is akin to Plato's (unfair) condemnation of democracy, where everyone does as they please. The Church, of course, demands obedience; it places demands on the individual, which are antithetical to the spirit of existentialism.

But ultimately, for the existentialist, it *is* necessary that persons place demands on themselves--authenticity ought to be an expression of this view. Authenticity demands honesty and courage; it too can require obedience when obedience is warranted. While the Catholic view of mankind and the existentialist view are admittedly very different, the authentic life ought not terminate in the "totally permissive society," in the unlimited consumer society, if you will, or in hedonism. Indeed, we will show later that hedonism is not consonant with the doctrine of authenticity.[31]

There is also a challenge in the objection that authenticity is an empty concept. If to be authentic is to be capable of any action whatever in pursuit of any state of affairs whatever, then how can authenticity be a moral concept? How can we strive toward an authentic existence if we cannot define it or delineate its limitations?[32] The strongest statement along these lines is that of Theodore Adorno.[33] Adorno claims that the language of authenticity is a deceptive ("inauthentic," as it were) language, weaving a spell of words, of rhetoric, of phony profundity, that takes the place of analysis. Authenticity consists in incantations. It is a subjective delusion seemingly operating to free us from reification (in the sense that this term is used by Georg Lukacs). Indeed, a Caligula might be as authentic as a saint.

Authenticity does not strike at the sources of the woes of society, but pretends that an individual can somehow avert these woes without changing the objective conditions that give rise to them. It provides the delusion that freedom is possible in the individual consciousness while oppression reigns in society. Particularly in the thought of Heidegger, all social content seems to be excluded from the idea of authenticity. Thereby, Heidegger has reified human subjectivity, rendering it unrelated to the world outside. Social problems are left out of consideration--the "jargon" of authenticity can contain no political program. And for Adorno, a sound political program ought to produce a rational economic system that would dissipate reification.

In his Critique of Heidegger (p. 183), Waterhouse also points out that for Heidegger, the public world is necessarily the world of inauthenticity, corrupting, and antithetical to the individual's attainment of authentic existence. With such a view of public affairs, it is not surprising that Heidegger himself failed so miserably in the public stance he adopted in Nazi Germany in the 1930s. Waterhouse suggests, in opposition to this view, that the

> public world is the only possible forum for the realization of meaningful authenticity, that it is only in terms of relationships with others that we can be either authentic or inauthentic, and that the attempt to realize authenticity as purely a mode of self-realization is vacuous.

These critiques are more compelling against a thinker such as Heidegger than against Sartre, for the latter became very involved in social and political affairs. Indeed, Sartre's efforts to become involved in a significant politics had almost a quality of desperation. Yet, it must be admitted that the doctrine even through its presentation by as socially-conscious a writer as Sartre tried to be in his post-World War II writings, is vulnerable to the criticisms leveled at authenticity by Adorno.

We will make efforts to vindicate the concept of authenticity by elaborating its implications and by proposing conditions, such as deciding on the basis of lucidity, that are required to found acts in authenticity. Thus, we shall hope to escape the criticism that authenticity has no end except for authenticity itself by elaborating the moral and rational requirements for authentic acts.

It would seem that to be responsible for acts, it is necessary for a person to be free. But this is not enough. To be simply and spontaneously free in the sense of pre-personal reflection would not relate appropriately to responsibility. To be responsible is to be able to choose a project and to sustain it (if we so choose), hence to have a personal identity.[34] Responsibility rests with the individual person, who, as has been argued, may freely choose to sustain a project. Ultimately, responsibility is a concept applicable to the individual as the source of consciousness, although consideration will be given later to the idea of the responsibility of nations. Another concern of the concept of responsibility will be to whom is reponsibility owed?

There are a number of responsibilities possible: to myself, to others, to being-in-itself, in some way, and to society and the nation. For there to be responsibility toward others demands additional arguments that will appear later. For now, it may be accepted that there are others, that others have an identity, and that others matter. The analysis of what responsibility might be borne toward being-in-itself has been provided in Chapter 2.

Responsibility is, in the first instance, related to authorship; the actor is the author of acts. This may have to be understood in an extended sense when collective responsibility is considered. Naturally, responsibility in the significantly moral sense requires that freedom exist for the individual. In the Sartrean notion of responsibility, it is a phenomenon of the prereflective cogito. What we author is done in connection with what Sartre refers to as our fundamental project, and this entails a noetic responsibility, whereby we author meanings.

Moreover, responsibility in this noetic sense extends not only to the meanings that we actually author, the meanings that "already are," but to the meanings that we might have chosen instead, to the "could have been." What we author in the nature of our activities and judgments is revelatory of our selection of an ideal self. We are in the process of creating an ideal image of what a human ought to be.[35] A being that is conscious of itself, that knows itself as a self with particular talents, passions, dispositions, and surroundings, assumes reponsibility, in this view, for everyone.[36]

By existing and being aware of existing in a certain manner, we undertake to "mould the world within which others will choose their lives," affecting vitally, as we shall strongly emphasize, others' freedom to realize ideal selves, for which reason we bear the attribute of responsibility; no one, therefore, is guiltless of the condition of the world.[37] Knowing this, knowing that we are abandoned to our own free decisions, knowing that our being is in our own hands, we are occasionally stricken with anguish.[38]

Although the moral aura of responsibility inheres in our free choice of ourselves or stems from others who so choose to regard our actions, Sartre provides a more basic definition that ought to hold regardless of moral implications, namely, the "consciousness of being the incontestable author of an event or object." This definition as interpreted by Sartre is very broad, for each for-itself is responsible, in the sense of authorship, for there being a world, for that is the nature of consciousnes. ". . . [W]hatever may be the situation in which he finds himself, the for-itself must wholly assume this situation."[39]

This view of authorship is acceptable only with some important reservations. Heineman is correct in saying that Sartre is wrong in making people responsible for actions they did not do and for situations they did not bring about. Moreover, if we accept a view of responsibility so all-embracing as Sartre's, we encounter the paradox that if everybody is responsible for all the activities in the world, then it transpires that no one is responsible for anything at all, a cogent point made by Flynn.[40] There must be some relevant answer to the question, who in this situation is in fact responsible, and to what degree are each of the participants responsible? Thus, in the period following World War II, it was possible for Karl Jaspers in *The Question of Guilt* to assess the degrees of responsibility each German citizen bore for the Holocaust.

Some heed also must be paid to the extent to which persons can be expected to understand the world in which they exist and the skills and abilities that they may possess or lack to accomplish their chosen goals.[41] As we will see later, it may be possible for particularly vulnerable groups or individuals to be, as it were, robbed of their right to assume a valid responsibility for their acts. In short, it is our opinion that Sartre makes responsibility too all-embracing a concept; it is not unlikely that he has exaggerated its scope in an effort to provide another arresting argument, a not uncommon literary device for Sartre. We have, Sartre avers, full responsibility for "the war," not only because we have not done everything in our power to prevent it, but also because we constitute the world in which this war occurs. Not to deny the element of truth in this view, it nevertheless is far too strong a prescription.[42]

On the other hand, it is possible to regard responsibility in a too-diminished fashion. There are collective and shared responsibilities that demand consideration. Responsibility does exist for the solitary individual, but it does not stop at this level. Responsibility is tied to collective structures. Each person does not simply belong to a nation, a family, or a rowing team. "I share in a myriad of meanings, customs, institutions, and the like, which I have not originated but to which I am committed, and thus responsible."[43] We exist a membership in such collectivities through being-for-others.[44] We all make use of collective techniques. Meanings are attributed to the collectivity or taken over from the practico-inert, meanings that may have been intended when the collectivities were in the process of formation. One chooses oneself through the ensemble, in Sartre's engaging terminology.

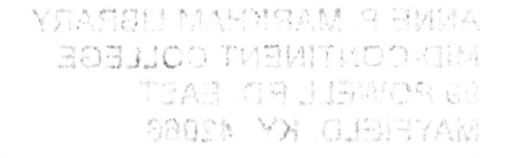

One may be immersed in a situation of oppression created by the institutions of society, but it is still the individual worker who can choose, within the collective, the future of the proletariat in relentless humiliation or conquest and victory, according to Sartre.[45] It is still the individual factory owner that accepts the reality of exploitation. Indeed, we would go almost as far as Sartre in accepting such a scope for responsibility in the collective: we are responsible for these undertakings that have fostered our own class interest, including racism, in the fruits of which we may partake, or colonial violence, even though we may be unaware of any particulars, and only after the fact.

We bear a responsibility for the past insofar as we partake of what the past has contributed to the present; we have some responsibility, that is, for the abominable conditions experienced by the working classes of the early 19th century, for we partake of the result of the system that oppressed them and produced our own present luxuries. We owe them their due in honest history, for one thing. As Sartre suggests, ". . . if I interiorize this multiplicity, I assume its overall project and that includes its temporal practical ensemble."[46]

Sartre has provided the additional concept of the "slippery fellow," a character who must certainly be vivid in the mind of any reader of Charles Dickens, who partakes amply in the fruits of the actions of his nation or class and ". . . who has done nothing for which to be reproached."[47] The decision that determines whether to acknowledge this guilt, of course, is itself freely selected. There is a moral implication here, certainly, which proceeds from the concept of authenticity.

But we must reemphasize our earlier criticism of Sartre on this theme of collective responsibility--failure to assign degrees of responsibility makes Sartre's discussions on this issue "extremely abstract and metaphysical."[48] Whereas guilt seems to attach to the actor and doer, there is also the guilt of the cowardly individual, who attempts to retire from the world of activity, for very fear of guilt. Nicolai Hartmann suggests the "courage to be under obligation," the sense in which one rejoices in responsibility.[49] Machiavelli extols the person who is courageous enough to make himself significant in the world, at the expense of assuming heavy responsibilities and guilt, the person of *virtu*. Unbounded purposive activity, avers Hartmann, means unbounded responsibility, responsibility for everything.

Thus, responsibility for a decision can be regarded as being quite far-reaching, although, to repeat, we cannot quite accept Sartre's extreme view. Yet, it is obvious that responsibilities may extend well beyond our immediate recognition of them. The decision to resort to the use of illegal drugs has an obvious effect on the person making such a choice, insofar as these drugs may well prove deleterious to the ability to perceive and act lucidly in the world. Such a consideration is connected with one's duty to oneself, a topic that is a prominent theme of Kant's *Lectures on Ethics*.

Drug use affects the ideal image of the person we want to project into the world. But there is an even wider range of implications associated with the creation of the illegal apparatus in the United States that is required to supply the addict. The addict becomes responsible for the national criminal apparatus that seeks profits through bribery, coercion, murder, and the perversion of political institutions; the addict is responsible for the expansion of the criminal apparatus into the ghetto, into the school yard, into the military. While some addicts may enjoy drugs in bourgeois gentility, they also lay the foundation for the despair resulting from drug use in the ghetto.

In addition, there is an international criminal apparatus, that the user also must accept the responsibility for helping to create, an apparatus powerful enough to control nations. The user condones the uprooting of subsistence crops and the development of a peasantry in Bolivia and elsewhere dependent on supplying the raw materials for drugs. Whole societies succumb to the penetration of the drug culture and its needs. The user becomes responsible for the massacres and the perversion of the political and judicial system of Colombia.

All of these ramifications fall within the addict's personal responsibility as a result of a choice to take drugs, and there is no need to force the definition of responsibility here. No choice is simple, of course, although some choices may not have repercussions quite as far-flung as a personal decision to use illegal drugs. But there is nothing in the vast ramifications of the individual choice to take drugs that cannot be lucidly perceived if the individual is to be authentic in such a choice.

Since human choice is arbitrary insofar as it relates to moral dicta from "out there," Sartre regards the effort to justify an act as a cowardly abandonment of freedom and responsibility. By an attempt to justify actions, we turn ourselves into things, into objects. From his analysis of consciousness, from his extreme absolute distinction between the for-itself and the in-itself, it may be seen how this conclusion must follow. And he follows this point up with his famous statement that whether I decide to die for justice or drink at a bar, the matter is indifferent.[50] In one sense of justification, this is true. In the sense of justification as rationalization, it follows as a matter of course. However, it is not necessary to accept the complete implications of Sartre's view.

There must be a place for self-analysis; insofar as our acts depict the ideal individual, and to the degree that our actions are valid for all mankind, we must seek to justify them. It is the moral point of there being a reflective cogito as well as a prereflective one. Justification would seem to be a concomitant of authenticity and responsibility and to require both lucidity and a sense of identity. We must within any moral and ethical stance justify our choices to ourselves. This is another reservation from the Sartrean position.

Notes

1. John Wild, *The Challenge of Existentialism* (Bloomington: Indiana University Press, 1955), p. 126.

2. Marjorie Grene, *Martin Heidegger* (London: Bowes and Bowes, 1957), p. 46.

3. Michael Gelven, *A Commentary on Heidegger's "Being and Time"* (New York: Harper Torchbooks, 1970), p. 189.

4. Marjorie Grene, "Authenticity: An Existential Virtue," *Ethics*, Vol. 62 (July 1952), p. 266. This fine essay is recommended for its coverage of its topic.

5. *Ibid.*, p. 267. It is necessary to stress that Heidegger has warned us that such terms as "lapsing" (Verfallen), "the they" (Das Man), and unauthenticity are not themselves ethical concepts. They refer to a mode of existence characterized by "forgetfulness of Being." Certainly there is some difficulty in bearing this in mind because of the very terms he has selected. It may be the case, that while the modes of existence--authenticity and inauthenticity--may form a basis for an ethics, they are not themselves ethical stances. This is, however, rather hard to believe. See Martin Heidegger, *Kant and the Problem of Metaphysics* (Trans. by James S. Churchill. Bloomington: University of Indiana Press, 1962), p. 243, fn 22, comments by Churchill.

6. Merleau-Ponty refers to an interesting case of brain damage, in which the patient, "Schneider," was only able to express himself in standard, inauthentic situations that lay on the near horizon of his diminished field. See Mallin, *Merleau-Ponty*, pp. 183-184.

7. This point is brought out by Grene, *Martin Heidegger*, p. 55.

8. Grene, "Authenticity," p. 271.

9. Martin Heidegger, *Being and Time* (London: SCM Press, Ltd., 1962), pp. 344-345.

10. A manageable initiation into these mysteries is *The Upanishads* (Trans. by Juan Mascaro. Middlesex: Penguin Books, 1965).

11. As significant a concept as authenticity would seem to be in Sartrean philosophy, it is curious, as Poster notes, that authenticity is mentioned in *Being and Nothingness* only in a single footnote, and that too is curious: "It is indifferent whether one is in good or in bad faith, because bad faith reapprehends good faith and slides to the very origin of the project of good faith, that does not mean that we cannot radically escape bad faith. But this supposes a self-recovery of being which has previously corrupted. This self-recovery we shall call authenticity, the description of which has no place here." Of course, one asks, why not? Perhaps at this point Sartre was looking forward to his work on ethics, which never appears. However, in his fictional works, *The Flies*, for instance, we have characters who represent an ethical life. See Mark Poster, *Existential Marxism in Postwar France* (Princeton, New Jersey: Princeton University Press, 1975), p. 89. Sartre's footnote may be found on page 70 of Barnes' translation.

12. Anthony Manser, *Sartre, a Philosophical Study* (New York: Oxford University Press, 1966), p. 163, suggests that Kant's categorical imperative, in its formulation of treating other people always as ends, never as means only, is similar to aspects of Sartre's authenticity. And see also Alfred Stern, *Sartre: His Philosophy and Existential Psychoanalysis* (New York: Dell Publishing Company, 1953), p. 171, who mades clear the difference in the basis for authenticity between Sartre and Heidegger. In both cases, however, the basis is also concerned with lucidity, or honesty to self.

13. Norman N. Greene, *Jean-Paul Sartre: The Existentialist Ethic* (Ann Arbor: The University of Michigan, 1963), p. 87. While not accepting the ontology that leads to this conclusion, Nicolai Hartmann, *Ethics, Vol. II, Moral Values* (Trans. by Stanton Coit. Atlantic Highlands: Humanties Press, 1974), p. 247, nonetheless expresses a comparable thought, saying that "moral life is a venture and requires courage at every turn. Along with the courageous deed must be classed the courageous word, conviction and opinion, bravery in truth, confession and thought; and not less, courage towards oneself and one's real feelings, one's own personality, the courage of great emotions." Hartmann was, of course, in the line of great German philosophers, as was Heidegger himself. Any analysis of the German situation of the 1930s and 1940s would probably conclude that the percentage of Germans who made authentic choices in the face of Nazism, a stance that would require all of the courage recommended by Hartmann, was certainly no greater, possibly somewhat less, than might have been the case among any other people or nation. Authentic decision must always, by its nature, be the minority of moral decisions with a polity. It is of interest that Heidegger chose to go the way of inauthenticity, becoming lost in an inauthentic being-with-others. This is disappointing to anyone who admires his contribution to philosophy, but it in no way detracts from his work. It may detract from his later work, however, because there will always be lacking in it any commentary, any mention, of the greatest moral debacle of our time: the Holocaust and World War II, and such omissions show a lack of lucidity; hence, a lack of authenticity.

14. Nor would brain damage be the only cause of such reversion. Evelyn Waugh, in *Brideshead Revisited* (Boston: Little, Brown and Company, 1946), p. 200, has one of his characters make the following assessment, "You know Father Mowbray hit on the truth about Rex at once, that it took me a year of marriage to see. He simply wasn't all there. He wasn't a complete human being at all. He was a tiny bit of one, unnaturally developed; something in a bottle, an organ kept alive in a laboratory. I thought he was a sort of primitive savage, but he was something absolutely modern and up-to-date that only this ghastly age could produce. A tiny bit of a man pretending he was the whole."

15. Jeanson, *Sartre and the Problem of Morality*, p. 117. In *Being and Nothingness*, pp. 90-91, Sartre provides an example illustrating lucidity, namely, the proletariat coming into class consciousness.

16. Joseph Halpern, *Critical Fictions: The Literary Criticism of Jean-Paul Sartre* (New Haven: Yale University Press, 1976), p. 68.

17. Mallin, *Merleau-Ponty's Philosophy*, pp. 183-184.

18. The analysis of authentic communication has become the focus of Jurgen Habermas. We will have reference to this problem again when we come to analyze the nation-state.

19. Olson, *An Introduction to Existentialism*, pp. 197-198.

20. Thomas C. Anderson, *The Foundation and Structure of Sartrean Ethics* (Lawrence: The Regents Press of Kansas, 1979), p. 61.

21. Olafson, *Principles and Persons*, p. 203.

22. Hartmann, *Ethics, Vol. III, Moral Freedom*, p. 161.

23. Manser, *Sartre*, pp. 56-57.

24. Hazel E. Barnes, *An Existential Ethics* (New York: Alfred A. Knopf, 1969), pp. 18-19, and p. 60.

25. Manser, *Sartre*, p. 163.

26. Simone de Beauvoir, *The Ethics of Ambiguity* (Trans. by Bernard Frechtman. Secaucus, N.J.: Citadel Press, 1980; first published in English in 1948, the Philosophical Library), p. 87.

27. *Ibid.*, p. 78.

28. Jeanson, *Sartre and the Problems of Morality*, p. 218.

29. John Wild, "Authentic Existence: A New Approach to 'Value Theory'", in James M. Edie, ed., *An Invitation to Phenomenology* (Chicago: Quadrangle Books, 1965), pp. 63-64. Paul Ricoeur, *Freedom and Nature: The Voluntary and the Involuntary* (Trans. by Erazin V. Kohak. Evanston: Northwestern University Press, 1986), pp. 348-349, mentions that even an "authentic existence" must be replete with lapses: "Consideration of the inevitable from a spectator viewpoint is my refuge when I am tired of willing and when the daring and danger of being free weigh upon me. . . . the hypostatization of character type, of the unconscious, and of life as fundamental exclusive natures are an alibi for fear and sloth, a pretext for non-being."

30. Herbert Marcuse, "Contributions to a Phenomenology of Historical Materialism," *Telos*, No. 4 (Fall 1969), p. 7. His citation of Marx refers to *Archiv* I.

31. This material is taken from a book review by Reid Buckley in the *American Spectator*, but the issue has eluded me. Pope John Paul II, who was responding to M. Frossard, had some additional comments on freedom as well: "The key is the way we understand human freedom. If freedom is the ability to 'do anything I wish' (or rather, 'anything I fancy'), then it is clear that, confronted with freedom in this sense, not only Christian morality... but any human system of morality can be considered restrictive. My neighbor's freedom is then an irritation and a threat to mine; that is what makes Sartre say, 'Hell is other people.' On the other hand, if freedom... is expressed in responsibility, that is, in the perception of the truth about human dignity—that of others and also mine—then Christian morality will seem 'liberating' in the inner experience of those who apply it conscientiously and honestly...."

32. Waterhouse, *Critique of Heidegger*, p. 188. G. J. Warnock, "Contemporary Moral Philosophy," in W. D. Hudson, ed., *New Studies in Ethics: Modern Theories*, Vol. 2 (New York: St. Martin's Press, 1970), pp. 416-417, also calls attention to this problem; if choosing freely is the highest value for us, then the choice of sock color is as significant as the decision to assassinate Hitler. Such a result is ludicrous, of course. Additionally, all choices must by nature be free—even though our excuses for our acts may seek to exonerate our actions by a resort to determinism or social coercion.

33. Theodor W. Adorno, *The Jargon of Authenticity* (Evanston: Northwestern University Press, 1973), p. 126. There is an apt summary of Adorno's argument in Leszek Kolakowski, *Main Currents of Marxism*, Vol. 3 (Oxford: Oxford University Press, 1978), pp. 370-371.

34. H. Richard Niebuhr, *The Responsible Self: An Essay in Christian Moral Philosophy* (New York: Harper and Row, Publishers, 1963), p. 65, agrees that "Personal responsibility implies the continuity of a self with a relatively consistent scheme of interpretations of what it is reacting to." We agree with this, and it provides some problem, which he has endeavored to overcome, with Sartre's ontology.

35. Flynn, *Sartre and Marxist Existentialism*, pp. 14-15. Sartre expresses the thought that "in choosing for himself, he chooses for all men," although it is not clear that this is the case unless we indeed choose to act authentically. See Sartre, *Existentialism and Humanism* (London: Methuen and Company, 1957, Trans. Philip Mairet).

36. Stack, *Kierkegaard's Existential Ethics*, pp. 125-126. Unlike the Sartrean position, however, where the individual's moral responsibility is global, for Kierkegaard responsibility is personal (Stack, p. 96). Farber criticizes this Sartrean view as unclear and ill founded: "It remains to be shown how an individual 'chooses all men' when 'choosing himself'...." See Farber, *The Aims of Phenomenology*, pp. 223-223.

37. Barnes, *The Literature of Responsibility*, p. 83.
38. Sartre, *Existentialism and Humanism*, p. 39.
39. Sartre, *Being and Nothingness*, pp. 553-554.
40. Flynn, *Sartre and Marxist Existentialism*, p. 169.
41. Olson, *An Introduction to Existentialism*, p. 161.
42. Sartre, *Being and Nothingness*, pp. 554-555.
43. Flynn, *Sartre and Marxist Existentialism*, pp. 28-29.

44. Of course, I have chosen my past and am therefore responsible for it, a responsibility I can take up (choose to recognize). My being-for-others is not founded on my own freedom, however, although since it is a dimension of my being that appears in the world, I am responsible for it as well. Olson, *An Introduction to Existentialism*, p. 178.

45. Flynn, *Sartre and Marxist Existentialism*, pp. 138-139.

46. Sartre, *Critique of Dialectical Reason* (London: NLB, 1976. Trans. by Alan Sheridan-Smith), p. 761.

47. Flynn, *Sartre and Marxist Existentialism*, pp. 140-141. Although orthodox Marxists do not attribute freedom to individuals in society, their condemnations of society and their frequent assignment of responsibility would suggest that they must regard individuals as in some sense free to make choices.

48. *Ibid.*, p. 168. Nicolai Hartmann, *Ethics*, Vol. II, p. 153, puts it quite well: "Guilt falls upon him who has power."

49. *Ethics*, Vol. II, pp. 246-247.

50. Wild, *The Challenge of Existentialism*, p. 164.

Chapter 4

Facticity and Bad Faith

The topic of facticity will be discussed here, leading to a discussion of the moral stance that is called "bad faith." In later chapters, certain themes elaborated here will be further developed, in particular when "situation" and "lucidity" are covered more fully.

Humans do not enter an empty world and proceed to create their niche *de novo*. Rather, humans are cast into a world, a society, a nation already extant. This is referred to by Heidegger as "thrownness," a term that is very apt. We discover ourselves to be mortal, amidst being-in-itself which possesses necessary laws about which we have had no say, in a society we did not choose, and in rules of logic that we discover (although one may also create new logics).[1]

So, while free will operates in the world, although we may be free to interpret the significance of the world to ourselves and to launch projects within the world, we are not capriciously free to invent entire new worlds. In fact, Sartre, in a very subtle analysis of human emotions, explains them as a reaction to our facticity--at the point when our path becomes difficult, when all ways to act seem to be barred, emotions manifest themselves as a magical way to transform the world, as a rebellion against facticity.[2] In the *18th Brumaire of Louis Napoleon*, Marx tells us, "Men make their own history, but they do not make it as they please: they do not make it under circumstances chosen by themselves, but under circumstances directly encountered, given, and transmitted from the past."

This puts the matter most appropriately. Although in *Being and Nothingness*, Sartre at times seems to ignore facticity, by the time he wrote the *Critique*, he had tempered his more extreme views. While Sartre was influenced by Husserl, he did not follow Husserl into idealism. His choice of the pre-reflexive cogito as the core of his phenomenological ontology, allowed him to posit being-in-itself, external reality, in a simple and straightforward way.[3]

Freedom in Sartre's view, which has been followed here albeit with reservations, is "a complete dialectical development," which can become "alienated or bogged down or allow itself to be caught by the traps of the other and. . .simple physical constraint is enough to mutilate it."[4] Sartre now goes so far as to state that "all men are slaves in so far as their life unfolds in the practico-inert field and in so far as this field is always conditioned by scarcity."[5] So, mankind is affected by facticity, which can also be defined as the "past."[6]

Political, social, and economic structures are the "totality," the historical "facticity," the practico-inert of our situation.[7] Freedom is relative, therefore, in the sense that the world and the body already exist for it. We cannot escape this fact, except through the illusory and temporary expedient of emotion. But even then, reality keeps breaking through. The "I" affirms itself only as involved in the reality of the body and the world.[8] This interpretation of freedom is, therefore, not so distant from that of certain Marxists, such as Adam Schaff who avers that "Man always confronts the real material world with its objective laws, and does not by his action annul those laws. His freedom does not consist in annulling necessity, but in recognizing and making use of it."[9]

We can agree with this, provided that we acknowledge the continual dialectical interaction between social directions ("laws") and human freedom. Society is not determined in any sense akin to that determination operating in the in-itself. And not only society; for that matter, the natural world is not independent of how it is acted upon by mankind. The evolution of the cow, the pig, and the numerous varieties of dog, has been greatly altered by human projects. All of this, of course, is determined dialectically within the facticity of genetic laws as these are selectively acted on by the human project.

Binswanger, a psychiatrist with existentialist views, has studied cases of individuals victims of *verstiegene*, a term referring to absolutized ideals applied to a fantasy world. In one case, so ethereal was the fantasy world devised by the patient, that bodily existence itself was endangered. The individual suffering from such a condition will eventually pay the cost of ignoring facticity. Binswanger notes that the goal of psychotherapy in these conditions is to free the patient from the tyranny of their false ideals.[10]

While freedom is the basis for the development of human projects, the acceptance of the real world is an aspect of that moral lucidity with which humans must assess their possibilities in the world. One consequence of a failure to take the real world, our body, others, society, into account when we frame free projects, may be the political decision to resort to violence. Stymied by facticity, humans may destroy and murder to overcome the unanticipated barriers to the realization of a project. This is a not infrequent event in political or national projects. It is the source of the anarchist problem, the assassination of individuals, a project criticized by Marx and Engels, who had a sounder perception of facticity.

Sartre himself, impatient with recalcitrant others and the practico-inert, was at times prone to the language of violence. Johnson[11] calls attention to Sartre's blood-thirsty preface to Fanon's *The Wretched of the Earth*, and this is not an isolated instance. Intellectuals are all too prone to play out their intellectual projects in the real world in uncompromising fashion, where these projects are resisted by the facticity of institutions and by other consciousnesses. Beneath even materialistic intellectuals often lurks an idealist, if not a solipsist. It is difficult to keep thought in touch with the real world, particularly for revolutionaries, who project massive changes in the practico-inert. In the later discussion on lucidity, an effort will be made to reconcile freedom with objective reality, to acknowledge both the possibility of freedom and social science.

Flynn observes that the flaw in Sartre's early reasoning was his failure to distinguish concrete freedom, the ability to realize a particular project in a situation, from ontological freedom, or freedom as "the definition of man."[12] Indeed, this error occurs from time to time among existentialists who hold both that man is condemned to freedom and that it is somehow our duty to "choose freedom." But a person acts freely in any case, for one always might have chosen otherwise. While we are free, there are situations in which our choices, depending on our projects, may be quite limited.

There are, then, two definitions of freedom here: freedom of the will, and freedom as defined most clearly by Hobbes as the ability physically and without external opposition to realize some project in a situation. The free subject in the phenomenological interpretation always is directed, as intentionality, as cogito, to that which is *not the subject itself.* The real world with its dense facticity faces the subject, who chooses a way of being-in-the-world. But this is not a matter of pure concrete freedom. The subject must also remain sensitive to a real world that he or she does not command.[13] Thus, not all projects are realizable in the face of facticity, although unrealizable projects are frequently pursued against reason. Certain possibilities are excluded, or, rather, certain possibilities appear doomed to failure in particular situations. Sartre himself emphasized this by the time he wrote the *Critique*.

In conclusion, it is necessary to recognize that despite ontological freedom, a person is also a being-in-the-world. We participate in a world of facticity through a material body, and emotions themselves have some physical basis.[14] The human sustains particular emotions, such as anger, desire, and so forth, and not others--is an animal capable, for instance, of sustaining a sense of the ludicrous? It is not that the real world contains meanings or values out there waiting for us, of course, but that the meanings and interpretations we provide it are projected freely onto the world as it is out there, already made, already practico-inert.[15]

It is not through some absolute initiative that we freely found ourselves as workers or bourgeois, says Merleau-Ponty, for if this were possible, then everything is possible and nothing is predictable.[16] It is an error to associate freedom with unpredictability in a simplistic way, although it is true that a system that contains the possibility of innovation is ultimately unpredictable. It is not necessarily an appropriate expression of freedom to strive to be unpredictable in one's acts. This is especially the case in political situations, where the politician or diplomat, recognizing personal freedom, need not choose to be unpredictable.

The exercise of freedom might be most rationally expressed in the selection of the decision that an adversary most expects, assuming that rationality might be the choice most conducive to a peaceful resolution of some dispute. Wherever one is thrown into existence must form a starting point in one's path through the world. But while the worker is conditioned by class, wage, and working conditions, it remains for him or her to decide what these conditions will mean. It is up to the individual worker to choose whether reform, revolution, or submission is the appropriate stance. Before the Marxist revolution, the worker must have developed class consciousness, and for the existentialist it is this that rests on a free choice.[17]

In light of the preceding discussion of contingency, how does it go with the concept of human nature? To review an earlier stand, there is no once-and-for-all human nature as a given, but all persons face a common world of facticity--all humans are limited by the body (including in the ultimate sense by the anticipation of the death of the body), by social structure, by the real world. All human beings are forced to limit any absolutely free choice of projects by facticity, and we all face this common condition. Humans, finally, are the sole creatures defined as anticipating death. As we will shortly see, humans are therefore creatures beset by certain emotional conditions, by the recognition of nothingness, by anguish. This is what is meant by a common human nature; it is a boundary-condition, in the apt phrase of Karl Jaspers.

Sartre exaggerates his position when he denies that man has a common nature, although we may still accept his formula, with reservations, that existence precedes essence. Existence, obviously, is never found without structure.[18] In less enthusiastic moments, of course, Sartre is fully aware of this. There are brute facts of life--the day is hot, the hill is steep. We are not free to change the slope of this hill or the heat of the sun, but we are fully free to choose our reaction to this facticity.[19] Merleau-Ponty agrees, first, that man is totally free, and second, that he is also totally part of his physical and social environment. It is a reconciliation of freedom in determinism.[20]

Simone de Beauvoir claims that the sub-human would recognize only the facticity of existence. This verges on Heidegger's realm of Das Man, the "they." This is an unauthentic stance for the reason that it foregos and fails or refuses to recognize freedom, the ability to transcend facticity. We transcend facticity not by ignoring it, but by recognizing that possibilities for free projects exist for the subject within the realm of the real world, even given facticity. And an authentic ethics, "is the triumph of freedom over facticity."[21]

Here, de Beauvoir mistakes two aspects of freedom, as we pointed to earlier, when she mentions the constrictive activities of man as a movement toward freedom, for freedom as ontological freedom is always present, and we make our choices freely and responsibly under any conditions; it is concrete freedom of which she speaks, the development of the economy, of art, of science, which create and open up to individuals new and more numerous possibilities for further concrete projects. It does not seem appropriate, given the basis for freedom in existentialism, to designate certain acts as unfree, some as free. To do this is to smuggle into the discussion our own personal evaluations of these acts. To do this is to provide a surreptitious ethics, without acknowledging the fact. Thus, it will be our contention that bad faith also must be a free choice, albeit a choice that ignores truth.

If we experience a sense of fear in the face of the world, the cause of this emotion is probably that some specific threat to us has arisen in the world. But anxiety, an experience akin to fear, occurs in the face of nothing specific in the world.[22] In viewing the world it would be comforting to know that there was a key to existence, a conumdrum to unravel, which, solved, would point us in a "correct" direction. But to discover that we confront the world without a guide--with no acceptable plan superimposed on our being-in-the-world is a disconcerting event, and it engenders anguish.

To experience anguish is to realize that we are free to choose a path, and free to renounce innumerable other paths. It is to realize that we are without support.[23] The world provides no necessary anchor for choices for the reason that humans are different than the world within which we choose ourselves. With no certain mooring, no necessity, experience reveals a void, a sense of nothingness. As for-itself, we are undefined, while the in-itself is tangible and necessary. In a way, the in-itself has a right to exist as it does, for it can be in no other way.

Emptiness distinguishes the human from the world.[24] Nothingness must be filled by human projects, but these are not sustained by any necessity or meaning by the world, by the in-itself. By themselves, these projects are fortuitous. As Heidegger puts it in his inimitable way, Dasein means to transcend what is by projecting itself toward what-is-not-yet, to be projected into nothing.[25] From Heidegger, therefore, Sartre has derived his theme that consciousness is completely transparent and, by itself, contentless. It is nothingness.[26]

Granted that anguish is an existential experience, it is still difficult to grasp Sartre's concept of non-being. For non-being in certain Sartrean formulations sustains a desire to be in-itself. As lack, the for-itself has the impossible project of becoming in-and-for-itself, a free consciousness that has founded itself. While Hegel accomplishes this reconciliation through the Absolute, Sartre regards this project as futile.[27] But to charge non-being in this way with desire or complex activity seems contrary to reason.

This is why a less Promethean ontology than Sartre's seems more plausible, at least to the extent of suggesting some reservations to his more extreme stands. Perhaps, the for-itself must be conceived of as not entirely empty. So that dread is not quite a recognition of nothingness; rather, it is the general feeling of finitude (which the for-itself certainly is) and limitations before the immensity of the universe. Consciousness is an existence conscious of its finitude, which is to accept the Ego in some sense as existent.[28] It is unclear how a for-itself as nothingness could distinguish itself as other than the in-itself.

The existentialist is concerned with anxiety, because it furnishes a clue to an authentic existence. Psychoanalysis as presented by Freud, on the other hand, is an effort to deliver us from anxiety.[29] Morris suggests the three forms of "nothingness" that arise from the concept of intentionality which are at the origin of existential anxiety: (1) The conscious relation is a "lack" for the reason that it requires an object outside itself to make an appearance in the world; (2) The conscious relation can project a nonexistent as its second term; and (3) For humans, there is not any fixed purpose.[30]

In the face of such nothingness, anguish is the recognition not only that we are free, but that we are conscious of this freedom.[31] We are conscious that, having no set purpose, we can pursue any one out of a vast field of projects. The unchosen projects that clutter our past, the might-have-been, that are not possible for us any longer, were possible at one time. We chose against them, and in finite time, the choice becomes irreparable.

The fact that humans experience anguish is the evidence that whatever they are and whatever they do is essentially unjustified. Anguish is a condition all humans can experience, another indication that there is a common human nature in the sense of a common condition. The fact of anguish is the reason that Sartre regarded the attempt to justify our actions in the world as a futile moralizing endeavor. Anguish stems from the fact that our projects, our activities in the world, are freely chosen; one must be content with this knowledge, because the attempt to reassure ourselves by justifications always results in bad faith.[32] Efforts at justification are a source of the "spirit of seriousness," as Sartre puts it, one manifestation of bad faith, which we will discuss.

Bad faith is one possible viewpoint on the self. Since it is a dishonest viewpoint, it would seem appropriate to avoid it if lucidity is a value for us. Barnes suggests that there may be bad faith in spending too much time contemplating our anguish.[33] Sartre has firmly avoided positing any general values or moral principles, and his promised work on ethics never appeared. He reminds us on several occasions that it is all one what one's project in the world might be. Yet, in the definition of bad faith, indeed in the very choice of terms he has selected to describe it, Sartre indicates that we ought to avoid falling into the condition of bad faith. Bad faith is wrong. Just why should this be? Since mankind is ontologically free, it cannot be that the choice of bad faith is not a free choice, for that is not possible. We are condemned to be free.

Although Sartre does not put the point this way, it must be obvious that in avoiding bad faith, we have elected to acknowledge our true condition, namely, that we are free to choose our projects. We have, therefore, by acknowledging freedom, elected to take responsibility for our acts. But since all projects are equal (if we agree with Sartre at his most contrary), what difference does our recognition of the true state of affairs of our human situation make? None, unless one posits a value that is enhanced thereby. And that value can only be honesty, or lucidity. How very quintessentially French Sartre really seems, when between the lines of his normless presentation one cannot avoid grasping the real core of bad faith, which is its violation of lucidity.

Thus, a person ought to select that stance, in the face of the world, that accepts the situation and the human condition as it really is, with no holds barred, with no crutches, with no reliance on a philosophical or religious *deus ex machina*. Honesty to oneself and, at least in this context, to others, is the supreme value hinted at originally by anguish. Thus, there is a true situation outside consciousness, although a number of interpretations concerning it might be adopted, depending, of course on one's project, and there is an inescapable human condition, namely, the freedom to choose with all that this entails, and lucidity requires that one ought to acknowledge the truth about these.

It was, therefore, to sink deeply into bad faith to have presented the false image of the Communist countries as unaffected by alienation, by pollution and environmental damage; the lie that was propagated became patent when these regimes collapsed or allowed realistic appraisals of their condition. Indeed, much of the propaganda of the radiant future of Communist reality was revealed as falsehood after 1989, and those that were involved in consciously ignoring the truth were involved in bad faith. The recognition of the truth of our condition imposes itself upon us as an obligation.[34] Since one may choose to acknowledge this truth, or, equally, freely elect not to acknowledge it and fall into bad faith, on what basis ought this choice to be made? What moral imperatives might we call to our aid? For the existentialist, the answer to this must be, there are none.

A choice is not grounded in any principle other than free choice, and any choice is equally grounded in freedom. Nothing commands us to choose lucidity. It is even an uncomfortable choice, and Sartre's depiction of the smug bourgeoisie of Bouville, who exist in bad faith, suggests that these individuals are generally pleased with their condition.

B. F. Skinner's disturbing but complacent woman in the haven of *Walden II* has opted for such a choice, and she seems to be presented as a fully worthy being, which shows, of course, how antithetical B. F. Skinner's viewpoint is to existentialism.

Lucidity or bad faith may be freely selected as a stance in the world, but there is the feeling that honesty requires the choice of the former; there is a subterranean feeling that it is better to be honest rather than dishonest concerning the world and ourselves. Thus, for all of his dissembling, there is running through Nikita Khrushchev's memoirs the impulse toward honesty. But there is no metaphysical foundation vindicating this choice. We might suggest that avoiding bad faith launches us into more interesting and hazardous possibilities, and this is probably the case, but it still does not follow that there is a moral imperative urging us to do so.

Faced with the decision of lucidity or bad faith, with perhaps the experience of anguish as a clue to an appropriate choice (depending on the meaning we provide it), we may freely elect lucidity. The moral opprobrium of the existentialists obviously seems to be directed against persons choosing bad faith, and the negative judgement is rendered because of the nature of the choice that they have made rather than that they did not choose freely, for, like it or not, lucidity brings us to the recognition that all persons are condemned to be free.[35]

The choice of lucidity is the creation by the chooser of a value. It is a value that by our choice of it we have thereby tacitly recommended it to all other persons. It ought to be a fundamental value in an existential ethics. Bad faith, on the other hand, is the futile attempt to deny that we choose freely, something that we can never escape from in reality.[36] The human motive for the choice of lucidity is similar to the motive that we may adopt in playing the game fairly; in playing, say, a game of chess, there are rules that establish the game as an intellectual skill--were we to cheat by removing, say, the opponent's pieces against the rules that we have chosen to abide by, we might win, but the victory would be an empty one.

Bad faith is a lie, essentially, and to oneself first of all. Furthermore, it is a lie in the face of the truth which we must know, namely, that we always choose freely, that we are always free to choose other than what we have.[37] Anguish announces the possibility that we need not be as we are, but that we have a myriad free possibilities of choosing ourselves.[38] But in bad faith we pretend the for-itself is an in-itself, that we are solely facticity, and that we could not have become other than what we are.[39]

In bad faith, one denies, except for the idea of the common human condition that we all must admit to, finiteness, mortality, that existence precedes essence. What we are is what we have decided to be, so that, in a way, we are never unalterably what we may be at the moment. We may always choose otherwise.[40]

But our existence does take us up to a point at which we have arrived now in the present, and the past, of course, is now our facticity, what we have made of ourselves, and this past is out there in the open for everyone to see. It is public domain. So we are not authorized to say, in another form of bad faith, that what you see in the facticity that we have made of our past, is not our true nature, that we are not really the politicians who have been bribed, the lieutenant who has ordered shootings at Tiananmen Square, the revolutionary who has assassinated a village mayor in order to sever the control of the central government from the rural districts . . . we are all of these if they represent our activity in the world; we are not pristine natures untouched by our deeds--we are our deeds.

The second form of bad faith, of course, is to adopt the position, which is not the lucid view of the human condition, that we are as you see us because of heredity, because of a childhood of poverty, because of the force of public opinion. This view may take two forms: (1) the objectivist view that what we are is determined ultimately by external forces over which we have no control, the position taken by B. F. Skinner among others; and (2) the immanentist view that what we are is the unfolding of an internal human nature, a position associated with Aristotle.[41]

Translated into political terms, the leaders of nations fall into bad faith when their nations fall into chaos, or when millions of peasants die in the collectivization. Of course, there is the matter of facticity: colonialism has marred the historical and economic past, or droughts occur. But there is not a determined history for a nation that operates inexorably despite the choices of the leadership. There is not Spirit in history that overwhelms whatever choices the leaders make. All of these excuses are brought forward to explain the killings and the deaths that are the direct result of the decisions of the leaders of nations. Leaders operate within a situation, but they also make free choices within that situation. It is bad faith to exaggerate the constraints.

Colburn in an article on Ethiopia makes the point, "If students of politics are to regard political actors as morally responsible individuals, rather than products of impersonal historical forces, then the quality of their stewardship is indeed a matter that scholars should be willing to observe, analyze, and, yes, judge. Elites may be constrained by their circumstances, but they retain large degrees of freedom."[42]

While we must accept that we are presently what is indicated in the facticity that is our past, that is, our past that we have chosen may not be denied in good faith, there is another form of the full recognition of the past that may also slide over into bad faith, and this is the project of sincerity. In this project, the past is viewed honestly, that is, objectively, but taken to be that which we are once and for all. This is a free project, of course, and it may include a lucid view of the past, but its bad faith is implicit in the denial that we are always free to be something different in the future. In the project of sincerity, the choice is to be once and for all, as being-in-itself, as a stone, a juggernaut through the world, a statue of the lawyer. And a choice like this is dishonest.[43] We cannot say, without bad faith, that this is what we are and that's the end of it.

Hazel Barnes suggests another aspect of bad faith that helps to underscore our interpretation of the existentialist ethics. All projects, as we shall see later, entailing predictions of the future and the consequences of these projects, are based, ultimately, on evidence that must needs be flimsy and incomplete. Still, in good faith, we must make all possible efforts to assure that what we believe to be true in a situation *is* true, even if full certainty can never be attained. There is a curious example of bad faith embedded in *The Second Treatise on Government* in which John Locke argues in vindication of slavery. He reasons that when an unjust war is launched against another nation, the victorious defender has the right to put to death those that have participated in that unjust aggression. Since one has the right to put the aggressors to death, it follows that the defenders might elect to allow the criminals to live but to enslave them. Thus, we have a defense of slavery that is a reasonable justification.

Aside from other problems inherent in the argument, the chief problem is that the slavery that existed in Locke's time could hardly have had the origin that he hypothesized. In fact, most slaves were probably forcibly rounded up by coastal tribes through unjust aggressions and then sold to European traders, a fact of which Locke was surely cognizant. The argument is therefore irrelevant. Moreover, it is likely that in his effort to defend human property, Locke was probably aware of the irrelevance of his argument and was rationalizing the situation in bad faith. Hobbes certainly emerged from his brief discussion of slavery in the *Leviathan* with more honor, using the argument of self-preservation as a justification of revolt from a condition of slavery. Examples of political bad faith similar to Locke's abound in international affairs: the French civilizing mission as a justification for colonial ventures is another such.

An individual trying to avoid bad faith will, regardless of knowing that there can never be total knowledge of any situation, accept responsibility for acts. In bad faith, the actor, knowing that all action, all beliefs, are insecure, will give way to whatever irrational impulses may prevail at the moment: since no consequences are fully predictable, runs this delusion in bad faith, all acts become equally valid in a situation.[44] This is a form of bad faith that anticipates later discussions of the concept of lucidity.

Literature and politics are crisscrossed with the paths of persons acting in bad faith. Macquerrie depicts the most common personality as "the man who...has no will of his own--the irresolute man, the man of bad faith, the scattered man. . . ."[45] Such a one is Oblomov, the character so effectively drawn by A. I. Goncharov, who thereby characterized an important segment of the 19th century Russian elite.

In Marxism, alienation is a result of exploitation, the abolition of which under socialism will also eliminate alienation. In existentialism, bad faith is the crux of alienation, because it alienates the person from a valid understanding of what it means to exist as a person. It is also apparent that the alienation resulting from bad faith may occur in any social system, because the possibility of bad faith is within the individual, not out in the society. While the abolition of exploitation may be a worthy end, it is not so because its elimination will abolish bad faith; at best it will eliminate some opportunities to live in bad faith. Thus, those who accept the social privileges of a ruling class are invariably living in bad faith, in one form or another.[46]

But the opportunites for bad faith are myriad. In the former Soviet Union, *glasnost* provided the opportunity to criticize the innumerable privileges of the *nomenklatura*. In another form of society, other opportunities to elect bad faith will arise. It is the easy choice of bad faith that allowed the comfortable bourgeoisie to stoically endure the fate of the factory workers who sustained them in relative comfort. But it was also the easy choice of the *nomenklatura* of the European Communist countries that allowed them the same satisfaction in bad faith. However, there is another Marxist concept even more closely related to bad faith, namely the social structure Marx and Engels refer to as "false consciousness." False consciousness and bad faith are quite alike in some ways, and both rest on the choice to avoid lucidity. Bad faith, however, characterizes the problem of the individual, while false consciousness depicts the ideological position of a class or society.

The other pitfall for the individual is the "spirit of seriousness." In the serious attitude, we confer too much reality on the world.[47] This may often occur in one stage of pre-adolescence, when the moral structure seems to be external, quite solid and infallible, a stage that Simone de Beauvoir suggests begins to crumble at about the time of adolescence.[48] We have already noted the complacent woman in *Walden II*, who must needs be a "serious person." This is the stage of civilization depicted by Emile Durkheim as the stage of "mechanical solidarity."

We might opine that in the case of human moral development, presented so cogently by Lawrence Kohlberg,[49] ontogeny repeats phylogeny. This is another instance of the potential value of biology and the natural sciences to existentialist thought, which has tended to ignore such important features of the past as evolution. It has done this to overcompensate for the fallacies that the sciences sometimes lead us into, such as the spirit of seriousness. The spirit of seriousness also permeates the work of the authors of many ethical texts, we hope not this one, in so far as they advance the belief that there are things good in themselves, and actions that are absolutely to be desired on account of their consequences.[50]

This is, we have earlier argued, a point of view apt to lead to false conclusions, for values are not found embedded in the in-itself, nor in the practico-inert which is social institutions. However, at a later stage, as we discuss society, we will suggest that the authentic person might opt to follow certain conventions, for the reason, agreeing with Hobbes' social contract argument, that formal moral systems may contribute to human order and well-being.[51] In any case, while we might authentically choose to follow conventions, we will make such a choice in the realization that these values are not transcendent, nor are they embodied in things.[52] We accept that we might choose to follow certain conventions without adopting the fallacious position of the grave man, of the soldier to whom the Army and its regulations are everything, the colonist who sacrifices the natives to build the road (or in Vietnam under the French, the 10,000 lives it cost to construct the railway from Hanoi to Saigon), the revolutionary blind to everything save some utopian goal.

This is the spirit of seriousness at work in the world, pursuing the futile end of making the for-itself an in-itself, of casting free personality in stone.[53] The spirit of seriousness is a false way to escape anguish, which announces that there is no support in the world and in society for our choices. Freedom produces our values, and these arise from nothing.[54] Kant also recognizes that moral concepts may not be abstracted from any empirical or merely contingent knowledge, and thus he would, in this respect, avoid the spirit of seriousness. On the other hand, he finds these concepts originating *a priori* in human reason, thereby formulating the for-itself as a receptacle for principles of morality, falling into another form of bad faith.[55]

For Marx, who denies an eternal human nature, the nature of man is the ensemble of social relationships, which would seem to indicate a society-wide spirit of seriousness. To be sure, most people probably do accept the dictates of the practico-inert of social institutions as the basis for their morality, but it is to avoid this spirit of seriousness that we endeavor to act in good faith.[56]

In a way, that is what Marx and Engels tried to do, for as good members of the bourgeoisie, they endeavored to adopt the standpoint of the proletariat, thereby escaping from the ensemble of social relationships that held for their own class. As certain existentialist psychologists try to do, the patient's *absolutes* and prohibitions, that is, the "spirit of seriousness," must be broken through so that they no longer block out the possibilities of choice that exist for them. The therapy is explicitly intended to release the ability to view alternatives.[57] The free person is dynamic and creative, not something fixed and with a "serious sense of duty."[58] We have already dealt with the spirit of seriousness insofar as it appears in the naturalistic fallacy. Much of Sartre's presentation on bad faith is also applicable to the refutation of naturalism.

We ought to opt, therefore, for good faith, but here Sartre's Calvinism, if you will, makes a reappearance, for he claims that the ideal of good faith, like the ideal of sincerity, is just another effort to attain being-in-itself, another futile effort to avoid anguish.[59] Try as we might, all our projects are doomed to be suffused with the spirit of seriousness. It hovers inescapable like original sin over our deeds. It is probably replete in this effort at extracting an ethics from the existential standpoint. Yet, Sartre may be guilty here of the either-or fallacy, and not for the first or last time, for this fallacy recurs in his thought. It may be that there are degrees of bad faith.

While the spirit of seriousness suggests that any system of authority in establishing decisions ought to be renounced, still, it is also true that persons free to choose anything at all, in the knowledge that all choices are futile, or decisions are all one in any case, may fall into indifference. As Rieff pointed out, paradoxically, "freedom does not exist without authority."[60] But to be in good faith, responsibility must be assumed for selecting our authorities.

Finally, to conclude this chapter, a word on conscience. In Heidegger's view, conscience is the call toward the authentic self. It beacons us from distraction, from engaging in this and that, from the "they," from, if you will, mechanical solidarity, to the reality that we are: free to choose and responsible for our choices.[61] Both Heidegger and Marcus Arelius appear to be motivated toward the concept of conscience by their recognition of our being-toward-death. Life is too brief to spend it trivially. Croce likens conscience to moral sensibility, as opposed to behavior based, say, on "historical necessity," or whatever.[62] Conscience is the self questioning itself.[63]

We must, of course, avoid as well the spurious voice of conscience in the form of the voice of the "they," recalling us back to the trivial world of this and that. There are some persons lacking in any moral depth, to whom the self seems not to make any appeal toward authenticity.

One such seems to have been Kurt Waldheim, the former head of the United Nations and a voluntary servant of Nazism in World War II. It became clear from his evasions and statements that he existed in a situation of bad faith. Indeed, Waldheim is a splendid study into the concept of bad faith in a political personality.[64] Waldheim was almost heroic in his bad faith. There is an interesting contrast to be made between the stance of a Kurt Waldheim and that of another and different Austrian, Franz Jaegerstetter, executed for his refusal to serve in the Austrian army. The tale of how he resisted numerous efforts made to convince him to renounce responsibility for his choice is a fascinating one.

To begin to encounter life in good faith, it is necessary, avoiding the "spirit of seriousness," to take responsibility for the choices we have made in the past. Waldheim has not publicly, at least, made any effort to acknowledge his responsibility for the past he made for himself. In the same vein, however, Martin Heidegger himself was culpable of evading public responsibility for his judgments under the Nazis. His refusal to say anything about his unfortunate role during the Nazi period was probably a refusal to take personal responsibility for this past. Both cases are failures of conscience.

Notes

1. Barnes, *The Literature of Possibility*, p. 31.

2. Sartre, *The Emotions: Outline of a Theory* (Trans. by Bernard Frechtman. New York: Philosophical Library, 1948), pp. 58-59. And, as Sartre suggests, the very fact that there are certain emotions we display in a repertoire, and not others, is an additional aspect of our facticity; *op. cit.*, p. 94. An additional possible view ought to be suggested here, namely that, as the for-itself arose as an upsurge from the in-itself at an evolutionary point in time, the emotions are still to some degree marked by the residue of the in-itself. It is unlikely that for-itself appeared suddenly and all-at-once, fully formed; it was perhaps a gradual process, a process of quantitative changes accumulating toward a qualitative change. Perhaps we see in creatures surrounding us stages in the direction of for-itself. Therefore, is it necessary to postulate the total emancipation of for-itself from its origin in the in-itself? We may not have arrived yet at the total emancipation of the for-itself, and emotions may well be a clue into the completedness of that project.

3. Desan, *The Tragic Finale*, pp. 134-135.

4. Sartre, *Critique*, p. 578, fn 68.

5. *Ibid.*, p. 331. A veritable paraphrase of Rousseau's famous, "All men are born free, but are everywhere in chains."

6. Sartre, *Being and Nothingness*, p. 118.

7. Smith, *Idealism*, p. 428.

8. Luijpen and Koren, *Introduction to Existential Phenomenology*, p. 103.

9. Adam Schaff, *A Philosophy of Man* (New York: Monthly Review Press, 1963), p. 86. Schaff is to be commended as one Communist philosopher who tackles opposing doctrine on an intellectual plane.

10. Izenberg, *Existentialist Critique of Freud*, p. 282.

11. Paul Johnson, "Jean-Paul Sartre: `A Little Ball of Fur and Ink'," *The Wilson Quarterly*, Vol. xiii, No. 2 (Spring 1989), p. 71.

12. Flynn, *Sartre and Marxist Existentialism*, p. 76.

13. Luijpen, *Existential Phenomenology*, p. 104 and pp. 204-205.

14. John Macquarrie, *Existentialism* (New York: Penguin Books, 1973), p. 156.

15. Charles E. Scott, "The Role of Ontology in Sartre and Heidegger," p. 294, in Schilpp, *The Philosophy of Jean-Paul Sartre*.

16. Merleau-Ponty, *Phenomenology of Perception*, p. 449.

17. Sartre, "Introduction to *Les Temps Modernes*, 441, in Eugen Weber, ed., Paths to the Present (New York: Dodd, Mead and Company, Inc., 1960). The translation is by Francoise Ehrmann from *Les Temps Modernes*, Vol. 1, No. 1, 1945. Intellectuals of the bourgeoisie have been intrigued with the problems of workers for decades. Lenin rightly points out that neither he nor Marx and Engels were workers, and Sartre, of course, was never a member of the proletariat. The proletariat have been incorporated into the free projects of a number of intellectuals.

18. Wild, *The Challenge of Existentialism*, pp. 162-163.

19. Warnoch, *Existentialism*, pp. 122-123.

20. *Ibid.*, p. 89.

21. De Beauvoir, *The Ethics of Ambiguity*, pp. 80-81 and p. 44.

22. The distinction is pointed out by Heidegger. Warnoch, *Existentialism*, p. 56.

23. *Ibid.*, p. 98.

24. *Ibid.*, p. 94.

25. Heidegger, "What is Metaphysics?" trans. by R. F. C. Hull and Alan Crick, in Werner Brock, ed., *Existence and Being* (South Bend: Regnery/Gateway, Inc., 1979), p. 337.

26. Warren, *The Emergence of Dialectical Theory*, p. 101.

27. See George L. Kline, "The Existentialist Rediscovery of Hegel and Marx," in Lee and Mandelbaum, eds., *Phenomenology and Existentialism*, pp. 125-126, and Desan, *The Tragic Finale*, p. 130.

28. Desan, *The Tragic Finale*, pp. 153-154. Heidegger is the source for this interpretation. See also Luijpen, *Existentialist Phenomenology*, p. 194.

29. Stern, *Sartre*, pp. 211-212.

30. Morris, *Sartre's Concept of a Person*, p. 27.

31. Manser, *Sartre*, p. 57.

32. Jeanson, *Sartre and Morality*, p. 182.

33. Barnes, *Existential Ethics*, p. 272.

34. It is difficult to agree with Sartre, given his ontological presentation, that one may not freely choose to live in bad faith. One who wishes to live in bad faith, disregards the truth of the human condition, which consists of freedom as absolute autonomy. But if this is the truth of the human condition, then the choice of bad faith would seem to be another example of (the misuse of) freedom. I think Sartre's argument is unacceptable. See Luijpen, *Existential Phenomenology*, pp. 209-210.

35. Marjorie Grene, *Dreadful Freedom: A Critique of Existentialism* (Chicago: The University of Chicago Press, 1948), p. 143, certainly recognized that "Good for the individual resides in the integrity with which he recognizes his freedom . . .Evil is the lie of fraudalent objectivity, the denial of freedom."

36. Mary Warnock (commenting on Sartre's *Existentialism is a Humanism* in "Existentialist Ethics," in W. D. Hudson, Vol. II, *New Studies in Ethics*, p. 402) proposes that Sartre, in the notion that by choosing, we choose for all people, reiterates a theme from Kant. But Kant might be guilty, as we will see later, in his categorical imperatives of a "spirit of seriousness." Sartre, furthermore certainly does not mean that our decision in a particular situation should thereafter be accepted by anyone as a moral prescription.

37. Sartre, *Being and Nothingness*, p. 48.

38. Jeanson, *Sartre and the Problem of Morality*, p. 178.

39. Klaus Hartmann, *Sartre's Ontology: A Study of Being and Nothingness in the Light of Hegel's Logic* (Evanston: Northwestern University Press, 1966), pp. 54-55.

40. Arthur C. Danto, *Jean-Paul Sartre* (New York: The Viking Press, 1975), p. 25.

41. Olson, *An Introduction to Existentialism*, pp. 140-142.

42. Forrest D. Colburn, "The People's Democratic Republic of Ethiopia: Masking and Unmasking Tragedy," *World Politics*, Vol. 43, No. 4 (July 1991), 586.

43. *Ibid.*, p. 145. It denies the constant possibility of choosing to be what we are not, according to Sartre, *Being and Nothingness*, pp. 62-63.

44. Barnes, *The Literature of Possibility*, pp. 54-55.

45. Macquarrie, *Existentialism*, 202.

46. Tony Smith, "Idealism and People's War: Sartre on Algeria," *Political Theory*, Vol I, No. 4 (November 1973), p. 436.

47. Joseph H. McMahon, *Humans Being: The World of Jean-Paul Sartre* (Chicago: The University of Chicago Press, 1971), p. 124.

48. de Beauvoir, *The Ethics of Ambiguity*, p. 40. De Beauvoir has been an observant teacher, apparently, of young persons. Her observations are quite in line with Kohlberg's stages of development.

49. See his *The Philosophy of Moral Development, Vol. I, Moral Stages and the Idea of Justice* (New York: Harper and Row, Publishers, 1981).

50. Warnock, "Existentialist Ethics," p. 409.

51. See Kai Nielsen, "Why Should I Be Moral?" in Kenneth Pahel and Marvin Schiller, eds., *Readings in Contemporary Ethical Theory* (Englewood Cliffs: Prentice-Hall, Inc., 1970), section 2, pp. 460-463.

52. Sartre, *Being and Nothingness*, p. 626.

53. Luijpen and Koren, *A First Introduction to Existential Phenomenology*, p. 233.

54. See Grene, *Dreadful Freedom*, p. 47, and Jeanson, *Sartre and the Problem of Morality*, p. 125. It is not that we ought simply to avoid acting by any general rules, or even by conventional rules; the point is that we must choose these rules and act with lucidity, rather than using general rules as "substitutes for decisions we are unwilling to face," Olafson, *Principles and Persons*, p. 55.

55. Immanuel Kant, *Groundwork of the Metaphysic of Morals* (Trans. by H. L. Paton. New York: Harper Torch Books, 1964), p. 79.

56. Kamenka, *The Ethical Foundations of Marxism*, p. 146.

57. Izenberg, *The Existentialist Critique of Freud*, pp. 284-285. He is discussing Boss.

58. Wild, *The Challenge of Existentialism*, p. 166.

59. Sartre, *Being and Nothingness*, p. 69, and Warnoch, *Existentialism*, p. 101.

60. Izenberg, *The Existentialist Critique of Freud*, pp. 285-286, is quoting P. Rieff, *Introduction to Sigmund Freud: The History of the Psychoanalytic Movement* (New York: Collier Books, 1963), p. 21.

61. Grene, *Martin Heidegger*, pp. 32-33, and Macquerrie, *3 Issues in Ethics*, p. 125.

62. Benedetto Croce, *Politics and Morals* (Trans. by Salvatore J. Castiglione. London: George Allen and Unwin, 1946), p. 128.

63. It need not be an inner voice speaking original thoughts, of course, a sort of "Voice of Latin Grammer," as Gilbert Ryle in *The Concept of Mind* (New York: Barnes and Noble, Inc., 1949), pp. 315-316, satirizes it.

64. Despite Waldheim's autobiography that claimed that he finished active service in 1941 after being wounded, he fought against the partisans in Bosnia and worked as an interpreter with the 12th Army Commando under General von Lohr until 1944. Lohr was directly responsible for the deportation of the Greek Jews. There is no escape from responsibility for this past, even if his role was only indirect. See Misha Glenny, "A Nazi Kind of Past," *New Statesman*, Vol. VIII (March 21, 1986), p. 21.

Chapter 5

Others

The discussion of the status of others may be entered by peremptorily disposing of the solipsistic argument. It is possible that a sufficiently cunning devil might cast a delusory spell over us so that we imagine a non-existent universe. This delusion is not philosophical idealism, which recognizes other points of consciousness. To read a play by Shakespeare, however, is to recognize the unlikelihood that the solipsist created it; the solipsist cannot remember so doing, and each page of *A Midsummer Night's Dream* would come as a new discovery on first reading.

There are too many such discoveries, technological, political, or artistic, that we come across, surpassing our own skills and ability to produce, to allow the solipsistic assumption of the social world as self-created to be plausible. An encounter with a speaker of French, when we have not mastered this language, is a convincing indication that there is someone else in the world. Of course, it could still be the illusion of someone else in the universe, but this relies on the hypothetical consciousness of one devil, at least.

Husserl in the *Cartesian Meditations* argues that it is the significance we find in the world that persuades us of its externality; this significance presupposes other subjects, who must on this account be given at the same time that the world is.[1] The only convincing conclusion is that we live in a universe of an in-itself that existed before our appearance in the world and that will continue to exist when consciousness is stilled. We likewise live in a social universe criss-crossed by the projects initiated by others. That there are other minds in the world is the only rational conclusion, and the moral problem for political philosophy is how do we treat these other minds? This is, once more, a fundamental question of politics, although it is not often treated as such.

Our immediate and thoughtless perception of other individuals must be in the objective mode, perceived as things among other in-itselves, as, inevitably, will be their perceptions of ourselves. It takes an effort of reason to grant them the same moral freedom that we appear to possess ourselves. While we can recognize that these others out there are the frustrating originators of projects that may expand to encompass us or to put up barriers to our own projects, this experience does not afford any immediate sense of their consciousness, which is always off-limits to immediate experience. Other consciousnesses can be posited at secondhand, but they do not come-to-life for us like our own, ever, for our own consciousness, at least, may become a close subject for the reflective cogito.[2]

Children experience the intervention of parents, one of whose projects may be the preservation of order in the household, and since this is a conflictual clash of opposing goals, it is evident to a child that one of these goals did not originate with it. Throughout life, we will live in the midst of these colliding projects, in the arena of conscious entities attempting to force submission to their projects or to thwart our own. Therefore, the social world is a world of conflict, and this is the source of all politics.

> The threat of an alien moral consciousness involves not just the threat of a conflict with my 'values', but the threat of my being absorbed into the moral [ethical] world of the other through being denied recognition as an autonomous being.[3]

The penetration of the consciousness of another individual into the world constituted by our own value-structure has the effect of reducing our values to lifeless "facts" and of reducing us to the status of an object. This is exactly the origin and core of the political.

By projection, we may accept that other beings are independent sources of evaluation in the world, much like ourselves. And if each of us can accomplish a projection of this sort (some psychopaths and sociopaths cannot, although this shortcoming does not prevent them from attaining rulership over nations), we can begin to realize the possibility of carrying out projects of mutual interest, of compromising conflicting projects. To the degree that each individual can respect his or her own ethical freedom, and provided that there is an attempt to act always in good faith, it will be evident that others will also be origins of free acts of evaluating the world, and by an extension of the meaning of the concept of good faith, it would clearly not be in good faith to refuse to acknowledge this truth.

To deny the existence of other free beings at some stage of our accumulated experiences in the world, would be to violate lucidity.[4] The force of reason brings us to the recognition of others as "morally autonomous beings" distinct from the in-itself. This is a preliminary stage of intellectual development, and it does not provide any immediate insights into how we ought to react to these understandings. To recognize others as autonomous, initiates a process of developing a sense of community, and among a limited number of other persons, perhaps, a moral community.[5]

There are at least two perverse orientations toward the resolution of the conflicts brought about by the existence of other minds. The first orientation is the sadistic, as Sartre indicates, in which others are regarded as objects, and projects are undertaken with the purpose of putting them into the position of objects and maintaining them there. In all societies, this has been the purpose of certain social practices, and, as Marx pointed out, it is the initial conscious purpose of ideology or "false consciousness." In the status of women, for instance, there has been the effort to reduce them to predictable in-itself--an extreme instance of this was the Chinese practice of footbinding, whereby women experienced excruciating pain for the end of appearing a more pleasing object to men.

Capitalism reduces persons in economic exchange relations to interacting objects, and in somewhat the same way, centralized planning has had a comparable effect in socialist societies. At the extreme, the concentration camps of the German Nazi regime took the reduction of others into objects to a macabre extreme. The sociopathic nature of the cadre running these camps was revealed years later as they cooly discussed with interviewers the problems of devising poison gases that could kill more rapidly, increasing the efficiency of the extermination process.

The position complementary to the sadistic orientation is that of the masochist, who in the face of the existence of independent others reduce themselves to the objects of other wills. Many such persons become members of fanatic sects and movements, to which they devote themselves "body and soul." It is not difficult to understand their motivations, for the recognition of freedom and the ever-present threat of the collapse of one's value structures, always poses a danger. The value structure is supported by this freedom, that is, by nothingness. This problem was discussed under the concept of anguish; it is as though from the top of the ladder, we could see that the bottom half had vanished. All persons have difficulty in establishing an identity and projects in the world--some people discover that the Party or the movement or the sect will do this for them.

The future adherents will experience a conversion, a sudden once-and-for-all illumination of the world, a solution of the problems they had hitherto vainly struggled to resolve, and they accept a doctrine that will provide for them a solid edifice. Now they have become as in-itself, spared from the buffetings of doubt and irresolution (although, most likely still assailed now and then by anguish), one with the juggernaut of history, solid and undeviating as a projectile. These are the superpatriots and fanatics of all societies and movements.[6]

It is obvious that the masochistic choice is in bad faith, for it is an effort, never fully successful, to annihilate the knowledge of freedom. We can always choose differently, and we know it. The wife who transforms herself to an object for an abusive husband can choose to leave or retaliate. Her object status is not a necessary fate. We do not want to choose to live in bad faith not because it contributes to immoral actions, although it can be shown to do so, but because bad faith violates lucidity and the acknowledgement of what the world is like. Sadism obviously contributes directly to immoral actions, but masochism also does so indirectly, insofar as it is associated with fanaticism; masochism is not so much a moral but an ethical problem, for it affects the way values are generated.

It should be noted here, that altruism commits the error of masochism, as Hartmann depicts it, by transferring "the centre of one's whole sphere of interests. . .from oneself to the other person."[7] The choice of altruism as a persistent project would violate our responsibilty to pursue our own unique path in the world. In most cases, altruism avoids the ethical problems that arise for ourselves by placing the onus of responsibility onto others. This argument also applies to the sadistic orientation, but sadism is a distinct moral problem in addition to its ethical aspects, for at the heart of sadism as a project is the treatment of others as things.

Just why ought we not to treat others as objects? Of course, lucidity forces the conclusion that other persons are independent sources of projects in our world, but over and above the acceptance of lucidity, what valid reasons might be recommended for a moral consideration of the other person? Kant's categorical imperative that we ought to accept other people as ends and not as means only does not justify itself--it is only a rule. (By the way, it is important to acknowledge that Kant realized that treating others as ends *only* was not quite possible: the injunction is "Never treat them as *means only*.")[8] Sartre concurs with statements such as, ". . .as soon as there is involvement I am obliged to want others to have freedom at the same time that I want my own freedom. I can take freedom as my goal only if I take that of others as a goal as well."[9] But this does not suggest any supportive reason why we ought to do so. Certainly it is not because our reason grasps this principle as an *a priori* one.

The crux of any argument toward the practice of morality is contained in the idea that

> I am a self-consciousness only if I gain recognition from another self-consciousness and if I grant recognition to the other. [Further,] [t]he vocation of man--to find himself in being, to make himself be--is realized only in the relation between self-consciousnesses.[10]

Without this recognition, the world collapses into in-itself, and the "social" disappears.[11]

The potential contribution of others to most of our own projects is a compelling and even self-interested reason for observing morality--the computer that eases my writing, the automobile that makes it possible to rest for this day at the beach, the book that owes its existence to the art of printing and book-binding, the contributions of publishers, retailers, and, above all, the author, whose thoughts I find stimulating, all of this is owed to the existence of other persons. Through our own projects, we have established evaluations in the world, and we find that occasionally others grasp and realize those values independently, for which we may admire them and even admit their intrusions into our own value structure with some gratitude.

The choice of the project of existence over annihilation, which was posited as the origin of ethical projects, rationally implies certain consequences. It goes with the pursuit of fullness of that existence. Provided that one can live somehow, it may be preferred to exist in a landscape of boulders rather than one of mere space (a rather bleak prospect bringing to mind the surreal landscapes of Tanguy), but the growth of a few plants enriches the meager landscape and it would be encumbent on us to tend them if we could; the appearance of mobile creatures, some of which might even pose dangers to us, increase the quality of the existence we have affirmed, enhancing it by increasing its interest and the nature and quantity of projects now possible.

But of far more impact is the intrusion of other free beings into our world, as Crusoe experienced the appearance of Friday. Finally, and of most relevance to this chapter, free beings increase the content of our existence most of all, even considering the danger they pose to our projects. The payoff is the far more intriguing world we may now experience. One line of argument as to why we ought to treat other beings morally rests, therefore, on the very fundamental choice of existence over annihilation.

Jaspers indicates that our reason for wanting to develop our capacities for social intercourse is that without the free contributions of others, we cannot attain our "natural growth of self-possession. There are some aspects of his own freedom which refuse to reveal themselves as long as a man restricts himself to the subject-object relationship."[12] Aldous Huxley has explored this problem of ignoring the social world for the in-itself, the clash between science and humanism, in several of his novels.

(There is a corollary argument we will note but briefly here, namely that a complex world containing representatives of all levels of in-itself and levels of consciousness, is better than one monopolized by any single representative only. For human experience to have a fullness of significance and interest, a complex and prolific world is to be preferred to a simple and entirely man-made one. This point was made in Chapter 1).

If our ethics, the values that grow out of the choice of projects in the world, include values such as scientific or philosophical truth, technological progress, art, or sports, it follows that by ourselves we can accomplish little; we build upon contributions of consciousnesses no longer present in the world, and those that are pursuing some of the same goals. Other persons become a necessary factor in the realization of projects. Science calls for intersubjectivity; sports calls for competitors.

But whether others are necessary in order that we may realize free projects, is only a first step toward a possible morality; a major consideration must be that for others to be necessary to our own projects, they must be able to contribute to the possibility of realizing our projects, making our own existence more interesting, and enabling us to evaluate our own being more accurately. This means that they must be free, speaking, of course, of concrete freedom, for no one can deny their ontological freedom. Expressions of admiration, love, concern, must be uncoerced.

A chess game against a computer offers some challenge to the intellect for the moves are made independent of our own thought process, but chess is not a sport unless we pit our mental capacity against another human who can also compete with us psychologically. The point is nicely illustrated in Ira Levin's fantasy, *The Stepford Wives*, where robots are programmed to exhibit qualities of admiring and submissive housewives; the result is a quite unsatisfying male victory.

As Sartre recognizes in many of his stories and plays, coerced responses are not psychologically satisfactory when we regard these lucidly, for we can value only freely accorded admiration. It is not the accolades of a terrorized multitude that can effectively meet the leader's requirement of adulation. Admiration must be freely accorded or it is worthless. Richard III could not have genuinely enjoyed the entreaties of the crowd that he accept the crown. Nicolae Ceaucescu of Romania was startled when a cowed audience suddenly turned surly and emerged from its object status in 1990.

The same demand for the concrete freedom of others suggests the need in a world we desire to know as fully as possible, always assuming an original project of existence over annihilation, for free communication between free beings. It is not satisfying for humans to talk to a parrot. We need to communicate, if communication is to be of any value, with beings who are self-contained and uncoerced, who can generate meaning independently. Communication is valuable when it is among independent persons.

All societies place barriers in the way of free intercommunication, of course, but some societies are more prone to do this than others. The Confucian system of hierarchical classes represented moral progress in its time, but as a system of ritual and hierarchical stations, it had the effect of inhibiting free communication. This hierarchical structure of boundaries between persons and classes is built into some languages. The Hindu caste system was even more rigid, since in China there was the possibility through the examination system of a career based on merit.

In British novelists like Jane Austen, Charlotte Brontë, and Dickens, we sense the difficulties of penetrating the barriers of class in the embarrassment and somewhat forced conversations between the comfortable classes and those beneath them, and this is noteworthy even when the author is emphasizing the magnanimity of the well-off. Habermas makes it a point in his notion of ideal speech to promote equal opportunity for discussion, "free from all domination, whether arising from conscious strategic behaviour and/or systematically distorted communication (internal and/or external constraints)."[13]

In the 20th century, however, transcending even traditional societies and the remnants of Victorianism and authoritarianism in national societies, fascist and Communist societies have been most blatant in their positive efforts to stifle free intercommunication. Although given as he was on occasion to dogmatic and abrasive argumentation, this was patently not the intent of Marx's dictatorship of the proletariat nor the period of transition toward the classless society, for Marx pointedly attacked the evident contradictions of capitalism that created estrangement and alienation between persons.

The implementation of Marxism via the avenue of Leninism and Maoism in the 20th century was not in accord with this end. A society that can elevate to the rank of a state hero a boy who turned his parents in to Stalin's inquisition is not a Marxist society, nor is it likely to become one shortly, for it violates the principles enunciated by the philsopher of alienation. Lenin set the tone of the coming Soviet state, when, called to account for his astringent criticism of others in the party, he admitted that, indeed, his arguments were

> calculated to evoke in the reader hatred, aversion and contempt.... Such a formulation is calculated not to convince, but to break up the ranks of an opponent, not to correct the mistakes of an opponent, but to destroy him, to wipe his organization off the face of the earth. This formulation is indeed of such a nature as to evoke the worst thoughts, the worst suspicions about the opponents, and, indeed, as contrasted with the formulation that convinces and corrects, it "carries confusion into the ranks of the proletariat."[14]

Lenin knew what he was doing.

In the People's Republic of China following the 1989 suppression of the democratic movement, such comments as "I invited you to come to our home for lunch . . . but I'm sorry you can't come . . . .They said foreigners should not come to our homes," are a commentary and a damning indictment against such a regime.[15] It is a duty of individuals valuing freer human communication to condemn such practices whether they accompany Leninism, fascism, Nazism, authoritarianism, apartheid, or bourgeois societies.[16] It is a duty provided that we have accepted to live life, for we rationally by the extension of this principle have also chosen thereby to live life as fully as possible. Without free others, this is not possible.

In seeking to widen contacts with uninhibited others, we are motivated at least by curiosity, some amount of self-interest probably (according to our projects), and lucidity. On the political level, this will suffice. It is beyond the secular intent of this book to advocate the love for others as a necessary motivation to respect their freedom. The advocacy of universal love, in the sense of honoring free communication, strikes us as abstract.[17] Protestations of brotherhood and love may even be an affront to humans determined to maintain their freedom of choice, because most lovers of mankind are proposing some rate of return on their unsolicited investments. By comparison with the lovers-of-mankind, Machiavelli appears more genial, for his unabashedly manipulative politics of *The Prince* make no demands on subjects. There is a certain variety of the love of mankind that invades our projects to violate our freedom.

It may well be that, although we want to be accorded a degree of respect, we may even want to be unlovable. This is a significant enough problem that Hobbes, in his witty way, has revised the Golden Rule to a negative formula, namely, do not do to others what you would not have them to do to you. But in those few cases, if these exist, in which protestations of universal love may be genuine rather than hypocritical, such a position is decidedly supererogatory for the political world.[18] And from Sartre, we note with agreement the idea that reciprocity is always concrete--it can only be based on the individual's praxis, as the realization of his or her project, not on an universal abstract bond like Christian charity.[19]

Earlier we noted that consideration for others as free entities, who, we have seen, are potential contributors to our world as we exist it, leads to the principle of impartiality, of treating all humans equally in the first instance.[20] In his *Science of Rights*, Fichte puts the matter correctly:

> I must recognize the free being as such in all cases, that is, must restrict my freedom through the conception of the possibility of his freedom,

which Fichte calls the "Relation of Equality" or the "Legal Relations."[21] This is also a chief principle of morality as we perceive it. Again, from Fichte,

> The Science of Morality shows that every rational being is absolutely bound to desire the freedom of all other rational beings,[22]

which we have accepted for the reason that it is an existence-enhancing principle, a principle leading logically to a definition of justice.

This moral conclusion is not a sentimental choice; it does not entail, as we have argued, love or liking of others. It is not the universality of benevolence that directs us to support justice, treating everyone equally under the law. Hiram Caton criticizes the Benthamite doctrine of universal sympathy as a recipe for constant frustration, holding that the person who tries to practice humanitarian sympathy to all would most likely be "a piece of physiological pathology and psychological neurosis."[23]

Hence, we cannot accept the necessity of *agape*, so cogently argued by Glen Tinder, as a political principle.[24] We will argue that justice and laws that treat persons equally are a necessity for human society and a basis for rights. Sartre is formally correct in his frequent criticism of the doctrine of equality and rights (although he does advocate a form of reciprocity in his group-in-fusion),[25] but the historical consequences that flow from ignoring rights have been dire. The doctrine of equality is the necessary basis of any constructive society. The attack on rights by Communist thinkers facilitated the advent of Stalin's monstrous regime. Kamenka quotes George L. Kline [26] as follows:

> When (A. A.) Bogdanov (pseudonym of A. A. Malinovsky) and Bazarov (V.A.; pseudonym of V. A. Rudnev) turn to attack not Kant's abstract will but his elevation of man as an *end*, and themselves substitute other ends, the servile character of their doctrine is finally confirmed. "The free man not only regards his neighbour as a means; he demands that his neighbor should see in him only a means. . .for the neighbour's own ends. The recognition of the individual person as an absolute principle has always been and will always be, alien to the proletariat." By 1920, the effect that thought of this nature was leading to had become painfully evident. Leon Trotsky, in his *Terrorism i kommunizm* repudiates scornfully the "Kantian-clerical, vegetarian-Quaker chatter about the 'sanctity of human life.'" The doctrine that individuals are ends in themselves is a metaphysical, bourgeois doctrine; the proletarian and the revolutionary know that where necessary (for the Revolution) the individual is and should be treated only as a means. The prominent party theorist A. B. Zalkind put the position bluntly five years later: "For the proletariat human life does not have a metaphysical, self-sufficient value. The proletariat recognizes only the interests of the . . . revolution."

This attitude was the basis for Communist legal doctrine, which, as advocated by Y. B. Pashukanis, regarded law itself as bourgeois. (Ironically, Pashukanis, a former head of the Moscow Legal Institute, disappeared in 1938, a victim of the purges. Attitudes like this helped Stalin establish his totalitarian system. B. F. Skinner, although arguing from a different basis, comes to much the same conclusion as these Communist theorists, for which reason his doctrine rather than accomplishing the salvation of humanity would more likely contribute to its destruction. But the lessons of Communism in its comptempt for individual human rights have not affected some lines of theory: the stage has been set for a replay of the same ideological fallacies by the more modern deconstructionists.[27]

Parfit[28] essays another significant problem, which would take us too far afield to discuss here, but which we ought to note: the consideration we owe to people belonging to future generations, a principle he calls Conservation. Our doctrine that existence ought to be life-enhancing should serve to address this important issue, which was done, albeit briefly, in connection with Chapter 1.

Justice, therefore, is the minimal principle stemming from the project of morality. It is the social requirement that follows from our basic choice of existence and the recognition of the potential and actual contributions to this existence of other free beings. Emotions toward others that transcend this basic level of morality are aspects of our ethical choices, that is, our choices of projects (other than the minimal one of morality) for making our existence meaningful. The choice of being a teacher, for example, should expand this basic doctrine of equality to include caring for those whom we teach.[29] These additional ties to others, going beyond the sense of justice, are the result of our additional ethical choices; it is beyond the scope of our present interest, which is in morality, to pursue these here at length.

For Scheler, Kant's thesis of equality is acceptable but too basic, in that Kant regards, as we do, the person simply as a cognitive ego. Justice, from this basis, is a formalism. Scheler wants to proceed further and transcend mere equality by according each person an essential and absolutely unique dignity.[30] Sartre, as we have observed in a previous chapter, eschews this attribution for the good philosophical reason that dignity posits an essence, and that this is unwarranted if existence precedes essence.

Sartre's reasoning seems correct here. Dignity in human beings is a potential attribute only, and we afford others dignity in accordance with the values generated by our ethical structures. As a general position, persons are to stand in our regard for the fact that possessing freedom they can potentially attain to dignity. Rights are extended to other beings for reason of their freedom. Dignity is extended to them as a result of what they may do with this freedom.

The consideration due others is by no means an easy doctrine to maintain, for our basic relationship to others is always ambiguous. The fact of other free beings coexisting with us is conflictual as a result of the basic ontological situation of human beings. To ourselves, we are the for-itself who constitutes the world as it ought to be, the free originator of projects in the world, but the intrusion of the other reduces us to an object in the other's eyes. There is an inevitable ontological confrontation in which the natural inclination, that of defending our own status as a free being, is to reduce the other to the status of in-itself, to an object. Mutual threat is inherent in every human encounter. We rationally infer that others are free consciousnesses, but we never know them as anything but objects intruding into our world.[31]

The very root of human interaction is inevitably conflictual, hence political. By reason, we can maintain a tenuous support for morality, but human society is inherently unstable. There is an ever-present tendency to use persons as means only, which is all the more reason to recommend loyalty to some system of rights. Sartre, because of his analysis of the impact of the existence of others on ourselves, is to some degree a Hobbesian. Humans are always, among other effects, a danger to other humans. The look of the other reduces "my freedom. . .into an 'attribute' of the 'thing' I am for the other."

This concept of alterity is Sartre's version of alienation, but where Marx's reconstruction of society would in theory eliminate all sources of alienation, alterity is an eternal social "pathology" for existentialism, because its basis is not private ownership of the means of production but the onological condition of mankind.[32] This origin of social conflicts is mitigated by reason but not eradicable.

Briefly, to return to Tinder's compelling point that a human society not based on Christian agape would not be capable of sustaining itself for long, nor capable of supporting human rights or a sense of human dignity, we have proposed as a support for rights only lucidity and a belief in equality and not the love of mankind. It seems to me that both lucidity and the belief in equality may suffice to uphold a doctrine of human rights, for both beliefs have reasonableness in their favor.

For most members of society, the force of the idea that the vagrant ought to be loved on account of the divine spark is less than the force of the alternative idea that such a person ought to be regarded in the first instance as due equal rights are the same, for the proposal that we must hold a genuine love for mankind is really only possible as a rare intellectual attainment, at least for all but the most unusual individuals. *Agape* provides no firmer support for rights, in my opinion, than the doctrine based on lucidity. Moreover, if we can claim honestly and dispassionately to regard the wino as deserving of equal rights, this is preferable to claiming falsely that we love the wino when we likely do not. Tinder's doctrine begs for hypocrisy.

So dire is the ontological condition in the human encounter, that even tolerance might be taken to be an aggressive stance affronting the freedom of others. Like Kant, we will later advocate the liberal democratic society, Kant's "Kingdom of ends in which all are, at least potentially, legislative members," if you will. The liberal democrat, in the spirit of tolerance, keeps the ideal of the good society separate from the ideal of the good person. Ethically, we may try to attain an ideal of the good person, and doing so, afford an example of a possible good life for others, but tolerance recommends that we do not force others to accept our values.[33] Kant's liberalism makes it a contradiction to even try to "deem myself obligated to promote [another's] perfection. For the perfection of another man as a person consists precisely in his being able to set his end for himself according to his own concepts of duty."[34]

These principles, which are the true interpretations of justice and the basis of an appropriate polity are attacked by Sartre as akin to coercion itself, for education and tolerance determine the situation of others regardless of their own determination of their possibilities.[35] Tolerance tries to steal the cause from potential rebels. "To realize tolerance with respect to the Other is to cause the Other to be thrown forcefully into a tolerant world."[36] We have thereby deprived the other of the possibility of courageous resistance.

Marcuse presents some similar arguments in his attack on the oppressive uses of liberal tolerance. Once again, we may be convinced by the philosophical point that is presented in these arguments against the tolerant polity, while denying the practical politics of the criticism. To accept that there are contradictions, if you will, in the liberal society is not to accept that it is therefore inferior or the same as intolerant systems of authoritarianism or totalitarian rule. It appears to be another of those paradoxical and extreme positions that Sartre sometimes liked to adopt.

But let us be clear on the concept of toleration, which we advocate for the polity in the same sense that John Stuart Mill presents it in *On Liberty*. It is not our duty to acquiesce in the foibles and opinions of others. Our values will clash with the values generated by free others, and it is to recognize them as ends that we afford them the freedom to express their values, but it is not the point of tolerance that we will refuse to confront those values and do battle with them. We may work to make certain some values do not prevail in the polity. The tolerant society does not require that we accept all values as equal.

Sartre is mistaken, therefore, to hold that treating persons as absolute ends means to pass over in silence the injustices of the age, such as colonialism or anti-Semitism (or Stalinism, Sartre ought to have added).[37] To have truly accepted other persons as ends requires not that we acquiese in their values, but that we attack those values we believe to be a negation of free existence. The sign of intolerance is not argument but the use of calumny, designed not to refute a position or argument, but to destroy the person offering it, as we have seen in the case of Lenin.

We accept reservedly, then, the philosophical point that supports Sartre's criticism of liberal society without accepting certain of what he takes to be its implications. As sometimes occurs in philosophical enthusiasm, Sartre commits the anarchist's fallacy: Since all societies are based on the principle of coercion, there is no plausible choice to be made among them. This is untrue: the alternatives open to people in Mao's society were far more restricted than the choices open in any liberal society. Intellectuals are too prone to conclude that the "cultural revolution" was a wonderful event, but only for the Chinese, not for themselves.

Comparable to the philosophical flaw of toleration, education is also inevitably an incursion into the freedom of others; indeed, because of the youth and lack of experience of these others, the dangers are even greater that education will become a weapon of ideological coercion. The aim of the educator, however, in the democratic society ought to be to import only what he or she believes to be the truth, emphasizing lucidity and witnessing. As Croce puts it in his recommendations on communicating with others, ". . .the overshadowing objective is that the life in people should be stimulated, changed, and enobled."[38]

The good educator will, as will the diplomat or the psychiatrist, be in the position sometimes of treating students as means, but also to be borne in mind is Kant's injunction that they must never be treated only as means (as good citizens, soldiers of the Reich, entrepreneurs of commercial society, etc.). Education ought to instill, along with substance, the truth of responsibility, lucidity, and freedom. As Barnes comments on Heidegger's extension of his idea of the "call of conscience," it affects *Mitsein* (being-together-with) by appealing to *Dasein* (the conscious individual) to "become the Conscience of the Other." But this emphatically does not mean to set the standards for the Other, but to "awaken him to his own possibilities for being and to inspire him to choose himself authentically."[39] This is the authentic aim of an appropriate education, and to some degree has inspired all the great educators from Confucius and Socrates to the present.

To the degree that conflict with others is based on human ontology, it is irremediable although mitigated by a constant dialectic with reason. But Sartre and some other thinkers also show another and aggravating source of conflict, which is scarcity. This is a consideration beyond ontology, but it interacts with it. Marx, of course, treats of scarcity, but it is for him not quite the fundamental concept that Sartre made of it in his *Critique*. Laing and Cooper recognize this as a major factor influencing Sartre's later thought. They point out that scarcity "makes real the impossibility of co-essential existence."[40] Human beings come to be viewed as excess, as purely interchangeable quantities. Each person becomes just one too many. And scarcity certainly exacerbates the danger people pose to one another. This is the ultimate social consequence of burgeoning overpopulation, that human life will be regarded as excessive, hence cheapened, so that people become things only, each one being just one too many.

Rousseau once asked a question raised by Aristotle in the latter's somewhat ineffective defense of slavery. Might there not be situations so unfortunate that one can preserve one's own freedom only at the expense of someone else's? Perhaps these circumstances, which certainly include scarcity, justify that to free some citizens, others must be slaves.[41] Although Aristotle argued that some are slaves by nature, he was really trying to justify slavery as a result of scarcity, because he sensed the flimsiness of the former argument. Although a society of independent peasants might produce an occasional *Works and Days*, who would not choose slavery (for others) if not to do so were to erase the Golden Age of Greece? And to so choose, would be to choose immorality and injustice.

Capitalism also supports immoral choices, if, indeed, it really needed child labor and 14-hour days during the early Industrial Revolution. Accepting our present status of comforts on the basis of these past injustices places those of us living at present in a questionable moral situation, which we will try to illuminate in a forthcoming chapter on history. To accept our present status of well-being as a matter of course is to forget the oppression inflicted on past others. For Sartre, as for Marx and the Marxists generally, the solution to the problem of social scarcity was the revolution. Most likely this would have had to be a violent revolution. After all, the bourgeoisie would hardly give up their social advantages peacefully.

Merleau-Ponty claims that revolutionary movements "are justified by their own existence," for they attest to the fact that workers are unable to live in society as it exists.[42] This appears to be Sartre's view, for he seemed olympically uninterested in any consequences of the revolutions he supported. Perhaps, he presupposed without further analysis that these revolutions would have desirable results. There is a degree of romantic rebellion that might be so justified, and Hobsbawm delineates revolts of this type in his *Primitive Rebels*.

Lucidity and responsibility, however, demand that the revolution we support be justified by its anticipated consequences, and at the last by its actual consequences. This demands a degree of political analysis that Sartre never produced. In fact, the revolutions supported by Sartre were not the means to overcome scarcity, as the repeated failure of collectivization shows; indeed, many of these systems collapsed shortly after Sartre's death.

Intellectuals are sometimes quite violent persons, at least vicariously. No land reform meets the approval of a certain type of radical intellectual unless accompanied by the slaughter of thousands of peasants. Somehow mass slaughter makes change appear more real. The mass grave serves to give notice of strenuous progressive effort. If you kill only scores, how can you be trying as hard as you should to do good? Yet, these forms of forced collectivism have been the sure road to agricultural stagnation. In *Being and Nothingness*, Sartre shows that the for-itself can never *possess* an object (or an other, for that matter), and the frustration resulting from this realization inclines the for-itself to violence. "Destruction realizes appropriation perhaps more keenly than creation does."[43] Yet, for the advocate of violent reform, the temptation to totally control the lives of others for their own good is ever present; destruction seems to underline the significance and success of such endeavors in the world.

With Sartre the choice always seems to fall on the violent path. Thody [44] accuses Sartre of holding a very cult of violence, with no clear or practicable notion of what kind of social system will replace the old. Poster defends Sartre by calling our attention, quite rightly, to the definition of violence in the *Critique*, where it includes the refusal to recognize the humanity of the other, hence, includes social oppression.[45] This, however, is not an illuminating definition of the concepts of violence and oppression; oppression is quite a good enough indicator for a state of obviating the freedom of others; and violence adds a distinct element as to how we deny the humanity of others. Sartre is not exonerated from Thody's accusation.

Whether we call oppression violence or not, there are still strategies of reform and non-violence that have worked more effectively for social good during past history. Sartre appears to want the violent means for their own sake, even when they are patently ineffective. And, it is also no defense to call on Sartre's demands for a level of civilized behavior far in excess of current norms before an ethics or morality can be established, as Poster does. Aron puts it thus: "What I hate is not the choice, *hic et nunc*, at a particular conjunction of circumstances, in favor of violence against negotiation, but a philosophy of violence in and for itself [the *Critique* is the issue here], not as means that is sometimes necessary for a rational politics."[46]

A more rational orientation here is that of Lenin's or Clausewitz's. The Supreme Court decision Brown v. Board of Education wrought far more effective change than the murderous tactics of John Brown, although it must be granted that the milieu was different on each occasion. Wendell Phillips, who advocated tactics of reform, like his predecessor Robert Owen, are responsible for more good results in the increase of concrete freedom than the Sendero Luminosa will ever be, however many peasants and others they manage to murder. Occasionally Sartre seems to be a leftwing Karl Schmidt[47] in his concepts of the "pledge" and the "terror," which bear an uncomfortable resemblance to the latter's perverse division of society into the Friend and the Foe.

In part, the cult of violence grows from an absolutist view of society. For Sartre, the bourgeoisie are unredeemable and unalleviatedly bad. Such a totalitarian mindset is well-known. Ulrika Meinhof, the ideologist of the Baader-Meinhof group in West Germany, was an avowed pacifist, whose initial aversion to violence masked strong aggressive impulses that when freed gave rise to a fascination with violence.[48] For quite other reasons, A. J. Muste, an inspirational figure to the New Left of the 1960s, argued that "a distinction between the violence of liberation movements and imperialist violence" [allows pacifists to] support some who are engaged in violent action."[49]

Strauton Lynd and Tom Hayden applied the same reasoning to their support of the North Vietnamese and the Khmer Rouge, asking rhetorically "How can we as pacifists support revolutionary violence?" In both the cases, the simple answer is that pacifists cannot support violence and remain pacifists, and to present themselves any longer as pacifists is an exercise in bad faith.

But the question is an important one, nonetheless, whether violence is morally admissible in any political situation. It is obvious that violence terminates the victim's freedom, sometimes once for all. The only satisfactory answer is that under many conditions, violence will be an immoral act in the means it uses to gain political ends, but that under certain conditions where other means are genuinely lacking to bring about situations in which humans can attain a measure of justice, violence becomes morally acceptable. Violence may be an authentic choice. After John Locke, we might say that this choice would become appropriate if a monarch or a group raise a tangible and dangerous threat to human freedom and leave no other predictably viable recourse to prevention of their ends. If any person or group is being brought irresistibly under the manipulative control of another, the time for violence has arrived.

For the Jews, the time for the recourse to violence occurred long before their incarceration in the extermination camps; for the Japanese incarcerated in camps in the United States during World War II, violent measures were also warranted under the existing unpredictability of events, although in the latter case the consequence would have been unfortunate: as it turned out, the Japanese were not on the path to extermination, although it is difficult to know this before the fact. Justice assumes a civil reciprocity among people. But the deviation from morality is so great in the case of political violence that the responsibility of lucidity weighs very heavily upon the perpetrator. Other avenues must first be explored and one must make all rational efforts to weigh the consequences of such acts.

On this basis, such monsters of iniquity, of the denial of existence and freedom, as Pol Pot, Idi Amin, Mengele, Heydrich, Hitler, and Stalin are targets for just assassination. Social conditions and countervailing power recommended, most likely, against the assassination of Huey Long and the attempted assassination of George Wallace. Indeed, in the case of George Wallace, from posing a threat to human rights, he may actually have grown in moral stature during the course of his career. Violence, however, although condonable in certain political situations, must always be a last resort, not a manifestation of romanticism. The burden of proof, of weighing the consequences of violent acts, is on the perpetrators.

It is well to be quite clear about violence in political situations, where violence is defined as the killing of people. Violence is the ultimate denial of the freedom of others, the absolute refusal of communication, the point at which debate gives way to destruction. Therefore, the choice of violence is the decision to put aside all morality, all considerations of justice. In this, at least, the view of the pacifist is correct, for the resort to violence is the decision to regard others as objects only. Thus, violence is in some versions of politics the very denial of the political, the designation of the opponent as the Enemy in the sense of Karl Schmitt.

If this is so, the decision to resort to violence is a fateful one to be made only under extreme circumstances. Since morality is a free choice, the choice to depart from the moral consideration of others is also free. The sole individual reason to make such a choice must be only within a situation in which there is a major threat to the individual's existence. This means that the individual's life is presently under threat; or, it means that the restrictions that prevent the projection of ethical goals have become so great as to limit the individual to an inhuman existence. Not that society presents some barriers to certain of our projects, for that is always the case, but that society has reduced persons to subhuman conditions. Locke and Hobbes understood the justifications for revolt, although Hobbes did not clearly admit this. The revolt of Spartacus would have been justified. The escape from Treblinka justified killing any guards of that camp.

But the resort to violence requires that the rebel take responsibility for a lucid view of the political situation. There were times and conditions in the 19th century when a proletarian revolt was justified. Toward the end of that century, in some countries, the justification for such a resort to violence was becoming moot. In addition, the Enemy in these circumstances is not cast once and for all in an inescapable role, but there may well come a time when human communication can reopen. Although the fanatic Nazi will probably remain obdurate, other opponents might not be carved in stone. For the individual, therefore, a departure from morality may have a moral justification. Later, the problems posed by the decision of nations to go to war will be discussed.

The revolution as self-defense may be justifiable. But there is also the revolution as a projection of perfection, as Utopia. Such a revolution sacrifices thousands of lives, and its transitional phases sacrifice a generation more who labor, not for their own amenities, but for the far future. (We are aware of course, in these analogies, of the important differences between time and place--situations do differ, and some, also, may appropriately call forth a violent reaction.) This is a Hegelian ambition, a totalizing Truth, which vindicates death and destruction for a final culmination of history; and who can predict with surety a final culmination of history? For Marx, this will be the classless society, and in a similar vision for Sartre and others, it will occur when there is a complete openness in intercommunication. This would mean, for Sartre, total transparence, for "secrecy and even privacy are forms of power retention and hence are alienating; they undermine true reciprocity".[50]

Sisely Bok quotes an interview with Sartre conducted by Michel Contat, in which Sartre advocates his universal transparency, "I can imagine rather easily the day when two men will have no more secrets from one another because they will keep secrets from no one, since the subjective life, just as the objective life, will be totally offered, given."[51] Whether this is a worthy objective, and in the face of human ontology it may well be unattainable in its extreme formulation, it is surely in keeping with the morality of treating all persons as ends. But whether such a goal could be ever attained among flawed creatures such as mankind, whether there is not always to be some merit in our defensive ability to retreat to privacy, is moot. The goal is probably not worth too high a price.

To summarize this chapter, which has discussed our relations with others, the problem of rights must be settled. While rights cannot be founded, in our view, on natural law or human nature as essence, there is nonetheless an appropriate argument in support of them. That argument as developed in this chapter is that rights are a free project, a stance freely adopted by the lucid individual toward others. The foundation for rights, therefore, is freedom; the free choice of life and the lucid recognition of how life is enhanced by the existence of free others provides the reasons that indicate why others ought to be accorded rights. This is admittedly a precarious basis for so important a political choice, since the responsibility for rights rests forever on the shifting projects of free consciousnesses.

But precarious though this support may be, that is the way it is: there is no more solid support than the freedom of individuals to choose to afford rights to others; precariousness is a quality of the human condition. Hobbes in his effort to provide a basis for absolute monarchy, tried to do so through a rational psychology. He was criticized for the weakness of the support this provided kings, a support apparently more flimsy than 'divine right." But divine right was no longer viable in Hobbes' day, and it was no longer a believable support for anything. This would seem to be the case for supports for rights in our own day.

In this discussion of others, we have chosen to discuss generalized others, with whom we share only a common humanity and the quality of freedom. In politics, however, there are at least three levels of our interaction with other individuals. We are associated in the first place with intimate others, on the basis of family and friendship. These are intimate others with whom we share a more substantial emotional input than required by political morality. In addition, we are associated with individuals with whom we interact in a political project at the national level.

As members of a society, we may owe such fellow actors a measure of regard beyond mere justice: This problem will be approached in the chapter on society and the nation. Finally, as members of a nation interacting in a world arena, we are also associated with persons beyond the boundaries of the political project of the nation: we will discuss the application of morality at this level of interaction in the chapters on diplomacy and international politics.

Notes

1. Caws, *Sartre*, p. 62.
2. Olafson, *Principles and Persons*, p. 194.
3. *Ibid.*, p. 195.
4. *Ibid.*, p. 212.
5. James Collins, The Existentialists: A Critical Study (Chicago: Henry Regnery Co., 1952), p. 239. It is interesting to find Fichte among the staunchest advocates of this view of respecting the freedom of others. See Johann Gottlieb Fichte, *The Vocation of Man* (Indianapolis: The Bobbs-Merrill Co., Inc., 1956), p. 146.
6. F. H. Heinmann, *Existentialism and the Modern Predicament* (New York: Harper Torch Books, 1958), p. 126.
7. Hartmann, *Ethics*, Vol. II, p. 268.
8. Sir David Ross, *Kant's Ethical Theory. A Commentary on the Grundlegung zur Metaphysik der sitten* (Westport: Greenwood Press Publishers, 1978. A reprint of the 1954 edition by Clarendon Press.), p. 94.
9. Sartre, *Being and Nothingness*, p. 54.
10. Jean Hyppolite, *Genesis and Structure of Hegel's Phenomenology of Spirit* (Trans. by Samuel Cherniak and John Heckman. Evanston: Northwestern University Press, 1974), pp. 166-167.

11. Flynn, *Sartre and Marxist Existentialism*, p. 20.
12. Collins, *The Existentialists*, p. 240, quoting from Jaspers' *Reason and Existence*.
13. David Held, *Introduction to Critical Theory: Horkheimer to Habermas* (Berkeley: University of California Press, 1980), pp. 323-344.
14. Quoted in Sydney Hook, *Philosophy and Public Policy* (Carbondale: Southern Illinois University Press, 1980), p. 119. It is from V. I. Lenin, *Selected Works*, Vol. 3, (New York: International Publishers, 1943), p. 490.
15. From the *Hawaii Tribune-Herald*, July 16, 1989, p. 2.
16. See Marcel, *The Existential Background of Human Dignity* (Cambridge, MA: Harvard University Press, 1963), p. 123; this is the William James Lecture, delivered at Harvard 1961-1962.
17. Marcel Eck, *Lies and Truth* (New York: Macmillan, 1970), p. 69. Luijpen, *Existential Phenomenology*, pp. 338-339, presents this thesis from the phenomenological view, that "Man himself *is* a certain 'ought' with respect to his fellowman. An age-old tradition calls the execution of this 'ought': 'Love,' and it understands this love as the acceptance, the willing, supporting, and fostering of the other's subjectivity, selfhood, and freedom." This analysis is agreeable to our viewpoint, which tries to relate this "ought" to lucidity rather than love, for we can will lucidity sooner than we can will love.
18. Findlay, *Values and Intentions*, p. 275, is cognizant of this problem, when he refers to "the lack of respect" in extending *our* schemes of happiness to others.
19. Sartre, *Critique*, pp. 109-110.
20. John H. Riker, *The Art of Ethical Thinking* (Washington, D.C.: University Press of America, 1978), p. 95. And see also Williams, *Ethics and the Limits of Philosophy*, pp. 59-60.
21. Fichte, *The Science of Rights* (New York: Harper and Row, 1970. Trans. by A. E. Kroeger), pp. 78-79.
22. *Ibid.*, pp. 129-130.
23. Hiram Caton, "Towards a Diagnosis of Progress," *Independent Journal of Philosophy*, Vol. VI (1983), p. 10.
24. See Glenn Tinder, "Can We Be Good Without God?" *The Atlantic Monthly*, Vol 264, No. 6 (December 1989), 68-85.
25. See Raymond Aron, *History and the Dialectic of Violence* (New York: Harper and Row, 1975. Trans. by Barry Cooper), pp. 29-30; Flynn, *Sartre and Marxist Existentialism*, p. 115; and Sartre, *Being and Nothingness*, p. 366, p. 408.
26. Eugene Kamenka, *The Ethical Foundations of Marxism* (London: Routledge and Kegan Paul, 1962), pp. 180-181, taking the passage from George L. Kline, "Changing Attitudes Toward the Individual," in C.E. Black, ed., *The Transformation of Russian Society* (Cambridge, MA: Harvard University Press, 1960).

27. See Dinesh D'Souza, "Illiberal Education," *The Atlantic*, Vol. 267, No. 3 (March, 1991), 51-79, for a short preview of the potential consequences to be brought on by the new nihilism. It is not the case that humans cannot learn from the historical past; it is the case, however, that they must learn the same lessons over and over again.
28. *Reasons and Persons*, p. 397.
29. Milton Mayeroff, *On Caring* (New York: Harper and Row, 1971), pp. 56-57.

30. Stephen Frederick Schneck, *Person and Polis: Max Scheler's Personalism as Political Theory* (Albany: State University of New York, 1987), pp. 60-61, p. 64.
31. We accept Sartre's presentation without reservations here. See Natanson, *A Critique of Jean-Paul Sartre's Ontology*, p. 35; Flynn, *Sartre and Marxist Existentialism*, p. 25; Ronald David Laing and D. G. Cooper, *Reason and Violence: A Decade of Sartre's Philosophy*, 1950-1960 (New York: Humanities Press, 1964), p. 175. "Try as I will, I never arrive at meeting [the other] as subject," states Barnes, *Existential Ethics*, p. 88.
32. Poster, *Existential Marxism in Postwar France*, p. 286.
33. Hare, *Freedom and Reason*, pp. 179-180.
34. William Galston, "Defending Liberalism," *American Political Science Review*, Vol. 76, No. 3 (September 1982), p. 623.
35. Greene, *Jean-Paul Sartre: The Existentialist Ethic*, p. 174.
36. Sartre, *Being and Nothingness*, p. 409; and see Izenberg, *The Existentialist Critique of Freud*, p. 268.
37. Flynn, *Sartre and Marxist Existentialism*, pp. 78-79, for Sartre's comment.
38. Benedetto Croce, *The Conduct of Life* (New York: Harcourt, Brace and Company, 1924; trans. by Arthur Livingston), p. 55. The educational principles of John Dewey are the classic formulation of what education ought to be about in a democratic society.
39. Barnes, *Existential Ethics*, p. 416.
40. Laing and Cooper, *Reason and Violence*, pp. 113-114.
41. Ellenburg, *Political Philosophy*, p. 162, drawing on the *Social Contract*.
42. Merleau-Ponty, *Adventures of the Dialectic* (Evanston: Northwestern University Press, 1973. Trans. by Joseph Bien), p. 226.
43. This is an insight from *Being and Nothingness*, p. 593; it is interpreted by McMahon, *Humans Being*, p. 119.
44. P. M. W. Thody, "Sartre and the Concept of Moral Action: the Example of His Novels and Plays," in Schilpp, *The Philosophy of Jean-Paul Sartre*, p. 436.
45. Poster, *Existential Marxism in Postwar France*, pp. 300-301.
46. Aron, *History and the Dialectic of Violence*, p. 192.
47. See his *The Concept of the Political* (New Brunswick: Rutgers University Press, 1976. Trans. by George Schwab). Schmidt's politics violate our idea of the moral at the very core, while Sartre usually pays heed to others.

48. Stanley Rothman and S. Robert Lichter, *Roots of Radicalism: Jews, Christians, and the New Left* (New York, Oxford: Oxford University Press, 1982), p. 367.
49. *Ibid.*, p. 187.
50. Flynn, *Sartre and Marxist Existentialism*, p. 193.
51. Sissela Bok, *Secrets: On the Ethics of Concealment and Revelation* (New York: Pantheon Books, 1982), p. 17. The interview is in *Le Nouvel Observateur*, June 23, 1975, p. 72.

Chapter 6

The Problem of Morality: Why Ought We To Be Moral?

Part I. Reasons for Adopting a Moral Stance

In reviewing Donald Wallout's essay "Why Should I Be Moral? A Reconsideration," Kai Nielsen criticizes the answer given to the question, namely, that ". . .one should be moral because this fits into a pattern of universal harmony of all things. . . ." a harmony that is the ultimate culmination of all existence.[1] An answer of this nature is, in the first place, too impressive for our purpose. Moreover, it may be doubted whether there is some ultimate culmination of moral existence, here harmony, a problem treated earlier. In addition, the answer would appear to beg the question, for one might ask why, exactly, a pattern of universal harmony is desirable. But the question itself--Why ought one to be moral?--is by no means easy to answer, nor is it irrelevant to our aims. An answer, therefore, must be attempted.

The basis of any tentative answer to the query must rest on the discussion of anguish stemming from the ever-present danger of the evaporation of the meaning-structure the individual has erected (one result of freedom) and the decision to be lucid; from such a basis, the choice of life over the termination of existence, Eros over Thanatos, has been commended. Later, an argument will be presented to show that the choice of life leads logically to the delimitation of our (free) selection of projects. Projects are those aims generated by an active human existence.

For now, it will be taken for granted that there are projects, different for each individual, according to each person's freely posited goals.

Let us suppose that a person has chosen the goal of *virtu*, as espoused by Machiavelli in *The Prince*. Such a goal will define for a person the meaning for him or her of the natural and social situations that arise along the path of attaining this goal. The choice of such a goal will certainly color the moral choices that will be made along this path, but it would be amoral to hold that all means are moral that further the attainment of *virtu* and that all means inappropriate to that attainment are thereby to be called immoral. This is not a morality. Insofar as such a stance posits a valued goal, it is an ethics, but an ethics that omits morality.

The amoral individual, and this is to be seen in extreme form among certain types of psychopathic personalities, would never do anything that deviated from self interest, defined according to his or her choice of projects. This is the formulation of morality that is generally attributed to Marxists like Lenin and Trotsky, although in their case it is presumably class interest as opposed to self interest that is to be furthered. In choosing to be moral, we choose under some conditions to act in ways that are not self-interested, and to refrain from certain actions that might be even more efficacious in propelling us closer to our goals. Morality is a choice to be less than fully effective, in some cases, in attaining certain of our aims. Morality places limits on our activity. Why would we freely choose to so hamper our efficacy?

This leads to the problem of others. In a solipsistic universe, morality is irrelevant. But lucidity, as indicated in the preceeding chapter, requires that we admit the existence of other beings such as ourselves, who have consciousness and freedom. It is the existence of others which is the chief reason for there being a moral problem. Our acts impinge on the existence of others, their's on ours. This fact raises the issue, over and above the goals that we may have chosen, that the path we pursue through the situations encountered in accomplishing projects will have important subsidiary effects on others; their projects, in turn, will affect us and will affect independently the situations we encounter.

The selection of a morality or the refusal to act morally, is an exercise in responsibility; it is our responsibility, if morality is the choice, to take others into account in our activities. Morality is the choice that others are of some account independently of whatever use they may be to the attainment of our goals.

In choosing to be moral, a person will sometimes desist from efficacious actions designed to facilitate a project, on the grounds that it would be injurious to others, because they must also be taken into account. A moral choice is often a choice that is not of direct benefit to the actor. Morality waives self-interest. Regardless of what we might want to do, or what the situation seems to call for as a direct response to attaining an end, we choose instead to do what we have determined that we ought to do on occasion. We choose to act morally.   Our projects represent values that have been freely chosen to create the kind of being we would be, to create the world as we would like it to be. Being free, we can also choose to take the straight and ruthless course to gain our ends. Or we may freely choose to accept limitations on our acts in consideration of the existence of others. Morality is a subsidiary project that guides value-projects under certain circumstances.

It is possible that the aims of Copernicus, Darwin, or Saint Francis are not consonant with our own projects, but these are beings who have contributed to the social setting in which we operate. They have acted on history to make it more interesting, possibly even more constructive. They have done so for the reason that they were individual consciousnesses free to choose and to pursue their unique projects. Morality accepts that other persons are potential and worthy contributors to the situations we encounter, so that we must come to terms with them. Morality is the way in which we come to terms with the existence of others.

Through moral choice, we determine that there are some actions we ought to forego in order that other free consciousnesses might continue to provide unique contributions to the world in which we seek to realize projects. To temper with morality our path through the world toward the realization of our own projects is to accept that it is better to admit into the world the independent contributions of many other free individuals. To put this conclusion in another way: "Reflection about how the individual should live is inseparable from reflection about the nature of the good society."[2] Morality is quintessentially a political problem, just as Aristotle and Plato regarded it.

One ought to be moral, therefore, because others exist and because their free projects can contribute independently to a better world than one that could be reconstructed from scratch by ourselves. This respect for the freedom of others is the core of an appropriate ethical theory, and without it any ethical system lacks passion. To conform to a system of rules opportunistically is not to be moral, for there are too many situations, each one unique, to be encountered and resolved anew, and rigid moral rules cannot be prescribed for each new instance. Morality, therefore, is not a set of all-purpose rules; rather, it is the general principle of regard for the freedom of others.

It should be clear that there is a distinction being made here between ethics and morality. Ethics we take to be a broader term than morality. It includes the ends we propose to infuse meaning into our lives and it includes also morality. Morality is only a part of ethics, namely, that part in which we take others importantly into account. In addition, there are the goals we posit for ourselves, which establish for us our view of the good life. Of the innumerable goals we might select in our path through life, only those that are consonant with life as against destruction are to be deemed ethical.

But in pursuing these goals, we have additional choices to make with regard to our treatment of others, and this is specifically a moral choice. Without this distinction between ethics and morality, it might seem appropriate to some thinkers to make a choice of the moral life as a chief end. But with the distinction in mind, it is obvious that the choice of goals, the selection of our vision of the good life, is a vital decision in itself; that is, we do not choose to live in order to be moral. Morality is the subsidiary choice. First we choose to pursue our vision of the good life, then we choose to do so morally on the way. This distinction is not general in the field of ethical thought, but it is made by Stuart Hampshire.[3]

The choice of ends has to do with establishing a meaningful existence for ourselves out of our thrownness. It is a selection out of freedom of values. A decision to become a pianist, an entymologist, or a baseball player is not in itself a moral decision, although it may be a highly significant decision for both the person and the world. Whether it is better morally to become a doctor, a lawyer or an academic does not enter actively into consideration, for morality as such is not *the* end; rather, morality is a relation between oneself and others as projects are pursued.

We may be free to choose, say, the end of the "perfectly moral individual," but this is essentially an empty and passive goal. On the other hand, the project of diplomacy is not empty, for it presents a whole array of exertions and aims toward goals of a varied nature, of those projects in the world selected by a diplomat as individual and national values, but there are both moral and immoral choices that may be made along the path toward these goals as diplomatic actions bring others into the national sphere of influence. How we treat others, the respect or the lack of it that we accord to their freedom, is the essence of a morality.

The distinction here is between all that which is valued, which we will regard as the broad topic of ethics, and what ought to be done with respect to others, which is morality. Projects may be assessed according to their value with respect to the choice of life over nonexistence, and this is the major purpose of an ethics. But morality is the assessment of our activities as they specifically affect other humans. If the experience of intense competition is valued, where our skills are pitted against the skills of other persons as in a sport, such competition need not be chosen for all others as a universal choice, but we will certainly be glad to find others willing to become worthy competitors. In games and sports, the need for independent others to exist and choose freely is of particular importance, as anyone knows who has ever tried to play chess against themselves.

It is, in any case, through our treatment of other beings as we pursue projects that we assert what ought to be universally accepted behavior. Values represent our unique choices of goals; scholarship is not the kind of goal that is posited as a universal one, for a world of scholars would probably not be viable. A world formed by numerous and different choices contributes to a more abundant existence. Such choices may be weighed according to the nature of the world that they will produce, and so they may be evaluated, but they are not selected as projects for all persons to adopt. But on the basis of how we value the freedom of others, the basis for a morality, we have chosen universally. Such morality will operate within the context of other values. Morality, that is, is subsumed under ethics.

Now it is true that a choice of what to value, projects, affects moral behavior. Moral behavior toward others may be more easily effected if we choose to pursue the project of scientific knowledge, because the contributions of other free consciousnesses are quite evidently necessary in the development of cumulative knowledge. Within a project of this nature, of course, other projects will also be pursued, perhaps subsidiary to this one, as that of lover, religious believer, teacher, and citizen. And within the ensemble of projects, behavior may be moral in pursuit of one or more of these. But it is not the pursuit of scientific knowledge in itself that renders one moral or immoral; rather, it is our relationship to others in the way that we pursue that goal that marks us moral or immoral.

In political projects, in diplomacy, bureaucracy, or the military, the very nature of the ends involved raises the issue of whether they may be conducted in a moral way at all. For all politics involve conflict among opposing interests, and some situations generate destruction and death, and it is within these kinds of situations that morality falls under immense strain. At the extreme, we might consider the moral implications of the choice of the pacifist as against that of the soldier. Neither stance is moral by definition, although pacifism might appear to be so; it is the consequences of each stance that must be taken into account. For although the soldier is trained for violence, the war may not come about given that it is deterred, or the outcome of the war that does come about may be preferable to the condition that results from passivity.

While we aver that ends are values, and values are not identical with morals, there is, nonetheless, a relationship. The foundation of this relationship between projects toward valued ends and the morality of the means toward those ends lies in an original choice, made probably unheedingly, and often without the application of a lucid analysis, of life as against non-existence. This choice infuses the world with potential meanings and precludes other choices that would contradict this fundamental choice. The necrophilia evident in the diaries of Heinrich Himmler is illustrative of a choice of non-existence, and Himmler's decisions and activities during World War II represent the logical consequences taken to the extreme of this basic choice; and so, such an original choice greatly affected Himmler's morality.[4]

Nietzsche fulminates against the principle of morality, although it might be better to say that he attacks moralism, the propensity to emphasize moral interactions at the expense of the pursuit of other projects. Thus, he inveighs against those who

> preach "Good and Evil, good and evil, the same for all," [since each individual] must discover the rule of his own health.[5]

But here, Nietzsche, mistakenly in my opinion, has not distinguished between values in the broader ethical sense and morality in its more restricted province. While our projects differ according to our values, morality can be, in fact, the same for all.

Morality is the manner in which we pursue values. It is a peculiar and separate value that may be selected together with our unique projects. Nietzsche is attacking the moralism that manipulates others for the moralist's own benefit, in this case the manipulation of the strong by the weak; he is attacking the morality that grows from what Scheler refers to as *resentiment*. Indeed, Scheler regards Nietzsche as wrong in thinking that genuine morality springs from resentiment, and we may agree that Nietzsche's attack here is directed against a certain type of morality only.[6]

Thus, we heed Hare's injunction to distinguish between the word "good," which applies to our ideals, and the word "ought," between judgments about goodness and those that concern obligations and duties, and between moral judgments that refer to the interests of others and those that do not.[7] Kupperman also recommends a usage that appeals to the point-of-view taken here between morals and ethics. In essence, morality is included within ethics. If we question whether to assassinate a dictator, this is both a moral and an ethical problem. But if we decide whether to devote our leisure time to intellectual activities or tennis, that is an ethical problem, the kind of problem, Kupperman points out, that exercised Plato, Aristotle, John Stuart Mill, and Moore. And this type of problem is not, in essence, a moral one.[8]

We may, then, agree with Sartre that values are "valued only within a definite individual project."[9] Values may define obligations that we accept for ourselves. If we value music as an aesthetic expression and adopt the project of a concert pianist, the choice obligates us to develop pianistic skills. But these are self-imposed obligations, whereas the obligations that stem from the choice of according other people freedom and independence are framed in the context of universal duties--in freely imposing these types of duties on ourselves, a choice is indeed made that is intended as a model for all persons. Only some of us will be obligated to develop our pianistic skills, fortunately, but the choice of relating our acts to others is a universal choice.

The process of applying moral rules to situations is called casuistry. Hartmann points to the error of casuistry, namely that rules cannot cover the complexity of the situations we encounter. Moreover, the structure of situations is also in part defined by the projects we pursue, so that to apply a preordained rule, a categorical imperative, is too mechanical. The crux of our moral decisions in any situation will rest on the fundamental choice of taking others into account, and we are responsible for defining what this means within any given context. "Casuistry," on the contrary, "lies in a dead rut, because it thinks to evolve from a principle and to discuss what only the unfalsified fulness of real life...is in a position to unroll....it is an abortion of the letter, which kills."[10]

That our view of lucidity in understanding the status of others is a basis of morality is buttressed by developmental studies, such as those of Lawrence Kohlberg, that show the apparent stages of moral growth. And casuistry, the mechanical application of rules with no subtle distinction is morality at an early and primitive stage, according to Kohlberg. Wilson refers to Aronfreed's evidence that in some societies internalized moral orientations never develop to a significant degree. Instead, externalized moral orientations, pharisaism, are the end points in some societies (and among many individuals in all societies).[11] Of course, the existentialists eschew "unconditioned values which would set themselves up athwart his freedom like things," for which reason intuitionism and categorical imperatives are likened to bad faith.

Simone de Beauvoir asserts, rather, that values come into the world through human existence. Free human existence is a lack, for we pursue projects in order to fill in a portion of the world that does not yet exist. Desire arises insofar as persons view the world as lacking in some way, and desires produce values.[12]

This view, uncannily akin to Buddhist psychology, has much to recommend it. Both Hare (prescriptivism) and Stevenson (emotivism) agree that values are chosen, not discovered out there in the universe. They would have as constraints on these choices, personal sincerity (honesty, let us suggest, and the acceptance of responsibility) and formal universality (in choosing, we choose for all mankind).[13] This formal universality, of course, we have not associated with goals other than basic morality.

We thereby depart from the Hobbesian argument that moralities are systems of principles whose acceptance by everyone as overruling the dictates of self-interest is in the interest of everyone alike.[14] This is Glaucon's argument that justice is what is in everyone's self-interest, which Plato attempts to refute by asserting that justice, on the contrary, must be good in itself. Hobbes, ever the astute thinker, posits that to define morality in this straightforward way also makes morality accord with reason only in those social conditions where there are rules of behavior recognized by everyone. Our definition does not agree with this definition, but we will defer our arguments against this important view at present--it is closely related to Sartre's conclusion that ethics is not possible until society is just. With Hobbes, of course, it is the social contract that makes the choice of morality reasonable.

In any case, we may undertake to evaluate values, in our argument on what, for us, will be the basis of a significant life, but we cannot define the values others ought to have. On the other hand, if we accept the worth of others, we can prescribe certain acts that are or are not moral. Value, or good, arises in the world through our individual commitments. Morality arises in the world as a result of the existence of other rational and free beings. The choice to act morally or immorally is freely made, but the basis for that choice is constrained by the existence of other humans.

In the case of all our ethical and moral judgments, we acknowledge that our evaluations could freely be otherwise. Even the foundation decisions to affirm life over non-existence and to view other people as independent and free entities, are open always to reevaluation. In both cases, the selection of foundation principles is intended to have consequences. We are responsible for these choices, being free, and there is the additional responsibility for the consequences of these choices. Accepting responsibility for consequences will demand that reason and lucidity be applied to choice.

If existence is taken as a value over non-existence, certain corollaries would appear to follow as reasonable inferences. For instance, it would be unreasonable to blind oneself and diminish existence. Other behaviors may be more difficult to judge: is it a contribution to our existence (morally speaking, we might ask, does it contribute to enhancing the existence of others?) to clear this forest and plant rubber trees? Through this deed, does existence gain over the weight of non-existence? This variety of question may be very difficult to answer, and part of the argument will rest on the choice of projects, part on the regard for others, and part on an interpretation of existence as opposed to non-existence. One inevitable result of the pursuit of values is the inevitable destruction of other values, and reason must enter into the weighing of gains over losses.

If others are to be taken into account as we pursue goals, it follows that some arguments will arise based on differences concerning facts.[15] Assuming that two persons agree that other persons count, they might still disagree whether an area of the city ought to be bulldozed and transformed into a housing project for the poor. If one is able to present a convincing argument that such projects in other cities actually decreased the quality of life for the inhabitants (indeed, the original inhabitants may even be entirely displaced), then we might be able to persuade another person that the project ought not to be undertaken. Of course, we might not be able to convince him or her that other people ought to count, but even then we might be able to demonstrate that the crime rate of the city may increase if the planned project is undertaken. Although a person such as B.F. Skinner does not accept that persons have "dignity" (so why take them into account?), an argument on the facts might prove persuasive.

As to values, it is possible that beliefs about the values defined by our projects may be logically based on reasons that other persons may entirely discount. They are our choices alone and not his or hers. Evidence in the context of these values may not count as evidence in the context of the projects another has chosen.[16] But there is generally little reason for anyone to try to convince anyone else to adopt projects of this kind. Here too, however, there are factual conditions to be taken into consideration. Lameness may prohibit the attainment of the goal of the gold medal in Olympic racing.

Ayer holds that ethical judgments are an expression of feeling, so that there is no way to determine, in the sense of logical positivism, the validity of any ethical system in any case. In short, ethical judgments have no supportable validity.[17] In a sense, this view is acceptable, for there is really no reason to convince others to accept particular ethical projects or evaluations as distinct from moral principles, although it might be persuasive to point to the enhancement of life accruing from some projects and not others.

So from a very different vantage point on ethics and projects, another might view certain accomplishments as good, while not in the least desiring the same goals. In the context of the projects we define for ourselves, however, there is ample room for arguments about consistency and consequences. There is every reason for an individual to consider the correct answer to ethical problems that arise in the pursuit of projects, if lucidity has been chosen and, of course, if others are to be taken into account, for efforts to solve moral dilemmas may contribute something to others, regardless of their unique projects, who desire to take others into account.

While ethical judgments partake of the cognitive-affective realm, they also enlist rationality, reasonableness, and intelligence.[18] So the cognitive-affective realm ought to be enlisted in support of moral judgments, if it is important that others be taken into account. For instance, it may be argued that your choice of not criticizing Iraq in the use of poison gas against its Kurdish population was wrong, for it is to ignore the fact that the Kurds are human beings. Furthermore, it is implicitly destructive to existence, to Eros, not to denounce this form of activity. Finally, omission of judgment at this juncture of history may affect many other persons later.

The great problem in justification is not morality as a portion of ethics, but values. Indeed, morality has its justification in the lucid decision to regard others as significant. Toulmin[19] suggests that it is not the business of ethics to try to justify "all reasoning about conduct." Indeed, this is true to the degree that we cannot really give any justification to treating others as real people rather than as objects to be manipulated for our personal convenience, although lucidity in assessing psychology, sociology, and history has afforded some basis toward justification. But a genuine *ethical* reason is difficult to envision.

By existing, a person has already made a tacit choice against non-existence, and a choice of projects will stem reasonably (or not so reasonably) from this fundamental choice. Certain minimal ethical choices, as justice or equality, may be rationally based on the choice of a world in which others taken as important beings may freely pursue most of their projects. This stance rests on an acknowledgement of human freedom. But a choice of the life of a diplomat or that of a concert pianist may rest to a great extent on attitude and personal predilection. It would seem appropriate to vindicate such choices as life-enhancing, but perhaps not with reasons that will convince a person unwilling to admit that existence is a greater value than non-existence.

Ayer is correct in asserting that the subjective answer to the question, *Are the things you value really valuable?* is *Yes, for the reason that I (or others) really value them.*[20] But this does not accept that there is ethical knowledge. Cognitive ethical knowledge would require that it be shown that (1) these values enhance existence and that (2) these morals take others importantly into account. But why must this requirement be met?

Perhaps it is a responsibility assumed by the decision to exist, but if so, the decision to pay heed to such a responsibility may be choosen or declined. To follow Ayer, we might accept that our values are correct for the reason that we choose to stand by them, knowing that we are capable of choosing otherwise. We are asserting an ethical system by our loyalty to it: The question for others may be phrased, "Is this admirable or not?" There is an attractiveness to the good life, or there ought to be, and this rests on other than strictly scientific or social scientific methods.[21]

Consistency is another aspect of ethics. It implies commitment. To live ethically, we propose that in situations of a particular nature, we will be prepared to make the same judgments as in like situations. Freedom does not imply lack of commitment, nor does it require unpredictability. An ethical personality is a committed personality, although in Sartre's view there is in such commitment the ever-lurking danger of seriousness--we ought never to forget that our commitments have been chosen freely and that other views of life are always possible to us. It is quite obvious, of course, that commitments may be made to what others regard as the wrong projects.

It is necessary in a view of an ethics that requires lucidity that there be "a harmony of subjective judgement and objective experience." The views we take within our ethical system "must never knowingly assume a view which conflicts with what is believed to be reality."[22] Honesty, lucidity, is an important criterion in the justification of an ethical system, a choice that is commendable, in our view. If the proletarian revolution is a value we choose to pursue, and we base our project on a patently false view of the role of the proletariat in Stalinist states, our value system must be ethically inadequate, and in some cases it may be dishonest. It is thereby refutable. Intentions in the real world must combine with predictable consequences to vindicate an ethical stance in the world.

Barnes points out that any ethical system must provide a "clearly ascertainable way of attaining the values which it promises."[23] A project of attaining being-in-itself-for-itself is humanly inaccessible; therefore, it is futile, for which reason its pursuit will probably turn out to be a destructive one. There is here a further requirement that if a project engenders values, the ethical actor ought to act consistently within this system. Otherwise, an individual will lack an ethical identity. In this, too, lucidity puts in a necessary appearance.[24]

To use logic in our stance toward our projects is also a recommendation of ethical being in the form of a commitment.[25] Certainly commitment by itself does not vindicate or justify an ethical system, but it may signify that the individual is attempting to act ethically. In addition, the aim of ethical discourse has got to be rationally motivated agreement, an agreement based on evidence and arguments rather than external or internal constraints on discussion.[26] That is, ethical discourse requires lucidity, hence, freedom. Therefore, let us underline here a departure from any Kantian type of ethical system, where a categorical imperative is "applied monologically to a given situation."

White posits a situation in which an old-fashioned father forbids an adolescent daughter from studying to become a doctor on the grounds that this profession is improper for women. In good conscience, there is no reason this might not be willed as an universal law. (Actually, this example might be somewhat unfair to Kant, for he may have viewed it as using the daughter as a means, but the point is still valid.) Our requirement is that any moral conclusion within such a situation ought to rely on free discursive communication, in which the daughter's unforced views must be taken into account, for she is a person who ought to count.

Participation among those affected by morality and ethics is a criterion that also may be (perhaps distantly) based on the requirement of lucidity. We need to have others able to freely express their own minds.[27] We need to have access to all the reasons affecting a choice, hence, all the reasons offered by free participants to that choice and by those affected by it. Lucidity in science requires that we do not ignore any examples under a concept, while in morality, it requires that we examine all the reasons that arise in an ethical situation that affects others.

It should be noted that much of the preceeding discussion has been about ethics, in the broad sense, as well as morality. Having brought the discussion through the question of why ought we to be moral, with some basic definitions and comments on method, some generalizations concerning ethics ought to be noted here. What principles, if any, have been generated? One principle that we have encountered is universalization. In morality, the thesis has been supported that people, conscious beings, ought to be taken seriously into account as ends. In the broader field of ethics, in the free positing of values, we might say that here too we have "chosen for all" by choosing our own projects.

But only some very general values were universalized here, namely those that distinguish between the enhancement and the denigration of life--specific values of lifestyle are not recommendable to others, save by example. Society needs, after all, a division of labor. The generalizable principles here concern authenticity: we aver that our choice is free and we accept responsibility for it; that is, we try to avoid bad faith insofar as possible. We try to choose with lucidity, with a clear analysis of the facts in situations--objectivity is possible despite the definition given the situations by our choice of projects. Related to the idea of responsibility and lucidity must be honesty.

More debatable, and unprovable, is the basis of all value selection, which is that if projects that bring us out of passivity, which would seem to be required if bad faith would be avoided, if existence as opposed to the possibility of removing ourselves from the game has been selected, then this may be taken to imply that values ought to be selected that enhance existence in a general sense rather than diminish it. This principle makes choices quite clear in certain cases, while it is moot in many others. Support for such a principle must be arbitrary; it is a free possibility that we have recommended, although there would appear to be some merit in regarding the choice of existence over nonexistence as an either/or choice that entails, or commits us, to additional freely accepted responsibilities.

There will be many principles, as we will see, that stem from the moral project. But the choice of existence and the generation of projects is, as it is in Nietzsche's view, precedent. The pursuit of morality as such as an end in itself has not been recommended. Altruism, therefore, need not be recommended--that is, while we pay heed to other persons, we are not committed to give more weight to their preferences than our own.[28]

It is possible, of course, and in keeping with many recommendations, that a person might choose a project of improving conditions for the proletariat, as Sartre purported to do. But there are some dangers lurking here, which will be considered later. Who gives us the right to determine how the conditions of others are to be improved? Of course, the contrary of altruism is also not supportable from our recommendations: we ought not to demand more from other people than from ourselves.[29]

Nicolai Hartmann and others enumerate and rank ethical virtues, but this is not, in the context of this book, necessary except in a rather cursory fashion (setting justice below certain of the other virtues). Shortly the minimal ethical requirements of justice will be considered, and from time to time a few comments on such values as courage will be offered, but these, we would argue, are derivable from more fundamental values, namely, honesty and responsibility. They may also be bound up with the projects one has chosen, which are the source of personal value hierarchies, although from time to time everyone will find themselves called upon to play roles outside their value systems. Although no list of moral virtues will be offered here, Philippa Foot's brief ennumeration deserves some comment; for her, there are four cardinal moral virtues: courage, temperance, wisdom, and justice.[30] Of course, it is hardly fortuitous that these are the same four qualities proposed by Socrates (i.e., Plato) in *The Republic*. By now it ought to be clear that if one were to accept the basis for morality and values argued in this chapter, that these four virtues might find a firm grounding, although only one is strictly a moral virtue. For instance, both wisdom and temperance might be derived from the requirement of lucidity. Courage might be derived from commitment. Morality would require justice.

The stress on the freedom to choose necessitates some words regarding obligations and duties. This is a particularly important moral area, for the reason that the selection of political projects may often entail obligations. To what degree, if any, ought obligations be freely undertaken, and how binding ought these to be? Although not considering the topic from the view of obligation, we have already advised freely accepting lucidity. We might consider lucidity a human duty. Such a duty as lucidity is freely accepted (or not), if the projects undertaken are to be pursued in a real world.

Some utopias demand that the world be something which observation shows that it is not. And while everyone interprets the world in their own way, there is still the in-itself out there that must be taken into account. Actions must correlate with the real world if they are to attain their intended ends. We might add that the person who exhibits intellectual penetration and honesty is more admirable than one who escapes into the various niches of bad faith. Bad faith, of course, might be freely chosen--and nothing prohibits regarding bad faith as an obligation that ought to be freely taken on. Indeed, some polities might demand bad faith and reward it. The Communist government of China following the massacre of students and other citizens in Tiananmen Square in June, 1989, required students to praise and accept the government's patently false presentation of the event.

Later, obligations undertaken voluntarily in society in the form of roles will be considered. While it would be a mistake to interpret ethics as a system of obligations only, which we do not, it is the case that obligations provide the polity with situations in which people can reasonably expect others to behave predictably. It contributes to social harmony and interpersonal trust. It is a requirement for nation-building. While we maintain that duties are forever open to question, the free acceptance of certain social duties is not a violation of moral autonomy. Existentialists have been too prone to praise the questionable projects of overthrowing the bourgeois societes in which they have lived and had the rare freedom to express themselves, to have grasped the mundane virtues of at least some of these obligations.

In fact, Sartre discusses duties in the development of the idea of the "pledge" in one of the more curious presentations in the *Critique of Dialectical Reason*. This would appear to be an instance in which Sartre's flair for drama and violence overcomes his lucidity. It is entirely possible that accepting the duty of the honest tradesman in a bourgeois society has, to date, done more historical good than the "pledges" of any of the revolutions of the 20th century. But the mundaneness of social obligations in imperfect democratic societies do, admittedly, lack drama, and often fall under the contempt of adventurous philosophers.

The basis for morality, namely that others ought to be taken into account, leads directly to a consideration of the social virtues of justice and equality. The first remark is owed to equality. If morality views all individuals as separate, free, and independent beings, as the fundamental assumption on which morality may be based, it follows that we may not require other criteria to support justice. We do not require that these independent beings be Aryan, male, peasants, or geniuses. . . .only the attributes of humanness are required. On this basis, these moral considerations are universal, not only as applicable to situations but to persons as well. Free expression, for example, a prerequisite for lucidity, must be vouchsafed all persons *qua* persons, and not selectively to college graduates or males.

We chide Plato for his sophistical comment about democracy as treating all men equal when it is evident they are not equal; obviously, people are equal in the moral view, which considers their humanness only. There is an argument that without the belief in a deity and the element of the divine in persons, there can be no foundation for equality consonant with dignity.[31] Not to deny the historical contribution of Christianity to human rights in the West, it is not clear that other bases, quite as firm, or tenuous for that matter, might not support the doctrine of equality. It is not obvious that religion provides a firmer foundation for a moral system that includes equality and human dignity, for historically it has been easy enough for fanatic believers to treat nonbelievers as infinitely unequal.

Justice is not one of the more glorious virtues, at the apex of the ethical hierarchy, such as that erected by Hartmann. Justice is a base point, so to speak, a minimal level from which the ascent toward more elevated ends can start, but it is a vital base point for all that. It is providing our fellow humans with their basic due in a world of scarcity. Toulmin regards it as a key factor determining the goodness of ethical reasons that they "correlate our feelings and behaviors in such a way as to make the fulfillment of everyone's aims and desires as far as possible compatible."[32]

This is how the moral code applies to society, and it is called justice. To the degree that society embodies the principle of justice, we should freely support it and follow this minimal social code. Hartmann,[33] too, suggests that justice is not a very high value; it applies, he says, to the most elementary of goods-values. But these goods-values, in turn, support every potential actualization of any higher values, and that is why justice has its unique moral import. That is why, undramatically, whatever just rules society contains ought to receive support.

This discussion provides a refutation to Hobbes' opinion that justice is what the law says it is, although we may agree with Hobbes that justice can never come into being outside some kind of social contract. Thus, if everyone is to be given their due as human beings, it follows that legal involuntary segregation, for instance, is a positive evil. But, if society enforces some of the norms of justice, it is entirely appropriate that we choose to be bound by them. Sartre and Merleau-Ponty have expressed themselves badly on this issue, rejecting too easily the acceptance of social norms.

The point they make is partly valid, for these norms may come to be embedded in the in-itself, or what Sartre refers to in his *Critique* as the practico-inert. But not all institutions degenerate into dead matter, or ought to; some deserve to be kept alive. Merleau-Ponty certainly is an advocate of the "recognition of man by man."[34] It would seem to follow that he ought to support social norms provided these contribute to justice.

Another doctrine that Hobbes presents in his *Leviathan* ought also to be confronted here. He argues that ideas of justice that call for the laws to meet some criterion, such as that of treating people as equal, are the source of disorder in the polity. There is some truth to this, for if someone believes that the laws ought to be consonant with some higher criterion, it is possible that they will refuse to obey laws that do not meet this standard. It is, in fact, the source of considerable social conflict not to regard justice as what the law proclaims. But conflict is, after all, the nature of politics, and Hobbes' *Leviathan*, just as Plato's *Republic*, is an effort to abolish politics, i.e., civil conflict. From our viewpoint, however, positive laws that do not take other people importantly into account are to be disavowed, changed.

The United States has had many laws of this kind, such as the miscegenation laws barring interracial marriages or those concerning segregation. In these cases, the violation of persons *qua* persons is morally outrageous, and when governments depart from the principle of taking persons equally into consideration in the law, the groundwork is laid for far worse abuses in the future. This kind of law must be confronted on the ground of morality. John Locke, in many ways a less impressive thinker than Hobbes, has in his critique of Hobbes' presentation on undivided sovereignty refuted the major basis of Hobbes' political system that holds extant law to be irremovable.

Justice, then, although it is one of the lower virtues, if you will, if ignored in favor of the so-called highest values will leave the latter to float in the airy heavens with no visible means of support.[35] To pursue only justice would lead to a pharisaical morality; but to ignore it would be unrealistic. Considering the belated nature of many of the 170 or so nations of the world, justice in many is a distant goal still far out of reach. Where it has been to a great degree established, however, justice is quite a minimal level of human attainment, and ethical pursuits of a much higher order open up for individuals, but not for the state. Justice is as far as the state should go: other values are personal. The liberal state is not an ethical state.

Finally, justice is the reasonable inference from human personalities as free and independent. It is not the outgrowth of feelings or liking.[36] Rights must be accorded to people we abhor. Fletcher is quite wrong to equate justice with love.[37] If justice depended on loving one's fellow humans, it would be a long and futile wait for it to appear in any polity. Fletcher has mistakenly merged a higher order virtue with the lower virtue of justice. And Tinder, in an article referred to earlier, does the same in his advocacy of the religious attitude of agape. Politics concerns justice, but it does not have a concern with love. While Luijden and Koren[38] grasp correctly the origin of justice in the person's subjective title to it, they too speak of love with relation to justice, surely an exaggeration of the intellectual sources of our adherence to it.

One cannot, it seems to me, become in any sense a champion of freedom in the world while rejecting the demands of justice. It is an unassuming quality, to be sure, but a vital bulwark at the same time of freer social interaction. But just laws may be best left to an abstract type of reason rather than to any emotions of love or hate. Politics is not the appropriate arena of love. We may not even want our fellow citizens to regard us with love, which is also an imposition upon us which mere justice is not.

Notes

1. Kai Nielsen, "Why Should I Be Moral?" pp. 454-483 in Pahel and Schiller, *Readings in Contemporary Ethical Theory*. Walhout's essay appears in *The Review of Metaphysics*, XII (June, 1959), 570-88.
2. George F. Will, *Statecraft as Soulcraft: What Government Does* (New York: Simon and Schuster, 1983), p. 135.
3. Stuart Hampshire, *Innocence and Experience* (Cambridge, Mass.: Harvard University Press, 1989).
4. See Erich Fromm, *The Anatomy of Human Destructiveness* (New York: Holt, Rinehart and Winston, 1973), especially Chapter 12, "Malignant Aggression: Necrophilia."
5. Foot, *Virtues and Vices*, p. 91. The quotation by Nietzsche is from his *The Will to Power*.

6. Max Scheler, *Ressentiment* (Trans. by William W. Holdheim. New York: Schocken Books, 1972). Scheler's own view, stemming directly from his phenomenological method, is that emotion acts analogously to reason in that it reveals to us a whole hierarchy of values. These essential values defy proof, but they may be described in ways that can convince others. For a summary, see Lauer, Phenomenology, p. 165.

7. Hare, *Freedom and Reason*, pp. 152-153.

8. Kupperman, *Ethical Knowledge*, p. 100.

9. Stern, *Sartre*, p. 244.

10. Hartmann, *Ethics*, Vol. II, p. 101.

11. Richard W. Wilson, "Political Socialization and Moral Development," *World Politics*, Vol. XXXIII, No. 2 (January 1981), p. 168.

12. de Beauvoir, *The Ethics of Ambiguity*, pp. 14-15. In *Being and Nothingness*, p. 626, Sartre comments, "Ontology has revealed to us, in fact, the origin and the nature of value; we have seen that value is the lack in relation to which the for-itself determines its being as a lack."

13. Anthony Quinton, "Utilitarian Ethics," p. 109, in Hudson, *New Studies in Ethics*, Vol. II.

14. Kurt Baier, "Why Should We Be Moral?" p. 437, in Pahel and Schiller, eds., *Readings in Contemporary Ethical Theory*.

15. Maurice Mandelbaum, *The Phenomenology of Moral Experience* (Baltimore: The Johns Hopkins Press, 1955), p. 280.

16. See Foot, *Virtues and Vices*, p. 111.

17. Kupperman, *Ethical Knowledge*, pp. 50-51. Ayer makes such arguments in "On the Analysis of Moral Judgements," pp. 231-249, *Philosophical Essays* (New York: St. Martin's Press, 1963) and in his *Language, Truth and Logic*.

18. Kupperman, *Ethical Knowledge*, p. 42.

19. Stephen Toulmin, *Reason in Ethics* (Cambridge: Cambridge University Press, 1960), pp. 162-163.

20. Ayer, "On the Analysis of Moral Judgements," p. 244. This kind of answer is quite Sartrean.

21. C.L. Stevenson, "The Emotive Meaning of Ethical Terms," in A.J. Ayer, ed., *Logical Positivism* (New York: The Free Press, 1959), pp. 266-267. The essay was originally published in *Mind*, Vol. XLVI.

22. Barnes, *An Existentialist Ethics*, p. 26.

23. *Ibid.*, p. 27.

24. Bambrough, *Moral Scepticism and Moral Knowledge*, pp. 91-93.

25. *Ibid.*, p. 111.

26. Thomas McCarthy, *The Critical Theory of Juergen Habermas* (Cambridge, Mass., The MIT Press, 1970), p. 312. Habermas makes some vital arguments about interpersonal communication, which is an important aspect of regard for others.

27. Stephen K. White, "Reason and Authority in Habermas: A Critique of the Critics," *The American Political Science Review*, Vol. 74, No. 4 (December 1980), p. 1015.

28. Hare, *Moral Thinking*, p. 129. While we are on the topic of altruism, let us consider a statement by Ayn Rand: "Altruism holds *death* as its ultimate goal and standard of value--and it is logical that renunciation, resignation, self-denial, and every other form of suffering, including self-destruction, are the virtues it advocates." Granted our own view of altruism as a project is not positive; this comment is a flagrant violation of logic, for it is not necessary that altruism be like this. Rand argues for a form of ideal capitalism, and there is no reason why an ideal altruism may not support life. In fact, the social virtues may well support life in ways that Rand's own version of capitalist virtues may not. We ought to take a broad view of what life entails. Rand's entire *The Virtue of Selfishness* (New York: The New American Library, 1964), interesting as it is (particularly in the essay on racism), is permeated with logical flaws.

29. Mackie, *Ethics: Inventing Right and Wrong*, p. 87.

30. Foot, *Virtues and Vices*, p. 2.

31. This argument is cogently presented by Glenn Tinder, "Can We Be Good Without God?" *The Atlantic Monthly*, Vol. 264, No. 6 (December 1989), 78-80.

32. Cited in Kupperman, *Ethical Knowledge*, p. 108.

33. In *Ethics*, Vol. II, p. 455.

34. Luijpen, *Existential Phenomenology*, pp. 212-213.

35. Hartmann, *Ethics*, Vol. II, p. 462.

36. Stace, *The Philosophy of Hegel*, p. 370.

37. Fletcher, *Situation Ethics*, pp. 105-106.

38. Luijpen and Koren, *A First Introduction to Existential Phenomenology*, p. 192.

Chapter 7

The Problem of Morality: Why Ought We To Be Moral? Definitions and Distinctions

Part II. Alternative Ethical Views

There is an objectivistic view of morality that regards consequences alone, discounting intentions. But is the objective, the concrete external action only, all that ought to be taken into account? The argument resembles that in the social sciences, which holds that scientific understanding is complete when we are able to predict events, while a contrary (and more convincing) view makes prediction just one aspect of explanation. The most appropriate view is that which takes the external act into account together with motive and intention. Both aspects of morality are important in determining the moral and value implications of human projects. The objectivistic view is, however, correct in one respect: it is difficult, particularly in the field of politics, to assess intentions.

In his coverage of free will, Van Inwagen suggests that we imagine that if person X chooses to accomplish Y, then he or she is responsible for Y coming about; but if for the sake of extreme example, person X is under the diabolical influence of W, then W can press a button and force X to commit Y even if X has not freely chosen Y. Then, under these circumstances, we cannot assume that X is responsible for Y, even if X seems to have freely brought about Y. But can we make this assumption? Clearly, if X has freely chosen to do Y, the case is different than if X had been coerced into committing Y.

Let us take a not too far-fetched example. I must choose whether to arrest the children of this village who are Jews to be exported to concentration camps. If I choose not to do this, the case will be the same, for the children will be gathered and deported anyway--it is inevitable whether I am an accomplice or not. But the responsibility for choice is still there: I am responsible if I have freely made that choice. This may not answer the example presented by Van Inwagen exactly-- for there, W has a means whereby he can control my actions entirely-- but the principle is the same: the temptations for acting in bad faith are very great, if in exoneration of my deeds I can argue that the consequences would have been the same anyway.

In taking people importantly into account, it is likely that we are aided by some reinforcement from the sentiments, although the doctrine that demands that we love mankind or fellow citizens has been found inadequate for the support of justice. While lucidity is a position that supports the rational consideration of others, Hume's doctrine of moral sentiments is at least suggestive. Reason without passion makes morality appear artificial. While projects may be selected for reasons other than that they may excite admiration or gratitude in others, the appearance of these emotions in others inhabiting our world allows a further ethical evaluation of these projects, and harmonizes the value structure of the project with the moral stance of regard for others. But it must be emphasized that reason is the essential origin of our moral view, lest our actions be cut off from the world.[1]

The merit of the objectivist morality is that it avoids the potential absolutism of subjectivism. Like a science that rests necessarily on the freedom of inquiry--for all theories must be open to question since no theory is capable of definitive proof--objectivism opens morality to argument, for consequences can be assessed.[2] While the source of moral value is not out there in the world, nevertheless, arguments revolve around the consequences of our projects, which have been the product of our generated values. Whether values have appropriate and intended results may be discerned in their consequences, and the fundamental criteria recommended for this assessment are at least two: (1) Are the results existence-enhancing; and (2) Do the results affect others in ways that preserve or enhance their uniqueness and freedom?

To the degree that objectivism regards some opinions as right and others as wrong, we agree with it: such judgments are necessarily to be made. But the criteria for making such assessments are by no means enforced upon us from the environment, as objectivism seems to imply. Some major objections to objectivism were considered when naturalism was discarded earlier.

Doctrines that hold that some actions are wrong no matter what their consequences, are deontological theories. They contradict so-called teleological theories, which, as in objectivism, rest assessments on whether consequences are good or bad.[3] Kohlberg's developmental view with regard to deontological theories seems sound, that these codes that emphasize the "letter of the law" are morally less developed: they do not enlist human reason and motive. An ethical theory that does not enlist free human activity in its judgment structure cannot be a full and compelling system. It remains a truncated and crippled structure. While this work recommends criteria for ethics, it also presumes to assess moral acts through consequences, a particularly important aspect of any system that purports to be about politics. Deontological systems may treat adequately, in the first instance, of justice, but they lapse into the practico-inert, merge with the in-itself, and become the corpse of a morality.

Yet, establishing criteria for judging consequences as we will try to do, denies relativism as one consequence. In addition, if judgments across cultures are accepted, it cannot be that ethical truth is relative to whatever system is accepted by individuals making whatever ethical claims they will.[4] For example, Dobu society in its classic depiction in Ruth Benedict's *Patterns of Culture* was morally wrong, for the reason that it annihilated social trust, and it did this for the reason that the system of human relationships it supported denied the positive moral significance of others. While maintaining that humans are free to choose, if existence against non-existence and the significance of others as against their being merely objects is accepted as a basis for political morality, such a morality provides a foundation that reasonably leads to regarding some acts as right and others as wrong, in whatever society these may occur. Such judgments may be made from within or from outside a culture.

A typical deontological principle is contained in the commandment "Honor Thy Father and Mother." While fathers and mothers will fall into the class of others for whom we ought to have regard, the non-deontological principle, "Honor They Father and Mother Insofar as They are Honorable," might seem more rational. After all, parents have included Adolph Eichmann and Joseph Stalin.

We now turn to some qualities of intuitionism. Without considering the doctrine in full, it is possible, as Hare avers, to argue that intuitionism is at least incomplete, for conflicts between duties *can* be resolved by a consideration of consequences, a resolution not possible in purely intuitive systems.[5] To develop Husserl's idea of ethical essences, it would also have to be shown how such disagreements could be resolved. Pure intuitionism would probably not make an attempt to solve such conflicts, nor could there be any argument showing any moral principle to be wrong. Once established that these are someone's intuitive principles, all further inquiry would be ended.[6]

And for any morality that purports to evaluate political situations, intuitionism would appear most inadequate. Intuitionism would eliminate reason as relevant, while we regard it as essential that situations be analyzed and consequences of projects as they affect situations be evaluated according to criteria of value and morality. Ethics does not reduce to a mathematical system, independent of persons or situation.[7]

In short, the idea that good principles or good intentions suffice to produce a morality is unacceptable. By oversimplifying the generation of principles, intuitionism neglects to consider major questions that ought to be evaluated in connection with ethical decisions, and, in particular, greatly reduces the role of lucidity, which in political situations must be an important attribute in ethical evaluations.

Intuitionism offers a clear demarcation between a mathematics of morality and those systems that consider actual consequences, such as utilitarianism. Utilitarianism will be treated quite briefly, important to political thought though it has been. The strong point of utilitarianism is its emphasis on the consequences of political and social activity, an emphasis compatible with our presentation. Where disagreement arises is in the kind of consequences utilitarianism is supposed to bring about, at least in most of its major formulations, namely, happiness.

Before embarking on the more serious claims of utilitarianism, however, hedonism ought to be considered, insofar as it bears some relationship to the ends sought by utilitarianism. That hedonism or the search for physical pleasure is ultimately self-defeating is the message of philosophy generally; the lesson is brought out pointedly in Joris Huysman's *Against the Grain*, a novel that clearly sets out the objections to hedonistic doctrine. Schopenhauer's insights should also be noted; he reasoned that consistent pleasure is unattainable without intervening pains to which it can be compared. There is some pleasure when the decayed tooth is finally pulled; there is joy in the death of the tyrant.

But if political systems are established with a view toward the greatest happiness for the greatest number, disappointment will be the most likely outcome, for the reason that happiness is not a tangible goal. The pursuit of happiness, as in the similar case of hedonism, is futile for humans. Its pursuit cannot be recommended as a valid social goal. In the case of happiness, it is usually found, almost unpredictably, as a concomitant of some other unrelated project. Paul Froelich recounts the intense happiness Rosa Luxemburg experienced during the four months of writing her *The Accumulation of Capital*: "The period while I was writing *Accumulation* belongs to the happiest in my life. I lived as if in a state of intoxication . . . .", she wrote to a friend.[8]

While most people would probably not attempt to pursue happiness by economic researches, the point is clear: projects are formed toward whatever free goals we select, but happiness is not an appropriate primary goal--it will occur, if ever, while we are writing *The Accumulation of Capital* or walking the dog. The error of hedonism and the pursuit of happiness is to pursue that which is empty. Bertrand Russell indicates that the doctrine confuses the notion that whatever we desire will produce pleasure when we gain it, when the pleasure often has its true source in the desire only.[9] As Moore stated in making the same point, hedonism commits the fallacy of confusing means and end.[10] Thus, Aristotle was wrong to hold as an end of the polity the happiness of citizens. Better to hold that the end of the polity is to afford citizens latitude to pursue their many projects in their own ways. Some citizens will thereby achieve some moments of happiness while they pen *The Accumulation of Capital*, build a chicken coop, or play badly a Beethoven sonata.

Restatements of utilitarian aimed at avoiding these errors are possible. What utilitarianism could propose that would be acceptable is that some minimum of justice and equality, which forms the basic starting point from which each individual can formulate his or her own project, ought to be provided by the polity. Some free projects, then, will conceivably contribute to happiness from time to time; others will certainly fail. In any case, it is dubious that on such a scale as the whole society it would be possible to weigh the sum total of happiness resulting from a just and equal polity, as compared with one that was unjust. Such an impossible assessment assumes that we know what makes everyone happy.

In fact, fascist polities, although denouncing individual happiness as a political goal, might even contribute to the greatest happiness of a population for whom the framing of free personal projects is an insufferable burden. Bad faith might be a plausible utilitarian goal, if that goal is posited on the happiness of the greatest number. We must be frank: freedom is not a happy fate--people voluntarily flock to sects and movements designed to deprive them of just such a necessity to choose for themselves. Sartre has delineated the innumerable and often comfortable sloughs of bad faith. To become a rock, to unite with the juggernaut, has been ever a compelling political choice. So it is unclear that utilitarianism could automatically recommend a liberal democracy over a totalitarian state.

In any case, the concept of the project as constituting a sound value system would seem to refute any utilitarian system based on a principle of pleasure/pain. Unless one's project was the selection of pleasure or happiness as a goal, do individuals really ever weigh the sum of pleasure/pain on an individual basis in making choices? People tend to maintain their principles, such as lucidity, freedom, or responsibility, regardless of whether these contribute to happiness. In social research, happiness is to discover the correlation between the dependent and the independent variable at 0.75; but having discovered one of 0.12, we usually bind ourselves to report the truth rather than falsify the data. Sir Cyril Burt, of course, sought happiness, apparently, in juggling his data on intelligence, but this was frowned upon by most of the profession.

Another problem raised against utilitarianism is that it treats of aggregate utility without regard to individuals.[11] While this is a real shortcoming in some utilitarian analysis, it would seem to be fixable within the structure of the doctrine. More to the point, according to the criterion that all persons ought to be taken importantly into account, some utilities ought not to be counted at all, if they, say, reduce (even acquiescing) persons to objects.[12] And this stricture follows clearly from our principles but not from those of utilitarianism.

As a doctrine of consequentialism, utilitarianism has some merit. But its sight is on the consequence that, for instance, history go as well as possible, regardless of the wrongs that may be committed in bringing this about.[13] This is probably not agreeable to our principles, although consequences are important. Let us ponder the events of 1936 when Hitler reoccupied with military forces the Rheinland. In a political situation of this nature, it is very difficult to assess the situation with a view to future consequences, although there were those--Churchill was one--who warned that the democracies ought to confront Germany at this historical juncture. Looking back, it is easier to see that the possibility was high that if the French and British (the United States, of course, being a self-selected non-actor, and therefore, pro-Nazi in allocating consequences) had chosen to confront Hitler with military force, committing wrongs, of course, in lives lost and depriving the Germans of what was a German-populated area, the next great war would probably have been averted, for Hitler would most likely have been toppled from power. Failing to do this, retrospection suggests that utility was not served. In this, the utilitarian view would be morally correct.

From the standpoint of the views we recommend, it is not clear that the choice would have been propitious; it would rest on the ludicity that one was capable of bringing to the analysis of the project. Of course, if the Allies had so acted in 1936, averting World War II, then there would have been no historical event to support the utilitarian choice, no event that would allow the conclusion, "You see, we were right; lives were saved!" In any case, the focus of utilitarianism on consequences is its strong recommendation.

Hare, in defense of the closeness of utilitarianism to the facts, to consequences, claims that it

> shows the lack of contact with reality of a system based on moral intentions without critical thought, that it can go on churning out the same defenses of liberty and democracy *whatever* assumptions are made about the state of the world or the preferences of its inhabitants.[14]

This interesting comment both supports and challenges our positions, which, as will be seen, logically support a democratic polity. What Hare is calling to our attention here is the fact that democracy has no roots in some societies. To apply principles sans social analysis, understanding of situations, or the careful evaluation of expected consequences has often been the road to disaster. Aristotle suggested that each people probably throve best under a constitution adapted to their conditions, a point agreed to by Rousseau and Mill much later. Lucidity demands realism. To fulfill projects and produce good consequences, effort must be expended to determine what others will actually do and how they will be affected.[15] Utilitarians are realistic in this way.

In addition, although projects may be framed in personal terms, goals being individual ends posited for ourselves, utilitarianism calls attention to the effects of these projects on the whole society. This is a valuable contribution, quite directly based on the moral doctrine of taking others into account. The principle should be mitigated somewhat, however, by basing projects and the means used to realize them solely on the degree to which these projects leave others free to pursue their own projects; that is, it is not necessarily a matter of assessing the sum of happiness of these others but rather, the sum of their freedom to act.

Moreover, it would seem to be possible, or at least capable of being imagined, that while a person might be able to pursue happiness for himself, one probably will not know how to seek the happiness of all others, as utilitarianism could be taken to recommend--may one supply free cocaine to addicts? Difficult as it is to seek happiness and well-being for oneself, how much more difficult it would be to meddle in the search for happiness for others.

A major shortcoming of utilitarianism reveals itself on a reading of Sidgewick, one of the great advocates of utilitarianism. There is an aura of irrelevance, of dryness, in this presentation of utilitarianism. It is more than a comment on the style of presentation alone, but, it seems to me, the dryness stems from the substance of Sidgewick's form of utilitarianism. Without concern for individual projects and the commitments that rest on these, ethics becomes a tedious discipline. Utilitarianism skirts the issue of the individual struggling to provide life with significance, an omission that Nietzsche clearly emphasized.

Kant's major principle that people are to be treated as ends, rather than as means only is a principle that has been incorporated into the system of morals we espouse.[16] In one formulation or another, this must be the cornerstone of a morality, and it is the reasonable result of the lucidity that reveals that other beings are also foci of consciousness and independent projects.

On this principle, there can be no quarrel with Kant, except that in political situations, the principle cannot be observed rigorously, and certainly not at all times. The question must be resolved in the context of the problem of realism against idealism and the assessment of the consequences of political acts, consequences that may be--as we have seen in the case of the Rheinland in 1936--very long in appearing. But, at all times, even in the breach, this principle ought always to be kept within our ken. Even so, the immoral act now might be acceptable if it is judged after painstaking analysis that it averts worse disasters in the future. But Kant's system, is an intuitive one, and hence, for that reason, unacceptable.[17]

Kant has also honored the principle of lucidity, but not always in appropriate ways. Lucidity penetrates the situation and illuminates consequences, operates in the empirical, as opposed to the abstract, realms of experience, more than Kant acknowledges. Kant concludes that

> rational creatures are negatively free because they exhibit a kind of causality by virtue of which their actions are not determined to any end by their physical or biological nature, [for which reason they are] creatures of a higher kind than others in nature.

So humans, according to Kant, have an end which their own reason must acknowledge.[18] This much seems sound. But for Kant, this leads to some ends that must be ends in themselves. His categorical injunction against lying is wrong, but it is based on plausible supports, namely, that the respect due to another as a rational creature forbids misinforming him, not only for evil ends, but for good ends also. In duping another, one deprives him or her of the free exercise of judgment, an admirable formulation.[19]

But this principle is acceptable only in part here, for in the political context of this book, lying must be weighed against telling the truth by regarding the consequences, long term and short term. It may be concluded, after assessing the consequences, that it is best to lie. A principle such as telling the truth should be regarded not as categorical but as hypothetical only, to use Kant's distinction. Realism would appear to require hypothetical principles only. In the *Phenomenology of Mind*, Hegel presents a brilliant critique of Kant, showing that the problem with Kantian ethics is that they are too abstract.[20] The Kantian ethics taken to its extreme is too capable of producing such political personalities as Robespierre and Saint Just.

Kant's ethics also appear to ignore at least a second major principle: that principle which espousing existence implies that it is the chief ethical business of humans to devise projects to bring to fruition in the world. As Donagan states, "A life the sole object of which was to obey the moral law would be aimless and empty."[21] Sartre correctly points out that the Ideas are imposed on everyone as a practico-inert exigency, or in Kant's term, a categorical imperative.[22] While the practico-inert is morally supportable in the form of the legal system insofar as that produces a minimal condition of rights and justice in the world, the higher ethical purposes must have the elements of free choice and enthusiasm to sustain them. Schopenhauer condemns Kant's legalistic absolutism as a "drill-sergeant theology of eighteenth century Prussia, with the drill-sergeant turned into an abstraction."[23]

It is time to lean back and contemplate where we are with Kant. Recall that our plan for ethics is comprised of two parts, of which the chief element was the ethical one, whereby in the face of a realistic appraisal of the universe, a fundamental choice was made, whether to be an upsurge and make a place in the universe for ourselves and our deeds, or to terminate existence. Selection of the former implied the formulation of projects for making a way in the world, and through such projects, freely chosen, values made their appearance into the world. Lucidity revealed that others are companions in this existence, and in coming to terms with this significant discovery, a morality of due regard for others seemed an appropriate free choice, such a morality being itself a free project within the larger ethical system.

This presents a standpoint for the interpretation of Kant's major categorical imperative, which goes, "Act only on that maxim through which you can at the same time will that it should become a universal law." And a law, Acton [24] points out, applies to everyone. Sartre has an analogous formulation of this principle in his idea that when we act, we act for all persons. In the case of the ethical principle of value creation and projects, this is not so, or it is so only to the degree that the claim presented to others is that these projects are a commendable (but not quite recommendable) choice in the face of the human condition.

It is certainly not to be expected that all persons ought to choose the same ends or to adopt the same values. At most, a life in accord with a free project is an example of how one life might be lived. Such a value system is one among many available systems. On the other hand, the project of morality is one that ought to be universalizable, but it is, unless we (wrongly) choose otherwise, a subsidiary portion of a lifetime of projects. Morality will speak frequently about the means by which other goals will be pursued. By placing so much emphasis on this universalizable moral aspect of our projects, Kant does risk either the fanaticism to which Hegel points or the Philistinism that Kierkegaard warns about.[25]

While Kant holds that moral considerations "have their seat and origin completely *a priori* in reason, Kierkegaard places morality in the person's potentiality-for-becoming-a-self, in a capacity for self-reflection. For Kant, the moral individual may spring fully made, so to speak, regardless of any other projects or encounters with experience he or she might have. Kierkegaard's is an existential view: it is not through *a priori* reasoning, but through cognitive-affective acts of choice that the moral person is finally produced (or defeated). The motivation for ethical beings is internal, not the result of laws that are encountered out there.[26] It is evident that Kierkegaard's critique of Kant resembles those of Hegel and Schopenhauer.

We may conclude that coercion and deception are the most fundamental forms of wrongdoing to others, an insight to which we are indebted to Kant.[27] It is Kant's presentation of these and his theory that supports his conclusions that are unacceptable. His lack of concern with consequences [28] reduces the application of lucidity to determining moral and ethical choices, which, in a sound political ethic, is a prime responsibility. The full view of a political moral act must take consequences as well as the purity of intentions actively into consideration.[29]

Marxism has been reputed to have no system of morality, and Lenin's quote, "I call any action useful to the party moral action; I call it immoral if it is harmful to the party," is often accepted as the last word in Marxist morality.[30] While Marxism obviously considers ethical principles, the problem is with its project of morality, which violates several moral principles generally accepted in other systems, namely universality and the regard for others. Lenin might even be viewed as an ethical Nietzchean.[31]

In fact, Leninist-Marxist systems have adopted a point-of-view which is defensible (debatably so) if history is determined to advance through revolution to the higher level of the proletarian dictatorship, and if the party is the true representative of the proletariat in this class struggle. And this is the moral position of Sartre, writing in his Marxist mode, when he recommends to intellectuals ". . .that all means are good if efficacious, *provided* they do not deform the end pursued."[32]

But the Marxist view also stems from a systematic program, which speaks to moral problems and reveals some (for us) acceptable principles. Marx himself was very interested in addressing moral problems, as one sees in his and Engels' *The Holy Family*.[33] Marxist ethics are, too, a form of consequentialism.[34] Marxism's consequentialism is both long range and perfectionistic. Actors are expected to produce the best possible outcomes given their social situation. Even more than the position set out in this book, which requires that others be taken importantly into account, Marxism avoids deontological rules, or any idea that under certain circumstances the right act might not be justified by the realization of the best possible end.

Indeed, Marx's ethical principles rest on the whole of his theory, for they depend on his analysis of capitalism and historical materialism. Although incomplete in part and suffering as in any human mental endeavor from gaps, Marx's is an attempt to see society, indeed all of history, as a total system. The most trivial-seeming everyday matter, fits rationally into Marxist thought, and it is easy to grasp its compelling effect in the 19th and 20th centuries. As with theory itself, ethics is lifeless unless combined with action. Like the existential concept of the project, praxis alone is where values arise and live, but for Marx, praxis must be guided by an understanding of social and historical change.

The emphasis on deed rather than on mere talk is a vital quality of Marx's early thought affecting ethics.[35] The ethical content of Marxism cannot, therefore, be separated from the context of his social and historical theories. As Adam Schaff puts it,

> All absolute ethical systems, so-called, erected on the basis of supposedly eternal and immutable moral truths, are helpless before the problems occurring most often in life, namely, situations of conflict in which doing what is thought to be right brings about evil consequences.[36]

Marx's concept of society is illuminating, too, for showing the effect of ideologies, in which the extant morality, the social principles inculcated into the subjects of society, plays the role of "false consciousness." This view resembles the existentialist critique in Heidegger of "das Man" and Sartre's of the practico-inert. *Nausea* among many other of Sartre's writings takes bourgeois values to task for the purpose they serve, which is to maintain things-as-they-are and as they-ever-should-be. This is a commendable accomplishment of both Marx and existentialism, that they show up the extant system of morals as open to criticism and not simply a natural condition of mankind. Marx and Engels critique the existing moral principles generally in order to debunk them and to look toward a future end where valid moral principles may come into being.[37]

The task in the present is to clearly understand the contradictions of (for Marx, 19th century capitalist) society in order that the class struggle can be initiated that will bring history to the next stage of development.[38] The crux of evil in capitalism is exploitation, and a clear understanding of exploitation coupled with class consciousness among the exploited, will remove these evils, most likely by way of a violent revolution. Now Marx did not necessarily refer to exploitation as wrong or evil, although it is difficult to believe he did not think them so, for the reason that at a certain stage of history, capitalism was both necessary and progressive. But it would be decidedly wrong to try to stall social development at the stage of capitalism, when the end of class struggle will be the attainment of Communism.

Communism is an historical stage that will overcome exploitation and alienation (and the additional contradictions under capitalism), which stem from the condition that people exercise power over other people. These wrongs will be transcended because under Communism productivity will be fully social and greatly increased, obviating scarcity; and class divisions, the origin of the exercise of social coercion, will have disappeared. At this stage, equality is achieved and people exist in actuality as ends rather than as means.

Mankind as species being has, in this culmination of history, no need for a system of morality, for theory has fully merged with practice; contradictions have disappeared, for scarcity has disappeared; and humans will not think about ethics and morality for the reason that they will unthinkingly, and as a matter of course, conduct themselves morally. The projects of individuals will automatically mesh with constructive social projects. By coming into its full realization in social practice, morality will have abolished itself as a philosophical pursuit.

In a fascinating exchange between Trotsky and Dewey, Trotsky defended the Marxist moral outlook. To attain the moral society, where social conflict is abolished and violence and lies eliminated, it is necessary to get to there from here by a violent revolution.[39] The means are, then, justified by the end, not in a simplistic way, but in the way that is justified by a correct analysis of historical change. So Trotsky claims that what is permissible is not any and all acts, but only the act "which *really* leads to the liberation of mankind."

But there is a "catcher in the rye." Trotsky, and Novack, who defends the same position, are fanatically certain that they have analyzed the true course of history, a queer conclusion when the Soviet proletarian revolution under Lenin led to the Stalinist "meat grinder" (Khruschev's term in his memoirs). But, of course, Stalinism cannot be an outgrowth of a valid Soviet conception of the proletarian revolution; it "is the product of imperialist pressure upon a backward and isolated workers' state . . . ."[40] This is a questionable retroactive analysis; dialectical materialism ought to have predicted Stalinism.

It may be suggested that not accepting the moral attitude toward the recognition of others as significant beings may have contributed to the collapse of the ideals of Communism. It is the danger faced by all systems that proclaim the necessity of entering the Millenium before morality can come into its own. The very fanaticism exhibited by Marxists such as Trotsky and Novack is a denial of others as significant beings, for it hinders communication and debate. But then, for those ideologies that know Truth, communication and debate is the outcome of the bourgeois "talking shop."

Marxism is astute in uncovering hypocrisy surrounding the doctrines of rights in bourgeois societies. Marxists are bourgeois democracy's most formidable critics.[41] But bourgeois statements of rights rest as well on the conception, if only hypocritically at first, that other persons are to be taken importantly into account. And social rights, even hypocritical social rights, can develop in society toward genuine effects. Kautsky recognized this in his criticism of Lenin's revolutionary society (see his *Dictatorship of the Proletariat*) and so did Rosa Luxemburg, for they both thought it a mistake to abolish all bourgeois rights in the revolutionary society. A contempt for rights in bourgeois society translates to a contempt for those rights in revolutionary society.

The blanket condemnation of the doctrine of rights does not stand up to careful historical analysis, for it leads (inevitably?) to a polity in which those rights are ignored. Of course, rights may be used to veil the realities of the social order, and it is well for critics to call attention to this, but in themselves, rights refer to correct moral principles and as ideals they are capable of developing within society, sometimes together with economic change or at times independently. The gradual expansion of suffrage in Great Britain shows this. But was not all this expanded right to vote phony? Partly; but partly not.[42]

It is the nature of non-fanatic principles that they may be gradually realized within the imperfect societies in which real people will have to pursue their ends. By positing the advent in the future of the perfect society in which human freedom needs no guarantee, Marxism in the present has denounced human rights as spurious.[43] In taking this view, Marxists have adopted a nonmoral stance that in state after state produced human disaster. The mistake was repeated by Sartre, who deferred writing an ethics for the reason that morality was not possible in society as it existed.

And, after all the hypocrisy, deaths, and destruction, the revolutions heralded by Sartre and others finally discovered the secret after 70 years of . . .the capitalist market! Trotsky's position, therefore, and that of most Marxists--that the means have no moral weight and do not enter into the moral scales, that only the purpose counts--must be rejected.

Furthermore, Dewey's major point was correct, namely, that all genuinely scientific laws are conditioned. There are no socially inevitable ends.[44] Marxists have been shown up as incompetent prognosticators of history, a fact that seriously affects their position on morality.

As a doctrine, Marx's analysis of history leads to another pertinent moral conclusion, namely, that as the class that will produce the revolution, it is the proletariat from which the ethical system of the future will spring, and that insofar as morality in capitalist societies is class-based, if there are any moral decisions to be made, it is from the viewpoint of the proletariat that these must be decided. Were Marx's analysis of history correct, it could support this view. But this is a terrible burden for the proletariat to have to bear, which history (as interpreted by the dialectic) has imposed. The ethics, then, of the proletariat, is, in fact, its class-consciousness, for its class-consciousness is its project, the unity, as Lukacs phrases it, of its theory and practice.[45]

By extension, the party, alone capable of a correct historical analysis, becomes the "active incarnation" of this class consciousness. To assume this, however, is to assume that movements generated by false theory do not succeed. Lukacs cannot really believe this; for one thing, it violates the notion of false consciousness. At most, what he might maintain is that the party must embody the aims of the proletariat, or the proletariat might fall away from it. In fact, this seems to have happened in the Polish election of June, 1989, and later throughout much of eastern Europe.

Lenin, of course, expanded the point further by maintaining that it was the party that espoused the true aims of the proletariat, which, by itself, could develop only a trade union consciousness. Thus, the project of the proletariat, correctly interpreted by the vanguard, could be the only effective project under capitalism, and Marx's analysis presented some strong reasons for this, while "true socialism," of which he spoke contemptuously, held to the abstract notion of a universal morality, the same for everyone, for all classes, under capitalism. That morality comes to life when charged with human projects, is an important Marxist insight. Thereby, morality is lifted from the level of cocktail-party chit-chat to praxis. Engels is quite correct in his criticism of the Feuerbachian theory of morals, "designed to suit all periods, all peoples and all conditions . . . ." and never and nowhere applicable.[46]

Morality disassociated from other projects is lifeless and ought not to be pursued for its own sake alone. But that morality is embodied solely in the project of the proletariat, which holds the project of bringing about a Marxist proletarian revolution, depends on the acceptance of Marx's entire theory of history. And that theory is flawed. In fact, it turns out that since Marx's day, it has been the alternative projects of reformism, such as those initiated by Robert Owen, the American Wendell Phillips, and innumerable soft-headed religious groups, that have had a solid and constructive impact in the hard-boiled world.

Some existentialists framed intellectual projects in favor of Leninism/Marxism. For Sartre, the intellectual may only understand the society in which he or she lives by adopting the viewpoint of the most underprivileged members.[47] There is no necessary reason for adopting this viewpoint, of course, other than a free choice of projects and values-- it is also presumptuous to advocate the viewpoint of others unless there is certainty of what that viewpoint is. Later, in his massive *Critique*, Sartre incorporated existentialism into a Marxist framework, a method he refered to as progressive-regressive. Like many another intellectual, Sartre appears to have been excessively uncritical of Marxism, seizing upon it as "the philosophy of the 20th Century" for unrevealed reasons.

(Contrariwise, however, Sartre is trenchantly critical of the orthodox Marxism that developed, or shriveled, under Stalinism, but he never seems to question that the party and the course of history would vindicate Marx's predictions. The "ends pursued by the masses," of which he speaks on occasion[48] would seem to be a very tenuous concept, and it is unlikely that Sartre or anyone else, even the cadre of the vanguard party, had any notion where those ends would lead. As even the members of the vanguard party realized, they could lead the party to ends it did not want to pursue, as, for instance, land provided to individual peasants as against communes.)

Merleau-Ponty's *Humanism and Terror*, written when he too was in the thrall of intellectual Marxism, is a typical example of the intellectual blindness that often accompanied the alliance between Marxism/Leninism/Stalinism and certain existentialists:

> (I)n the Soviet Union, violence and deception are official while humanity is in daily life; in the democracies, on the other hand, principles are humane, while deception and violence are found in practice.[49]

One might ask where Merleau-Ponty found the empirical evidence to support this statement. Since the date of Merleau-Ponty's book, there have been many works that penetrate to Soviet daily life under Stalin, real products of socialist realism, such as Vassily Grossman's epic *Life and Fate*, that have given the lie to his airy statement. In fact, Anton Ciliga's *The Russian Enigma* was published in Paris in 1937; it was the eyewitness account by a genuine Communist of the perversion of the revolution within the Soviet Union. It is one result of the contempt sometimes shown by existentialists for logic and empirical analysis that they could be guilty of such unfounded positions in political affairs.

Kohlberg's six stages of moral development is an interesting empirical scheme[50] that shows how the mind attains certain moral capabilities during individual maturation. It suggests the importance to ontology of evolutionary theory, and Kautsky among the Marxists has developed just such an evolutionary theory of ethics. Marxists were quite intrigued by Darwin's theory of evolution, which, as Engels interpreted it, seemed to vindicate the process of dialectical change in nature. Kautsky treats society as subject to the natural laws of evolution.

Presumably by showing the process of how we evolved ethically up to now, the theory indicates how we ought to evolve in the future. Moore, however, is very convincing in his criticism that evolution involves survival, plain and simple, and is regardless of the survival of traits or beings that are morally good.[51] In his non-Marxist expostulation of an evolutionary theory, Huxley also encounters problems in drawing moral concepts from biological clues. The fact that ant societies may have slaves does not count for much on the human level. Huxley does stress that we must honor the individual, but it is not clear how this follows from an evolutionary foundation.[52]

Even were evolution progressing toward some goal, there is no compelling reason why that goal ought to be regarded as good, although one might choose to so regard it. Finally, although evolution is suggestive, and although the mental capacity of *homo sapiens* has developed through time, to equate social change with biological evolution is no better than any argument by analogy. The Huxleys recognized this problem.[53] For Kautsky, such traits as trust, obedience, defense of a common interest, are not the product, as with Kant, of a higher intellectual order, but the products of the animal world.[54]

Perhaps, however, the evolutionary course of morality is presently irrelevant. It is certainly acceptable to a doctrine of free will that mental capacity has evolved; in fact, not enough attention has been given to the implications of this fact. Somewhere along the route of biological progress, trust became possible. We hypothesized that at some stage, freedom came into being as consciousness split from the in-itself to become for-itself. It is probable that this did not happen as a sudden qualitative change unprecedented by quantitative changes along the way. In fact, it is unlikely that the process is complete, and, at least in many individuals, those with low IQ or brain damage, it is unlikely that the freedom to choose is greatly developed.

The problem for humans, however, is not that there is the possibility of trust, which may well be attributed to the development of mental capacities during the long course of evolution, but what is to be trusted. That is, evolution ought to be of interest to any philosophical ontology, but it provides no ready answers to fundamental moral or ethical questions.

Can the existential program provide an ethics that supports a morality? There are reasons to suppose that it cannot, although this book has been an attempt to provide just such a program. If, in the thrownness of the human situation, or its absurdity, the choice of projects and principles is ontologically free, then, what anchor exists for morality? How can human choices escape arbitrariness? The projects a person chooses have as the result that they will establish an identity--the individual becomes that person who acts as he or she does.

Guided by projects, individual identity will be gradually revealed in the world, to his or her self, and to others. These projects that establish human identity as persons exist them are freely chosen, constrained, of course, by contingencies, such as the body, the country, the entire in-itself. But Sartre correctly holds that constraints are also chosen, in accord with the values we decide to pursue. This entire project structure rests on the primary decision to exist, to bear with it, to face death resolutely in Heidegger's phrase. If we affirm existence, this is already a very basic ethical decision, namely, that existence is better than non-existence.

It is logical that this affirmation be extended to the world at large, which, since the choice has been made to affirm existence, supports this existence or hampers it. In such a spirit of affirmation, one selects the projects to pursue that comprise his or her setting out on a path through the world. Thus, human choice produces values in the world and the fundamental choice of existence is a broad guide as to which values are life-enhancing and which are not. Needless to add, some persons never make a definitive choice, oscillating between acceptance and denial of life.

Lucidity assures us that we are not alone in the world. Indeed, there are other independent foci of projects that may coordinate or clash with our own. One could choose not to be lucid in following out this line of discovery, but there are ways to distinguish reality from illusion. So long as one chooses to exist in the world, it follows as a matter of honesty that we ought to comprehend this "in the world," our environment. Lucidity and a concomitant honesty concerning our situation recommend themselves as life-enhancing, for lucidity helps us follow through with our projects--it is a prerequisite of engagement with the world.

Honesty requires the recognition of others' existence as well, and we posit other free consciousnesses. Without these, life would be barren indeed, or, rather, quite impossible. The individual can appreciate the free contributions others make to his or her well-being, as well as confront hostile projects. Free choice and existence recommend the basis of morality, however, which is to regard others as free and to enhance their abilities wherever possible, consonant with our own projects. The existence of others provides an arena of conflict, however, that gives rise to politics.

Politics, then, is the conflict of projects, and the most important political question is whether to let politics happen, a decision that requires that others be accorded concrete freedoms, or whether to suppress politics, as did Plato, Hobbes, and B. F. Skinner in their political theories. These, then, authenticity, which is bound to freedom and lucidity, the choice of existence, and the positive evaluation of freedom for others, despite continual conflict, are the bases of an existential morality and ethics. Any of these choices may be freely disavowed--it is very difficult, given Sartre's ontology, to imagine that by free choice we may not choose to live in bad faith, although, to be sure, this is inauthentic, dishonest, and non-lucid.

Therefore, a morality is the free choice that a morality become a project for us, and this choice is based, so far as a person is capable, on a lucid analysis of the human condition and the appropriate status others ought to be accorded. There may not be a human nature, but there is a human condition, putting all persons on a par in relation to some universal facts. The need for a lucid analysis of the human condition rests in the first instance on an analysis of human ontology, an analysis that is "capable of being checked by evidence accessible to all."[55]

The ambiguity of this decision rests, of course, on the fact that this morality and these choices are free commitments, and a person can choose to commit himself otherwise. There are no moral imperatives or any natural set of rules to adhere to as the result of the decision to take others importantly into account.[56] The choice to regard others, once made, can also be unmade, and it continues to prevail only by our decision to sustain it. Having chosen to play the game by means of a lucid understanding of the human condition, a person should scorn to lie to themselves. This sets the terms for our engagement in the world.

Freedom, as such, it seems, cannot be the universal value in this sense, for it is difficult to see how freedom might be avoided in Sartrean ontology; thus, in the ontological sense, freedom is not a choice. What might be avoided is only our recognition of this freedom. Values, that is, are choices. (Speaking of emotivism, Warnoch asserts, correctly in my view, that Ayer, in his positivist *Language, Truth, and Logic*, has a similar view of values, namely, that, in the final analysis, using Engels' favorite reservation, they are neither analytical nor empirical. They are choices. In the view expounded in this book, however, values, although they are also choices, are in addition based on the logical implications of ontological analysis. Obviously, too, the undertaking of ontological analysis and the decision to base a case on the result of such an anlysis is also a free choice.)

Since one freely engages the universe in terms of the moral and ethical choices suggested here, there follows a responsibility for these choices and for the consequences that they bring about. This responsibility, too, is a choice, but it is the choice that a person must make to retain authenticity.[57] Now, the choice to be moral is the logical outcome of a lucid recognition that there are other valuable and independent beings in my world. In the course of a choice of other non-moral ethical projects in one's engagement with the world, morality may become a project as well, but only one among many. Through the free choice of morality, the choice is made to pursue other projects according to some means and not others.

At the extreme, to accept the subsidiary project of morality may be to accept the failure of our ethical projects. Since this is a free choice, all individual existences pose a potential threat to others, for the choice is always open to choose otherwise than according to morality. But this danger exists even if an individual accepts a set of moral rules written in the heavens or in some good book or other; the choice to deviate from the rules can always occur. People are always a potential danger to other people, and this is one result of freedom.

One cannot claim universality for those projects that define our values. Some projects are commendable if we propose that existence is to be enhanced. Regarding morality, it might be stated that if one is to choose any project worthy of being designated a morality, it would have to be based on taking others importantly into account. In this sense, morality is and must be universalizable. While other ethical choices are relative from person to person, from society to society, morality is not, and a society that denies a morality of consideration of others can be invidiously compared to another that does.

Through the choice of projects and morality, individuals make demands on themselves that they cannot rightly enforce on others. The values of one person can only be commended by that person existing them.[58] The award for authentic choices is not success, happiness, or acclaim. There is only the personal satisfaction that one has tried to perceive the true condition of human beings, has made an effort to be lucid in the face of the world, and has tried to uphold life as against nonexistence. Does this suffice to define the good life?

Stern in treating of Sartre's doctrine suggests that the viewpoint is one of absolute ethical idealism, whereby ideas are affirmed not in the expectation of advantages accruing from them, but solely for the sake of the kinds of values bound up with such an affirmation.[59] The for-itself has thrust itself forward into the world so that values may exist, in a manner of speaking.[60] Thus, ethics and morality are always in the process of coming into being. It is important to reiterate that one ought not to be in pursuit of moral purity, for, as Hartmann makes clear, "He who is pure does not actualize; his ethos is not a pursuit of ends."[61] And this is the genuine wisdom of Nietzsche, who focuses solely on ethics as opposed to morality. The better position, however, is that morality can be adopted in terms of a good life but that it must not abolish ethics by monopolizing it.

The last topic that needs to be covered in this already over-crowded chapter is whether any authentic morality can be pursued in society as it presently exists. Ought morality to be deferred to a more auspicious future? De Beauvoir puts the point nicely: ". . . if man is waiting for universal peace to establish his existence validly, he will wait indefinitely: there will never by any *other* future."[62] Since de Beauvoir regretted writing her work on ethics, it cannot be certain that she would maintain this principle, with which Sartre disagreed. For instance, in the introduction to Sartre's *Search for a Method* (xxvi), Hazel Barnes notes that for Sartre, "the ethics of a philosophy of freedom is not possible in a society where men are not free." Yet, it is de Beauvoir, in this case, who is correct.

There are several problems with Sartre's position. First, *Being and Nothingness* presents an ontology that supports a radical freedom. The for-itself there is unattached, as it were, to any in-itself. Of course, consciousness ceases when the physical brain dies; on this there is no argument. Freedom is therefore provided by Sartre as the support of ontological analysis. Therefore, how can one not be free? Certainly, one can choose to escape into the innumerable forms of bad faith and (freely, one presumes) choose to follow the strict letter of the group mores. But this cannot determine the for-itself. Bad faith will simply continue to be nagged by anguish.

This viewpoint led to some social conclusions that Sartre, the philosopher as social advocate, did not want, and he was roundly criticized for such statements as that the slave in chains is still free. Such a view conflicted with Sartre's social projects, for which reason we find a somewhat different definition of freedom emerging, which is that of Hobbes' *Leviathan*, that freedom is the ability to select alternative projects without hindrance. This is Sartre's "concrete freedom." The slave is still ontologically free, of course, but once emancipated, his free choice to own, say, a ten-acre plot outside Rome becomes more realizable.

As Rousseau put it in his *Social Contract* (which has many affinities to Sartre's *Critique*), "man is free, but he is everywhere in chains." So, in the later *Critique*, Sartre focuses on the problems wrought in society by scarcity. The solution of the problem of scarcity is the meaning of the phrase that "I cannot be concretely free until all are free."[63] This is Sartre's reason for not developing his promised work on ethics, that purity of action in unjust society is impossible, that truthfulness and effective political action are incompatible in the world as it is (Machiavelli's point, who also eschewed morality).

But these reasons are not sound. To await the utopia before considering moral action may be one way of never attaining a better world. Thus moral perfectionism leads to two errors: first, that if morality does not fit in the imperfect world, actions cannot take it into account and anything goes; second, that morality must be fitted into the world as though it were a perfect world. Sartre makes the first mistake; Kant sometimes commits the second.

Kant, therefore, makes the other kind of error, one that Sartre plainly avoided. According to Kant, and this is the essence of any morality, ethical behavior is not concerned only with the interests of a limited group, but with the possibility of a universal community of free persons. And the error stemming from this abstractly correct principle is the advice that we should act morally as though this community already existed. So Lukacs criticizes Kant and Fichte of constructing an ideal image of society in which our devotion to "duty" may be applied as though the world were without conflict.

If the ideal world existed, the way to ameliorate all social contradictions would be to follow the strict dictates of the moral law. But as Lukacs points out, not all the moral problems of society can be resolved by the formal postulate of practical reason.[64] So Kant's error is the opposite of Sartre's, to apply the perfect ethical doctrine to an imperfect world. The moral problem is to relate oneself morally to the imperfect world, in which compromises may be necessary, where duties really do clash with other duties, where it is not always possible to affirm existence and at the same time give this person, this group, its due, while working toward an improved society. Sartre's attitude is that nothing positive can be accomplished in an unjust society, which is simply untrue.

To defer morality to some future utopia is more than an error, for with this attitude goes the tendency to sacrifice the present generation to the Utopia to come. Morality, if it is of any import, must be of use now in the imperfect present. Now in the time of human conflict. When will there ever be another time?

Notes

1. These issues referring to Hume are very well presented by Foot, *Virtues and Vices*, pp. 76-80.
2. Bambrough, *Moral Scepticism and Moral Knowledge*, p. 43.
3. The distinction is based on Broad's coverage in his *Five Types of Ethical Theory*, and is cogently presented in Toulmin's *Reason in Ethics*, p. 141.
4. Kupperman, *Ethical Knowledge*, pp. 65-66.
5. Hare, *Moral Thinking*, p. 26.
6. Stroh, *American Ethical Thought*, p. 213.
7. Harrison, *Our Knowledge of Right and Wrong* (New York: Humanities Press, 1971), p. 108.
8. Paul Froelich, *Rosa Luxemburg: Her Life and Work* (New York: Monthly Review Press, 1972), p. 159.
9. Russell, *Human Society in Ethics and Politics*, p. 63.
10. Moore, *Principia Ethica*, p. 90.
11. Mervyn Frost, *Towards a Normative Theory of International Relations* (Cambridge: Cambridge University Press, 1986), p. 139.
12. *Ibid.*, pp. 142-143.
13. Derek Parfit, *Reasons and Persons* (Oxford: Clarendon Press, 1984), p. 37.
14. Hare, *Moral Thinking*, pp. 167-168.
15. Parfit, *Reasons and Persons*, p. 30.

16. Kant, *Groundwork of the Metaphysic of Morals*, p. 95, contains a formulation of this principle.
17. Sir David Ross, *Kant's Ethical Theory: A Commentary on the Grundlegung zur Metaphysik der Sitten* (Westport: Greenwood Press Publishers, 1978; a reprint of the 1954 edition by Clarendon Press, Oxford), pp. 21-22.
18. Alan Donagan, *The Theory of Morality* (Chicago: The University of Chicago Press, 1977), p. 237. A very interesting neo-Kantian presentation on the topic.
19. *Ibid.*, p. 89.
20. For additional comment on this critique, see Georg Lukacs, *The Young Hegel* (Trans. by Rodney Livingstone. Cambridge, MA: The MIT Press, 1976), p. 153.
21. Donagan, *The Theory of Morality*, p. 11. Sklar also notes that "Kantian moralism never acts at all. Passivity, indeed paralysis, is built into this state of mind . . . .Kantian moralism is fit at most for judging, not acting." Sklar, *Freedom and Independence: A Study of the Political Ideas of Hegel's "Phenomenology of the Mind* (Cambridge: Cambridge University Press, 1976), pp. 182-183.
22. Sartre, *Critique of Dialectical Reason*, p. 302.
23. The citation is from Fletcher, *Situation Ethics*, p. 129. See Arthur Schopenhauer's critique in *On the Basis of Morality* (Trans. by E. F. J. Payne. New York: The Bobs-Merrill Company, 1965). Although Schopenhauer is severe with Kant's moral doctrine, it must be remembered that he had a high regard for Kant's philosophy, much of which he took for granted in *The World As Will and Idea*.
24. H. B. Acton, "Kant's Moral Philosophy," in Hudson, ed., *New Studies in Ethics*, Vol. I (*Classical Theories*), p. 326.
25. Soren Kierkegaard, *Fear and Trembling and the Sickness Unto Death* (Trans. by Walter Lowrie. Garden City: Doubleday Anchor Books, 1941), p. 174.
26. Stack, *Kierkegaard's Existential Ethics*, p. 169.
27. Christine M. Korsgaard, "The Right to Lie: Kant on Dealing with Evil," *Philosophy and Public Affairs*, Vol. 15, No. 4 (Fall, 1986), pp. 333-334.
28. Broad, *Five Types of Ethical Theory*, p. 117.
29. Grene, *Martin Heidegger*, p. 46.
30. Leszek Kolakowski, *Main Currents of Marxism*, 3 volumes (Oxford: Oxford University Press, 1972), pp. 515-516, is an assessment of Lenin on morality.
31. Odd as it may seem, interpretations of Nietzsche's views on morality did have an effect on Russian Marxists. (Even on Jack London, as in his strange novel, *The Iron Heel*, an amalgam of the thought of Darwin, Nietzsche, and Marx, interpreted of course by the author.) Kamenka (*The Ethical Foundations of Marxism*, pp. 178-179) citing G. L. Kline, shows A. V. Lunacharsky (later Lenin's People's Commissar for Culture) and Stanislav Volsky (a pseudonym of A. V. Sokolov, 1880-1936?–there is significance in the date of death and the question mark) drawing on Nietzsche and upholding the individual as a free

creator of values as against the conception of rules and moral obligations.

32. Sartre, *Between Existentialism and Marxism* (New York: Pantheon Books, 1974), p. 263. Sartre's lucidity is often at its dimmest when he is in his role of proletarian revolutionary.

33. Karl Marx and Frederick Engels, *The Holy Family, or Critique of Critical Criticism* (Moscow: Progress Publishers, 1975), circa page 200. Needless to say, Marx is particularly sharp in finding holes in bourgeois morality and forms of "false consciousness."

34. Steven Lukes, *Marxism and Morality* (Oxford: Oxford University Press, 1987), p. 142.

35. Popper, *The Open Society and Its Enemies*, Vol. 2 (Hegel and Marx), p. 201.

36. Schaff, *A Philosophy of Man*, p. 33. Some praise is due to Adam Schaff as one of the first post-Stalin Marxists to break away from the dogmatic and inert doctrine that Marxism had become and to confront other philosophies, in this case, existentialism, on their own merits. Under Stalinism, Marxism was reduced to the status of rules, to the practico-inert, and critics, including Sartre, were dealt with ad hominum. Glasnost, initiated beginning in 1985 by Mikhail Gorbachev, might have the effect of infusing more life into Marxism.

37. Alain Gilbert, "An Ambiguity in Marx's and Engels's Account of Justice and Equality," *The American Political Science Review*, Vol. 76, No. 2 (June 1982), p. 328.

38. *Ibid.*, p. 333.

39. Leon Trotsky, John Dewey, and George Novack, *Their Morals and Ours: Marxist vs Liberal Views on Morality* (New York: Pathfinder Press, Inc., 1973). The quotation was taken from *The Basic Writings of Trotsky*, edited by Irving Howe (New York: Random House, 1963), p. 387.

40. *Ibid.*, (Basic Writings), p. 380.

41. See Lukes, *Marxism and Morality*, p. 28, on this.

42. Engels is partly correct in viewing moral theories as the product "in the last analysis" of the economic stage which society has reached at a particular epoch. (See his *Anti-Duhring*, pp. 104-105.) But he is not correct in the assumption that moral ideas are only the product of their social epoch and have no history of development of their own. Both Marx and Engels admitted this later.

43. Lukes, *Marxism and Morality*, p. 62. And see also Conway, *A Farewell to Marx*, p. 198.

44. Stroh, *American Ethical Thought*, pp. 95-96.

45. Georg Lukacs, *History and Class Consciousness* (Trans. by Rodney Livingstone. Cambridge, MA: The MIT Press, 1971), p. 42. For years, Lukacs, when at his best, was the sole worthy expositor of Marxism.

46. Engels, *Ludwig Feuerbach*, p. 36.

47. In Sartre's *Materialism and Revolution*, pp. 219-220, he reviews the potential contributions of existentialism to revolutionary theory as compared to naive materialism. Most of the points he makes are unexceptional, such as that the "system of values current in a society reflects the structure of that society and

tends to preserve it," a point that Marx and Engels had already made clearly. That "any collective order established by men can be transcended towards other orders" suggests a stronger support by existential views than by the naïve materialists. Despite all this, it was an historical error for existentialism to align itself with the kind of revolutions that have occurred in the 20th century.

48. As in the course of his *Between Existentialism and Marxism*, pp. 262-263.
49. Quoted in Lukes, *Marxism and Morality*, p. 134.
50. For an exposition of this empirically based scheme, see Ted L. Huston and Chuck Koret, "The Responsive Bystander, Why He Helps," in Thomas Lickona, ed., *Moral Development and Behavior, Theory, Research, and Social Issues* (New York: Holt, Rinehart and Winston, 1976, p. 277. Other essays in this book are also of interest here.
51. Moore covers evolutionary theories in his *Principia Ethica*, pp. 45-48.
52. Thomas H. Huxley and Julian Huxley, *Touchstone for Ethics* (Plainview: Books for Libraries Press, 1971; original copyright, 1947). The book contains both "Evolution and Ethics" by T. H. and "Evolutionary Ethics" by J.H.
53. *Ibid.*, p. 27.
54. Karl Kautsky, *Ethik und Materialistische Geschichsauffassung* (Stuttgart: J. H. W. Dietz Nachfolger, 1922), pp. 62-63.
55. Wild, *The Challenge of Existentialism*, p. 126.
56. Jeanson, *Sartre and the Problem of Morality*, p. 218.
57. For Kierkegaard, for example, although his focus is primarily on intention as against consequences, responsibility entails introspection: concerning oneself with what one has been, is, and is becoming. This is a form of responsibility denied by the nihilist or the aesthete. See Stack, *Kierkegaard's Existential Ethics*, p. 154.
58. Olafson, *Principles and Persons*, p. 52.
59. Stern, *Sartre*, pp. 235-236.
60. Fell, *Heidegger and Sartre*, pp. 138-139.
61. Hartmann, *Ethics*, Vol. II, p. 216. This entire section is engrossing.
62. De Beauvoir, *The Ethics of Ambiguity*, p. 119.
63. Flynn, *Sartre and Marxist Existentialism*, pp. 183-184.
64. Lukacs, *The Young Hegel*, p. 151.

Chapter 8

The Political Situation

Projects are not pursued in a void; all humans are thrown into a situation that is not originally of their own making. They are like castaways, according to Ortega y Gassett, on an unpremeditated globe.[1] The free project develops, first of all, in a milieu that is given, but all givens are open as well to interpretation, and how our projects fare is a factor in how we choose to interpret the situations we encounter. Freedom exists in a world that it may affect and interpret but which is not self-created.

In phenomenology, the world is given as the world of objects (populated as well by conscious beings), which objects become phenomena, objects as meanings, as they are presented to a consciousness.[2] The situation is not invented by us, but it also is not entirely a given; consciousness perceives the world, not piecemeal, but in its totality, and in the relationship of objects to itself, that is, as phenomena.[3] We have already commented in connection with Heidegger's later philosophy of being, that being is always out there in some form or another; a barren planet is amply in-itself. In-itself cannot be destroyed, but the forms it presents to us may change.

Therefore, if we speak of the destruction of being, we are speaking in highly interpretative, human terms; we are defining the situation and distinguishing among the forms of being-in-itself. The tangible world is distinct from for-itself; the in-itself exists independently, but for-itself imposes relationships onto the in-itself.[4] Only consciousness can reveal relationships. This view, which might resemble idealism is not that, for our world is not self-created, nor does the in-itself rest on mind only; but it is consciousness that rescues it from blankness and provides whatever meanings it may acquire.

Through our fundamental choice of the project of existence, we live the human reality, and that reality is being-in-the-world. To be in the world is to pursue whatever our projects are in that world, to make our impact on the world, to leave our mark. Thus, our surroundings are the in-itself, the practico-inert of human institutions, and other conscious beings, but the situation consists of more besides, for the practico-inert comprises economic systems, ideologies, social mores, and so forth; it is infused with our own meanings as well--the situation is a synthesis of the individual consciousness and the nonsubjective conditions into which we thrust ourselves.[5]

Freedom does not operate arbitrarily and capriciously, although an individual might elect to pretend that it did; rather, our projects are based on the situations into which we fall, and our freedom is exercised according to the situation, over which we may have some impact, some control, and an ability to bring it under an interpretative structure. In fact, Sartre makes it very clear that the existentialist act has little in common with Andre Gide's "gratuitous act," as in his *Lafcadio's Adventures*. Gide, he states, has no concept of situation, so that Lafcadio's acts are purely capricious and are not united with any other acts in a project.[6]

There is, in one sense, nothing to provide gratuitous acts with the continuity essential to attribute them to an individual, an identity that can claim responsibility for them. While it is Sartre's point that ". . . a freedom encounters no limits but those within itself,"[7] this is to be taken in the sense that while the situation is open to innumerable interpretations--and there are many projects we might choose to pursue--this does not vitiate the fact that there is a dialectic between for-itself and in-itself. To be sure, I am free to interpret and choose, but if my choice is to invade a neighboring country, I will be forced, despite my desires, to conduct a war.

The reality of the situation includes as well the presence of the projects of innumerable other consciousnesses. As Engels expressed this idea in a letter to Joseph Bloch,

> . . . history proceeds in such a way that the final result always arises from conflicts between many individual wills, and every one of them is in turn

made into what it is by a host of particular conditions of life. Thus there are innumerable intersecting forces, an infinite series of parallelograms of forces which give rise to one resultant—the historical event. This may in its turn again be regarded as the product of a power which operates as a whole *unconsciously* and without volition. For what each individual wills is obstructed by everyone else, and what emerges is something that no one intended.[8]

Both Marx and Engels were fully alert to the complexities of social and political situations. While the outcomes of these situations are never quite what anyone had intended, the outcome can hardly be the result of *unconscious* forces.

While Engels and Marx denigrate the impact of individual projects on the situation, it might seem that the existentialists exaggerate that impact. But this is not so, for Sartre, at least, was fully cognizant that the actor

> ... is completely in Nature's clutches, and at any moment Nature can crush him and annihilate him, body and soul. He is in her clutches from the very beginning, for him being born really means "coming into the world" in a situation not of his choice, with *this particular* body, *this* family, and *this* race, perhaps.[9]

Freedom, therefore, is not an arbitrary manifestation; it is always a freedom that discovers its aims submerged in a situation.

The dialectic of the human political life, therefore, occurs between the in-itself and the for-itself, between the chooser and the situation. The choice to exist and to thrust oneself into a situation through the pursuit of a project is *engagement*. Engagement in a situation is a manifestation, in the first instance, of the fundamental choice of existence. One could submit to situations as an object, the masochistic choice, the choice of surrendering our will and submitting to the project of another. This is to relinquish our own existence, whereas to engage ourselves in the situation is to try to control our destiny, to be, in Henley's melodramatic words, "Masters of our fate, Captain of our soul."

The individual is always responsible for the situation, whether he or she chooses to pursue projects of their own devising or passively await what happens; but engagement means, regardless of how much or how little power one wields in the political and social situations in which we are plunged, that we are responsible for the situation, for our engagement, whether active or passive, for the projects we attempt to pursue in the situation, and, however complex the situation, for its outcome.

Natanson [10] points out that insofar as other consciousnesses pursue projects within the situation where we, too, are engaged, that we are responsible for them, as well. We are legislators for the situation, political sovereigns, as it were. However, while Sartre, who exaggerates our responsibility, holds the extreme view that we are *absolutely* responsible for the situation (whereby, since everyone is absolutely responsible, it turns out that responsibility is trivialized), that we "have the war we deserve," we accept a that there are degrees of responsibility.

In political situations there are always varying degrees of responsibility, according to such variables as one's possession of power, one's education, one's projects. If we elect to join the Hitler youth, advance upward into the Schutzstaffel as a loyal supporter of Nazism, regardless of our individual power or specific deeds, we will bear a large measure of responsibility for the destruction wrought by Nazism.

Such is the responsibility of the moral fonctionnaire, Kurt Waldheim, former Secretary-General of the United Nations, then President of Austria. A volunteer in Hitler's army of the Reich, with service in Croatia, he bears a responsibility that he has never admitted for the deeds of Hitler's minions. On the other hand, if one were one of the few Germans who actually opposed the regime, the burden of responsibility is of a very different degree. Unfortunately, this does not seem to be Sartre's formulation.[11]

In that we have in a situation made a choice, or made no choice, claimed an ethical or moral stand, we are indeed totally responsible for having done so; however, our responsibility for the outcome of these choices is mitigated by the complexity of events and the difficulties of prediction. The official who chooses for his or her country out of a range of alternatives is responsible for that choice, but in the allocation of praise or blame, it must be considered that only some alternatives were realistically available.[12]

As Merleau-Ponty recognizes, the inextricable tangle of our projects and those of others in the situation, to which Engels alluded in his letter, rules out, as it were, an absolute freedom "at the source of our commitments, and equally, indeed, at their terminus."[13] Yet, despite this, the manner of our engagement in any given situation is our choice. We may select a project even when we recognize its probable futility. It is still our ethical position that infuses the situation with values.

To be sure, political and social situations make certain calls on us, call for our participation in apartheid, xenophobia, a campaign for civil rights, the denunciation of traitors. But it is the individual who heeds these calls, or ignores them, or confronts them. The projects which constitute ethical choices, will determine what choices we will define as good or bad in a given situation. The situation poses its demands on the individual according to that person's projects.

Because of the complexity of society, in view of innumerable and competing projects, and in view of the ontological basis for human freedom, it is quite unlikely that politics, which is the very stuff of competing projects, will ever be superseded. There is a viewpoint that has been voiced chiefly by technocrats, sometimes by psychologists, that we now know enough about the human psyche to banish the need for politics. Such a program has been suggested by Eysenck and by Kemeny. It is inherent in the outlook of B. F. Skinner. But such a denouement is unlikely considering the great complexity of projects generated in society. It is also unlikely that Sartre's state of pure transparency will ever be a desirable one, given the likelihood that many projects of others will continue to compete with our own, even if scarcity of tangible goods is overcome.

The curious aim of some of the great political thinkers, such as Plato and Hobbes and Marx, is not to facilitate politics (taken as civil conflicts in the public arena), but to abolish politics. The ultimate abolition of the political is a utopian projection. It is also not a desirable goal, given that those who would abolish politics would do so to implement their own ulterior designs. The general characteristic, frequently, of the call for suppressing politics and authority, is that it is made by those who desire to be in control. The common call to do away with politics in any situation almost always veils an urge for power and control by one or another group.

Engagement also implies that there will be degrees of engagement. There are projects of activity and projects of passivity, depending on how we choose to impose our values on situations. We may move with the tides, we may elect to be a "camera," or we may exert efforts to impose our goals on political situations, to see these as problems in which the course of our actions must be worked out.[14] There is also a real difference in the nature of engagement whether events are viewed from the idealist position or related through political theories to praxis. The basis of an interpretation of reality, whether it is an idealistic, with an overemphasis on mind, or a dialectical view that beyond consciousness is a real world raised upon matter devoid of thought, will make, as the

Marxists aver, a distinct difference in the manner of engagement in the world.[15]

Thus, the situation is the situation for the individual, for the individual consciousness, and while my situation is comparable to the situation you encounter in many ways, it is never the same, for a situation is the amalgam of facticity, in-itself, and freedom.[16] Actions are the result of human engagement in situations, while happenings . . . just happen. Actors signify motives.[17] As we maintain projects, seek to impose our ethical evaluations on the world, so we become agents, so we are an upsurge in the world. Our freedom consists in the ability to project ourselves into a world that does not yet exist in the way that we prefer and that might never come about without us.

This definition of the situation shows how difficult it is to assess the morality of acts. We cannot restrict the "scope of the purview of moral judgment . . . to motive [only], to act, or to consequences . . . . " When we judge the morality of any act, we must take the whole situation into account, including the circumstances in which the act was performed, the contingencies of that situation, the past, the ethics of the agent and the facts that were known to or concealed from him or her at the time.[18] Thus, the nature of the situation is pertinent to any moral judgment.

We must not focus on any too-limited an aspect of the situation in the exercise of such judgments. Moreover, the circumstances comprising a situation in which an actor exists may be morally indifferent until the actor takes a stand or pursues a project within the situation.[19] And it is this nature of our ethical and moral principles that makes them so different from those of Kant, who could propose his system even if a person were inert and pursued no goals. His system just won't suffice for an active for-itself pursuing free projects. Kant focuses on morality to the detriment of ethics, or the values we seek to realize in the world.

There are at least two interrelated reservations that must be made concerning the nature of the situation from the existentialist viewpoint. It resembles, in some ways, the Gestaltist psychology, or Kurt Lewin's field theory. But Sartre attacks this theory in his "Reply to Lefort"[20] for its tendency to apply the principle of readjustment, namely, the idea that social groups [ought to] change within a field (a society) just for the purpose of repudiating change and establishing equilibrium with the field. Each Gestalt is thus more or less autonomous and in control of the projects it contains. This objection of Sartre's has merit. But Gestalt theory also makes some pertinent points that are not unacceptable even from the existentialist point of view, provided that no necessary recommendations are drawn from field theory in favor of some status quo.

Human freedom is not a freedom with no limitations, although the actor may also exercise a degree of control over those limitations, depending on the projects he or she selects. But we cannot manipulate the world magically--there are some resistances to our activities, and field theory shows how some of these ressistances are the result of fields of social forces. Moreover, we are defined by others within the situations, like it or not, as Sartre shows on several occasions (as in his *Anti-Semite and the Jew*). We are in certain situations a woman, a slave, an untouchable. To seek to make something else from one's station as slave, however, one must first adopt the world's point-of-view, that is, our slavery, before we can project a revolt.

One can accept a status as an oppressed being in a number of ways, although in the first instance it is an enforced status, either by resigning ourselves to that status, or by seeking to change it.[21] By the time of writing the *Critique*, while still holding in a sense the notion that no situation is freer than any other, Sartre pays far more heed to the limitations imposed on the free actor. The worker has *no* effective choice but to sell his labor-power at the going rate; the practico-inert of the economy has a certain control over the worker, so that a meaning has been imposed on one, but one can still choose one's personal commitment to the status, one's own view of the job.[22]

Between *Being and Nothingness* and the *Critique*, Sartre's outlook changed, in part as a response to criticism. Thus, field theory and the recognition of a Gestalt is not inimical to an existential stance. Indeed, lucidity demands that we take into account the effects of the overall social relationships within which we find ourselves; field theory can enhance that lucidity. In international relations, too, it is necessary to observe, the nature of the system also provides constraints to action. Nations as well as individuals operate within a field that has to be taken into account by decision-makers.

Christie and Geis in their fascinating empirical study of Machiavellianism concluded that there was a crucial difference between the high-Machs and the low-Machs, which contributed to the success in competition of the high-Machs. Those who were high, on encountering a situation, sought to structure it on lines beneficial to themselves, while the low Machs tended to be more passive in the situation, accepting the structure that others, generally some high-Mach in the group, had placed on the situation.

The existentialist approaches the situation, with the philosophy of engagement, like the high-Mach in these experiments, for he or she engages in the situation and proposes ethical projects that structure its meaning. The Marxist, as well, with the concept of *praxis* is in a position to structure situations. Both philosophies are philosophies of action. Christie and Geis also found the low-Machs susceptible to affective involvements that interfered with their ability to assess situations in reasonable and self-interested ways.[23]

This tends to underline the point made previously, that to pursue a project of morality, *per se*, in political situations, is to cease to act effectively in the world. The realists in politics, those defined by Hans Morgenthau in his *Politics Among Nations*, are therefore correct in the sense that to follow morals *as goals* in local or national politics and in international politics is to lose the ability to cope, to lose the chance to obtain other goals, including, perhaps, national security. Politics, therefore, can most likely not be successfully engaged by moral principles alone. It is our ethical projects that make us effective actors in the political arena. This is not to say, however, that politics, including international politics, and morality are mutually exclusive.

As we pursue existence by way of posing free projects in the world, we interact with the situation, which is both encountered and produced. Two questions arise which, if we choose to be lucid, must be answered: (1) What is there really out there in the situation in which we are engaged? (2) How do projects impinge on the situation to organize its values and disvalues, including, if it is one of our considerations, morality?

One necessary method of dealing with the world is analytic. The world is viewed by analyzing it into its components and studying the concatenations of cause and effect, with the purpose of relating all this knowledge to our projects. (Of course, one possible project may be just this objective study of elements of the situation; this is the project of science, and it may become a worthy pursuit in its own right.) In an analysis of a situation, one would be a fool to ignore the findings of natural science, such as mechanics and biology. But note Aristotle's thoughtful points, that people who have no fixed aim are not given to deliberation --projects engender our interest in the world.[24]

Scientific knowledge is intersubjective knowledge. Perceptions of the situation may be checked with other observers and thus we will arrive at truths (always considered, of course, realistically with a lowercase "t"). We may grant there is some merit in Thomas Kuhn's interpretation of the scientific paradigm, for we enter even the realm of scientific research with a framework and are not totally open to experience, since bracketing is never complete. Yet it is our point that there are tangible truths that mark all situations.

It is also the case, that despite the projects we pursue in the situation, that our acceptance of many of these truths does not always conform to personal desire.[25] We fully agree with Wilson that to accept statements as true, there are three qualifications: (1) We must understand the statement; (2) We must know how to verify the statement; and (3) We must have good evidence before we believe it.[26] None of these considerations include that a true statement must conform with our preconceptions of it.

Rather than treat the scientific project with contempt, the effort, at least, ought to be made at critical times to view the world objectively, undogmatically, and severed from our preconceptions of it. This is a way to remain open to the world.[27] Fanatical and closed versions of the world stagnate and cease to grow--that we will to impose our projects on the world is not to say that we will to choose dogmatism, for to be effective in the world, it is required that we also see it as it is out there in our absence. This does not violate the phenomenological view, which is not that truth is a matter of the subject's arbitrary choice, but that truth is always objectivity-for-a-subject.[28]

Phenomenology also strives for intersubjectivity. We eschew the tendency in some existentialists such as Kierkegaard to overemphasize the manner in which we think a thing, as contrasted to the, for him, less important matter of whether or not what we think is objectively true.[29] We renounce the position that Heidegger takes, that th

> so-called logical, so-called analytical objectivity, the arrogant claims of positivism and the illusions of verifiability/falsifiability (Popper's model) have led Western man to personal alienation and collective barbarism.[30]

In fact, lucidity, without which we slide into bad faith, requires our recognition of objective truths. In view of the anti-scientific bias of so many political movements of Heidegger's own day, and the barbarism that stemmed from these, his objections to science and positivism lack force. His own unfortunate failure to cope authentically with the German world of the 1930s may be attributed to this disparagement of objectivity. More attention to "so-called logical, so-called analytical objectivity" might have saved Heidegger--although not necessarily--the embarrassment of alignment with the Nazis.[31]

In thus proposing that lucidity also partakes in logic, science, and an effort at objective observation, we probably have departed somewhat from the tenor of existentialism. Kierkegaard, in particular, set the tone of existentialism by his attacks on abstract thought insofar as it ignores "the concrete and the temporal, the existential process, the predicament of the existing individual . . . ."[32] The existentialists are on strong grounds in attacking the analytic viewpoint for its frequent lapse into a sort of directionless pragmatism.

Life subjected to positivistic analysis becomes a disconnected series of situations, situations that are neither yours nor mine, which are reduced to certain objective conditions through which we may pick our passionless way, avoiding mishaps here, picking up some emotional or physical gains there, all without the sense of a guiding personality. And this analytical opportunism is the danger encountered by certain forms of pragmatism based in the main on an objective assessment of reality. For the ethical person also brings projects, reasons for existing, hence, caring, to the situation. The wise person, then, as Foot depicts him or her, knows the means to certain good ends, but also knows how much particular ends are worth.[33] A person is authentic only so long as he or she is engaged in the world through personal long-range projects and commitments.[34]

In his critique of analytic rationality, Sartre embarks on an insightful sociology of knowledge that relates the development of this form of thought to the rise of the bourgeoisie. He is quite compelling and essentially correct in discerning the fallacies to which reliance on analytical thought alone might give rise. Insofar as he pursues an enlarged technique of analyzing the situation to include other aspects of knowledge, including the ethical, he rectifies the limitations of analytic thought in presenting an adequate and full view of the situation.[35] Then, in his *Critique* he draws the distinction between totalities and totalization, holding the former to be inert and a proper subject, perhaps, for analysis, rather like a finished object such as a table, while the latter is a living process, a unified culmination of history, thereby transcending analytic understanding.[36]

This distinction, however, seems to violate the position of *Being and Nothingness*, in which human consciousness is treated as individual, which it certainly is, whereas now in the *Critique* the emphasis turns human consciousness into a form of social consciousness, which it is not. Totalization would of necessity reduce others to objects, pervert their freedom to choose, impose a final goal on society, and close off possibilities. This view presents the threat of all historicisms. We hold against Hegel, against Marx, and, in this instance, against Sartre of the *Critique* that there is no such totalization. There is no sound reason to sacrifice persons to some future end where individual consciousnesses are somehow unified.

We do not hold that there is no hope for mankind or society; in fact, there is no one great hope, but there are many smaller ones. There may be many projects that transcend our abilities to analyze them objectively, but none is a totalization. Scientific analysis has its place beside freedom as a buttress to lucidity. It is not all there is, and must be tempered with passions and the sense of projects, but it is contributory to a human path through the world.

Objective analysis also helps strip the pretense from poses by other consciousnesses and from "false consciousness." We need not apologize for seeking truth in the world, for trying at some juncture to deal with the situations we confront by the effort to see things as they are, in terms of themselves and in terms of how others act in the world. This is why Machiavelli's effort was sound, though not necessarily his conclusions: His intent in *The Prince* was to present the political world as it really was rather than as the Mirror of Princes that we might prefer it to be. To do this successfully, as we must to attain lucidity, requires that our tools of perception include scientific analysis, mathematics, and logic. Otherwise, we will never be able to expose "false consciousness."

Truth comes into the world through the individual consciousness, relating itself to other consciousnesses, which alone can sustain truth in the world. To seek truth is also a duty, provided we have opted for a lucid stance within the world. According to Heidegger, who is correct in this, the primordial human relationship to the world is to put it to *use*, to view it as "ready-at-hand." To be able to see the world as it is in itself, or "present-at-hand," to use the Heideggerian language, is a derived relationship. But both relationships are an important aspect of our being-in-the-world, that is, if we will to be lucid.[37]

Farber, who presents the phenomenological technique of increasing our understanding of the world, is both trenchant and witty in attacking the lack of solid and logical thought in the existentialists Marcel and Jaspers.[38] Too often the tendency in existential thought is to disparage lucidity. Although trained as a medical psychiatrist, Jaspers is sometimes slipshod in supporting his views. Sartre is generally less vulnerable to this criticism, but at times Sartre, too, does not include among his characteristics of the free act, the necessity, proposed by Leibnitz and others, of basing one's actions on rationality.[39] This omission is critical, in our view, for the reason that any effort to avoid bad faith must include the virtue of lucidity.

Through logic and analysis, we *choose* to limit our freedom in some ways, but we do so in order to gain the more effective use of freedom, embodied in successful projects. We desire to bring about certain consequences by means of projects, and this cannot be accomplished unless freedom is voluntarily restricted with reason; that is, reason may be freely elected as a technique with which to face the world. In particular, the political situation requires for the avoidance of bad faith and failure, that we pay attention to facts and know what facts are pertinent to goals. It is not enough to will peace in the world; we must also apply ourselves to the analysis of the forces that affect peace and to the consequences of our actions. Once again, good intentions do not alone suffice to create moral outcomes.

Nevertheless, Sartre's admonitions concerning the shortcomings of the analytical technique are quite astute, some of them, and acceptable to a critical stance. Indeed, no rational engagement with the world can ignore the fallacy of basing acts solely on logic and scientific analysis. Many arguments concerning rational analysis are misguided, because rational analysis is only one of the techniques of uncovering the truth of the "present-at-hand," and attempts to refute it as a failed technique are often just efforts to refute it as the sole method of engaging reality.

In this connection, let us briefly consider the technique of polling as a means of assessing aggregate attitude in society. The first major problem is that of accurately distinguishing genuine attitudes from deceptions. The scales for "authoritarianism" are well enough known that most people know how to answer these so that they can avoid being known as "authoritarian personalities." In this and other regards, Jahoda and Christie have brilliantly assessed the theoretical and empirical shortcomings of the classic study *The Authoritarian Personality*. One of the shortcomings they show is how through quasi-scientific jargon, one can seem to show that the lower classes are more authoritarian than the educated elite: but the conformist thinking of the authoritarian is present among both groups; it is just that in the educated group, authoritarianism is veiled in arcane jargon; it is more difficult to perceive. Thus, a seemingly scientific technique has failed to make proper distinctions, and has therefore produced a biased conclusion.

The second major problem with aggregate analysis through polling is that it represents an ideal mathematical model of the distribution of attitudes (usually posited on the distribution of attitudes in the aggregate form of the normal curve--which is never empirically realized), under the mathematical assumption that we have obtained a true independent, random sample of a target population, which, once more, is never attained. Thus, we would be foolish to ignore the approach to reality that is afforded by statistical devices, but we would be less than lucid in accepting the data generated by these techniques as hard and irrefutable evidence. Even economists in their more honest moods know that the data they use are seldom correct within three or four percent of their figures. To regard, say, the IQ measure as a solid indicator rather than the flimsy construct that it is, would violate the very canons of science that lucidity requires that we uphold. Hence, Jensen's "evidence" that IQ is 78 percent the result of heredity is quite spurious as a scientific finding related to the real world.

A third major problem that particularly exercises the existentialists is that all statistical analyses of persons are reductive: We collect data on a number of indicators (all shakily defined, none mutually inclusive and exclusive as they ought to be), which cannot possibly present to us a full picture of any individual personality. To do certain kinds of social-psychological research requires that we reduce living beings to the most elementary stereotypes, as when we analyze "economic man" or the "closed personality." We are operating in a realm of unreality in order to seek clues that may relate to a real and complex social world.

But for all of this, provided we use psychometric tools as only a portion of our efforts to seek truth in the situation, whatever precarious knowledge accrues from them is frequently of some value in attaining lucidity. Thus, we need other modes of analysis together with our analytic tools, including, perhaps, a sense of the dialectic.

In a study, for instance, of the revolutionary movement in the context of the Tsarist regime of pre-1917 Russia, we can grasp much of value by seeing the interactions of the two opposing forces, the authoritarian state and the opposition, each acting upon the other to change the structure and behavior of both the government and the movement. This is the revealing viewpoint that the Marxist dialectic, properly applied, provides. Part of the tragedy of the revolution of 1917 is probably attributable to its dialectical interaction with a dictatorial and backward political regime. And Sartre's *Critique* is sometimes a valuable contribution to such dialectical thought. However, his own political projects would have been improved had they been better informed with empirical research.

It is well beyond the scope of this work to critique the method of phenomenology. Some phenomenological analyses seem to honor the so-called phenomenological method more in the breach than in the application. However, phenomenology has several aspects that recommend it as a possible technique in revealing the essences of things, of events, of processes, and even of institutions. For one thing, it is intended to be intersubjective, so that appropriately applied, an intuition of the essence of an event or object must be seen by others in the same way. It is also objective in the sense that conducted according to the *epoche*, historical, cultural, social, and even scientific paradigms are put aside in assessing our "essential" intuitions. It is intended as a "controlled process, which justifies itself from beginning to end."[40]

Objective essences are to be discovered in a way independent of contingent existence and freed from any arbitrary meaning that a subject might *want* to give them. Phenomenology, therefore, if it is possible to conduct such an investigation, is an investigation of pure consciousness, which is, after all, the only manifestation of which we may have certain knowledge, without the assumptions that underly science. But such an investigation, based as it is on intentionality, reveals not the world as it actually is without consciousness intruding (as Kant's thing-in-itself), but a world that exists for (my) consciousness, a world-for-us.[41] Existentialism does not intend objectivity to this degree. It brings the being of things closer together with the being of consciousness.[42]

Thus, an adequate view of the world must be the result, in part, of an effort to gain empirical truth, even prior to the interpretation of that truth for us. Some of these empirical truths may not even apply to our projects in the world, such as the knowledge gained by astronomers concerning the age, the size, and the components of the universe. Yet, even this knowledge will affect our lives in intangible ways as we ponder it, for in a very real sense, this too is part of the human situation.

The Renaissance Church was correct insofar as it recognized that the theories of Copernicus were not irrelevant to human concerns. Our worldview depends as well on the acceptance of the idea that humans are free to choose, and this assumption infuses the situation and reveals it to us over and beyond the empirical knowledge we have of the situation. In addition, our projects in the world produce a structure of values on the world we seek to analyze, a structure that transforms it by binding together the disparate bits and pieces that analytic reason has made of it.

We agree with other existentialists that, taken alone, analytical thought is too atomistic, too prone to take such concepts as equality as objective objects in the world, and too given to manipulative practices

The Political Situation 163

that see other beings as objects only. The system of B. F. Skinner is indicative of the final result of analytic thought alone.[43] Thus, we bring to the situation an intentional structure based on the projects that we intend to exist.

And no *epoche* ought to discard these while action is at issue, for they make the situation ours--unique. Once the world as it is "present-to-us" has been determined, persons recognized as free, and our projects are imposed upon the situation, then the alternatives offered in the situation as thus constituted will emerge. This is the responsibility of lucidity: to understand ourselves, to view the world as it really is, and to acknowledge the status of others in this world.[44]

By positing others as more than objects, we are additionally required in examining political situations to use such techniques as empathy, further analyzing the situation into how it affects others and how our potential acts in the situation will affect them. This is an additional burden we have laid upon ourselves, voluntarily, through the choice of morality.

All of these are aspects of an understanding of a situation. All human acts ought to strive through the various techniques available to us to attain total lucidity regarding situations. But in political situations, a complete lucidity is always beyond our grasp. As Mason points out, situations are often far less illuminated than our actions require, time is too short, and others may try to deceive us.[45] International politics, in particular, exhibit the crisis situation, in which core interests are affected, the time for analysis is limited, and information is lacking and uncertain.

So, in the case of the Jewish Councils during the Nazi perpetration of the Holocaust,

> no realistic definition of the situation was ever available to the Czerniakovs and Rumkovskys, the Cohens and the Asschers.

We must often take the responsibility of acting on very meager and uncertain data. The Councils did this and failed to act properly. In political situations there will be times when "Caution," the "Virtue" of deliberating "whenever and so long as deliberation is judged to be required even though powerful impulses urge us to immediate action"[46] must be foregone.

The prudence advised by the political realists must always be relative. In any case, an authentic act in the world must be based on due care; we may be ignorant of certain facts, but our culpability lies in not trying to uncover them. In spite of all, our attempt to be lucid and to act authentically may still be defeated in the world of complex politics, but we must not be faulted for not trying to be lucid.[47] Moreover, full responsibility still adheres to acts based on perceptions clouded by alcohol or drugs, for reduced perception in such cases is a free choice. It is this type of consideration that makes responsibilities to oneself a moral obligation. In the political realm of the diplomat, it is neglecting one's responsibility of searching for the truth of a situation to rely on briefings only. The diplomat fills a role in which the search for truth is one requisite.

There is a specific aspect of lucidity that best comes under the concept of witnessing. If we have chosen the project of lucidity, which, if we are not to slip into bad faith, we ought to do, we bear a responsibility, not only to ourselves and the prospects of our own projects in the world, but to others. This is evident in the scientific project, where the role of scientist requires openness, intercommunication, and honesty, all of which a person accepts with the role of the scientist. By accepting the role, a tacit promise is extended to others; and others deserve to be taken importantly into account.

In politics, no such promise to others normally goes with the project, although if persons act within a democratic society, they may have voluntarily accepted certain limitations. And we assume that we will also have chosen the limitations that accompany the choice of morality. The project of morality calls for treating others as equal and having concern for them to the degree that we include them with concern in our assessments of situations. This means that we will not only concern ourselves with how their projects threaten and impinge on ours, but that we are aware, within the situation, of the pleasure or suffering wrought by our projects or by the sum total of competing projects. This is part of the lucidity that we owe to the decision to be authentic beings and to having accepted lucidity as a project as a consequence.

But as there are other consciousnesses involved in the world, and since these others are rational beings, whom we also rely upon insofar as we are willing to extend trust for reporting truths and matters beyond our own limited range of experience, we owe them, reciprocally, as rational beings, honesty in reporting on the situation. This is the case, even though we have not chosen the aims of the scientist or the journalist. In addition, lucidity requires, as we have seen in connection with our view of the situation, a taking into account of participants of the political situation. Taking them importantly into account requires that they receive a truthful rendering of their status within a situation. This is the nature of (secular) witnessing, which rises above the minimal level of justice, the basic concern we take of others according to our acceptance of morality.

Thus, we try to expound the truth concerning political situations so far as we are able. Rotenstreich touches on our position, perhaps goes beyond it, when he states that

> By lying a person denies the special position of truth in the world of values generally, *and admits to a lack of attachment to this world*, insofar as he himself is formed by the world of values.[48]

(Our reservation is that the world of values rests on the projects and fundamental decisions we have formed, of which, certain of these may indeed support Rotenstreich's position.)

Thus, humans bring the meanings of situations into being, and witnessing requires that these meanings be based on truth and on taking others importantly into account. The metaphysics of "clearing," which Mallin holds is firmly established in existentialism, posits that "my whole essence . . . *is to make visible.*" [49] Since each participant in a political situation is responsible at various levels for that situation, we bear a measure of guilt if the situation is destructive of existence and causes great suffering for other beings. While we may sometimes be powerless to alter the situation, we always have alternative projects to pursue, and lucidity requires that one of these be witnessing, the true accounting, the penetration into the suffering of others. Years after the Holocaust, some Germans still avoided recognizing the truth. The avoidance of witnessing is a descent into bad faith.

Witnessing occurs in a variety of political contexts. It creates a conflict at times between our free choice of projects and our devotion to lucidity and morality. Witnessing can be religiously based, as it is, for instance, in Christianity, drawing from such parables as that of the Good Samaritan, recounted in Luke 10: 29-37. Thus, Marcel makes much of the concepts of testimony and witnessing.[50] In Buddhist thought, the Bodhisattvas take upon themselves to renounce their final entry into Nirvana in order to remain among people as witnesses to the true path. Criticism might be leveled against missionary activity for the consequences of the proselatizing project on foreign cultures, but in Korea under the Japanese, most missionaries did not remain silent in the face of colonial brutalities: "No neutrality for brutality" became their motto.[51] They did their secular duty as witnesses.

All persons, if they accept lucidity as a value, are charged with witnessing. Some persons take upon themselves projects and roles in which the responsibility of honesty weighs even more heavily. This is the case of scholars, journalists, writers, and artists, in particular all those who have chosen communication with others as their significant project. For Camus, the artist has an inescapable responsibility to act as a witness for those who cannot speak for themselves. In *The Myth of Sisyphus* he writes:

> The miner who is exploited or shot down, the slaves in the camps, those in the colonies, the legions of persecuted throughout the world--they need all those who can speak to communicate their silence and to keep in touch with them.[52]

Amnesty International as a non-governmental agency has accepted this vital task proposed by Camus on an international level, and it has generally conducted its witnessing with fairness and lack of bias. Sartre held that the writer, in particular, "must see to it that no one can ignore the world *or call himself innocent*."[53] At times Sartre violated his role, as in the matter of suppressing valid information on the Soviet gulags; among other sources, Simone de Beauvoir's *The Mandarins* recounts this. Indeed, on the subject of the new Communist world many persons refused to witness the truth. Marx himself, for all of his stature as a scholar, was not exempt from temptation to falsify reality.[54] Journalists such as Walter Duranty knew the truth about the brutalities of the collectivization program in the Soviet Union, the heinous "Revolution from above," when, "dizzy with success," the Stalin regime killed some six million of its own people, yet many reports deliberately presented a false picture.

Emma Goldman, an advocate of the Soviet revolution, on the other hand, was a lucid witness to the realities of the early regime under Lenin. Her *Living My Life* (Vol. II) is a valuable testimony from an honest witness.[55] Sartre, himself, met his responsibilities clearly in his forewords to Fejto's *The Rape of Hungary* and Henri Alleg's *The Question*; the latter book is a grueling account of torture perpetrated by the French in their effort to retain Algeria. Contrarily, however, Sartre's two-hour interview to a reporter from *Liberation* was a pastiche of lies; as Paul Johnson put it,

It ranks as the most grovelling account of the Soviet State since the notorious expedition by George Bernard Shaw during the early 1930s . . . . Indeed, he maintained, "There is total freedom of criticism in the USSR."[56]

By 1970, according to the account by Francois Bondy, Sartre had retracted many of these extreme positions and had become aware of "his own contradictions," but the false witnessing had nonetheless been done.[57]

The advocates of revolutionary visions often violate lucidity, as Anna Louise Strong admitted in one of her newsletters from Mao's China, "I am not allowed to admit that anyone in these three years ever starved to death."[58] It is the case of many advocates, for the new vision or the old world, that they are penetrating witnesses of the opposing force, and that they are silent concerning the consequences that result from their own movements. It is a simple case of bad faith.

Finally, intellectuals, whether they are specifically writers or not, bear special responsibilities for lucidity, in obvious consequence of their vocation as intellectuals and scholars, for who, if not intellectuals, ought to try to ferret out and report the truth? So Edgardo Angara, the President of the University of the Philippines, reprimanded them, saying,

> I regard [Benigno] Aquino's murder and the events that followed as an indictment of the intellectual class in our country. It is a class that has indulged its own fantasies at the expense of its real obligation to provide a clear and coherent picture of Philippine reality.[59]

In a review of books about Ethiopia, Colburn comments,

> Scholars may not have, or want the responsibility of judging right from wrong and of fingering the perpetrators of acts of gross immorality. Yet at the least, their work should make it clear who did what and with what consequences for human welfare and life.[60]

Intellectuals are tempted by political regimes, who hold favors and appointments in their power, to violate their role of lucidity; moreover, intellectuals are frequently advocates of various political movements, so the inclination is great to ignore the consequences perpetrated by the causes they advocate, thus violating their freely chosen role and living in bad faith. Even more than artists, who, admittedly, are often apolitical and may not be well-informed, intellectuals are responsible for witnessing or for neglecting to witness. While some intellectuals perform this responsibility admirably, for example, The Czech writer and political figure Vaclav Havel, who is praised by Pavel Tigid as a "life in truth,"[61] Johnson in his comments on a number of intellectuals comments that "One thing which emerges from any case-by-case study of intellectuals is their scant regard for veracity."[62]

This idea of witnessing is contained in the preceding presentation on truth--it suggests that there is intersubjective truth. It admits that although situations are open to interpretations depending on the projects that one brings to them, that there are elements of inescapable reality in situations as well. It is bad faith to fortify illusions concerning a situation by remaining in a state of voluntary ignorance.

In his *Roots of Evil*, Ervin Staub refers to

members of the community of nations [who] have an obligation to be active bystanders [and] who act as mirrors in which other nations can see themselves [that is, as witnesses].[63]

He also considers the question whether witnesses have an obligation to take action. For both nations and individuals, such action may well be supererogatory, and not called for in the context of our own minimal morality. Whether or not action is warranted would appear to rest on the ethical values the individual advocates. For nations, the topic will be covered later when we discuss the problems of intervention.

There is another aspect of lucidity which in international relations falls under the dual rubric of realism and idealism. E. H. Carr's *The Twenty Years' Crisis* was one of the first works that clarified these different outlooks on foreign policy situations. Realism has been set forth as a series of principles in Hans Morgenthau's classic *Politics Among Nations*, principles which are actually hypotheses about the effects of certain behaviors between nations. Realism tends to stress consequences; idealism focuses on intentions. The one draws from utilitarianism, the other rests on Kantian doctrine. Stanley Hoffman remarks that "All realist theorists agree. . . on the wisdom of an ethics of responsibility instead of an ethics of conviction. . . . "[64] At least as it has developed in the study of international relations, realism has tended to focus on the lack of authority in the world arena and the nature of power relationships among nations, while idealism has emphasized the melioration of power and anarchy by way of international organization.

Finally, there is the usual difference between political realism and idealism in their differing assessments of "human nature," where realism tends to stress conflictual propensities and idealism the cooperative. Consequently, Machiavelli is the political realist *par excellence* as opposed to, say, Peter Kropotkin. Both tendencies purport to provide a true picture of the world of international affairs, but both are subject to distinct delusions. Since the trend in analysis in international relations since World War II has been to favor realism, let us remark that we are not accepting one of the inferences from Machiavelli's teaching, that is, that there is "an incurable division between politics and morality"; that idealism means ethics, and realism means politics.[65]

Where idealism, stressing intention, slips into any doctrine of absolute ends or categorical imperatives, it is most likely to stray from the real world, and as Kant was sometimes inclined to do, posit principles that could work only in the ideal world of the "kingdom of ends." The realist is not likely to propose ideal solutions in political situations and instead, resorts to an "ethic of compromise," choosing among varieties of immorality, or lesser evils, so to speak. The idealist, on the other hand, fearing to sink to the level of proposing any evil at all, may withdraw utterly from the necessity to choose. Purity becomes abstention, but abstention in the name of morality has also dire consequences.

The neutrality pose of the United States in the era of the 1930s was an abdication of responsibilities with concomitant bad consequences.[66] This tendency to shy away from the hard and tangible world of international politics and to cultivate an inactive purity is one of long standing in American politics, as evidenced by Secretary of State Bryan (yes, an idealist as Secretary of State; perhaps, "only in America"), who in his Prayer Day Address of October 14, 1914, presented the thesis that peace and preparedness for war were incompatible, for the threat of force leads to suspicion and war, while America had a better way of dealing with nations, and that was on the basis of moral principles and the goal of peace.[67]

It is also in bad faith to decline taking responsibility, to step back from those acts made necessary by our projects, to let others dirty their hands for us. If a relative evil must be perpetrated in order to avert a probable greater evil, it ought to be done if there is no other plausible alternative (a matter that would require an effort of analysis to determine), for consequences count in an effective political morality. To finally choose the least of several evils does not means that morality is not operative in international affairs. Rather, an effort has been made to propose a morality that works. But a moral principle that usually works may not always be effective, and acts that are seem immoral in the limited view may appear necessary for probable good ends in the long term. This was a major consideration in the U.S. decision to drive Iraq from Kuwait by force in 1991.

There is also the foible of idealism become moralism in its sometimes puerile emphasis on trying to change the attitudes of actors who possess powerful conflicting interests, not that this effort is always unavailing. Marx was quite strong in his denunciation of the moralism that tried to impose the principles of cooperation on societies that were organized to inhibit cooperation, a moralism that took an abstract view of persons torn from the concrete social situations in which they lived.[68]

Thus, the world witnessed the crusade of American religious leaders, infused with good intentions, ignoring politics and history, to produce such flimsy sand-castles as the 1928 Kellogg-Briand Pact outlawing war, which they hoped would work because it was morally desirable.[69] Far from being a benign, if useless, intrusion into international affairs, such a pact was genuinely deleterious. Its presumption helped prevent real measures for peace. As Senator Carter Glass commented, who voted for the treaty,

> . . . it is going to confuse the minds of many good and pious people who think that peace may be secured by polite professions of brotherly love.[70]

In the idealist, the will to improve the future is likely to outrun the possibilities inherent in situations and to replace lucidity with wishful thinking.[71] There are forms of pacifism that exhibit a number of violations of lucidity and good faith. There is a certain form of pacifism that retains moral purity by standing aside from the events of the world. There is another variety that proposes through the act of denouncing all violence that if all the world did likewise, there would be peace. This is as tautologically true as was Calvin Coolidge's maxim that "when more and more people are out of work, unemployment occurs."

But beyond this is the problem that political situations with their power relationships embrace us whether we will or no, and the pacifist, seeking to avoid power politics falls into the midst of these, contributing to the power of one actor or another. During the 1930s, the unfortunate result of pacifism was to embolden and strengthen the camp of Nazism and fascism. The pacifist has to be aware that he or she is partaking in the balance of power.[72] Reinhold Niebuhr asserts,

It is not unfair to assert that most pacifists who seek to present their religious absolutism as a political alternative to the claims and counterclaims, the pressures and counterpressures of the political order, invariably betray themselves into this preference for tyranny. Tyranny is not war. . . . It is a peace which results from one will establishing a complete dominion over other wills and reducing them to acquiescence.[73]

And in the situation in 1990, when Iraq invaded Kuwait, the pacifistic sentiment against warfare was a direct contribution to the brutalities perpetrated by Saddam Hussein on the Kuwaitis. In addition, and without intending it, pacifism contributed significantly to the climate that produced World War II. One would believe that religion was particularly guilty of the pitfalls of idealism, but this is not necessarily the case. Saint Augustine, Saint Thomas Aquinas, and Reinhold Niebuhr were singularly tough-minded realists. As another religious thinker, Jacques Maritain, puts it, ". . . conscientious objectors play the game of the conquerors."[74]

If idealism exhibits a tendency to slip from lucidity and responsibility, so realism is not immune to political fallacies. It is easy enough to accuse idealists of believing that good intentions necessarily produce good consequences, but we may forget that "realism," the choice of intentions that are selected to fit the situation and which may not be morally best, may also have untoward consequences. Just as the idealist may err by overestimating the benevolence and good intent of opposing actors in a situation, so the realist may err by overstating their malignity.

Recent historical research by Herbert Butterfield and Philipp Moseley show that this was the case with the French and British misperception of Russian intentions concerning Turkey that produced the Crimean War. It seems to have been the case that Russia did not have designs on Turkey and would have liked to have avoided this war, but realists overestimated the threat. There are additional traps in the realist position. One of these is the realist's avoidance of the risk of being "taken in." To be regarded as a "realist," is to distrust human motives and to rest one's case, always, on the pessimistic view, the worst case scenario. By avoiding any risk of getting taken advantage of, the realist seems to appear more adequate to international situations than he or she deserves. "It is not want of sense," wrote Henry Fielding in *America*, "but want of suspicion, by which innocence is often betrayed."

Thus, does the realist avoid getting ensnared by guile, but the result may be consequences that are less advantageous than they might have been. The realist view may generate more conflict where there might be less. Finally, there is the "realist" of historicism, who assumes the "tough" stance toward the inevitable March of History, the person always "talking about the hard lesson of facts," but who sees only the facts that fit his image.[75]

This is a very destructive form of realism, a realism that on close investigation may not be realistic at all. The tough historicists who formed the governments of East Europe following World War II, found their constructs collapsing about them by 1989; the march of history had been a false vision, the sacrifices of tough realism along the way useless to any good purpose. Such historicists may also commit a fallacy referred to earlier, that of awaiting the future age for the advent of morality, assuming that for the present pure morality, hypermoralism, as Maritain calls it, is not applicable--therefore, since moral perfection is inapplicable, no morality is applicable, and anything goes.[76]

While realism tends to err in the direction of the status quo, the idealist is usually dedicated to making the world a better one. Idealism is always to some degree revolutionary, for it looks beyond the extant reality.[77] Hartmann merges in a critique the two trends as well as anyone:

> A sense of reality, guided by a sense of its values, is the secret of the wise man. With him to overlook the fulness of values is just as much a sin against life as to make Utopian claims which are incapable of being gratified.[78]

This comment also puts the matter into our own context, wherein the actor is always in the business of balancing the claims of lucidity, responsibility, morality, and ethics.

From the realist camp, comes the admonition that is particularly apt in any balancing of idealism and realism in an appropriate mix, that in political struggles there is generally some justice and some injustice on each side. Political actors are, by nature, impure. The genuine realist, as opposed to the historicist or the fanatic, recognizes the complexity of the world. As diplomat, the realist will be involved in some situations at one time or another in activities that partake of injustices and immorality. The wrong solution to this is to preserve in bad faith the utter purity of abstaining from action. One must make the best of circumstances, and act. "Relative justice," writes Lefever, "is the very heart of both ethics and politics."[79]

It should be noted, however, that realism does not protect the advocate from error, for international politics is a complex field. In his interesting chapter on E. H. Carr, Smith shows how that thinker was an advocate of appeasement, a position that is often regarded as the province of weak-minded realists. However, the tough position of the realist might be put as that however bad we may think Nazism and Fascism, we must still have the fortitude to do business with them, for one cannot expect to treat only with moderate persons in international politics. The realist will have us forego our moral scruples to deal with dictators, if it can be argued to be in the national interest. In this case Carr was wrong-- indeed, he deleted these arguments from the second edition of *The Twenty Years' Crisis*.[80]

What is proposed is that morality does play a vital role in international affairs. What has to be sought is morality with lucidity and responsibility and attention to consequences. In a criticism of the stand of such realists as E. H. Carr, Hans Morgenthau makes the point that some form of moral assessment, some ideals, are necessary in dealing with power, lest we become the type of realist for whom, lacking any other ethical bearing, power becomes the sole consideration, and whoever is the superior in power becomes "of necessity the repository of superior morality as well," only on that account.[81]

Notes

1. Ortega y Gasset, *Some Lessons in Metaphysics*, p. 62.
2. Erazim V. Kohak, in his translator's introduction to Ricoeur, *Freedom and Nature*, xiv.
3. Jeanson, *Sartre and the Problem of Morality*, p. 123.
4. *Ibid.*, p. 148.
5. Greene, *Jean-Paul Sartre*, p. 35.
6. Sartre, *Existentialism is a Humanism*, p. 305.
7. Jeanson, *Sartre and the Problem of Morality*, p, 185.
8. In Karl Marx and Frederick Engels, *Selected Correspondence* (Moscow: Progress Publishers, 1975), p. 395.
9. Sartre, *Materialism and Revolution*, p. 236.
10. Natanson, *A Critique of Jean-Paul Sartre's Ontology*, p. 97.
11. So Albert Speer, who bore a substantial degree of responsibility for the results of Nazism, spoke as follows: "It is true that I did not know what was really beginning on November 9, 1938, and what ended in Auschwitz and Mardanik, but in the final analysis I myself determined the degree and the extent of my ignorance." Albert Speer, *Inside the Third Reich* (Trans. by Richard and

Clara Winston. New York: The Macmillan Company, 1970), p. 135.
12. Dennis F. Thompson, "Moral Responsibility of Public Officials: The Problem of Many Hands," *The American Political Science Review*, Vol. 74, No. 4 (December 1980), p. 909.
13. Merleau-Ponty, *Phenomenology of Perception*, p. 454.
14. Mallin, *Merleau-Ponty's Philosophy*, p. 10.
15. Ortega y Gasset, *Some Lessons in Metaphysics*, p. 158.
16. Flynn, *Sartre and the Marxist Existentialists*, p. 26.
17. Warnock, *Existentialism*, p. 118-119.
18. Joad, C. E. M., *Guide to the Philosophy of Morals and Politics* (Westport: Greenwood Press, 1969), p. 291.
19. Collins, *The Existentialists*, p. 87.
20. Sartre, *The Communists and Peace, with an Answer to Claude Lefort* (London: Hamish Hamilton, 1969. Trans. by Irene Clephane), pp. 236-237. Except for the "Reply," this essay shows Sartre at his ideological worst, with little argument and numerous unfounded assertions *ex cathedra*.
21. Olafson, *Principles and Persons*, p. 173.
22. Herbert L. Dreyfus and Piotr Hoffman, "Sartre's Changed Conception of Consciousness: From Lucidity to Opacity," pp. 237-238, in Schilpp, *The Philosophy of Jean-Paul Sartre*.
23. Richard Christie and Florence L. Geis, *Studies in Machiavellianism* (New York: Academic Press, 1970), p. 288 and p. 352. Like all small-group studies, this one too suffers the problem of generalization onto the larger society. But the experiments are clever and the findings are suggestive.
24. The point is made in his *The Eudemian Ethics* (Cambridge, MA: Harvard University Press, 1961. Trans. by H. Rackham, M.S.), p. 295.
25. Edward A. Tiryakian, *Sociologism and Existentialism: Two Perspectives on the Individual and Society* (Englewood Cliffs: Prentice-Hall, Inc. 1962), p. 160. There is some ambiguity here in both pragmatism and existentialism regarding our ability to accept truths that may offend us.
26. John Wilson, *Language and the Pursuit of Truth* (London: Cambridge University Press, 1967), p. 76. Nor are we averse to a good deal of the positivistic program on verification. To the existentialist, this forms a part of the "letting be" of reality and a respect for and acceptance of what reality is. We accept that objectivity is possible to a major degree. See Luijpen, *Existential Phenomenology*, p. 322.
27. Wild, "Authentic Existence: A New Approach to 'Value Theory'," pp. 64-65.
28. Luijpen and Koren, *A First Introduction to Existential Phenomenology*, p. 77. See also pp. 94-95. And from Sartre, *Anti-Semite and the Jew* (New York: Schoken Books, 1965. Trans. by George J. Becker), "How can one choose to reason falsely? It is because of a longing for impenetrability. The rational man groans as he gropes for the truth; he knows that his reasoning is no more than tentative, that other considerations may supervene to cast doubt on it. He never

sees very clearly where he is going; he is 'open'; he may even appear to be hesitant. But there are people who are attracted by the durability of a stone. They wish to be massive and impenetrable; they wish not to change. Where, indeed, would change take them? We have here a basic fear of oneself and of truth . . . Since they are afraid of reasoning, they wish to lead the kind of life wherein reasoning and research play only a subordinate role, wherein one seeks only what he has already found, wherein one becomes only what he already was." As an indictment of the anti-Semite, this is brilliantly insightful. From Sartre, it is also a very interesting positive position toward research and social science.

29. Warnock, *Existentialism*, p. 10.
30. This is a common view, characteristic of Heidegger in some moods, as shown in George Steiner, *Martin Heidegger*, p. 154. To stoop to an *ad hominum* argument, although it is also pertinent to the issue, this position is hardly feasible for a supporter of the Nazi regime in the 1930s. There is some point in the idea that positivism has had an alienating effect on 20th century persons, in the same way that the Copernican theory had done, and that was the content of some of the opposition of the Catholic Church. An exaggerated positivism may also violate the fullness of the truth of situations, for there are other factors that we must take into account in our appraisals. But, barbarism? The 1960s resounded in Heideggerian-style arguments, as in Roszak's attack on the social sciences in *The Making of A Counter Culture*, an attack well answered in Natanson, *Phenomenology, Role, and Reason* (Springfield: Charles C. Thomas, 1974), pp. 340-341.
31. Hazel Barnes, *An Existential Ethics*, p. 422, makes the comment that "The Freiburg speech and Heidegger's writing since then reveal the great drawback and positive danger of Being-philosophy. The idea that truth is a direct communication with absolute reality not only serves as an excuse for not investigating political and social problems and for not committing oneself to action which one can justify. It positively impedes the development of any consistent human value structure."
32. Soren Kierkegaard, *Concluding Unscientific Postscript* (Trans. by David F. Swenson and Walter Lowrie. Princeton: Princeton University Press, 1968), p. 267.
33. Foot, *Virtues and Vices*, p. 5.
34. Wild, *The Challenge of Existentialism*, pp. 140-141.
35. Fell, *Heidegger and Sartre*, p. 333, and Sartre, "Introduction to *Les Temps Modernes*," p. 436.
36. Fell, *Heidegger and Sartre*, p.421, and Poster, *Existential Marxism in Postwar France*, pp. 274-275.
37. Gelven, A Commentary On Heidegger's "Being and Time," p. 56.
38. Farber, *The Aims of Phenomenology*, pp. 206-226. Even admirers of these thinkers must admit a certain flacidity in their presentations.
39. Aron, *History and the Dialectic of Violence*, p. 167, fn. 10.

40. Lauer, *Phenomenology*, pp. 61-62. In addition, see Joseph J. Kockelmans, *A First Introduction to Husserl's Phenomenology* (Louvain: Duquesne University Press, 1967) and Farber, *The Aims of Phenomenology*, and, of course, Edmund Husserl, *Ideas: General Introduction to Pure Phenomenology* (London: Collier Macmillan, 1962. Trans. by W. R. Boyce Gibson.)
41. Lauer, *Phenomenology*, p. 88. Husserl's *Ideas* present a thorough discussion of the purpose of phenomenology.
42. Olafson, *Principles and Persons*, pp. 66-67.
43. Joseph S. Catalano, *A Commentary on Jean-Paul Sartre's Critique of Dialectical Reason, Volume 1, Theory of Practical Ensembles*, p. 79.
44. Follesdal, "Sartre on Freedom," p. 402.
45. Mason, *Imponderables*, p. 112.
46. Sidgwick, *The Methods of Ethics*, p. 236.
47. Donagan, *The Theory of Morality*, p. 130.
48. Rotenstreich, *On the Human Subject*, p. 92. The emphasis is mine.
49. Mallin, *Merleau-Ponty's Philosophy*, pp. 158-260.
50. Marcel, *The Philosophy of Existentialism* (New York: Citadel Press, 1968), in particular the "Testimony and Existentialism," pp. 91-103.
51. Samuel H. Moffett, "The Independence Movement and the Missionaries," *Transactions of the Royal Asiatic Society*, Korea Branch, Vol 54 (1979), p. 29.
52. Charlesworth, *Existentialists*, pp. 32-33.
53. Flynn, *Sartre and Marxist Existentialism*, p. 146.
54. Marx occasionally misquoted for effect; and in a letter to Engels dated 15 August 1857, he wrote, "Note Bene—on the supposition that the dispatches we have got up to now are correct. It is possible that I may be discredited. But in that case it will still be possible to pull through with the help of a bit of dialectics. It goes without saying that I phrased my forecasts in such a way that I would prove to be right also in the opposite case." See Leslie R. Page, *Karl Marx and the Critical Examination of His Works* (London: The Freedom Association, 1987), p. 124.
55. There is a balanced and fair account of the numerous tours of enthusiasts to the Soviet Union during the 1920s and 1930s in David Caute, *The Fellow-Travelers: A Postscript to the Enlightenment* (New York, N.Y.: The Macmillan Company, 1973), "Conducted Tours," pp. 60-131.
56. Johnson, "Jean-Paul Sartre: 'A Little Ball of Fur and Ink,'" p. 70. Sartre retracted this interview many years later and admitted its untruth.
57. See his "Jean-Paul Sartre," pp. 78-81, in Maurice Cranston, ed., *The New Left: Six Critical Essays* (London: The Bodley Head, 1970).
58. Quoted in Edward Friedman, "Maoism and the Liberation of the Poor," *World Politics*, Vol. XXXIX, No. 3 (April 1987), p. 422.
59. Quoted in Richard Gott, "A Whiff of Havana Blows Over Manila," *The Guardian Weekly*, Vol. 133, No. 9 (September 1, 1985), p. 9. We must be well aware in our judgment of other intellectuals of the sanctions that may be brought

against them by a dictatorial regime, which include banishment to minor colleges out of the bustling capital, at the least, or possiby even murder.

60. "The People's Democratic Republic of Ethiopia," p. 577-578.

61. Pavel Tigid, "Havel destined for leading role in Czech reconstruction," *The Manchester Guardian*, Vol. 141, No. 22 (December 3, 1989), 11; reprinted from *Le Monde*.

62. Johnson, *Intellectuals*, (New York: Harper and Row Publishers, 1988), p. 269. He exempts Edmund Wilson from this blanket condemnation, who did try to verify his earlier attitudes toward the Soviet Union.

63. Ervin Staub, *The Roots of Evil: The Origins of Genocide and Other Group Violence* (New York: Cambridge University Press, 1989), p. 254.

64. Stanley Hoffmann, "Raymond Aron and the Theory of International Relations," *International Studies Quarterly*, Vol. 29, No. 1 (March 1985), 15.

65. Jacques Maritain, "The End of Machiavellianism," p. 137, in *The Range of Reason* (London: Geoffrey Bles, 1953). Morgenthau makes this point clear, too, holding that the so-called realist is dedicated to a morality applicable to problems of concrete action and attention to consequences, while the idealist tends to uphold abstract formulae.

66. Ernest Lefever, *Ethics and United States Foreign Policy* (New York: Meridian Books, Inc., 1957), pp. 23-24.

67. Cited in Robert Endicott Osgood, *Ideals and Self-Interest in America's Foreign Relations* (Chicago: The University of Chicago Press, 1953), p. 203.

68. Kamenka, "Marxism and Ethics," in Hudson, *New Studies in Ethics*, Vol. II. p. 312.

69. Lefever, *Ethics and United States Foreign Policy*, p. 18.

70. Quoted in Osgood, *Ideals and Self-Interest in America's Foreign Relations*, p. 349.

71. Macquarrie, *Existentialism*, p. 201. Riker, *The Art of Ethical Thinking*, p. 96, puts it thus: "One can have all the warm feelings for humanity possible, but without the cultivation of the powers of reasoning and imagination, there is little reason to believe that those feelings will ever issue into any kind of effective moral action."

72. James Burnham, *The Machiavellians* (Chicago: Henry Regnery Company, 1943), pp. 144-145.

73. Reinhold Niebuhr, *Christianity and Power Politics* (Archon Books, 1969; a reissue of Charles Scribner's 1940 edition), p. 16.

74. In the "End of Machiavellianism," p. 161.

75. Barnes, *The Literature of Possibility*, p. 79, fn.

76. Maritain, *op. cit.*, puts it, ". . . nor does [morality] consist in waiting, before saving one's neighbor, who is drowning, to become a saint . . . ."

77. Ortega y Gasset, *Some Lessons in Metaphysics*, p. 137.

78. *Ethics*, Vol. II, p. 243.

79. In *Ethics and United States Foreign Policy*, p. 21.

80. Michael Joseph Smith, *Realist Thought from Weber to Kissinger* (Baton Rouge: Louisiana State University Press, 1986).
81. Hans J. Morgenthau, *Dilemmas of Politics* (Chicago: University of Chicago Press, 1958), p. 357. Morgenthau includes Carr among other representatives of this group, such as Adam Mueller and Carl Schmitt, concluding "It is a dangerous thing to be a Machiavelli. It is a disastrous thing to be a Machiavelli without *virtu*."

Chapter 9

Projects and Practice

The problem of political practice is inextricably bound to situation, for we intrude into situations with our projects. By means of our projects we make our way through the world. Situations arise before us; they are interpreted in accordance with our projects, which, in turn, leave our mark upon them.

Having chosen existence and made the world our home, we have thereby committed ourselves to engage in the world. In Spinoza's *Ethics*, life is assimilated to activity. "Nature does indeed teach life and its preservation as the authoritative law, but life means activity . . . . ,"[1] a view close to ours and, as Cropsey shows, unlike Hobbes' tendency to advocate passivity and acquiescence. The difference might be attributable to a fact mentioned earlier, that Hobbes appears to advocate a polity in which politics is abolished. In Feuerbach's words,

> Not mere will as such, not vague knowledge—only activity with a purpose . . . he who has no aim has no home, no sanctuary; aimlessness is the greatest unhappiness.[2]

These projects open up the political, social, artistic, scientific situations encountered in the world; our focus, of course, is the political. There are, as suggested previously, choices to be made prior to any political commitments. Initial commitments include such projects as lucidity (or its opposite, dogmatism or fanaticism), authenticity (or bad faith), the acceptance of responsibility for our acts in the world (or irresponsibility), and morality (or immorality), whereby we take others into account (or treat them as objects in the world). All of these choices will have most likely preceded any of our political choices. They will furnish a foundation for later political projects in the world. I t i s important to realize that excepting the project of morality, the political projects we essay in the world are not usually taken on in the name of obligations, nor are they to be regarded generally as universally binding on others. Taking others importantly into account as we pursue goals is accepted as a moral obligation; such stances as lucidity and responsibility are not obligations, as such, unless they might be regarded as obligations to ourselves as the image of the persons we want to become.

Other projects are our own assessments of what is valuable and what is not; they are our projections of the possibilities we would like to produce in situations; they are not disinterested in the sense that Kant regarded all virtue. Rather, the evaluations we impose upon the world grow out of our assumed purposes, and a purpose implies something desired rather than something required. In the ethical sense, we have therefore defined 'good' both as that in which we have an interest[3] and as that attitude we adopt toward others, the latter comprising morality as such.

Thus, we come to political decisions bearing already a considerable number of important commitments, provided we have freely accepted these, that will affect our further choices as we engage the political world. The crucial mediatory goal in politics, regardless of what our other political projects might be, is power. Indeed, power enters into whatever our ends might be, whether political or not; whenever we transcend a situation, try to bring about a new situation that this one is not yet, in the midst of other human projects within that situation, we require power. Projects (*praxis*, ends) constitute any active life and require the acquisition of power. Power is a requisite constituent of life.

In the political arena, we necessarily encounter the complex of other projects than our own, some of these hostile to the values we seek to realize, others compatible, some indifferent. Hence, power, the ability to have an impact on political events, becomes the intrinsic political means, crucial to whatever other ends we might seek. This viewpoint has the imprimatur of all realistic writers on politics, for instance, Morgenthau, who writes,

Projects and Practice

> ... man's aspiration for power is not an accident of history; it is not a temporary deviation from a normal state of freedom; it is an all-permeating fact which is of the very essence of human existence."[4]

Indeed, Machiavelli seems to advocate power as a surrogate for human freedom.[5] According to the distribution of power in a political situation, one set of values or an opposing set will prevail. Power is the ability to prevent certain ends from being consummated in political situations; it is the ability to bring our set of goals to fruition. Thus, power blocks the acts of some people and realizes the aims of others. The political situation is one where conflicting projects vie for hegemony. It follows that if the goals we favor are to be realized, we will have to confront competing ones, ally ourselves with compatible projects, garner resources to increase power, and enter into conflicts of varied intensity.

Whatever our other goals may be, power is one element in the political situation that cannot be ignored, or all else will fail. Indeed, power is fundamental to ethics as a whole. Frost comes to the conclusion that the normative theorist is a player in the game of power.[6] Ethical values are unrealizable in the political world without the power to effect them. No effective political actor will eschew power: it was used very effectively by Lincoln, Gandhi, Martin Luther King, Lenin, Woodrow Wilson, and so on and on.

Thus, the decision to exist implies that power will become one among other ends, the better to make our way in the world and to realize our projects. But power, rightly viewed, is not an end in itself; it is an end from which other ends can be sought. Even Machiavelli did not praise the pursuit of power in itself--he had in mind an end beyond power, namely, glory, magnificence, or, in the final chapter of *The Prince*, the unification of Italy. The decision to exist, therefore, is a decision to not only frame an ethics of values but to realize them in the world. Persons who have made such a decision are internally oriented people who recognize their responsibility for their acts in the world and hold others responsible in the same way.[7] This is, if you wish, Nietzsche's "will to power," and it can be life-asserting and proud.[8]

One way to decline engagement in the political world is the choice of the passive individual, who Phares refers to as "externals," people who attribute less responsibility for acts to themselves, and who place the locus of their motivations on forces external to themselves. These are the individuals most prone to various forms of bad faith. There is also however, another active relationship to power, which is not life-asserting, but which in the throes of Thanatos opts to destroy: the spirit of nihilism.

In the 20th century, we have seen power sought and put to use in this fashion by the Nazi movement. Hermann Rauschning captured the spirit of the movement in his *The Revolt of Nihilism*. Indeed, the positive aspects of the movement were vague, but the program was quite tangible in its efforts at death, destruction, and the stifling of free human culture. One of the dangers of nuclear arsenals is that while nuclear theory assumes that these forces are controlled by persons for whom life is a value, there are many individuals, and some who will gain power over nations, for whom existence is a disvalue.

Therefore, power and the effort to gain power is not intrinsically immoral, despite the bad reputation of power politics. Power is a positive aspect of ethics. Ethics posits values in the world, while power enables their fulfillment. Scheler's interpretation of power is a compatible one, namely, that power is a necessary ingredient in realizing all other values. It can be productive and creative, "even to the extent that the experience of power is at the root of subjective self-awareness."[9] Empirical research into internal control and self-esteem seems to support this philosophical view.

Those who attack the state because it is the possessor of power do not generally do this because of some pristine moral purity, although they may claim some such attribute. There is often a good deal of self-deception and hypocrisy in regarding the opponents of state or institutional power as automatically well-intentioned. The anarchists are prone to romanticize their rebellion against the state, as Emma Goldman idealized the nature and motives of young Leon Czolgosz, the assassin of President McKinley. In fact, Czolgosz was probably mentally confused and incapable of acting according to any sophisticated principle. Usually, it is the case that, as Meinecke alleged, the opposition to state power is brought about

> because the state constituted a barrier to their own power goals.... More often than not, cynicism and illusion were secret partners.[10]

Rather than free their fellow beings, anarchists and revolutionaries, of whom Sergei Nechaev is a common type, are more interested in controlling them.

If this interpretation concerning power as a universal means to attain human ethical goals is accepted, then we have, according to Kenneth W. Thompson, denied the core of Judeo-Christian morality. Indeed, many interpretations of Christianity, have tended to be otherworldly, emphasizing the City of God above the political city. And otherworldliness and the decision that activity in the here-and-now is futile, logically lead to a stance of passivity, an attitude that this-worldly striving is distracting if not downright bad. And we disagree with Thompson who goes on to state that

> The power relation in any ultimate sense is a denial of this respect [for man as an end in himself], for power at root involves the use of man as a means to the end of another man.[11]

If this were so, all goals ought to be avoided except the goal of morality, and this would reject an active life for one of passivity. Politics is possible without exceptionable immorality, certainly at the domestic level in some polities, but it is not possible without the exercise of power. Thompson, it seems, at least in this instance, errs by elevating morality to a too-pristine purity. Even Kant, for all his formalism, meant by his imperative that we ought not to regard other humans *only* as means. If the Judeo-Christian morality did actually eschew power relationships to the degree suggested, then such a morality is, quite simply, "too good" for this world.

The one consuming evil that stems from the necessary intermediate goal of gaining power is the attempt to gain power in an absolute sense, a form of the nihilist fantasy. In particular, in international affairs, nations that strive to obtain total hegemony or total security, which in reality are one and the same, are particularly dangerous to other nations. The lesson of power as a potential contribution to humane projects, is that limitations apply, and that no cause ought to be granted or to seek absolute power. As justice must be seen as a relative goal, and as it must be always in view that justice is never totally in the possession of any political actor or group, so does no nation deserve total power. Nations that seek absolute security are as dangerous as movements that seek to attain perfect ends.

Having elaborated on a number of basic commitments that precede political goals, we ought to comment at this point on some essentially political values. Ethics, we repeat, we regard as a system of values, as the hierarchy of the individual's value structure, in which morality is one aspect only. Morality is that portion of ethics that relates to the treatment of others. We have already treated of that minimal value arising from the moral stance, justice and fundamental human rights, in which view we opposed the position of some other existentialists.

Ethics, taken broadly, has to do with how we evaluate the quality of life: What are the good things we seek as individuals in order to infuse our lives with interest and significance? Seeking these goals among other projects, we will encounter opposition--politics is the clash of opposing projects; it concerns conflict. Although we may reduce social antagonism, there will always be "contradictions among the people," even in the classless society, as Mao was insightful enough to perceive. (It is one of the important topics that we will cover in a later chapter as to just how much and what kind of conflict is warranted in relation to asserting goals against opposing values.)

According to the principles proposed in the course of this work, what we ought to end up seeking by the use of power in political situations, therefore, will be concrete freedom for all individuals (not just equality, although the concepts are related). This is not to speak of ontological freedom, which is ineradicably present for everyone to begin with; as a political goal, we seek to expand concrete freedom, the ability of humans to pursue goals without encountering untoward or artificial social obstacles.

There are always barriers to goals, of course: success in the field of medicine requires considerable intellectual effort. The remediable barriers to a successful pursuit of a medical career consist of the money and social freedom necessary to pursue the goal, as well as the requisite intelligence and will. Social obstacles include restrictions on acceptance into medical school by race or sex. There are also restrictions based on grades, hence, to some degree, on intelligence, but it is assumed that restrictions of this type are germane to the successful pursuit of a medical education.

It is also a remediable social barrier that a young person may not have enough money to pursue the many years of education required for a medical career, and, in spite of a willingness to sacrifice, may find the avenue to a medical career closed. Inadequate elementary and high school education, whereby it is possible to progress through 12 grades without learning to read or write, is also a remediable but recalcitrant social barrier. To reduce remediable barriers in the way of constructive careers to a minimum is an important and possible ethical and moral political aim. It is also obvious that there will be social barriers erected against certain other goals, in particular, those goals that erode the freedom of others. Society can seek to maximize concrete freedom; an orderly society, however, can never admit the total freedom of all persons for whatever goals they may choose to pursue. Even a "free society" will produce Freud's discontents.

According as our values are life-asserting, we will also be in conflict with projects that, as we evaluate goals, are destructive, and in this confrontation, we will engage against their realization. Some of these destructive projects will contain as their aim, or subsidiary to their end, reducing people to objects. Some will reduce the potential complexity of the in-itself. But, despite a righteous intolerance and active opposition toward certain social goals, our chief goal in society ought to be to achieve a society in which opportunities are widely available to all individuals, and where the political system is open to the pursuit of innumerable ethical projects.

This is the crucial political goal that rests logically on the fundamental projects we have earlier proposed. This is the political end called for by authenticity and justice. This is the criterion that allows us to judge some polities as better than others. In seeking the goal of a free society, we will play out roles in two differing arenas, where two different political situations will be encountered: the domestic arena and the international arena. Both of these arenas will be treated in separate chapters.

It is important to understand that our distinctly political goals are to expand the alternatives available to others as well as ourselves, that is, if morality is taken seriously into account. It is not the happiness of these others that we ought to seek to further, for that is their business and is dependent on their ethical value-structure, nor is it their "goodness," but it is their concrete freedom to posit and follow their own ethical bent.

There is a peculiar problem related to popular culture here, including television and sports. It is related to Heidegger's discussion of Das Man; whether to work to banish the "trivial" in our culture; to move against kitsch. It would be too puritanical to banish football, baseball, the Marx Brothers, Wodehouse or Sherlock Holmes from society, and that is not the intent of this aside. However, popular culture has the ability to soak up our projects, as it were, leaving us passive and personally unengaged in the world. A person who views television 60 hours a week experiences the world of politics only vicariously. His or her projects are vitiated.

While movies such as *Becket* or a play such as *Henry V* are calculated to open new vistas to us and to point to the possibilities of transcending situations, most popular culture leaves its consumers unmotivated and unenlightened. This is the crucial difference between great literature and so-called popular culture. Sartre conducts an illuminating discussion of the problem in his *Critique* in connection with his concept of serialization.

The appropriate view, it seems to me, on the basis of the concepts of equality and freedom, is to leave the "high" culture open and accessible to all; for the rest, cultural matters must be left to survive on their own merits. No violent crusades are warranted to preserve quality in culture, although complete agnosticism is unadvisable. The criteria of culture is similar to that of good politics, namely, the values that it propagates. Unfortunately, some of what is regarded as high culture is accessible only with effort; kitsch is generally accessible with little effort. Whether that effort is expended or not depends on the socialization structures that include the family and the schools.

To commit oneself to political goals is an individual decision, whether to join a party or a movement or to propose change as a lone actor. And in making such a commitment, it ought to be acknowledged that it is a free choice for which we bear responsibility. Now if we are to have the power to realize goals, we will most likely want to join others who seek the same goals. Assuming that among the political ends we seek for ourselves and others will be justice, individual rights, and concrete freedom, it makes a difference what kind of a movement we join in order to bring such goals into existence. A genuine commitment to freedom requires that we engage the political situation through movements that allow us to retain our own freedom. The surrender to a movement that requires blind faith and stifles lucidity, movements of fascism, communist vanguards, and racist groups suppress individuality--they are means that are contrary to an expansion of human freedom, whatever other goals they may propose.[12]

Therefore, they are not likely to expand freedom when they have gained the power they seek to affect the political system. The means adopted to gain the end of political freedom affect that end. Although Marxism is aimed toward the goal of a classless society, the means of the vanguard party, as enunciated in Lenin's *What Is To Be Done?* are hardly appropriate to bring it about. Indeed, the Menshevik Martov warned Lenin about this. If ends are intended to expand human freedom, care must be taken that the means employed recognize justice and equality and other persons as significant ends, insofar as is consonant with the prudent use of power. Insofar as it is possible, there must be guarantees of projected political aims through the activities that are adopted here and now.

If these minimal moral values are violated, if others are manipulated by the use of deceptive united fronts, then the goal will inevitably become contaminated by these means. One has to agree with Ellul, "You can't fashion a just society using unjust means."[13] Saint Thomas Aquinas, too, speaks of means as "proximate ends, which enter into the end sought. . . ."[14] Commitment, therefore, must be made lucidly and responsibly and ought to include a due regard for others at all stages of the pursuit of goals, some degree of empathy toward other consciousnesses, and a due regard to means as well as to ends. With Aristotle, it may be argued that

> All men's well-being depends on two things; one is the right choice of target, or the end to which actions should tend, the other is finding the actions that lead to that end.[15]

One of the most germane debates on this issue was argued between Trotsky and John Dewey, a debate to which we have already referred. Trotsky's view was that scientific analysis, dialectical materialism, revealed the process through which the Communist society would be ultimately established. Since the end was good, and it was presumably consonant with the historical process of change, the means were therefore established by the end, namely, those means which could effectively bring about the proletarian revolution, which would place society on the correct path toward the classless society and the abolition of exploitation and alienation. The heady goal of the Marxist utopia need not necessarily condone immorality, although compared to more limited goals, it is far more likely to engender the propensity to treat other persons as objects. It does, for example, limit the use of violence--the original doctrine of Marxism did not condone random assassinations, for instance, and Marx carried on a vituperative argument with anarchists like Bakunin on this very issue.

Dewey, however, made a number of telling points in his critique of Trotsky's presentation. In particular, he criticized the Marxists for not examining *all* means that are likely to attain their end--there is a fixed preconception in Marxism that the end *must* be attained in a particular way.[16] In fact, however, the means cannot be simply deduced from the ends sought by the Marxists. Rather, Dewey, following pragmatism, recommended that the means must be chosen through an inductive examination of means-consequences, that is, he posited a genuine interdependence of means and ends, where class struggle may turn out to be a possible project to the goal, but other means may emerge as even more efficacious, or, if not more efficacious, at least appropriately effective and less destructive.

Class struggle may be conducted in many ways. History is relevant in this analysis, but Dewey disavowed that there is any *fixed law* of social development. Above all, Dewey criticized orthodox Marxism for the view that it "shares with orthodox religions and with traditional idealism, the belief that human ends are interwoven into the very texture and structure of existence...." Indeed, Communism is much more a matter of faith than a matter of scientific analysis, and it is obviously dependent on the assumption that essence precedes existence. (For which reason, in particular, it is curious that Sartre found in Marxism the significant doctrine of the 20th century.)

In his remarkable defense of Trotsky's position, Novack claimed that Dewey's criticism was unfounded, for the laws to which Trotsky and other Marxists refer are not imposed upon society by the Marxists, but rather, "had been drawn from a prior comprehensive study of social processes over many generations by strictly scientific methods." There is some merit to this argument, of course, and Marx was a significant if sometimes dubious scholar of society, but Novack's conviction violates the tentative quality of all social knowledge.

In his introduction to the *Critique*, and omitting any painstaking scientific research of his own, Marxism was accepted whole by Sartre. Indeed, Sartre once criticized a person for resigning from the Communist Party (because of the Hitler-Stalin pact of 1939) on the grounds that "it has driven him out of history. He no longer has any agency through which to help change the world..."[17] Preposterous statements like this mark Sartre's not infrequent descent into the "spirit of seriousness," his unexpected blind devotion to dogmatisms and violent causes.[18]

Revolutionary doctrines were Sartre's bad faith. In common with many intellectuals, his efforts at developing authentic political projects seem strained and self-conscious. He resembles a shy person trying desparately to be extroverted. Yet, while his foibles may deserve some sympathy, the genuine damage that may have resulted from his awkward projects in the political world cannot be ignored. On the one hand capable of brilliant commentary, as in the play *Dirty Hands*, he is found on the other hand an apologist for Mao's energetic social engineering.

Politically, we seek active projects to bring about our ends, and in acting within the arena of power and conflict, we are apt from time to time to violate our own principles of morality. With Kant, we are unable to treat people as ends only. While we may avoid lying to persons in domestic politics, where honesty is owed to others bound together in a social contract supporting certain minimal political rules of due process, honesty at all costs may be foolish in international affairs. In that arena, the lack of accepted due process except by persuasion (successful when mutual interests exist) or coercion renders ties to other persons uncertain. By lying, as Kant recognized, we deprive another person of the ability to form behavior on a true basis; that person is therefore being used as a means. Yet, we sometimes will engage in such short-term immorality, in particular in international situations, in view of the predictable consequences of practicing truthfulness. Faced with a seeming necessity, therefore, to violate the purity of our good intentions, we may be seduced, wrongly, to a policy of abstention. Abstention, too, it is clear, has its consequences. We are responsible for the consequences of a life of passivity, "for to refuse to act is to support by default those things which one might have prevented . . . ."[19]

In his idiosyncratic approach to this problem, Sartre has Mathieu commit a crime in *Age of Reason*, drawing the philosophical lesson from this incident that a crime, a tangible deed in the world, is at the least the potential beginning of a committed life. Mathieu has begun to have political projects.

> Consciousness *must incur guilt* in order to overcome its paralysis. Before he committed his crime, Mathieu was even reproached *because he was to blame for nothing*. . . .Consciousness is no longer wholly transcendent, it has entered the world and has *made history*.[20]

The lesson, though oddly illustrated, is nonetheless well put; to exist, to become at last a person who chooses to exist, is to accept the risks and the "dirty hands" of engagement in the world; and in the world of international politics, acts must sometimes be done that may indeed be taken to be crimes against morality, at least in the short term.[21]

It is also true that the farmer who builds a chicken coop, or the bureaucrat who, in the face of intimidating red tape, succeeds in having a playground erected (as in the Japanese film *Ikiru*), that these actors have also entered history; for acts need not be world-shaking to be humanly significant. Too great a propensity toward the dramatic act is, in many instances, the reason that intellectuals have tended to recommend violence. The meaningful small activities of everyday bureaucracy, which are sometimes effective and constructive, are well beneath the notice of world-shaking intellectuals. In any case, to desist from political action also is not to escape from the stigma of injustice, for we are also responsible for what we might have prevented.

Engagement through various projects is what constitutes a person as human. Through engagement within the world we transcend the situations before us by imagining that they might be different. Engagement brings us into contact and communication with others, through conflict and trust, loyalty and hatred.[22] Manser supposes that there might be produced machines that could respond to colors presented to them by formulating words to describe those colors. The machine would not really be saying anything; it would not be making a statement, for it would have no point in uttering these words.[23] Machines can determine no projects of their own; it is human others who build projects into machines. Our projects in the world make us human, for once having chosen to assert life, it is human to project values onto the world.

For the same reason, we may seek to transcend the everyday world of gossip, where we would soon be bereft of meaningful projects and our engagement with the world would be enfeebled. Aristotle noted that the life of action, of self-imposed tasks, was what raised mankind above the vegetable or animal world. This attitude marked the Greek concept of leisure; leisure to the Greek philosophers was not relaxation, but significant activity.

Thus, a life of practical activity is necessary to be fully human; contemplation alone does not suffice, nor do many leisure activities in the usual modern sense.[24] This is what Aristotle had in mind by stating that persons are not fully human except in society. Hence, there is a human need for projects, engagement, and commitments. Rawls, citing Royce, puts this point succinctly:

> ... a person may be regarded as a human life lived according to a plan. For Royce, an individual says who he is by describing his purposes and causes, what he intends to do in his life."[25]

And this is also Marx's lesson concerning the merger of theory and practice, as paraphrased by Lukacs,

> Knowledge that counts must be more than abstract knowledge of conditions inside our head. It must be "practical critical activity".[26]

It is here that existentialism, Marxism, and pragmatism come together in agreement, for all these views are philosophies of commitment and action. Compare to Lukacs' comment, Sartre's

> Man is nothing else but what he purposes, he exists only in so far as he realizes himself, he is therefore nothing else but the sum of his actions. . . .[27]

It is this position that so recommended Sartre to younger Communist intellectuals, namely, his notion of engagement.[28] We may also note the same of William James, who emphasized the immediacy of experience and *the union of thought and action*.[29]

An important consideration if we intend to take a position of lucidity in the face of the world is to examine not only the situation but the predictable consequences that arise from projects. We noted that lucidity requires a weighing of consequences, contrary to the deontological view, which was rejected, that there are some things that must be done regardless of the consequences. Once more, Kant epitomizes the view we reject:

> A good will is not good because of what it effects or accomplishes—because of its fitness for attaining some proposed ends: it is good through its willing alone—that is, good in itself.[30]

In fact, we accept that both intention and consequences are significant in any full view of morality or ethical valuation. Of course, one can exaggerate either consequences or intent. Under Stalin, any economic failure was viewed by consequence alone, so a project of economic development that went awry was proof that those in charge were guilty of sabotage.[31] Both intent and consequence is of significance in morality, and in addition it is required for authentic acts in the world that the actors must weigh causes and effects, and must make all reasonable efforts in their power to predict outcomes.

This is why the orthodox Marxists were more admirable than the rebels of the 1960s, for at their best they expended considerable intellectual efforts in an analysis of society, while many persons in the New Left were derelict in any effort to make a connection between their acts and consequences in the world. The neglect of social analysis and the assessment of consequences is responsible for such inane statements as Marcuse's "In fact, only revolution can change history."[32] Perhaps the reason certain intellectual fads such as deconstructionism became potent in the 1980s is that these exonerate adherents from serious efforts to understand texts and analyze society. Laziness and a lack of attention to details can find thereby an impressive intellectual vindication.

When we judge an action, then, to be a right action on the basis of its intended consequences,

> ...we are judging that it is such as a man will perform who desires to produce certain results which he believes to be good results, who is qualified by native endowment, by training and by education to make a reasonably accurate estimate of what the results of the action are likely to be, and, we must add, who takes the trouble to obtain all the data, or as many of them as are available, which are relevant to the making of such an estimate."[33]

Again, it is required that ethical judgement pay heed to the intent, or we may not have a full picture of whether an agent's action is a good one or simply an accident.[34] There are many cases, as well, when we might exonerate an agent, or mitigate a condemnation, because conditions may be particularly recalcitrant, the effect of the practico-inert devious, so that the intended consequences become perverted from the original intention, a result referred to by Sartre as counter-finality.

A later chapter will show how some persons and groups may be particularly vulnerable to having their projects diverted from the intended goal, stolen from them, as it were. But the mitigation of moral blame is possible only if the actor can be shown to have made an effort to assess the probable consequences of the act. The ability of situations to rob projects of significance is dramatized in Hemingway's *For Whom the Bell Tolls*, where the actors in a Spanish Civil War situation act out a project that the total situation has drained of all purpose. The poignancy of political projects in their great complexity is that we are often unable to encompass all the factors that affect and misdirect our efforts in the world.

So, an action

> necessarily sets on foot a chain of consequences. And because this external world is the sphere of contingency and unreason, I cannot foresee all the consequences of my act.... Then, the right of the subject...is that the subject should be held *responsible* only for what is in his *purpose*.[35]

But this Hegelian position is acceptable only given that the actor exercised lucidity to the best of his or her capability; and in fact, for Hegel, "purpose" includes all the necessary consequences of an act.

We may, in fact, depart essentially from the Sartrean vision of the project as pursued in the world through the unreflective consciousness, since responsibility for consequences calls for an alliance with the reflective consciousness which exercises lucidity. If consequences were the result of an unreflective consciousness pursuing its fundamental project through the world, responsibility would be attributable to the actor only in the same way that a materialist might assign responsibility to object-man.[36] Reflective consciousness at some junctures of activity is necessary to human projects.

In any case, it is partly on the basis of consequences that we weigh the goals of Marxism/Leninism, of nationalist liberation movements, and of capitalist imperialism. How could Novack undertake a defense of the class struggle leading to good results, when in 1965 the sole examples were the former USSR, Mao's China, and the East European totalitarian regimes? And in 1989, these regimes collapsed completely. Nicolae Ceausescu left Romania as a final parting gift from his version of Leninism/Stalinism, with violence and more mass graves. Other regimes went out with more dignity, leaving a legacy, albeit, of economic stagnation, corruption, and environmental destruction.

And was this why we ought to have supported revolutions? Was this the message of historical materialism as Novack reads it? Was it for this that Marxism ought to have been the significant doctrine of the 20th century? Still, the responsibility for consequences is not unlimited. In general it is related to those consequences we ought to have been able to predict.

This does not go as far in some ways as to include even all of the immediate consequences of an act, but it does include some subtle considerations. For example, as Thompson shows,

> To reject a plea of ignorance, we do not have to show that an official should have foreseen the specific act of some particular official (for example, that an aide would misinterpret an order in exactly this way). It is sufficient that the official should have realized that mistakes of the kind that occurred were likely.[37]

Among foreseeable consequences of this kind might be the lucid understanding of the dangers of loose talk: For example, the propaganda during the 1952 political campaign advocating the liberation of the East European satellites, "rolling back the Iron Curtain," was really intended solely for domestic consumption and was not directed toward any tangible efforts overseas that the United States intended to support; but it was also taken literally abroad and contributed to the futile revolt in

Hungary in 1956, a bloody revolt in which the United States stood aside.[38]

In the aftermath of the Gulf war in 1991, President Bush recommended that Saddam Hussein be overthrown by his own people, which probably contributed to the risings against the Baath regime that were put down with ruthless ferocity. It was probably unclear to the participants in these revolts that the United States intended to provide them no aid whatever. This is the type of consequence stemming from positions taken publicly in the world that are in a broad sense foreseeable and for which we are, therefore, responsible.

But we can never know all the consequences of political actions, ever, and the full meaning of our projects will never be known to us but "only to the backward glance of the historian who himself does not act."[39] President Carter's pursuit of human rights in Iran under the Shah contributed to the advent of the Khomeini regime, which by 1982 accounted for many of the world's most heinous human rights violations. Carter's responsibility in this case is mitigated by the lack of knowledge concerning the Ayatolla, for the CIA did not perform its informative function effectively. It is also typical of the immense complexity of foreign affairs, generally, that predictions are peculiarly difficult.

Thus, consequences must be taken into account. If we have been active in promoting the campaign against Salvadore Allende in Chile, we bear responsibility for the slaying and tortures that accompanied the rise of General Pinochet, even if that was not the intended result. If we supported the Khmer Rouge guerrillas in Cambodia, even indirectly by providing materiel to alternative groups, we may not avoid implication in the terrible consequences of that regime.

Above all, we are additionally required to be witnesses to these consequences. As actors, we are simultaneously witnesses to our actions. To ignore consequences is to remain, in the worst possible sense, in a condition of bad faith. Conscience is the human attribute lacking when we refuse to witness the consequences of political projects. Silence can also be an outrageous lie.

Notes

1. Joseph Cropsey, "Liberalism, Nature and Convention," *Independent Journal of Philosophy*, Vol. IV (1983), 23.
2. Ludwig Feuerbach, *The Essence of Christianity* (New York: Harper and Row, 1957), p. 64. This is one source of Marx's famous merger of theory with practice.

3. H. A. Prichard, "Does Moral Philosophy Rest on a Mistake?", p. 410, In Pahel and Schiller, eds., *Readings in Contemporary Ethical Theory*, originally published in *Mind*, XXI, 1912. Arthur N. Prior, *Logic and the Basis of Ethics* (Oxford, at the Clarendon Press, 1949), p. 4, relates the argument to Mandeville, who held the view that virtue was not only not in my self-interest, but not in anyone else's either. The gist of this view is quite acceptable to the doctrine of project, except that ethically, virtue is *not* related, as Mandeville defined it, to self-denial. Sartre posits a fundamental project which we are. This is the original choice, made in childhood in many cases, that constitutes a basic relationship to being. It is above all a choice to become being-in-itself-for-itself, which Sartre regards as futile (hence, the "useless passion"). See Benjamin Suhl, *Jean-Paul Sartre: The Philosopher as a Literary Critic* (New York: Columbia University Press, 1970), p. 120. In the ethical propositions I have proposed as prior projects, the choice to exist is a basic one, although this is not what Sartre had in mind. His original project unifies all our other projects in the world into an ensemble of projects which we are. Anguish alerts us to the possibility of changing this fundamental project, which can occur in a radical self-transformation, a conversion. Although Jeanson suggests that we from time to time may abandon the unreflective plane of consciousness and adopt a reflective view, at which point we may even devise projects that contradict the fundamental choice we have made, these projects will be hypocritical, out of character, and in bad faith. We have chosen to defer any conclusions on this fundamental project, the basis for existentialist psychoanalysis. Sartre builds some controversial portraits of Jean Genet and Baudelaire on the idea of fundamental choice. But, except for the choice to exist or not, our doctrine of projects, although associated with a unified personality, will lean instead on Merleau-Ponty's view of the existence of a "natural self." See for discussions of the fundamental project, Sonia Kruks, *The Political Philosophy of Merleau-Ponty* (New Jersey: The Humanities Press, 1981), p. 23, fn 5; Barnes, *The Literature of Possibility*, p. 281; Jeanson, *Sartre and the Problem of Morality*, p. 178; and Sartre's own works on Baudelaire and Genet.

4. Hans J. Morgenthau, *Dilemmas of Politics* (Chicago: University of Chicago Press, 1958), p. 240.
5. Cropsey, "Liberalism, Nature and Convention," p. 23.
6. Frost, *Towards a Normative Theory of International Relations* (Cambridge: Cambridge University Press, 1986), p. 71.
7. Phares, *Locus of Control in Personality*, pp. 102-103. This empirical study touchs on much that we say here. A related concept to internal/external control is self-esteem. The decision to engage in the world to realize projects has something to do with a person's self-esteem. See Victor Gecas and Michael L. Schwalbe, "Beyond the Looking-Glass Self: Social Structure and Efficacy-Based Self-Esteem," *Social Psychology Quarterly*, Vol. 46, No. 2 (June 1983), 77-88.

8. For some corrective comments, however, on Nietzsche's doctrine of power, see Robert B. Pippin, "Commentary Notes on Nietzsche's Modernism," *Independent Journal of Philosophy*, Vol. IV (1983), p. 15.
9. Schneck, *Person and Polis*, p. 88.
10. Richard W. Sterling, *Ethics in a World Of Power: The Political Ideas of Friedrich Meinecke* (New Jersey: Princeton University Press, 1958, p. 61.
11. Kenneth W. Thompson, *Ethics and National Purpose* (New York: The Council on Religion and International Affairs, 1957), p. 14.
12. Barnes, *Existentialist Ethics*, p. 93.
13. In Patrick Chastenet, "An Interview with Jacques Ellul: Socialism Yes, But Not Just Any Kind Will Do," *The Guardian*, November 15. 1981, p. 14.
14. Fletcher, *Situation Ethics*, p. 121.
15. Aristotle, *Politics*, Book VII, 13, p. 282.
16. The entire debate is in Trotsky, Dewey, and Novack, *Their Morals and Ours*. See in particular for this section, pp. 70-71, p. 73, and p. 81.
17. McMahon, *Humans Being*, p. 141.
18. On this concept, see de Beauvoir, *The Ethics of Ambiguity*, pp. 89-90; Barnes, *Existentialist Ethics*, p. 299. By proposing certain ethical principles and rules concerning morality, we have ourselves fallen into the "spirit of seriousness"; indeed, it is probably impossible not to when presenting a work in ethics.
19. Barnes, *Existentialist Ethics*, pp. 92-93.
20. King, *Sartre and the Sacred*, p. 161.
21. It ought to be clear, that in a morality of consequences, immorality judged in the short run ought to be intended as morality in the long run. Herein is the danger of this doctrine, however, and another reason to eschew dogmatism, for we can never be fully certain how events may work out in the long run. We can only do our best.
22. Macquarrie, *Existentialism*, p. 185.
23. Manser, *Sartre*, p. 110.
24. Renford Bambrough, *Moral Scepticism and Moral Knowledge* (Atlantic Highlands: Humanities Press, 1979), p. 149.
25. John Rawls, *A Theory of Justice* (Cambridge, MA: Harvard University Press, 1971), p. 408.
26. Georg Lukacs, *History and Class Consciousness* (Trans. by Rodney Livingstone. Cambridge, MA: The MIT Press, 1971), p. 262.
27. Sartre, "Existentialism is a Humanism," p. 300.
28. Poster, *Existential Marxism in Postwar France*, p. 111.
29. Stroh, *American Ethical Thought*, pp. 99-100.
30. Kant, *Groundwork of the Metaphysics of Morals* (Trans. by H. L. Paton. New York: Harper Torch Boods, 1964), p. 62. See also Mackie, *Ethics*, p. 154.
31. Sidney Hook, *Philosophy and Public Policy*, p. 120.

32. Marcuse, "Contributions to a Phenomenology of Historical Materialism," p.
34. Surely Marcuse knows more history than that.
33. Joad, *Guide to Morals and Politics*, , p. 219.
34. Hartmann, *Ethics*, Vol. II, p. 401.
35. Stace, *The Philosophy of Hegel* (New York: Dover Publications, 1955), pp. 397-398. This entire section in Stace is of interest.
36. Sartre, *Being and Nothingness*, p. 471.
37. Thompson, "Moral Responsibility of Public Officials . . ." p. 913.
38. Lefever, *Ethics and United States Foreign Policy*, p. 41.
39. Hannah Arendt, *The Human Condition* (Chicago: The University of Chicago Press, 1958), p. 233.

Chapter 10

The Nation

Part I. A Core of Values

In our definition of morality we proposed that among ethical projects, morality held a subordinate, albeit important, place. We regarded it as a minimal value, giving due recognition to others as independent origins of consciousness, while pursuing our more prominent ethical values. This due recognition was socially translated into what is commonly referred to as justice, and, unlike Plato, we regard justice as giving everyone their due regard as conscious persons.

Equality is a logical extension of this idea. To be sure, every subject may be equally treated in a totalitarian system, but this is not our meaning, because due regard for conscious beings, capable of free projects, requires an equality on a more elevated level. Additionally, due regard for persons, stemming from the doctrine of equality, demands adherence to other human rights.

The existentialist critique of justice and rights had some merit, in our opinion, for pointing out that equality, justice, and rights become part of the practico-inert, the in-itself of society, laws, and institutions, and, as such, were external rules interfering with free choice. Ricouer criticizes that

> segment of modern literature [which makes] it appear that to appeal to values which the mind recognizes rather than institutes would be the

principle of alienation. Freedom then can appear only as a rupture of all nascent fidelity to the the point of indignation and revolt....[1]

The individual, in our interpretation, is wrong to revolt for the sake of revolt, and it is unnecessary to disavow all ready-made values without giving these due consideration. Despite the danger of falling into a "spirit of seriousness," the doctrine of justice was recommended to our free choice as productive of better consequences than its omission. From time to time in history, particularly where justice is lacking, it re-emerges as a controversial and living doctrine. It is most viable where it is missed. Moreover, an ethical being pursuing existence can elect to freely adhere to the minimum requirements of justice, to freely accept external rules. Not to do so would be immediately to renounce any effort to expand freedom for all and to reject the minimal condition of a civil society. To opt for extant values after lucid consideration is not automatic bad faith.

Now these minimal requirements of justice are embodied, if they are to be found anywhere, generally in congeries of institutions we designate as nations, and international relations is the interaction among nations and other such aggregate groups, such as corporations, terrorist organizations and international institutions. The compelling subject of this chapter therefore, will be to examine what loyalty, if any, is owed to an institution such as the nation.

Marx and his successors, of course, were quite clear that the ties of a proletarian to the class superseded those owed to the nation. Marx was also shrewdly aware of the attitude toward the nation of some business persons, willing to sell arms to national enemies for profit. The chief good of the capitalist is profit; if there are additional loyalties to which entrepreneurs adhere, these are in addition to those of the economic system and do not logically follow from the working of that system.

The doctrine that the proletariat had no state, but had more in common with the proletariat of other nations, was the doctrine of all socialists before World War I, when national loyalties unexpectedly overwhelmed the workers of Germany, Russia, France, Austria, and England, causing the collapse of the Second International, the internationalism of which was shown to be hollow, although carried on by a small minority, such as Lenin, Rosa Luxemburg, Karl Liebknecht, and, in the United States, Eugene Debs. The diplomat and the political leader are situated in a role that exemplifies, above all, loyalty to the nation, that requires the furtherance specifically of the national interest.

What moral and ethical values might rationally be realized through the free choice of such a loyalty?

As one approach to this problem, we may consider the anarchist position, with which Marxism has some affinities (as well as some crucial differences). Were anarchism to prevail in the debate, the problem of nations would be resolved and we need not have to treat of the subject of this chapter, save, perhaps, to call for the worldwide and immediate abolition of nation states. The anarchists are correct in designating the nation as a source of power and coercion. Historically, all nations rise in part through violence.

The anarchists are wrong in sometimes refusing to distinguish between the nature, the purpose, and the extent of the use of force, regarding all nations as equally coercive. Earlier the point was made that there are great differences among nations in this respect, and it suggests a lack of intellectual discrimination to refuse to make distinctions between Sweden, Libya under Gadhafi, North Korea with its cult of Kim Il-sung, Great Britain, Kuwait, and Iraq under Saddam Hussein. The anarchist is wrong to make no discriminations among states, for it is obvious that some states are more oppressive than others. This is the fundamental anarchist fallacy.

Assuming that the anarchist is brought to admit differences among states, the argument that all states to a degree are repressive *is* sound, for that is what the state is about, and that states are based on the use of force is admitted by all social contract theorists. But social contract theorists like Hobbes and Locke would have the original contract bring rational people first into a society, so that society, in the first instance, is the repository of power and the use of force. Normally, the anarchist neglects the potentially repressive nature of society itself; whether such power is eventually delegated to a government or not, it is still inherent in society.

With relation to the concrete freedom of the individual, there may be no more oppressive societies than some of those that operate without an evident state structure; in the unsophisticated past, these were referred to as primitive societies, the primitive communism of which Marx speaks. From our viewpoint, it is notable that the individual may be completely submerged in the *Gemeinschaft* (community), or mechanical society, by comparison to the emergence of individuals in the *Gesellschaft* (society), or organic societies.[2]

The distinction is particularly important to the existentialist view, because empirical research shows that children from many non-Western societies do not evince the decline of the externalized orientation of moral judgment; that is, they continue to make moral judgments solely on the basis of extant social rules. They do not develop the tendency of members of the *Gesellschaft* groups to take an internalized orientation to morality, that is, to develop a personal morality that is to a degree divorced from external rules.

In the Sartrean view, they continue to exist in bad faith; it is the development of society beyond the level of the *Gemeinschaft* that makes it possible to consider escaping bad faith. In an organic society, it is more possible for individuals to oppose segregation, even if segregation is the law and required by the prevailing social mores.[3] In any case, whether constituted within a state or in a society, power is a fact of life when there are competing ethical projects or subjects to be instilled with loyalty to the group. Indeed, the class that will, according to the dictates of history as interpreted by some historicists, command the loyalties of the workers will demand and enforce the greatest loyalty to its aims, realizing the repressive dictatorship of the proletariat.

The non-national fused groups treated by Sartre in his *Critique*, through terror over their membership, exercise extreme coercion. The new Irish Republican Army is just such a fused group, and it has always enforced its doctrine with the utmost severity. Although not accepting the terrorist techniques of the Baader-Meinhof anarchist group, the editors of *Freedom*, the anarchist journal founded by Prince Peter Kropotkin in Great Britain, did exonerate their actions to a degree in the face of what they regarded as the greater force exercised by the state.

Nevertheless, the anarchists are ultimately wrong to attribute the use of force to the state only, and to propose, futilely, that groups, even pacifist groups, will by displacing the state, establish a society that will dispense with the exercise of power. All groups exercise power and coercion, a number of them to a far greater extent than the states they aim to replace. Of course, any nation that must be held together by force alone will be a nation lacking any form of a social contract. The foundation for the social contract assures that force is a last resort only.

Another anarchist argument, which deserves some consideration, is that people are "by nature" (hence, for many anarchists, accepting that "essence precedes existence") cooperative, and it is the state that makes some of them perverse and dangerous to others. This Rousseauean doctrine has been the stimulus for establishing innumerable cooperative groups and communes, all of these more or less failures. Of course, we may not ignore the arguments of Robert Owen and others that the cause of failure was the lack of education (socialization) into natural cooperative behavior, for the members of cooperative societies bring into them the competitive mores of the previous society. Many small groups find it impossible to survive the intrusion of the larger society. Yet, some groups have succeeded for long periods, and these have generally been those infused with religious or ideological unity, and as a result, they have inhibited concrete freedom as much or more than the greater society.

Admirable for courage, intentions, and devotion to an ethical cause as individual anarchists may be, their goal is a chimera. Their search for a society that need not exercise power is doomed to fail. We must return to the social contract theorists to determine for what purpose they believed states were formed; in their presentations of why societies might have originated, they make good sense.

The democratic John Locke and even the absolutist Thomas Hobbes were convinced that the establishment of the state, the second step following the formation of society out of the "state of nature," was intended to preserve some minimum level of justice, equality, and (for Locke) human rights. For any of these to exist, it may not be necessary to state, security is a basic contribution of the state. It is the state to which is delegated the task of enforcing a minimal justice in the society, and, lacking the coercive state structure, how is justice to be brought about? If it is to be brought about at all, probably only by some non-state force.

The first test in assessing the value of any state is the degree to which it preserves for its citizens a basic justice, some formal equality, and certain human rights, founded on some measure of physical security. Some states perform this function so badly that they ought to be overthrown; others, faced with the overwhelming problems of scarcity and disunity, may perform better than the probable anarchic strife were state structure to exist; and a minority in the 20th century perform acceptably enough that to overthrow them would be a grave mistake.

The basic function of the state, therefore, is to preserve minimal justice and security against social groups and individual projects that would violate it. Some of the loyalty due the nation represented by a diplomat must stem from the nation's ability to realize these minimal demands of morality. No state, of course, can elicit our unstinted praise; in fact, the United States fails to afford its citizens even minimal security within many areas of its large cities, particularly at night, when sections of urban areas return to the state of nature.

However, as a rule, the nation signifies much more than an institution to preserve a minimal degree of justice. Nations have come into existence as the active project of many persons, and it rests on projects that concern a common history, religion, language, an economy, in short, all of those qualities that comprise the topic of nation-building. Frost rightly claims that a

> state is not a political reality that exists independently of the ideas and norms which people adhere to. Amongst other things the existence of a state always implies the existence of a large groups of people who are in some way bound together, in large part, by a set of normative commitments and obligations.[4]

These attributes, as they contribute to the development of the nation-state, are the subject of Karl Deutsch's research into nation building, the security community.[5]

The topic of nation-building has a direct relationship to the doctrine of the social contract. In fact, most social contract theorists seem to have taken much for granted as they propose the motivations that cause people to gather into societies and to establish government. It is generally held that the social contract is a rational agreement for those in the hypothetical "state of nature" wanting to ensure security (Hobbes) or additional values such as liberties and property rights (Locke). But it is often neglected to note that such agreement also requires a degree of preliminary trust, and trust rests on a basis of some minimum of shared values ensuring predictability among people.

Thus, most social contract theories are too abstract, for they ignore the factors that are preliminary to forming a society, namely, all of those factors that lead to the modicum of trust that is necessary for society to hold together. Even John Rawls overlooks these bases in his initial standpoint of the veil of ignorance. Granted that there have been social groupings in the past that have adhered through coercion alone: That is, there have been "societies" lacking a social contract. There have also been groups within societies not a part of the social contract, as the slaves within Greek city-states, who lacked the dignity of citizenship.

But social contract theory demands, if it does not remain entirely abstract, that there be some preliminary attributes of social cohesion prior to the contract, which will support a society. That is, for a society to be formed under the principles of social contract, and for the social contract to remain viable for any society, demands a basic trust between the members of society, and that basic trust rests on a vital core of shared values. Societies, therefore, are affected by centrifugal and centripetal forces. If the former are too powerful, the society loses its cohesion: The values shared are not strong or numerous enough to bind people into a coherent society.

The Yugoslav state was experiencing such problems in 1991. If the latter forces are too powerful, the social grouping suppresses all individuality. Thus, like organisms in nature, the social group, the nation, is preserved, if at all, by a precarious equilibrium of contending forces. In the case of the former Soviet Union in the early 1990s, we observe that centrifugal forces in many of the republics have become very strong. In republics such as Estonia, Latvia, and Lithuania, the mutual values and trust could hardly have been developed following the forcible incorporation of these areas by Stalin in 1940 and the ensuing decades of totalitarian suppression.

In Nazi Germany in the 1930s, the social contract abruptly changed and ceased to include former members of German society, most significantly, of course, the Jews. In the difficult decades of newly secured independence, African nations frequently experienced bloody internal strife between groups for whom no common social contract appeared possible. Indeed, despite many values that ought to have preserved the union, the United States also fought a bloody civil war to enforce its own national unity.

The United States has peculiar problems of preserving a social contract, for the reason that it is composed of numerous ethnic and racial groups. There is a constant tendency in such a society for the centrifugal forces to overwhelm the centripetal tendencies. By the 1980s one battlefield of the social contract was the core curriculum of the schools and universities, which became a subject of bitter controversy. Founded on the principles of a Western heritage that was rooted in ancient Greece, Palestine, and the Mediterranean littoral, this tradition has much to recommend it, and in the conditions that gave rise to these traditions, much to regret.

But this is the core, and the values contained in the tradition, at their best, are not racial doctrines, are not gender-related doctrines; rather, they are values that transcend time and place. With a core structure of such values, other values may be adapted to the framework through cultural accretion, so that a parochial vision can expand to embrace the universal values that have arisen in India, China, the Arab areas (already strongly embued with the same core structure), and other cultural centers of the world.

The Western tradition has shown increasingly a remarkable ability to absorb the virtues of other and alien societies: In the 18th century, the Enlightenment was quite open to new sources of bureaucratic knowledge from China; in the 19th century, the first translations of the Vedas of the Uphanishads appeared in Europe, and Schopenhauer found them in some ways compatible with his own doctrine of the will.

The remarkable psychology of Buddhism, a product of non-Western thought, has been compared to the depiction of the for-itself by Sartre: The point is that knowledge of Western philosophy provides a point of comparison for Eastern thought, which, without a previous mooring, would likely find no haven at all. In short, the core Western values function as an open system, in contradistinction to the closed values of many other societies. To expand them is in keeping with their spirit; to eliminate them would contribute to social disintegration.

The point is clear: A society must have a core of values, even if that core ought to be open to expansion and alteration. Indeed, all developing traditions at first try to be closed systems, impenetrable by other influences; gradually, certain traditions become more flexible, more amenable to external influences, and this has seemed to have been the case with Western tradition, which at times in past history has certainly appeared impermeable. Indeed, it is to be expected that immigrants into the United States will make contributions to the core.

The more knowledgeable an individual in the core values of Western civilization, the more open that person will be to the values of other and foreign traditions. To know Machiavelli's *The Prince*, a work that is intrinsic to Western civilization in its values and in the values it attacks, a work grounded in Plato's depiction of Thrasamachus, in Aristotle's discussion of tyranny in his *Politics*, is to more easily encounter and comprehend the political works of the Chinese Han Fei Tzu or the Indian political philosopher Kautilya. I would suspect that the Western person ignorant of Machiavelli is quite unlikely to encounter or be interested in Han Fei Tzu, in any case. To be ignorant of Machiavelli is no virtue whatever (indeed, it is also not a *virtu*).

To preach destruction of Western tradition is to preach the ultimate destruction of any tradition whatever, with the consequent nihilism that object would achieve. Ignorance of the values of one's own civilization results in a mind closed forever and completely to any other source of values. The attack on this core is sometimes misguided, sometimes malicious. Successful, it will result in a society with no foundation at all for a social contract, and the eventual dissolution of that society. Some attacks lack historical basis: It is not true that exponents of Western civilization have some form of diabolical human essence that causes them to oppress others.

It is not true that only the Third World has suffered the oppression of others. Indeed, all peoples in Europe (the East Europeans most recently) have had a history of oppression by others, and it is only ignorance of history that neglects this fact. The Belgians had to rise against the Spanish, the Spanish against the Moors, the Germans were decimated during the Thirty Years War. It is not true that the West has spared itself, somehow, the effects of oppression. It is also untrue that the West in its world imperialism, while witnessing calls on the historian to record in all its details of strife and destruction, was entering societies that were pristine utopias.

Any history of the Third World, say, the history of Southeast Asia, reveals a history full of oppression of one people by another, of imperialism and of massacre: To neglect to notice this is to be egregiously ignorant of history. Western culture does not contain particular evils; the industrial revolution and the technology that led the West to the age of "discovery" simply made the West more powerful than other areas of the world. And the development of Western tradition did not end in the fifteeth century but has continued to the present, in which some of the narrowness of the tradition has been overcome. The attack on Western tradition is misguided, insofar as that tradition remains open to change, to the contributions of recent immigrants to the United States.

Some attacks, however, seem more properly to be intent on fomenting ethnic and racial conflict.[6] Values are, indeed, always in conflict. Antonio Gramsci's concept of hegemony is based on this. For Gramsci, the proletarian revolution is the replacement of a bourgeois culture by a proletarian one; but Gramsci does not mean, with that, to disavow all the values of Italian society. That would have violated the concept of the dialectical synthesis.

The preservation, enhancement and expansion of the core of values that constitute the nation is to some degree the responsibility of intellectuals. It is also the responsibility of everyone to be witnesses to the truth, for the nation never lives up to its primary value, its *raison d'etre*--it claims to value justice and it denies one race the right to vote; or certain values within the original cultural core are deleterious to human development, to justice or equality.

It is the mark of irresponsibility for anyone to be ignorant of these values, or, in ignorance, threatening the wholesale overthrow of the values that furnish the only basis for a social contract among members of the nation. The existentialist serves the critical function of placing all values in question, but to mindlessly ignore tradition or propose its total annihilation is criminally irresponsible. Indeed, the doctrine of consequences furnishes a basis for there to be responsibility.

What are the core values of the United States? It would be too far-afield to pursue this very interesting topic. It is mentioned in Gunnar Myrdal's *The American Dilemma* as the "American Creed." Seymour Martin Lipset discusses these values in his book *The First New Nation*.[7] Hirsch undertakes to enumerate these in an empirical way, and, while occasionally amusing, his list of concepts that constitute the American tradition as it exists at present, those concepts with which any individual as a member of the national social contract ought to be familiar, is at least suggestive. Hirsch makes no pretense, of course, that these concepts are the crucial values of Western civilization: his point is that lack of familiarity with them indicates lack of familiarity with the tradition and its values as well.

Knowing the term "Plato" does not ensure that one also knows something about "justice," but it becomes somewhat more likely. Values are always, of course, in question from the point-of-view advanced here. However, it is not necessary to indulge in self-contempt, as though the United States, among a pure world of naïve and gentle altruists, were striken in its essence by evil. Let me repeat that to be open to alternative values it is necessary to stand on a firm foundation of values already assimilated and critiqued. To destroy what there is of a core of tradition in the United States is not to let in a set of new values that will somehow replace these *in toto*; rather, it is to reduce the society to its pre-social contract status, to the state of nature.   The demands of morality are in the first instance a rational conclusion based on the existence of individual loci of consciousness. There is no call here for liking our fellow humans, or even for sympathizing with them; commitment to equality and justice may be entirely a matter for lucidity. It is the existence of additional emotional ties to nation and society that may expand the reasons for commitment to justice to include additional commitments. Besides an intellectual commitment, personal, affective ties may produce an additional bond to a nation. However, despite these additional and affective ties, the commitment to justice remains essential to social existence.

Andrew suggests, and we have also remarked earlier in a similar vein, that justice is intended to treat everyone as a stranger and not as a friend.[8] This may sound harsh, but it affects the attitude of the judge before whom appears a person of a different race, class, and style of life; he ought to receive a sentence according to the law. Both Hobbes and Locke are advocates for "indifferent" judges.

Justice is the minimal projection of morality onto the polity, the result of the rational realization that since all persons are centers of independent consciousness, they are all potential contributors to the enhancement of my world, for the reason that they too can frame free projects. To paraphrase Plato, justice is the recognition of the equality of persons, whether they are "equal" or not, and that is the intended consequence of the law. (Plato, of course, found this democratic principle unpalatable.) As soon as any person or group receives treatment that is not equally accorded to others, as in the segregation laws of the United States, the dialectic of group interaction reduces that person or group eventually to a position of permanent social inferiority.

The Supreme Court decision in Brown v Board of Education in 1954 referred to a number of sociological studies showing that segregated groups inevitably become regarded and treated as inferior. Major dangers to equality and the position taken by the Court in 1954 are posed by the Ku Klux Klan, neo-Nazis and racist groups of all kinds, all of which violate the principle of equality which supports the structure of political justice.

Such attitudes should be confronted in the political system, and, for the liberal who supports the principle of free speech, there is a further responsibility involved if movements that threaten the equality and the lives of other groups are allowed freedom of speech: It follows logically that if these groups gain the degree of power necessary to put their measures into effect, the advocates of free speech who allowed them the freedom to organize and advocate must now protect the equality and lives of the endangered, even at the expense of their own lives.

If they are unwilling to do so in the event, they ought not to advocate complete freedom of speech. This responsibility, it seems to me, flows directly from the liberal doctrine of free speech. The liberal must be willing to give his or her own life to protect those who come into jeopardy as a result of the freedom afforded radical groups to organize and advocate. Or else, free speech must be rethought and perhaps limited. The liberal, above all, is committed to keeping conflict civil within a system of laws so long as justice and due process remain possible, but this tolerance of divergent views does not require acquiescence or silence. The liberal position demands a large degree of civic courage, and at times, a stance of confrontation.

To repeat a point made earlier, the rights stemming from justice do not require "love for mankind" and do not presume any well-formed concept of human dignity, beyond a minimal quality of concern. Justice is accorded to others on the basis of rationality. Dignity is a further addition accruing to some beings, according to our ethical principles, on the basis of their existence--by being there, they ought to be treated justly; by living according to values enhancing existence, they acquire dignity. This violates the Christian attitude, most cogently presented by Tinder, that by being, simply, all persons have dignity; the Sartrean position on this concept is, of course, that having such an attribute as dignity constitutes an essence that preceded existence; hence, humans do not have it.

Most societies into the 20th century had little conception of justice.[9] Indeed, until 1789, French subjects had no conception whatever that they might have any rights at all. (Is this the condition that some existentialists want to return to?) The revolutionaries attempted to convey to them a concept of rights in the new designation of persons as "citizen," in the Greek sense of people who count for something in society, who share the social contract.

Thus, a three-tier hierarchy of concern has been established. First, the choice of life over the contempt for life, requires, lucidly, a choice as well of a basic humanness with regard to all living things. Animals, which do not partake in rights, fall into this area of concern, which also includes the environment, generally. Second, the existence of human consciousness of a high order with freedom marks humans as the special recipients of justice and rights. This is otherwise a value-neutral choice; we value the innovativeness and potential contributions of free choice in a general sense. Finally, there is the matter of human dignity, or what each human makes of his or her freedom. The origin of the possibility of dignity rests ultimately on freedom, but the evaluation that assesses dignity is a judgment of how the individual has manifested his or her concept of the good life through existence.

Although agreeing with the shortcomings of rights pointed to by the existentialists that they are a set of external rules that eventually come to be petrified in the practico-inert of society, the symbology they represent is an important counterweight to the power of centralized states, and when justice is violated for too long a time, at least in those societies with some history incorporating an experience of rights, the slogans and cliches surrounding rights may quickly take on new life and meaning.

There is a real difference historically between a doctrine such as Locke's affording people rights and the right to rebel if the representatives of the state surpass their legal limitations, and a doctrine such as Hobbes' in which there is no doctrine of inalienable rights and no manifest right to revolt. Justice and rights is the foundation for any modern state capable of observing concrete human freedom.[10] Of course, rights are not embedded in human genes; we adopt the position that people have rights freely.

Justice, as we have derived it, is not accorded to institutions or groups as such--it treats of individuals rather than of aggregates. It is in individuals that consciousness resides; an institution has no group awareness, nor is it a locus for existence in a human sense. For that reason, justice is indeed a product of modern society, since in many more ancient societies there was little or no concept of the individual. The individual had no existence independent of the group. There is every historical indication that the ideal of equal rights owes some part of its development to the growth of modern capitalism. Indeed, it was associated with the right to possess private property, although as Locke and others were careful to argue, not the right to an unlimited amount of property. How much property individuals needed in order to assert their individuality, pursue their legal projects, and enjoy rights is always politically controversial.[11]

Capitalism has been criticized as an atomizing institution, reducing human beings to individuals with no ties other than the mercenary with other individuals. There is some truth to this; "economic man" is a typical capitalist construct. But on the other hand, the social reductiveness of the developing capitalist system also focused attention on individual projects (generally projects of profit accumulation), which were to be left freely-determined by the individual. In so doing, capitalism contributed to the doctrine of individual rights. Marxist criticism of Sartre's *Being and Nothingness* was on the right track: there is an emphasis on the individual consciousness in that work that owes a great deal to the development of the bourgeois doctrine of rights out of the capitalist industrial revolution. Nevertheless, the origin of a doctrine neither condemns it nor recommends it.

It should be clear that rights are protected in a technical sense by due process, the same for all. The state ought to play no favorites, and this was the basis for Hegel's questionable claim that for the reason of its supposed impartiality, the bureaucracy represented the "universal class."

The view also colored Weber's ideal type of the rational bureaucracy. Because modern economies have spawned gigantic and powerful corporations, which should probably be regarded as *social* institutions, the principle of equality in hiring and promoting ought to apply to these too.

While the idea of corporations as social institutions may be an argument for socialism, the basic doctrines of rights and justice still concern individuals, for the compelling reasons that the locus of consciousness is there, not in the class, not in the corporation, not in any group. It is true that full rights for all have not been achieved by any society, no matter how progressive, but that there are contradictions in bourgeois society is no reason to disavow its contribution to the concept of justice and to the realization of rights for some members of society, at least.

To flee these contradictions in favor of a society based on no doctrine of justice or rights has led, over and over, to disaster.[12] We are too skeptical to believe that the doctrine of justice, for all its emotional aridity, may be dispensed with in some future society where the need for it will have disappeared.[13] Both Sartre and Marx argue the origin of the concept of justice on the basis of scarcity and the opposition of interests in society, but, to cite the teachings of the Buddha, human society will most likely always be defined by scarcity, whether of tangible or intangible goods, and conflicts among ethical projects.

The doctrine of justice can create a degree of cohesion in a society, but, unlike the contract theorists, we do not agree that modern states were formed simply around a core idea of human rights. That would have been quite unlikely. There have to be other reasons for national unity, such as it is, that develop within the modern state system to contribute to social cohesion. Social contract theory touches shallowly on the origins of nations, although granted that it also contributes importantly to the doctrine of rights. The topic of national cohesion has been adumbrated in the very brief coverage of nation-building, but the topic calls for a fuller expatiation.

What ties exist that draw persons to the support of a particular polity? Where justice is the very basic relationship, lucidity prescribes between myself and others as consciousnesses, and rights form a partial argument in favor of some societies, the loyalties, if any, that I grant to a particular nation are the result of other ethical considerations--the ties to the nation are the consequent of projects I have in common with others of that society.

A society that enables me to select from a large number of alternatives, to follow my projects unimpeded by state busybodiness, so long as I observe the laws, comes to be a society in which I can observe the realization and embodiment of the values I pursue. This is never a single project, ordinarilly, but an ensemble of projects, including such goals as family life, religion, literature, physical culture, and so on. Some of my projects will be political, no doubt, such as the effort concerted with others to bring the laws into a closer semblance of justice.

For a society to draw loyalties also demands that the people comprising it be predictable. Compatibility is an element in predictability. Another ingredient in this is trust. A society is a bounded group of persons among whom I am relatively comfortable, with whom I may communicate, not in the sense that I can trust everyone in that society, but that I can predict with some assurance who can be trusted and who cannot be. This is the reason that the lawyer who steals funds from a trust, a government employee who allots public funds intended for housing to a wealthy friend, or the broker who misinvests his clients' savings recklessly are so culpable, in fact, more heinous than the urban mugger, because it is social trust and predictability that they violate; their acts have repercussions throughout the society.

In the *Leviathan,* Hobbes is quite clear about this, holding the lawbreaker who is also an official more culpable than the common citizen. At bottom, a society is a system within which I can anticipate certain fundamental mores to be observed. On this criterion, no nation measures up to the definition of a true society, although some succeed better than others. We are suggesting here, that although the *Gemeinschaft* has been abandoned at the level of the larger society (maybe retained among some subgroups), and the *Gesellschaft* has entered history, that some aspects of community must be retained at the level of the larger society to maintain national loyalties.

There are some ties that are necessary for nation-ness. The problem of South Vietnam, in part, and in the face of external dangers, was that while subgroups commanded loyalties, no ties were ever substantially developed toward the nation; that is, there was no nation to defend, and it was every person and group for themselves. In his day, Marx was quite correct in finding that the proletariat generally did not really participate in the society defined by the hegemony of bourgeois culture, for there was little to draw their loyalty to the larger society.

Yet, within the worker schools founded in Europe during the 19th century, it was the Western tradition that the proletariat undertook to learn. Milovan Djilis in his autobiographical *Land Without Justice* describes a prenational Montenegro, with few ties of trust and civil due process, in which the clan was the furthest extent of human sociability. For a nation to command any loyalties from its citizens, therefore, it must comprise, to some degree, a moral community.

The nature of the nation that arises from these considerations does not rest on the common assumption that societies must grow from integrated races or limited ethnic groups. That the origin of some nationalism does rest on particular ethnic foundations is natural enough, for the reason that common language and common history contribute to ease of communication and predictability. But where the nation is defined by race or ethnic group, the intense hostilities that often arise between ingroup and outgroup mark this form of nationalism as narrow and limiting to human experience and potential. While most nations owe something to the trust that originally rested on common ethnicity, society must also develop an ability to expand human horizons. It must grow beyond its ethnic or racial beginnings. This is why Lord Acton noted that

> A state which is incompetent to satisfy different races condemns itself; a state which labours to neutralize, to absorb, or to expel them, destroys its own vitality; a state which does not include them is destitute of the chief basis of self-government. The theory of nationalism, therefore, is a retrograde step in history.[14]

Meinecke also advocated a non-xenophobic nationalism in terms of "tolerance, its openness toward alternatives, and its capacity to absorb new experience."[15]

The United States originally developed as a nation on the basis of a British past, or, more broadly, a Western European culture. This formed the original viable core for a moral community, despite the vast expanse of the country. Through much of its history, at least in settled areas, it was possible to wander into out-of-the-way areas and feel at home. One did not feel surrounded by threat and potential malignity, or unpredictable behavior.

This sense of community, however, was not universal, indicating how far the United States has always been from comprising a moral community: Consider the plight of a black person walking through a white residential community in the 1950s. But while state entities like the former USSR, which comprise many ethnic groups, were empires, built by extending the sway of the center over other potential nations, the United States comprises many ethnic groups that are absorbed into it from the outside. The Soviet Union finally broke apart on the basis of its geographic, ethnic divisions.

More homogeneous nations, such as France, Britain, Ireland or Sweden, may have a better basis for social cohesion than the United States, which has undertaken a very risky empirical test: Whether it is possible to draw together, around its diminishing original core, innumerable representatives of many other cultures, southern Europeans, Hispanics, African-Americans, Mexicans, Vietnamese, Japanese, Germans, Iranians, and so forth, and still retain a moral community.

For the negative, there have been the racist historians, Monroe, for instance, who believe that this enterprise is doomed to fail. There is opposing evidence, on the other hand: Values that were distinctly American were held by Michael Dukakis, a son of Greek immigrants, who ran for president in 1988. A number of tests might be suggested to determine the degree to which a moral community actually exists. For instance, how many individuals cheat on their income tax? How many people without children of their own, or with children grown and out of school, willingly vote for school bonds? There are oases of retired persons who have opted out of the society, developing closed subgroups. These are the retirement colonies, that resist inroads from the greater society.

It is possible in America to wander into large areas of the cities, where threat and unpredicatability announce that one has left one society and re-entered a state of nature. Considering the fissiparous tendencies of an immigrant society such as the United States, the retention of sufficient ties to other persons within the nation needs to be an active political project.[16]

Humans strive to realize our projects, whatever they are, in a social system that supports a culture. The culture influences us to accept portions of it or to rebel against other portions, but no one is exempt from coming to terms with it. In his inimitable style, Heidegger writes,

> In terms of the "they," and as the "they," I am "given" proximally to "myself." Proximally, Dasein is "they," and for the most part it remains so. [Did you get that? Heidegger is saying that the individual imbibes the culture in which he or she lives.] If Dasein discovers the world in its own way and brings it close, if it discloses to itself its own authentic Being, then this discovery of the "world" and this disclosure of Dasein are always

accomplished as a clearing-away of concealments and obscurities, as a breaking up of the disguises with which Dasein bars its own way. [I think that this suggests that one need not disavow one's culture to remain authentic, although there are tasks to be done to maintain authenticity.][17]

Being a free individual does not require a total negation of the social, as Max Stirner advocated, for, to note Izenberg's shrewd comment, this is *not* a way to escape society but a way to be tightly embraced by it; for the rebel is quite dependent on what is rebelled against.[18]

Indulge me in a far-fetched analogy to a production of a play, such as *Hamlet*, by which I hope to illuminate the relationship of the free person to social mores. Innovative producers love to produce Shakespeare in various garbs, wrenching his play from its proper historical milieu. One such production was done in modern street clothes. The idea behind this was to suggest to the audience that costuming in a Shakespearean play is irrelevant, and that it is the words that count. But the audience, alas, misses the words because attention is focused on the clothing, which seems so singularly out-of-place. One feels that the actors ought to wear the right costumes and get on with the play.

So it is with manners and social usages; why be imprisoned in them by so-called non-conformity, which is always attending to them and is thereby obsessed by them? One can conform to civility and get on with the ethical projects that count. Existential authenticity, so often perverted, does not require that we sever ourselves from the society in which we live; it requires that we exist it critically, that we pick our conformity lucidly. We will internalize the society in which we live, not from some absolute necessity, but freely. This is the *ethos* of Max Weber. It also shares something with the civil religion of Rousseau, in his peculiar and perverse last section to the *Social Contract*.[19]

Insofar as we have taken up some common characteristics of Americans, we are sharing in the culture of the United States. If the culture of the United States is foreign to me, for example, in the case in which I am not granted equality and rights, the sociologist may find that I partake of a class culture, or a ghetoo culture, or some other subculture that may be at odds with the culture that enjoys "hegemony."[20] This is the view of Trotsky and other orthodox Marxists, for whom the norms of the larger society are vacuous, while the norms of class membership are decisive.[21]

But this, in the light of historical events and the effects of norms on workers, is probably an overemphasis of the differences of the norms of social groups within most nations. Since the United States is an amalgamation of so many groups, races, classes, and ethnicities, indeed, this in itself is a characteristic of our culture and an object of positive pride, the critical question as to whether there is a moral community at all depends on the ties uniting individuals within these groups with individuals in other groups and in the larger society.

Sartre analyzes the nation by the use of the term *series*, which refers to groups that are bound into the general society by the seriality of the collective. A series is held together by feeble ties, just as beans in a bag may comprise a collection, in such mutual associations as viewing the same television programs, listening to the same political speeches. In his *Eighteenth Brumaire of Louis Napoleon*, it is seriality that Marx claims is the characteristic principle of peasant cohesion--that is, peasants hardly form a class. Yet, their lesser culture is nonetheless bound into the larger one.

While this is a meager form of socialization, it is also quite basic to a society of the type of the *Gesellschaft*, and although Sartre appears to develop the idea in a negative context, serialization ought not to be denounced. In mass societies of 200 million individuals, it is probably a good thing that we do not have to waste emotional resources on most of our everyday affairs. Serialization in one sense may be alienating; but it allows us to get along with most of our fellow citizens, while we reserve our energies for our more significant communications. In addition, the organic modern society affords us the opportunity of keeping some of ourselves private, which enhances rather than diminishes our freedom. So, two cheers for serialization.

In the greater society, we ought to be allowed to pay a minimal heed to most of our everyday affairs, on Das Man, meeting our expectations on the basis of justice and equality, so that we might reserve the greater part of our commitments for our ethical projects. This is why the organic society has some advantages over the mechanistic society it has superseded, for the mechanistic society permeated the individual to monopolize his or her freedom. In fact, individuals rights do not arise in such communitarian groups.[22]

Existentialism would not have found a home there. The social contract of John Locke is, for this reason, far superior to the concept of Rousseau, who desired to reduce all persons to the common cause of the polity and to reduce their private interests to zero. Madison of the Federalist Paper Number 10, in which he advises against trying to abolish factions, is the great liberal antithesis to Rousseau's version of the social contract.[23]

There are dangers in serialization, too, which are brought out by Heidegger--one can lose one's life in the organic society too, by a life of chit-chat and mass culture. This occurs when culture, meaning the whole fabric of what society contains, impinges upon the individual only superficially and inauthentically.[24] Society in this sense is the society of the practico-inert, the totality, as opposed to the totalization, where effort and free choice are still possible.

In the analysis of Machiavellianism, the high Machs were resistant to social influence and were oriented to cognitions so that they could initiate and control the structure, while the low Machs tended to succumb to social influence and to accept the structures of the situation as a given. It is *not* the case that the high Machs, however, refuse to accept the mores of society, but that, comprehending these, they seek to use social givens to increase their own values.[25] But the totality is not to be scorned, either, but accepted for what it is and can offer, and then, by the free individual, it can be transcended.

Part of our social loyalties depend on the degree to which such transcendence is possible. In Hegel's view, we cannot invent moral principles *de novo*; we find some principles embodied in the concrete everyday life of the community, and if the environment of the community is amenable, we can then proceed to develop our own powers to the full.[26] Desan provides a nice analogy:

> An empty house . . .would be *practico-inert*, but once inhabited, it becomes a home and the center of that unifying activity which is called "totalization."[27]

So it may be with society.

Notes

1. Ricoeur, *Freedom and Nature*, p. 179.
2. Ferdinand Toennies, "Gemeinschaft and Gesellschaft," in Talcott Parsons, et al., eds., *Theories of Society*, Vol. I (New York: The Free Press, 1962), p. 191.
3. Justin Aronfreed, "Moral Development from the Standpoint of a General Psychological Theory," in Thomas Lickona, ed., *Moral Development and Behavior, Theory, Research, and Social Issues* (New York: Holt, Rinehart and Winston, 1976), p. 67. These empirical studies based on the conceptual scheme developed by Kohlberg are very suggestive and offer some support for our positions.
4. Frost, *Towards a Normative Theory of International Relations*, p. 62.

5. See Karl W. Deutsch, *France, Germany, and the Western Alliance: A Study of Elite Attitudes on European Integration and World Politics* (New York: Scribner, 1967) and *Nationalism and Social Communication: An Inquiry into the Foundations of Nationality* (New York: Wiley, 1953).

6. See the interesting commentary on the New York task force on curriculum, Scott McConnell and Eric Breindel, "Head to Come," *The New Republic*, Vol. 202, No. 2 and 3 (January 8 and 15, 1990), 18-21.

7. Lipset, Seymour Martin, *The First New Nation* (New York: Basic Books, 1963).

8. Edward Andrew, *Shylock's Rights: A Grammar of Lockian Claims* (Toronto: University of Toronto Press, 1988), p. 35.

9. Rhoda E. Howard and Jack Donnelly, "Human Dignity, Human Rights, and Political Regimes," *American Political Science Review*, Vol. 80, No. 3 (September 1986), p. 802.

10. *Ibid.*, p. 806.

11. *Ibid.*, p. 807. See also Hartmann, *Ethics*, Vol. II, p. 23.

12. Fell, *Heidegger and Sartre*, p. 390, covers Sartre's critique of rights. Stalin's USSR is one such disaster.

13. Conway, *A Farewell to Marx*, pp. 104-105.

14. Acton, Lord, "Nationality," pp. 403-404, in Talcott Parsons, *et al.*, Vol. I, *Theories of Society* (New York: The Free Press, 1961).

15. Sterling, *Ethics in a World of Power*, p. 190.

16. The disposition and treatment of the American Indians and the Hawaiian people are a specific moral problem that has not been treated here.

17. Heidegger, *Being and Time*, p. 167. This is one of the great works of the 20th century. Macquarrie and Robinson have spared us the Herculean task of reading it in German.

18. Izenberg, *The Existentialist Critique of Freud*, pp. 276-277.

19. Steven Muller Delue, *On the Marxism of Jean-Paul Sartre in the Light of Jean-Jacques Rousseau: An Analysis of the Critique De La Raison Dialectique* (Doctoral Dissertation: University of Washington, 1971), p. p. 194, fn 24. Don't avoid this work because it is in dissertation style; it marvelously illuminates the often turgid *Critique* by showing Sartre's great debt to Rousseau. The doctrine of the "general will" has also contributed vastly to Mao's social interpretations.

20. Aron, *History and the Dialectic of Violence*, p. 101. The concept of hegemony here is taken from Gramsci.

21. Trotsky, *Their Morals and Ours*, p. 379.

22. Howard and Donnelly, "Human Dignity, Human Rights, and Political Regimes," p. 815.

23. On Rousseau and his relationship to Sartre's alarming group-in-fusion, see Delue, *On the Marxism of Jean-Paul Sartre in the Light of Jean-Jacques Rousseau*, pp. 232-233.

24. Philip Selznick, *The Organizational Weapon: A Study of Bolshevik Strategy and Practice* (The Free Press of Glencoe, Ill.: 1960; copyright, 1952, by the Rand Corporation.), p. 285.
25. Christie and Geis, *Studies in Machiavellianism*, p. 285.
26. Plant, *Hegel, An Introduction*, p. 160.
27. Desan, *The Tragic Finale*, p. 76.

Chapter 11

The Nation

Part II. Nationalism and the Moral Community

No society into which one appears as a thrown consciousness will exhibit an adequate ideal of human mutuality. Inevitably, some political projects will concern raising the minimal standards of justice and rights and extending these to all citizens; other projects will be efforts to realize individual values that may contribute to the prevailing culture.[1] Logically, it is possible to sustain an effort to improve the rights of all citizens solely on the basis of a passionless lucidity, but "this commitment is most evident within the context of friendly relations."[2] This is why it is so difficult to exist within large, modern, mass communities.

Dissatisfaction with the moral communities in which we exist should not serve necessarily as an impetus to sever ourselves from these communities, by misanthropy or revolution, however. Any lack of community, if the foundation of the community is politically sound enough and improvable, ought to stimulate us to improve the society in accord with our needs and desires, our ethical projects, and our sense of morality.[3] We are not purists in relation to society any more than we are perfectionists in relation to international politics. Thus, we lean toward Berdyaev's fourth type of relationship between the self and society (the first being the total integration with society, the mechanical solidarity of Durkheim), where the Ego honors its solitude and chooses at the same time to heed the needs of society. The prophet is Berdyaev's exemplar of this stance, but we perfer to manifest our contributions through relationships in social life, art, scholarship, and science.[4]

It is in such ethical projects that we truly carry out our valued duties to our societies; the contribution of Pasternak to Russian society was far more lasting than the officially sanctioned contributions of so many ersatz social realists (social sycophants as opposed to the few honest social realists), and the fateful but mostly destructive contributions of the vanguard party. In any case, Berdyaev's is the authentic existential project of the self in its relationship to society, neither engulfed by it nor severed from it.

It is a life-enhancing relationship to our social system that is commendable rather than the self-consciously rebellious and destructive stance sometimes advocated by Sartre. Sartre's hatred of the bourgeoisie goes beyond the pale of lucidity. One is convinced that the proletariat never could have realized his high regard for them. How well, indeed, did Sartre know the working class? And, if he had been as familiar with workers as he certainly was with the bourgeoisie, would he have supported them then? The intellectual's selection of the proletariat (or, later, the students) as the universal class has been a tremendous burden for the workers.

In contradistinction to Sartre, it is the strength of Jaspers that he, like Berdyaev, recognized the benefits to the individual of partaking in society. In the more just societies, minimally, we are at least freed from some of the unpredictability of brute force. It is on the basis of the totalities, of the practico-inert, that we may rise to a higher level of values.[5] It is best if we elect to accept some duties with regard to the whole society. And the largest society in which the ordinary individual's presence is felt is probably the national society, that is, if that society supports a just system. The livable state affords the basis on which the higher ethical values can be pursued.

In a state in which concrete freedom can exist, there is room for associations and subgroups within the larger society. This, too, is the nature of the *Gesellschaft*, or the organic society, as opposed to the *Gemeinschaft* societies of the past, to which Rousseau and various of the totalitarian movements of the 20th century would want to return us. In the total community, in the communitarian society, the whole does not afford any latitude to parts or subgroups. To form a subgroup, the aims of which deviate from the unity of the whole, is a treasonous undertaking. So it is in Sartre's group-in-fusion. Where justice and equality prevail, there is also a propensity toward assimilating the parts into the whole, a tendency toward atomization that marks all large modern nations.

The existence of recalcitrant ethnic and language groups within the greater society is a potential source of conflicts, for there are barriers between the larger society and each such subgroup; distrust and suspicions arise on the boundaries marking these subgroups. The just principle on the part of the major society is to leave members of such separatist subgroups alone, except for such general requirements of participation as taxation, and so forth. For the critical intellectual, it is also necessary in the ongoing critique of social values, to assess the values of such subgroups, which may make worthy contributions to the whole.

The principle of justice suggests that such ethnic enclaves or religious minorities must be countenanced, just as we leave the individual a sphere of privacy. In the nation, there is no reason for conflict between the larger society and these smaller ones, at least insofar as justice prevails. The conflicts arise, just as they do in the international arena, as groups contend for hegemony as a protection for their own continued existence against the buffetings of the mass society. Equality requires that in our treatment of individuals as members of subgroups, we recognize their rights based on their membership in the larger grouping.

The principles of morality are the minimal principles we extend to all persons, *qua* persons. Galston comments on the corrosive effect of liberal culture on subgroups, and the ultimate destruction of some of these self-contained communities is not necessarily to be welcomed.[6] It is especially evident when a *Gemeinschaft* community comes to be absorbed into the larger *Gesellschaft*, as has happened in Hawaii, and in areas where Indian tribes have been displaced or absorbed. In particular, the homogenization of society decreases the potential ethical richness of that society. As Hartmann declares,

> The more the single persons differ from one another, the richer in values becomes the whole of the community.[7]

But an important portion of our loyalties must be to the large society and the principles of justice and morality; our duty to subgroups of which we are not members is not to segregate them, but to tolerate them. The demise of such subgroups is a matter to be resisted by their members.

These comments relate as well to the problems of immigration. The principle for a rational immigration policy would seem to be enough continual immigration to maintain variety and the infusion of new ethical outlooks, but not so much as to suddenly alter the whole fabric. A public school system in a nation such as the United States exists to socialize persons into the broad society, into the nation as a whole, and not to establish enclaves of separatist subgroups. Thus, the purpose of bilingual education is to facilitate socialization into the nation, not to preserve the permament distinctiveness of subgroups. While subgroups ought not to be hindered in their pursuit of distinctness, theirs is a project in addition to that of the broader society.

Marcuse suggests that the mode of production of a society creates segments of society, which are related in certain ways to the productive process. This is, of course, the Marxist interpretation, which stresses that it is these segments, the classes, that become the agents of history. And, therefore, in the Marxist analysis, classes become

> historically more basic and authentic than the urban community, the country, or the nation which seems to include them.[8]

The proletariat may in fact come to view their situation from the experience of a class-in-itself. They are aware in the development of industrialization that they are viewed as objects. The individual worker becomes one with a group that is "a definite practical relation of men to an objective and to each other."[9] So we get a group-in-fusion within the bowels of the nation and the prevailing bourgeois society. And, as Karl Korsch stated the phenomenon,

> As the revolutionary bourgeoisie had enlightened itself as to the principle of the new industrial society in the new science of *Political Economy*, so did the proletarian class assert its revolutionary aims in the Critique of Political Economy.[10]

As the true universal class, which Marx had discovered in pondering Hegel's *The Philosophy of Right*, the proletariat is the group within the whole of society that would revolt and implant its own cultural mark on the whole.[11] But for all the profound analysis Marx applied to the problem and the very real divisions within capitalist society between the classes, the proletariat was not the universal class of historical materialism after all; in the event, it failed to realize the destiny mapped for it by intellectuals. It failed Marx and Engels, Lukacs, Korsch, Novack, and, alas, Sartre.

As Merleau-Ponty points out in the *Adventures of the Dialectic* (p. 170), the workers generally did not follow the commands of the party in the demonstrations of June 2, 1952, which drew the comment from Sartre that this meant that the proletariat was not at issue, since the proletariat is obedient to the Party. At times like this, Sartre seems to proceed by definition or axiom; rather in the fashion of the scholastics of an earlier age, we have a variety of the ontological proof of the existence of the proletariat as the universal class.

In Sartre's political essays, notoriously *The Communists and Peace*, we learn by definition apparently, rather than any empirical evidence, that the working class has no sense of solidarity with the main society, or that the working class is pacifistic--at least Marx and Rosa Luxemburg had made certain efforts to prove assertions such as these empirically. The exaggerated distinctions advocated by the Marxists between the working class and the bourgeosie are, therefore, probably unfounded. But classes are present in society, of this there can be no doubt, and the ability of society to extend justice and rights to all groups is the mark of its ability to be worthy of survival.

Sartre's analysis of groups in the *Critique* is often powerful and subtle, but his orientation seems always to be that there is a potential group-in-fusion that organizes to overthrow the extant larger society--it is an apocalyptic vision, an absolutist analysis of the structure of groups.[12]

Sartre introduces a term, *alterity*, to depict the condition of social impotence, numerical equivalence, separation, pseudoreciprocity and specious unity. This is the "passive activity" of Das Man.[13] Marx analyzes similar phenomena under "alienation," and in sociology, "anomia" and "anomie" are cognate concepts. Modern mass societies, the organic societies of Durkheinm, are most liable to evince alterity. In the communitarian societies or within religious or ideological subgroups, the self was infused with the norms of the social group to the degree that the individual scarcely existed. Modern society has freed the individual from the oppression of the group norms of the *Gemeinschaft*, so far as the larger society is concerned, at any rate. It has made people potentially more free, but there has been a cost in the condition of alterity. The process of utilizing concrete freedoms is a painful one of self-motivation, internal control, and the risk of failure.

It is not surprising that many individuals avoid responsibility and choice and in the condition of fallenness, select total conformity to such social norms as the society or some subgroup offers.[14] The extant social structures will buttress the identity of the conformist, and, like the masochist, he will seek to be dominated by them. This is the problem of authenticity.[15] Existentialist analysis would sometimes make it seem as though all conformity to norms was somehow inauthentic, but by now it ought to be clear that such an extreme notion is unacceptable.

Even the most simple forms of courteous address have their use in easing the path to intercommunication, although what on the one hand might be a straightforward courtesy may on a different occasion be the deceptive veneer for an inauthentic stance toward the world. Aron accuses Sartre of regarding the entire process of socialization as one of alienation or enslavement.[16] Much of his analysis, and that of some other existentialists, is guilty of this indictment.

We regard socialization, on the contrary, as potentially compatible with authenticity, although if experienced as alterity only, it will be inauthentic. Still, Sartre's depiction of what he calls seriality, collectives of people such as the radio audience, the newspaper readership, and the free market is quite astute as analyses of the impersonality and passivity of modern society.[17] While on the one hand criticizing the inauthenticity of conformity to social norms, Sartre in his compelling analysis almost seems to regret these absent norms:

> Seriality . . . reflects the force of the external [social] inert materiality on each individual in the "collective."[18]

In Western (that is, modern) societies, empirical research shows that members of these societies may use their cognitive capacities (lucidity) to arrive at "principled values of self-direction which go beyond the more obvious kinds of external constraints." In other, less modern and nonindustrialized societies, there is what students of moral development refer to as a more externalized perspective, that is, a conforming and pedestrian view.[19] Comparative research, then, indicates that if modern society is beset by alterity, it is also that society in which individual choice becomes possible.

We transcend purely conformist ethics, if at all, by rising above the social values retailed for us, by developing our own ethical system of evaluation. If we do not do this and fall completely into conventional ethics, the most likely ethic of choice in an industrialized society will be an ethics of success.[20] (Of course, increasing numbers of persons in the United States exhibit neither individual nor conventional ethics. They are essentially not part of a civilization or a culture. This condition, too, is a result of alterity.)

A system based on success has been well depicted by many novelists of the industrializing societies, from Defoe, to Sinclair Lewis to Tom Wolfe. The conformists are, by virtue of adhering to the social mores, bound to be good citizens, but, as Hartmann has indicated in the preceding note, and as Aristotle commented in *The Politics*, the good citizen may not be synonymous with the good man. To a certain degree, conformity may be consonate with authenticity, but an uncritical conformity may reduce an individual to the status of object, a status exhibited by many of the apostles of success.

Thus, the program of B. F. Skinner, for whom the purpose of morals is to preserve society, is subject to the criticism that there are polities and forms of society that ought not be preserved.[21] Thus, the case of Eduard Schulte, a bourgeois head of an established mining corporation in Germany, who grew to detest Nazism, and cooperated with Allied intelligence from 1939 to 1943.[22] Such an individual is representative of the rescuers, the witnesses, who are connected to others--to family, group, or to people--in contrast to persons disconnected and passive.[23] Such behavior ought to be regarded as admirable, and it rests on a critical view of society.

There are many examples of total conformity--the epitome of the total conformist is the *fonctionaire*, to devise an appropriate term. Kurt Waldheim is a fine study. He was probably not a real Nazi, but he became a Nazi when Nazism was in power; in the United Nations, while internationalism was not his project, he was an internationalist. If a Stalinist regime had been formed in Austria, though not a convinced Communist, he would have been a very good Stalinist. He seems to be representative of the social object *par excellence*. The personal seems to have shriveled. He was probably somewhat puzzled at the furor caused by the discovery of his service in a particularly active area of German occupation and atrocities, although he did show enough moral sensitivity to lie about this period of his activity. Less excruciating examples can be found in David Riesman's well-known *The Lonely Crowd*.

Were society the construct of a totalitarian leader, then total conformity would be the goal of reducing everyone to object-status, an achievement that was sought by Hitler, Salin, Pol Pot, Kim Il-sung, and, it must be said on the basis of innumerable statements, Lenin. This was not the intent of Karl Marx, however, to whom we owe his brilliant expositions on the reduction of persons to objects in modern industrial capitalism. Sartre has drawn heavily on Marx in depicting the serialization of the marketplace.[24] Marx had earlier shown the power of money to turn humans into subject beings determined from without. Through the market, mankind becomes reduced to a commodity.[25]

Marx's analysis on how people become ensnared in the practico-inert, how mankind has become alienated within the products of its own invention and labor is a lasting sociological contribution. Drawing on Hegel, Marx extracted a body of thought under the concept of reification that explained how human actions come to be independent of humanity and begin to control the actors. The analysis of this process is carried a stage further by Georg Lukacs (*History and Class Consciousness*). There is no doubt that economic systems have this effect, and in the capitalist system in particular, people easily become the objects of exchange, labor and consumerism.

Thus, the capitalist economic system is at root immoral, for it reduces its subjects to the status of objects. It is immoral in the sense that we have interpreted morality, for not taking people into account as free and individual *consciousnesses*. Under the capitalist system, our orientation to other people becomes solely commercial, a relationship of seller to buyer, rather than a relationship of conscious beings to one another. In large factories, the person at the center of any particular stage of manufacture may be replaced without emotional qualms by any other person.

It is evident that this bloodless outlook has also contributed to the concept of equality, for which very reason Sartre attacks the bourgeois concept of equality. But, although perhaps immoral in its origins, social equality also has the potential to support a more adequate structure of justice than existed under feudalism and previous historical stages. Moreover, equality can rest on other bases than the capitalist market.

In fact, through the immense productive power of industrial capitalism, scarcity has been greatly alleviated, a result that Marx and Engels both noted in the *Communist Manifesto* but that Sartre stints-- indeed, if the alleviation of scarcity is a desirable goal, as Sartre avers in the *Critique*, it would more likely occur within a tempered capitalism than within the overly-bureaucratic communist economies, a tacit admission that Teng Tsiao-ping and Mikhail Gorbachev both made.

For all the recognizable shortcomings of the market, most socialist systems have been brought to adopt it as the least bad alternative. Can it be that 70 years of human terror and sacrifice, idealism and cynicism, utopian hopes and gulags have at last stumbled unto the discovery of . . . the market? The momentous events of 1989 in East Europe would make it seem so.

For all the brilliant analysis of its founders, Communism showed no evidence that it could create a system in which persons became less alienated, less objects than under capitalism. Indeed, by 1990, the collapse of Communism in the most advanced countries where it was maintained by a vanguard party attested to its failure. Let us make a few reservations here. In the first place, Marx did not intend to analyze a Communist society that had not yet been formed, and his projections of Communist society were made from the data drawn from that economic society to which he had access--capitalism. (He did occasionally, if briefly, provide hints about the composition of a future dictatorship of the proletariat, as in his analysis of the Paris Commune and his *Critique of the Gotha Program*).

In the second place, there are conditions necessary for the kind of revolution Marx had predicted. In the *Class Struggles in France* (p. 43), Marx shows that the proletariat can come into being only *after* the development of the industrial bourgeoisie:

> Only bourgeois rule tears up the roots of feudal society and levels the ground on which a proletariat revolution is alone possible.

Marx was not talking emptily when he said this, but in recognition of the social changes wrought by the capitalist system that he had analyzed so carefully.

This is the Marxist theory on the basis of which it may be questioned whether there has ever been a genuine Marxist revolution; certainly not in Hungary or Poland, where there were few supporters of the Communist party that claimed to rule in its name, and not in Cuba, not in Vietnam, and not in Mozambique, none of which were capitalist societies at a highest stage of development.

To be sure, Lenin argued in his work on the Russian economy at the end of the 19th century that a Marxist revolution was possible there, but a compelling contrary view is presented in Karl Wittvogel's *Oriental Despotism*. In any case, central planning, like the market, also has the effect of reducing humans to interchangeable things. The revolution as a solution advanced by Marx and Engels in the 19th century, when it made some rational sense--a lucid thinker might well have come to many of Marx's conclusions--and Sartre and others in the post-1917 years, when it made no sense whatsoever, has to be disavowed.

Capitalism is, of course, no final goal of history, for there is no such thing, but for the time being, it is a system with certain immoral characteristics that works fairly well. Its productivity and social mode of production have made people far better able to develop independent lives, despite the pressures of alterity, and its equalizing effect has released persons, for good and ill, but potentially for good, from the bondage of communitarian systems.

In addition, there are large areas of our social life in which we may want to be released from emotional involvements, including a large proportion of our economic interactions, so that we may concentrate on the involvements we choose.[26] The market, after all, does maximize personal autonomy, provided the system of distribution in society is not too grossly unequal, as it may be in the United States. Some inequalities of wealth or prestige, of course, are bearable within a just society; others are unacceptably degrading.

Existentialism, as some Marxist critics are aware, has grown out of the modern social and economic severance of people from tribal, clan, and feudal ethics. While existential viewpoints can be found in almost every age and social system, including some remarkable "existentialist" poems from Anglo-Saxon literature in Britain, it has only been the advent of individualism in developed societies that has provided its full development. The constructive-destructive effects of capitalism have made such questions askable, as, how must an individual come to terms with the world? *Being and Nothingness* would not likely have been writen in the Cham empire or Assyria. (Oddly, however, such a work is just barely conceivable in the Chinese traditional system, where Taoism always played the role of the flexible alternative in the more rigid Confucian structure.)

Nevertheless, we may agree with a comment offered by Emmet Tyrrell [27] that neither capitalism nor socialism can substitute for higher moral and cultural commitments, and quoting Michael Novak, he points out that the commercial virtues "are not sufficient to their own defense." The point is obvious: while the free market system or variations thereof may have important social contributions to make, it does not offer a full social philosophy. Capitalism demands a concomitant social philosophy to mitigate its operation. Two major social viewpoints are necessary for the constructive operation of societies.

To counteract the evident problems of seriality, Heidegger's fallenness, Sartre presumes to undertake an attack on society through revolution, and, drawing on Marx's precedent, to transcend the impotence of seriality in modern society, by positing the group, the collective in which like-minded individuals regain the power to challenge the status quo. The purpose of the group seems to be to overthrow the extant society and to establish another, which would somehow empower persons rather than emasculate them.[28]

But this is absolutism in another and worse form--the seriality of organic societies is a condition in which we presently exist, and while persons and groups may rise above this status, it is unlikely that any technological society would banish the problems of alienation or alterity. These are ongoing problems of modernity to be continually confronted, but never once and for all resolved. Revolution is an unpredictable and, historically, a frequently futile activity for this utopian end. The avoidance of the fallen condition is a matter the individual must deal with for the reason that the locus of consciousness is individual.

Occasionally, he or she will unite with others into groups. On some occasions these groups may be well-advised to conduct revolts. But violence and revolution are not a solution to the social problem of alterity. Having severed our mooring to communitarian systems, we are now cast adrift to make our own way and to form our own ties, somehow. *The* Revolution is a myth and violates lucidity. This is to say, in addition, that reform is possible, and reforms have greatly altered conditions under modern capitalism since the 19th century; these reforms are quite tangible and were occurring at the very time that Marx was developing his doctrine of necessary revolution.

The abolition of the poll tax (now there is an unexciting reform for advocates of revolutionary grand guignol) in the United States; the removal of miscegenation laws (which used to exist in some 36 American states); female suffrage--reforms such as these are piecemeal, important, and successful efforts to remove sources of alienation. Cumulatively they create the differences in society that revolutions are intended to accomplish at once. But reforms sometimes improve conditions; the revolutions of the 20th century have almost never improved conditions, and have frequently made them worse.

The issue arises, since we have criticized Sartre's calls for revolution, his own form of "useless passion," about whether violence can ever be condoned within nations. Just how much violence is warranted in the conditions, say, of a moderately liberal, ameliorated capitalist system? The good end of political projects, as has been stated, must be the ultimate expansion of the concrete freedoms of people. The quintessentially moral project was the civil rights movement that began in the 1940s and bore legal and social fruits in the 1950s and 1960s.

We may conclude at the start that violence for the long-term purpose of dominating others is ethically and morally evil, though occasionally it may be necessary, to avoid greater evils. For instance, when the police apprehend a serial murderer, they dominate the criminal, but there is also a larger social purpose served. In an ethical project determined to expand human freedoms and possibilities for existence, violence may enter as one possible means.

We have suggested that it is right to revolt against some regimes. John Locke has got it about right: that, since the government ought to be considered as in trust to the society, any group or monarch that violates the limitations on power set by a freely-contracting society has placed itself in a "state of nature" against society and may be violently deposed. Locke even located in governments that were self-perpetuating a major origin of such potential for violation, an idea directly applicable to the typical vanguard party.

Marx had incisively analyzed the ethics-laden concept of exploitation in the 19th century, where people were reduced to commodities, to being conveyers of labor-power. To the end of releasing workers from the conditions enforced upon them in the 19th century, the idea of a revolution made sense. In the Marxian theory, the goal of overcoming alienation and exploitation, even if we discount the utopia of a classless system as illusory, made the violence of revolution an acceptable path out of the status quo.

But the further development of industrial economies, beyond anything Marx had thought possible, has raised the quality of life since Marx's day sufficiently for most in the population, that by the time Eduard Bernstein presented his *Evolutionary Socialism*, a revolution was no longer plausible as the appropriate way in advanced countries to further human emancipation. A Marxist revolution of the proletariat was no longer in the historical works.

There was still, however, room enough for doubt, so that the debates between the revisionists and convinced revolutionaries like Rosa Luxemburg, retained an aura of lucidity. But the calls for revolution in advanced societies for the purpose of emancipating the workers following World War II had ceased to be intellectually conscionable. Only a person who did not weigh historical data or an intellectual poseur could still advocate the revolutionary position in advanced, democratic, industrial states.

A society the aim of which is justice, rights, and equality of opportunity, which intends that people ought to be importantly taken into account when decisions are made, and that offers processes for bringing about real change, should be made effective use of before any thought can be given to violent means. To exhort any class or group to violence when change can be effected through voting and political pressures is a game for the bloody-minded armchair theorist of revolution.

Lenin himself called upon his followers to combine legal forms of struggle with illegal means, and this was within an autocratic state.[29] Where legal techniques can lead to actual emancipatory results, it would seem inadvisable to simultaneously undermine these techniques by combining them with illegal or violent ones. Illegal means applied when unnecessary lead to distrust and the undermining of equality and justice, where these exist.

So Lenin's advocacy of participation in the Duma, or parliament, was for the purpose of

> . . . working within parliament for the success of the Soviets in their forthcoming task of dispersing parliament

which the Bolsheviks accomplished in January, 1918.[30] Lenin effectively used extra-legal means against a government never dedicated to democratic forms, but through these means, he established another autocratic government. We may criticize his ends in this case, although the nature of the Tsarist state provided an excuse for his means.

While it is almost never justifiable to use violent means to diminish the concrete freedoms of ordinary people, there are circumstances at the extreme that call for defense of concrete freedoms through violent resistance, even in democratic societies. In the course of labor organization, there were cases of reaction to violent means by the state and the owners of the means of production that were defensible, even though, in the long run, the movement might have achieved as much without resort to violence. Nazi movements, the white supremacists, the Black Panthers for a period in the 1970s, as advocates of violence go well beyond the boundaries of civil debate. A strongly democratic society might contain even these groups, but their threats are quite real. A tangible threat to the physical security of their targets may be justifiably countered by violence.

But the society that maintains that minimal security afforded by a moral system of justice ought to inhibit violence. In such a society, violence ought rarely to be necessary, and always as a last resort. At best, such a society can allow even bitter debate to be carried on between individuals, who can still retain a respect for each other's basic being as consciousness. The morality of political life "is that as citizens the members of a party must stand above the party conflicts."[31]

In Communist societies, this degree of morality did not prevail. Mao's antagonisms between the people and the enemies of the people, antagonisms defined, of course, by the state elite, the vanguard, culminated in the Cultural Revolution, the antithesis of social civility, in which hatred, fanaticism, and the "spirit of seriousness" devastated society.[32] Indeed, it was not so much a cultural revolution as a revolution to obliterate culture.

Leszek Kolakowski pointed out that the spirit of the left is a critical spirit, which always calls into question the status quo and advances emancipation and freedom. This is acceptable as a civil movement, although in the same essay Kolakowski proposes that the left is a seeker of utopias, and this is potentially dangerous in civil societies. Ashley puts the political point across well:

> . . . the logic of politics is an intrinsically dialectical logic, at once depending upon, anticipating, and calling into question the dominant social order. On the one hand. . . political logics always involve a questioning of the truth content of the dominant, habit-linked order. This occurs as subordinate classes, sectors, and coalitions struggle to recover and creatively combine experiences, remembrances, traditions, and understandings which the dominant order forgets, represses, or otherwise denies full social significance. Once recovered these experiences, traditions, and their understandings afford a critical vantage-point upon the dominant order, allowing parties to see that there are alternatives to that which is habitual and, hence, that the habitual order of domination is historically contingent and susceptible to change rather than natural and eternal."[33]

In the democratic society, such struggles may become very heated, but civility must ultimately survive. Thus, the democratic society, flawed as it is, based on some structure of laws founded on equality and justice, is the true civil religion that Rousseau ought to have stressed, that allows people to pursue conflicting ethical projects without bloodshed. Lucidity informed by history ought to be able to refute any doctrines of absolute perfectability. Absolute doctrines have generally been associated with a great deal of unnecessary bloodshed.

Ethical projects ought not to burst their limits and wreak havoc and death on fellow citizens. Indeed, it is the tendency of absolutist doctrine and utopias that makes them frequent transgressors of civil boundaries and the cause of mayhem and death that mark these as evil, that is, destructive of life, and immoral, that is, oblivious of taking others into account. It is in undemocratic polities, where oppression and the systematic denial of justice occurs that revolts and revolutions are morally defensible, for no one has a right to reduce another's status to that of an object. This removes our relationship from the category of person-to-person and under many circumstances justifies a use of violence in self-defense.

This is what Locke and other social contract theorists refer to as a government placing itself in the state of nature against society. The tragedy of many successful colonial revolts is not that they were unwarranted in the face of dehumanizing oppression, but that the consequences were often the overthrow of one source of inhumanity and the implantation of another. We have referred to the dehumanizing aspects of capitalism, which when Marx analyzed it, may have justified action as extreme as revolution. The development of political liberties, in part caused by the forces released by capitalism itself, have allowed some mitigation of these effects.

Capitalism in many ways is still immoral in the sense that it reduces people to objects, but society also has the ability to prevail against the worst abuses of the marketplace without bloodshed. Finally, let me make a brief comment on a position mentioned earlier, proposed by both Sartre and Marcuse, the oppression of the tolerant liberal society (and a position that makes some valid points): An oppressive system, it seems to me, is always more oppressive than a tolerant system. The triteness of this last phrase was intended.[34]

Thus, we have argued ourselves into support for Mill's social views advanced in *On Liberty*, which is not a very exciting denouement. We had hoped to be able to advocate at this juncture of the argument something more cataclysmic. As intellectuals we have the sneaking suspicion that a land reform in which a few people are injured cannot be as important to humanity as one in which millions are done to death. How can virtue be attained without shedding rivers of blood?

After a journey of some length, we find ourselves facing not Everest but a molehill, in Marx's sour observation. We have actually been brought to propose the mundane, the shoddy, against the possibility of a great apocalypse of utopianism. Lucidity has forced us to take responsibility for such an undramatic choice. Indeed, we see society as always the arena of competing projects, never fully unified in a single great cause, and never brought into some post-historical final state, whether of the classless society (Marx) or total translucency in interpersonal communications (Sartre).

In the society we anticipate, we expect always to find enemies but no Enemy. As Gentile put it, "Political life is a struggle which draws us out into society and gets us involved with people of disparate mentalities and diverse interests."[35] This will most likely be the case so long as diversity exists. This is why Cavour is such an interesting political study, for he was convinced that the only real progress is slow and wisely ordered. *Lasting achievements*, in Cavour's estimation, were not usually the result of insurrection or conspiracy.[36] Worthwhile changes depended (wherever these were possible, we might add) on the use of "legitimate authority rooted in a country's traditions." Gramsci's pregnant analysis of competing hegemonies, which are broad ethical, cultural, and ideological projects, is most suggestive here, although Gramsci did not hesitate to participate in rebellion.[37]

The question arises, why does violence have such an appeal for intellectuals in situations where violence seems, lucidly considered, to be unwarranted? Referring to Hegel, Popper writes,

> The tribal ideal of the Heroic Man, especially in its fascist form [Popper is too severe on Hegel], is based upon different views. It is a direct attack upon those things which make heroism admirable to most of us—such things as the furthering of civilization. For it is an attack on the ideal of civil life itself; this is denounced as shallow and materialistic, because of the idea of security which it cherishes.[38]

In Sartre, the idea culminated in his concept of the fused groups.[39] Sartre's unmitigated hatred of the bourgeoisie, many of whom exhibit the all-too-human qualities of bad faith, as do many workers, is based on his preposterous belief that some system might ultimately banish these qualities, and his unprovable thesis that the working class, which he knew rather superficially, would somehow bring this about through violence.[40]

In part then, this inexcusable inclination for violence above all other means is an aspect of Sartre's and Marcuse's and others' absolutist goals. In this they share traits in common with Robespierre, including an intense dislike for certain other people. Or, in a particularly effective passage by Mao, later eliminated from the official published version of "On the Correct Handling of Contradictions," in the 1950-1952 campaigns against counterrevolutionaries,

700,000 were killed [and] after that time over 70,000 more have been killed. But less than 80,000 . . . . In the past four or five years we've only killed several tens of thousands of people.[41]

Accompanying Sartre's and Marcuse's absolutism is a total lack of empirical analysis to back certain of their opinions, in which they differ fundamentally from Marx. For a notorious example, read Sartre's *The Communists and Peace*, which advances an unalleviated conspiracy theory of the most simple sort involving the bourgeoisie. The entire book can only be regarded as a shallow satire.

Walter Schwarz explains the syndrome, which violates the project of lucidity, as follows:

> This love of ideas without facts to upset them keeps alive an entire industry of "intellectuals," who produce regular books in beautiful and brilliant language and are given great prominence on the television. For a decade they all admired the Soviet Union. Then they all found out about Stalin, and admired China, until they all found out about Mao. Then they admired Ho Chi Minh and they have not yet recovered from that illusion.[42]

Although the point is probably nailed down, an additional quotation is pertinent here:

> There is one side to the nature of intellectuals which finds fascination in power and even cruelty. Nazism attracted men of this type, but Stalinism did infinitely better because it could draw on the benefits of socialist phraseology. The intellectual's main fear is--and the Webbs are a good example--that he is not being heard, that he is talking to himself or a minute circle of like-minded readers. Hitching his wagon to a powerful cause is one infallible way of making sure that his voice will be heard.[43]

This is a possible reason for the not infrequent bad advice of the intelligentsia, which would plunge us into an exciting hell. The pluralistic conclusions of less tumultuous minds would be preferred by most people.

We have attempted to ground an ethical doctrine so far as possible in a plausible ontology, and, risking the reprehensible descent into the "spirit of seriousness," have proposed a few principles of morality founded on lucidity, the reflective position of seeing the situation as it really is. Our presentation has taken us to a most remarkable conclusion: the morally supportable society is a democratic one. Moreover, the democratic societies owe their origins to various intellectual and economic sources, for instance, Christianity (which we have not surveyed here but which provided crucial roots for equality and individualism in Western societies), and, most recently, to the development, through all its partly destructive and oppressive path, of modern capitalism.

As a start, we end by supporting the very bourgeois system of rights initially bound to the interests of that class, a doctrine therefore flawed. But Howard and Donnelly are quite right to suggest that although the idea of rights may have its origin as a tactic of the bourgeoisie to protect its class interests, "the logic of universal, inalienable personal rights has long since broken free of these origins."[44]

All democratic societies, therefore, are improvable, probably without resort to violence, relying on the principles of justice that they espouse (but do not always realize) and the constitutional and legal mechanisms of due process. This requires that equality ought to be achievable at least to the degree in which, domestically, the strong (the wealthy and educated, and skilled in organization) do not so outweigh the weaker that they have no motive to cooperate with the weaker and acknowledge the results of due process.

The ultimate goal toward which democracy tends, provided our projects bring about change, is free communication among persons. Sartre and Habermas propose this as the culmination of a moral society, although Sartre proposes complete translucence, barring any form of privacy, which may be both extreme and utopian.[45] In the fully democratic society, there will be fewer external pressures toward inauthenticity and bad faith, although it is unlikely these will ever be banished from social relations.[46]

While not all ethical projects within society will be treated with tolerance, the arena of social conflicts will be an open one, enterable by all. The arena will be one in which morality applies to everyone. No one will have the society automatically closed to his or her projects for the reason that society has refused to initiate them into the system, nor will passivity be enforced on some persons or groups. We are a long way from this future.[47] The maximum possibility of integrity and self-development (but not necessarily happiness, which it has been argued remains a by-product of other pursuits) is the objective of the democratic political order.[48]

Hobbes, who accepted the humanist doctrine that existence has a value and that people ought to be able to pursue their individual purposes, was nevertheless wrong to advocate absolutism for the law and order he believed it to produce.[49] It is almost unnecessary to say that the experience of the 20th century has provided the refutation of absolutism, within which law and order are largely spurious and ill-maintained. Sartre's ultimate goals are not really that far removed from the values of liberal society we have expressed, but he has espoused his views sometimes in convoluted ways, and he was wrong to assert the necessity of violent revolution and to deny the effect of reforms on the extant system. Genuine democracy has already made gains in bourgeois society.

Finally, there are some responsibilities if our goals include a democratic society. First, lucidity underlines our obligation to enter the political arena informed and critical.[50] Second, to quote an author not noed for his devotion to such ends, we need to exercise civil courage:

[This] consists in a steady loyalty to the dictates of one's own conscience in speech and action, and in the acceptance of a complete responsibility for one's conduct in one's relations to others."[51]

In the brief presentation of some of the factors involved in nation-building we touched on a topic that should be specifically addressed at this juncture. What identity does the nation have in the world? Let us consider this problem.

Nations present different faces to the world. Since some of the emergent former colonies after 1960 represented arbitrary colonial fiat rather than a nation-building process, and some of these are now in the throes of seemingly interminable disunity and uncivil conflict, these countries have not yet appropriated a national identity in the international world. In a pluralist society such as the United States, the question is whether a sufficient minimum of social solidarity can be maintained to warrant speaking of a national identity.[52] Needless to say, the United States has in the latter years of the 20th century a different identity than it presented to the world at the time of Madison or Lincoln. Nations greatly change over time, while retaining threads of continuity.

Germany in the 1930s presented something of the unity of the fused group, with an aim in the world of territorial expansion and racial domination. Liberal societies disavow by their nature any such solidarity and absolute goals, leaving ethical goals, in the main, to the province of individuals. Nations with identities of fused groups are a danger to the stability of the international system. They give rise to the necessary reactive strategies of containment. While the basis of morality calls for its universal applicability, the arena in which individuals can most effectively pursue moral and ethical concerns is the national. That is, the extent of any person's influence is normally bounded by the nation at the greatest limit.

Insofar as the nation represents a system, a person's activities in altering one aspect of the nation will reverberate to all other sectors of the nation. The international system is much looser, and it is difficult to deem it a moral community, except tenuously. Of course, in the far future, it may come to comprise a moral community. But for now, the nation comes to be a natural boundary containing our ethical and moral concerns. On the national level, individuals may have an effect; beyond the nation, they have less control and act amidst alien communities.

The history of our community ought to be of great concern to us, as it represents the basis of our present situation. The language of the nation carries with it at least some common loyalties, concerns and meanings that allow facilitated communication among fellow citizens. Some nations lack this aspect of unity, of course. Persons are embedded in a culture, normally (but not always, as in the United States), to a degree such that an epic, speaking of such literary products as Homer's *Iliad* or Camoens *Lusiad* will have an emotional effect; people will find the epic in some degree stirring; it will raise historical and cultural memories.

It is very unlikely that any epic of the United States would stir all the citizens of the polity.[53] Attempts at an American epic, *John Brown's Body* and *Western Star* by Stephen Vincent Benet have been of questionable success, that is, as national epics. And to the degree that we internalize the norms of the society in which we live, as members we designate ourselves as "we." To the degree in which we are free to follow out our political projects, we must assume some responsibility for the activities attributable to the nation. As we exert influence, so we guide national activity in the world. We also, if we accept our national identity as a "we," are assuming some responsibility for the nation's past behavior.[54]

Nevertheless, there is no locus of consciousness in the nation as subject, but only a multiplicity of individuals, who, partaking in a common culture and a common political system of justice and rights, seek to pursue projects, some of which will intend effects beyond the national boundaries. These projects will have some common identity for the reason that they have emerged from a domestic milieu, a situation. Autonomous wills have come together in some form of common practice that can be called the national interest. Characteristic acts in international affairs will be held together by some common threads.

The basic goal, of course, insofar as each group, after experience with colonialism, is best suited to determine its own affairs, is to preserve national continuity or sovereignty. The goal of self-preservation unites interests into some sense of national identity. Steiner in interpreting Heidegger's concept of Dasein, suggests that the
> heritage which the there-being assumes in authenticity, ... is not simply its individual history but somehow the heritage of the entire people *with* which it *is*."[55]

In constituting a personal identity, we maintain consistency in our behavior by promising, giving our word, standing by our commitments.
> Promising creates the human self; breaking one's word is dehumanizing, regardless of the profit.[56]

Domestic society is partially held together by the keeping of promises. This is suggestive for the nation as well, though it is a totality without a will; continuity and "promising" have created a sense of national identity through history, by analogy with individuals. But, for all that, we must never forget that so-called "collectives" such as the nation, do not themselves act, but that they are always to be understood as the sum total of individual human wills.

If it were the case that our attachments to the nation depended solely on moral considerations, on taking others into account, we would extend the same consideration to all persons throughout the world. Indeed, the universality of morality calls for just this, and rationality would not allow a consciousness that is Somali to receive any less consideration in our projects than one that is American. Presumably, loyalty to a society, emersion in a moral community, rises somewhat above this minimal level of morality. It rises above this minimal level, because as members of the nation we share trust and some common values within a coherent culture with other members. In the first place, provided that our country has embodied some of the basic principles of rights and justice, which, although based on a minimal morality, are not evident in all or many nations, we have some motivation to regard our society more highly than some others.

There ought to be some additional attachment to the culture of our society, the product of fellow nationals, past and present, in the form of art, literature, architecture, family structure and the variety of accomplishments that mark the nature of projects manifest in the nation. Connected with the cultural attributes of the nation, will be the social attachments, the likings, developed in the pursuit of ethical projects within the nation. It is these that constitute a nation as a moral community. These are the further aspects of society that have a claim on loyalty.

It is interesting that in the surveys reported in Almond and Verba's *The Civil Culture*, Americans often showed pride in their political institutions, an important factor in our national identity. (Later studies suggest that this pride has diminished.) The Italians, however, generally had a low opinion of their political institutions (remember that these surveys represented opinion in the 1950s, in which decade the Italian system did not work very effectively), but found, on the other hand, a common national identity in their artistic and literary culture. Interestingly, the Mexican respondents also showed a fair degree of cultural unity centered on the events and effects of their revolution of 1911. These are the national aspects of loyalty.

Participation in culture, insofar as we are participants, sets up attachments with others that will move us to put the needs of these national others somewhat above outsiders, who have no immediate cultural claims on us, and this is the significance of the "social contract." The nation has some claim on our preferences as we enjoy a measure of mutual interaction, mutual alliances in the pursuit of projects, national emotional attachments, and a boundary within which trust is more easily verified than outside that boundary. If none of these ties exist, and if society does not afford a measure of justice and protection of rights, it is not certain why patriotism or nationalism should have any force. Loyalties might halt at the border of the neighborhood or village.

For the Vietnamese under the empire, the bonds of loyalty were said to end at the "bamboo fence" surrounding the village. Yet, in the French invasion of the 19th century, the national identity was rekindled as it had been when the Vietnamese fought off Chinese hegemony. It is evident that nationalism is inclusive of particular groups, and exclusive of a great many others: these others rightly come under the concerns of morality, but not necessarily those additional ethical concerns stemming from cultural attachments.[57]

In this interpretation, nationalism need not be a threat to others, although it engenders sometimes the strife that national groups wage for independence and security. Historical experience seems to support wars of national independence, because the history of colonialism (and all the present states of Europe, too, were once colonies), indicates that basic morality, consideration for others, rights, and minimal justice--all those things brought under the rubric of the "moral community"--are more possible when national or ethnic groups are independent than when other groups try to rule them, even "for their own good."

The "white man's burden" was really the man of color's burden; no group has the right to assume another's burden. If there is one sure principle of international relations, it is that no distinct people are fit to govern another people. It is a principle that is constantly being reinforced by events: in the late 1980s, it was illustrated by the destructive rule of the Chinese over the Tibetans.

Nationalism, therefore, is generally a constructive force in the world when it strikes out for independent cultures based on a system of justice. But nationalism is also a threat to the stability of the world, when its exclusivity becomes extreme: this occurs when the nation is made an absolute goal, subverting individual projects, often in connection with a particular racial group, with all non-nationals not only treated as outsiders but conceived to be absolute outsiders, that is, non-persons, nonentities, objects. This was the view of all ancient societies, well expressed in the Old Testament, but even present among the ancient Greeks of a later and more sophisticated age.

This extreme view of nationality occurred over and over again as Europeans encountered American Indians, African blacks, Tasmanians, Hawaiians. Some of the oriental cultures were already culturally unified and stubbornly resisted Western proselytization and cultural imperialism. Absolutism based on racism was the core of the Nazi belief system: the Aryan people against the Slav, Semitic, and all other non-people. Thus, nationalism becomes inauthentic, based on myths that violate rationality. The for-itself is consciousness simply, and it is not Aryan or Christian or Chinese consciousness. That consciousness to which moral regard ought to be accorded is not a national consciousness, after all, but it exists equally in persons everywhere. Mackie[58] is correct in saying that "patriotism may have outlived its usefulness," if he has this more extreme view of nationalism in mind.

Some form of the social contract has come to bind most people within national entities. It requires that we be more socially responsible to some people, those within our society, than to others outside the sphere of our particular social contract, outside the purview of our usual social activities. Within the boundary of this hypothetical contract, ties are more easily developed with others.[59]

Indeed, if a person cannot develop social ties with those who live within the same nation, it is likely that his or her emotions are stunted--if an individual professes to a "love for all mankind," while holding his fellow nationals in contempt, this profession ought to be highly suspect. The integration into some form of moral community, as it still exists, though diminished, in the *Gesellschaft* of modern entities, is a step toward humanization.

All of these considerations in this chapter will be pertinent later, when we come to view the profession of the diplomat. For it is the diplomat who occupies that very precarious position at the edge of society, tied in one way to the culture he or she defends and on whose behalf negotiations are carried on, facing outward toward inhabitants of other nations, to whom he or she ought to accord a moral standing.

Notes

1. Olafson, *Principles and Persons*, p. 224.
2. Delue, *On the Marxism of Jean-Paul Sartre in the Light of Jean-Jacques Rousseau*, p. 389. He is here commenting on some points raised by Aristotle's *Nicomachean Ethics*.
3. Olafson, *Principles and Persons*, p. 215.
4. Tiryakian, *Sociologism and Existentialism*, pp. 235-236.
5. *Ibid.*, p. 141.
6. Galston, "Defending Liberalism," p. 627.
7. Hartmann, *Ethics*, Vol. II, p. 116.
8. Marcuse, "Contributions to a Phenomenology of Historical Materialism," p. 30. See also Leon Trotsky, "Their Morals and Ours," in Irving Howe, ed., *The Basic Writings of Trotsky* (New York: Random House, 1963), p. 379.
9. Flynn, *Sartre and Marxist Existentialism*, p. 404, note, quoting from the *Critique*.
10. Karl Korsch, *Karl Marx* (New York: Russell and Russell, 1963; first published in 1938). It is not clear how the proletariat did this. One imagines numerous workers in the shops poring over Marx's *Critique of Political Economy*, but like many intellectuals' visions of the worker, this seems a bit abstract.
11. See also Sartre's reply to Lefort, in *The Communists and Peace*, p. 232.
12. For commentary see Flynn, *Sartre and Marxist Existentialism*, p. 115; Desan, *The Marxism of Jean-Paul Sartre* (Gloucester: Peter Smith, 1974), pp. 233-234; Gila J. Hayim, *The Extential Sociology of Jean-Paul Sartre* (Amherst: University of Massachusetts Press, 1980), pp. 98-109; and, of course, the *Critique*.
13. Flynn, *Sartre and Marxist Existentialism*, p. 95.

14. In falling, Dasein, the person, loses himself in the "inauthentic being-with-others," which is called the 'they' or again in the busy-ness of his concerns with the world of things. This concept of falling forms an interesting topic in Heidegger's *Being and Time*. It is also discussed in Macquarrie, *Existentialism*, pp. 168-169.
15. Mallin, *Merleau-Ponty's Philosophy*, p. 270.
16. Aron, *History and the Dialectic of Violence*, p. 100.
17. Flynn, *Sartre and Marxist Existentialism*, p. 145, drawing from the *Critique*.
18. Delue, *On the Marxism of Jean-Paul Sartre in the Light of Jean-Jacques Rousseau*, p. 120.
19. Justin Aronfreed, "Moral Deveopment from the Standpoint of a General Psychological Theory," in Thomas Lickona, ed., *Moral Development and Behavior, Theory, Research, and Social Issues* (New York: Holt, Rinehart and Winston, 1976), p. 69.
20. Hartmann, *Ethics*, Vol. II, p. 110. The entire section from page 106 is of interest.
21. Kohlberg, *The Philosophy of Moral Development*, p. 67. Good, for Skinner, is "cultural survival," and he also adopts the position of moral relativism, that "each culture has its own set of goods . . ." whereas our position is that each culture ought to provide a morality based on the sense of taking each person into consideration. Of course, within each culture, other ethical pursuits may indeed differ.
22. See Walter Laqueur and Richard Breitman, *Breaking the Silence* (New York: Simon and Schuster, 1986) for this case.
23. Staub, *The Roots of Evil*, p. 167.
24. Poster, *Sartre's Marxism*, p. 70.
25. Kamenka, *The Ethical Foundations of Marxism*, p. 60.
26. J. Roger Lee, "The Morality of Capitalism and of Market Institutions," in Tibor R. Machan, ed., *The Main Debate: Communism versus Capitalism* (New York: Random House, 1987), p. 91, suggests that we do not have the emotional resources to help everyone, but the impersonal operations of the market allow a substantial amount of uninvolved assistance to others.
27. J. Emmett Tyrrell, Jr., *The Liberal Crackup*, p. 213.
28. Delue, *On the Marxism of Jean-Paul Sartre*, pp. 120-121.
29. Lenin, *Left Wing*, p. 77.
30. *Ibid.*, p. 62.
31. Hartmann, *Ethics*, Vol. II, p. 120.
32. See Nien Cheng, "Life and Death in Shanghai," *Time*, Vol. 129, No. 23 (June 8, 1987), 42-56. These are excerpts from her book.
33. Richard K. Ashley, "Three Modes of Economism," *International Studies Quarterly*, Vol. 27, No. 4 (December 1983), p. 478-479.

34. Cranston, in "Herbert Marcuse," pp. 85-116, Cranston, *The New Left*, provides a devastating analysis of Marcuse's positions such as the tyranny of toleration and the suppression of conservative ideas.
35. Gentile, *Genesis and Structure of Society*, p. 176.
36. Smith, *Cavour*, p. 29.
37. See Gramsci's *The Modern Prince*, a Marxist classic of the 20th century. See also James Joll, *Antonio Gramsci* (New York: Penguin Books, 1977), p. 129.
38. Popper, *The Open Society and Its Enemies*, Vol 2, p. 75. Popper is referring to Hegel here, but the quotation is probably even more appropriate in criticism of Sartre.
39. In the *Critique*, of course; for a summary of Sartre's philosophy of revolution, see Barnes, *The Literature of Possibility*, p. 258.
40. See Manser, *Sartre*, p. 11.
41. The discriminating intellectual will be happy to learn, however, that "basically there were no errors; that group of people should have been killed." This is quoted from Andrew J. Nathan, "The Road to Tiananmen Square," *The New Republic*, Vol. 201, No. 5 (July 31, 1989), p. 33.
42. Walter Schwarz, "Souvenir of a belle epoque," *The Manchester Guardian*, Vol. 131, No. 11 (September 9, 1984), p. 8. Schwarz is discussing the French intellectuals, but the thought has wider applicability.
43. George Urban, "A Conversation with Leszak Kolakowski," *Encounter*, Vol. LVI, No. 1, (January 1981), p. 25.
44. See their "Human Dignity, Human Rights, and Political Regimes," p. 805.
45. Flynn, *Sartre and Marxist Existentialism*, p. 193.
46. Macquerrie, *Existentialism*, p. 148.
47. McMahon, *Humans Being*, p. 258; also Flynn, *Sartre and Marxist Existentialism*, p. 195.
48. Morgenthau, *Dilemmas of Politics*, p. 112.
49. Galston, "Defending Liberalism," p. 626.
50. Thomas R. Nilsen, *Ethics of Speech Communication* (New York: The Bobbs-Merrill Company, 1974), p. 75.
51. Gentile, *Genesis and Structure of Society*, p. 95.
52. Plant, *Hegel*, p. 231.
53. Parfit, *Reasons and Persons*, p. 284 ff. Parfit is quite interesting on the subject of identity, although the issue is framed in the individual context.
54. See Flynn, *Sartre and Marxist Existentialism*, pp. 141-142.
55. Steiner, *Martin Heidegger*, p. 112.
56. Edward Andrew, *Shylock's Rights: A Grammar of Lockian Claims* (Toronto: University of Toronto Press, 1988), p. 75.
57. Melvin E. Bradford, "Sentiment and the U.S. Immigration Policy," *The American Spectator*, Vol. 17, No. 4 (April 1984), 20.
58. Mackie, *Ethics: Inventing Right and Wrong*, p. 123.
59. Rawls, *A Theory of Justice*, p. 473.

Chapter 12

Implicating Others Unawares

The ontological origin of freedom means that individuals in one sense cannot be deprived of their ability to choose freely. Politically, the problem of free choice is less simple. The conditions of an authentic choice, such as we have outlined in Chapter 8, include the application of lucidity to the analysis of the situation, and we must conjecture that the true qualities of any situation are never fully known. There is additionally the difficulty of fitting a value system to the situation, determining how values will structure the situation with relation to ethical projects.

Finally, the effective attainment of a lucid view of the situation is dependent on experience and education. What the consciousness can take in may be the same for all, provided there are unimpaired senses, but what can be understood on the basis of this data is dependent on qualities of the understanding. Is it ever possible that bracketing in phenomenological analysis will provide each human consciousness with an equal contact with essence?

With regard to an individual's value structure, lucidity and a critical outlook are at stake again, in order that the person is capable of forming an authentic choice regarding the external values offered by society. It is ordinarily not likely that any values will make an entry into the world, *de novo*; there have been few ethical innovators in history; these are probably as rare as innovators in scientific discovery. Two major problems emerge from these tasks that are involved in assuring an authentic choice in good faith, and these are (1) that many individuals and groups do not have the requisite knowledge and skills to make an authentic choice; and (2) that the situation may be posed deceptively, because it is subject to manipulation and false interpretations.

Raz puts it in terms of the autonomous person, who is at least in part the author of his or her own life.[1] One the one hand, autonomy is to to have options available from which to choose; on the other hand, there is a need to possess the ability to search and question the alternative available. We turn to a general discussion of these issues in the context of implicating others unawares in our own projects.

The fundamental position on morality taken in this work ought to be clear, namely, that it is the minimal regard for others; this basic concern for others ought to be adopted for the reason that as individual consciousnesses, they should be accorded a fundamental right as for-themselves to freely pursue the projects they select. If such a right prevails in the surrounding world, an environment usually bounded by the nation, then everyone's world will be enhanced. Parenthetically, although this basic morality should be sufficiently supported by this time, Popper points the interesting results of studies of rats, which show that raised in an enriched environment, rats show both more activity and brain growth than those raised in depleted environments.[2]

According freedom to others must result in an enriched social environment for humans. This is the significance of the doctrines of justice and equality, and it requires no necessary major project, unless one chooses to devote political energies to expanding the concrete freedom of others by influencing society to move in the direction of democracy--in fact, this is a logical major political goal, if politics are among one's important projects. In Chapters 10 and 11, we arrived at the dramatic conclusion that the ethical principles we espoused supported a democratic regime. In some political situations, such a project might require immense courage and a considerable devotion of time, the political project becoming all-embracing, as it did in the case of Andrei Sakharov in the Soviet Union in the 1980s, or in the case of the Czech playwright Vaclav Havel during the oppression of the Gustav Husak regime after 1968.

But in other cases, the problems to be resolved in the political situation may be less compelling, and the political project may be subsidiary to other more compelling projects. This is the only real meaning of the tyranny of tolerance; democracy may deprive the individual of taking a dramatic stand against oppression, although there is probably no political situation that does not call forth some measure of possible improvements. In addition, we may agree with Camus, that it takes substantial courage against existence constantly threatening to collapse into absurdity simply to carry out our mundane projects. In some respects, the accomplishment of a reform takes as much persistent courage as the strident call for violence. For some intellectuals, the dedication to revolution masks the reluctance to participate in politics.

But politics is conducted on the basis of power, and, indeed, so are all the ethical projects. We may, wrongly, try to flee the issue of power by shunning politics, but it will become evident that whatever the ethical purpose, save for abject passivity, it will be power-related. Power enables us to make our way in encountered situations, with their contingencies and the conflicting projects of other persons. To be a force in the world, as author, politician, artist or reformer requires some degree of internal control, some positive self-esteem, some ability to project values onto the situation. It demands if our projects are not to come to naught, that power be exercised so the goals sought do not recede from view as we approach them, like some mirage. Thus, power, which is also enhanced by the ability to grasp the situation, is necessary to a the ethical life, which is the life of goals.

But power may be put to other uses. The possibility always exists that projects might be facilitated if we are able to enlist the aid of others in the pursuit of ends. There is nothing immoral in concerting one's efforts with the efforts of willing others, provided our projects mesh and are the result of open discussion and free collaboration. But the temptation is strong to enlist the aid of others, whether their projects are compatible with ours or not--to draw others into our projects, although they may be ignorant of the true aims. This use of power is to implicate others unawares in our own projects.

To arrive successfully at goals in such a case will realize our own projects while cheating unheeding allies of realizing the projects to which they wrongly believed themselves committed. Suddenly the situation they believed they were engaged in becomes an entirely different situation; the value structure of the situation is transformed; the scales fall from their eyes. The free projects to which others believed themselves committed have been rendered nugatory, highways to nowhere, and the controlling project of another has been realized. The for-itself has chosen freely, but the alternatives presented were false ones. The situation was spuriously defined, and the others have been robbed, as it were, of the consequences of their free choice; their concrete freedom has been stolen from them. They have been tools. They have been reduced to the status of objects. The Party that promised them land reform was controlled by the great landowners, and reform has been stultified and crippled in bureaucratic red tape and legal conundrums. Or the Party that promised the dictatorship of the proletariat now controls the workers' unions and outlaws strikes. The soviets are abolished, according to plan.

With relation to the principle of justice and regard for others as authors of free choices, which were the fundamentals of morality, implicating others unawares in our projects has effectively reduced them to objects in someone else's world. To implicate others unawares in this fashion, therefore, is the essence of immorality. The practice is common enough in political events, and it constitutes a political evil. Aside from aggressive violence, which is sometimes associated with implicating others, manipulation is the prime political evil. It cheats others of purpose and meaning. Free choices have accomplished the opposite of their perpetrator's intent. Ethical projects might as well not have been.[3]

Sometimes the world itself, the contingencies it presents, the hapless predictions we make concerning what might bring pleasure, transform our goals against our intent. These are the risks that exist for everyone in the normal course of choosing. We accept these risks, that we might be wrong after all, that despite a fanatic devotion to music, we really did not have the skills requisite for the career of concert pianist. But to fall unsuspectingly into the meshes of the projects of another adds an element of deception and danger to the world that ought not to have been there in the "normal," unblemished situation. It is a human addition to the situations, although the phenomenon is not unknown in the animal world, as witnessed in the "bait" that turns out to be the predator's tongue.

The in-itself provides a blind resistance to projects; it does not plot our failures. It is not under the control of the fates as in the Greek drama. Of course, we are responsible for our choices, even if the immediate consequences of these were unintended, provided that additional available knowledge and lucidity would have allowed us to predict those consequences. But implicated unaware in the project of another, we find ourselves responsible for an outcome that we neither intended nor predicted, nor could easily have averted.

Such an intrinsically political evil is directed at nullifying the very ontological freedom of the for-itself, which, tangled in a web of deception, may go on choosing freely but always futilely. Haering considered such a tactic as among

> sins that are in very particular ways, directed against human freedom and people's capacity to grow in it. Among such transgressions might be enumerated all manipulations that diminish a person's self-interpretation, self-awareness, and his or her active insertion into the history of liberation.[4]

In the format of game theory, what happens to others is that their subgames, to which they apply themselves in interpreting situations as they seem to appear, turn out to be part of a supergame, which really controls the entire situation. Players of subgames are engulfed in the machinations of the controllers, who are actually conducting the game that counts.

If one seeks the origins of projects that have implicated others unawares, it is likely that somewhere close to the point of origin will be an intellectual. The reason for this is that it is the vocation of the intellectual to understand situations and to convey interpretations to others. The forte of the intellectual is words--words used effectively and persuasively. It is significant that Sartre entitled the autobiography of his youth, *Words*. Thus, the intellectual, having mastered the skills of communication has mastered, as well, the skills of deception. Words allow us to communicate information to others; words also allow us to communicate misinformation to others.

For the reason that the intellectual as interpreter and artisan of words may also be little integrated into the situation he or she interprets, the intellectual is also capable of self-deception. The intellectual devises the ideology of the working class without having worked in a factory. The intellectual is always, to some extend, involved in abstracting from reality. Self-deception violates the responsibility of lucidity, but it may not imply any conscious intent to deceive others. The chemist cannot practice self-deception in science for long--at some point, a chemist will confront recalcitrant reality that forces him or her to rethink theory and hypotheses. Thus, for the social philosopher, Marx's call for an alliance of theory and practice has a special significance, for it is through practice that the social philosopher becomes immersed in the world he or she purports to interpret. As Husserl asserts for his phenomenological technique, practice takes one "to the facts themselves."

But the intellectual represents a rather feeble source of physical power.

Removed generally from the reins of control of military or state apparatuses, the intellectual must, to effect certain projects, enlist others voluntarily into his or her project, and the temptation is great to do this in whatever way possible, even by deception. Skilled in searching for truth, the intellectual will be equally skilled in the use of untruth.

For this reason, the intellectual may reach out to other social groups, to the peasantry or the proletariat, to whom is delegated the task of bringing the intellectual's projects to fruition. We propose the historical burdens for others, for the Proletariat, for the Aryan, for the blacks, for the poor, or for the students. In addition, the intellectual has interests, including prestige and wealth, but above all the interest that his or her words be taken seriously and make an impact in the world. Among other important interests, the intellectual, as do all committed people, has ethical projects to realize in the world.

The critical question for the intellectual is authenticity, but there are also those who have, in bad faith, sold out, often to the prevailing ideology of the state. Sartre attacks this group as the false intellectual, who, pretending to the claim of rigorous reasoning, the intellectual's supposed stock-in-trade, always comes out in favor of the *status quo*. Sartre applies this argument to condemn the false intellectuals as those who espouse reformist arguments as against radical and revolutionary solutions. This book stands condemned for its reformist recommendations. However, to let the arguments stand on their own merits, I would suggest that Sartre has created here a false dichotomy. There are innumerable phonies on all sides.[5]

Let us liken the role that the intellectual has assumed to that of the Chinese mandarin appointed to the office of the Ming Dynasty Censorate. To have accepted this office, which was not infrequently a dangerous assignment, a mandarin has pledged to seek out the inadequacies of imperial rule for the good of the governed as well as for the interests of the Emperor and the imperial government. A convinced Confucian would be duty-bound, for the reason that having assumed the mandarinal role is to have extended a promise to heaven and to important others, bureaucrats and subjects, that one will be sharp-sighted and honest, whatever the consequences. The mandarin in the censorate took on the duty of witnessing. Cases exist of mandarins, the bearers of tidings the Emperor did not want to hear, being executed for their pains.

So with the role of intellectual, to assume such a self-appointed role, honesty and painstaking analysis is owed to everyone, particularly to the vulnerable of society. If Stalinism or Maoism has been the route we recommended to the future society of free beings, we would have to confess to being a false intellectual in Sartre's meaning, for we have missed the truth. To linger on this interesting problem a while longer, one can see the skill of the artisan of words: by defining the problem as a dichotomy between the Marxist/Leninist revolutionary and the reformer, by implication, between the one and only authentic path to a better future and the advocate of undramatic reforms, the latter interpreted as intending no change whatsoever, Sartre has won his point by definition. And he has done so by citing no evidence whatsoever.

Sartre's political stance is a *tour de force* of words, a triumph of the intellectual. This is far too easy a victory over reformism, so we will opt to stay awhile longer in the field of combat. Sartre's argument is not without some force, however; the danger of falling into the position of spokesperson, subaltern, to a form of false consciousness is very real. It is the indictment of Sartre's philosophy itself by some in the Marxist camp, such as Lukacs and Garaudy.

Let us clarify here the definition of "implication unawares." The person thus caught up is not coopted. Cooptation implies that the person, sometimes an intellectual, is aware of the purposes for which he or she has been coopted. Thus, the dictator has promulgated a new constitution, the purpose of which is to consolidate his power. The articulate young scholar has been requested to present the official explanation of the new document to the peasants, the unions, and the schools. At stake is the promising academic career in the major university, contacts with the powerful, and the good life for self and family. The young scholar decides to comply with the official request and to explain the constitution in official terms, but the choice is not made unawares, for the scholar knows full well the nature of the cooptation, and the projects advanced are quite clear.

At this point, we might consider a question concerning social roles. Since ethical projects in the world are self-imposed, to whom is honesty owed? It is at least a feasible project and, at times, a more lucrative one, to join, say, the legal profession with the single-minded view of amassing a fortune. What is wrong with that? Admittedly, the connection with morality, that is, justice, is a tenuous one in the choice to be rich, but if the worthy goal is a free society in which people can be genuinely considered ends in themselves, it is a deception of others as meaningful individuals to not be what one appears to be, thus, in a sense, implicating others unawares in our subversive legal projects.

As a journalist, it is my duty to be a reliable witness to events, to not use information for the purpose of blackmail, to not dedicate reporting to an ulterior ideology that causes one to omit certain fact. As a lawyer, the chief goal ought to be to serve justice in the sense of applying rights to everyone equally. As a scientist, the scientific role requires testing and reporting hypotheses about the in-itself accurately and fully. As as an intellectual, we must penetrate the veils of "false consciousness" and evaluate situations fully and honestly, attack projects that deprive others of their concrete freedom, expose inauthenticity and bad faith, and come to the aid of others who have been implicated unawares in manipulative projects.

To fail in any of these tasks, to violate the nature of the role, is to contribute to distrust and suspicion and to do injury to the moral community that is the frail fabric of any potentially better society. Sartre rightly castigates the false intellectual who practices self-censorship, who renounces his or her "ability to question the world," for that is the role intellectuals impose on themselves.[6] Thus, the intellectual above all must avoid Machiavelli's advice to the Prince,

> to seem to have this last quality [religion, and also "mercy, faith, integrity, humanity...." are the qualities Machiavelli refers to], for men in general judge more by the eyes than by the hands....[7]

But the intellectual's is a peculiar role, dependent as it is on words, on concepts, on interpretations of day-to-day reality from which some intellectuals find themselves to be quite severed and alienated. There is a tendency for the world to be interpreted in "abstractions and general categories," as Rothman and Lichter remark of Rudi Dutschke:

> For all his celebration of the individual, there is very little recognition of individuality, particularly in his speeches and tracts. People and social institutions alike are reduced to abstractions and general categories,

a characteristic of the German New Left, according to the authors.[8]

This common failing of the intellectual is related to other shortcomings. Whatever else the intellectuals represent, they also represent interests of their own quasi-class, as well as personal interests. Superior in knowledge and skills to many other groups in society, the intellectual is capable of masking these interests by projecting them onto others. Gouldner[9] quotes Bakunin, "It stands to reason that the one who knows will dominate the one who knows less." And like others, the intellectuals are themselves frequently Machiavellian, "resorting constantly to a conscious or unconscious deception of the masses," according to Max Nomad.[10] Needless to add, the intellectual is also subject to resentments and jealousies--as a capable interpreter of situations the question must occur, why has he or she not become powerful and wealthy? Why do those with very limited understanding attain success, and not the deserving intellectual? The intellectuals purport to interpret society and to uncover its mechanisms and its desired future.

In Marxism, which is a quite superior intellectual construct, everyone is assigned a role in the society, the peasant, the bourgeoisie, the proletariat, the small shopkeeper, but the theorist somehow transcends all of these groups, for he or she can analyze society independently of any social station. From Olympus, the intellectual is able to discern, not the contending criss-cross of innumerable individual projects, but some one all-embracing project, that depends for its culmination on the proletariat. (Or, if the intellectual was a Narodnik, on the Russian peasant as the bearer of Slavic destiny.) So Lukacs, ". . . the proletariat has been entrusted by history [not by God, mind you] with the task of *transforming society* consciously . . . ."[11]

Well, and it is a damn heavy burden, and the proletariat had better not shirk their historical duty. Thus, the proletariat as a group (that is, some of them) has been enmeshed for years in a typical intellectual project, which has implicated many of them unawares. If they should have the audacity to fail their destiny, the intellectual may designate others to replace them, for instance, the students in the 1960s movements. Thus, a new and purer group is assigned the role of realizing human destiny, while the worker has now become a bourgeoisized common clod.

But should any individual assign the onus of realizing destiny on anyone else? Is there, in any case, a destiny transcending the individual? Our opinions concerning the existence of some ultimate destiny were provided earlier. Is there a universal class? Implicated in such a project, the proletarian finds him- or herself deprived of individuality, for "this [class] consciousness is . . . neither the sum nor the average of what is thought or felt by the single individuals who make up the class."[12]

Rousseau, out of his sometimes paranoid outlook, was very suspicious of the philosophes, those intellectuals *par excellence* of the 18th century, for he noted that

> . . . these intellectuals constitute a new party, a "new class," a new church

of secular priests seeking lawless power. While supporting their antifeudal and anticlerical mission, he sees that they act not for the people's interest but their own.[13]

Yet, Rousseau himself was guilty of advocating the "Lawgiver" or "Guide" who draws the people to do the right thing by making them believe they have made free choices.[14] Left to their own devices, of course, the workers can be relied upon to betray the high expectations of history and develop only trade union and bourgeois consciousness. Only the vanguard party can rescue them for destiny. Trotsky wrote that "the liberation of the workers can come only through the workers themselves. There is no greater crime than deceiving the masses."[15]

He is denouncing Stalinism, of course, in this passage, but the very notion of the vanguard is too easily subject to Stalinist misuse. How well, indeed, do intellectuals know these other groups? Turgenev warned Herzen that the "instinctive socialism" of the Russian peasant on which Herzen rested his hopes for the future was a myth. Turgenev, who knew the peasants somewhat better (as his observations in *A Sportsman's Sketches* show), knew that for many of them to obtain land and become a bourgeois was the desirable goal.[16] Of course, to attain to a state of bourgeois comfort and complacency is a most contemptible goal, as any bourgeois intellectual can attest.

A major movement that has drawn support from workers and peasants in the 20th century is the Communist party, organized by Lenin under the concept of the vanguard. This crucial interpretation of Marxism, the vanguard concept, was proposed by Lenin with such statements as

> the workers can acquire class political consciousness only from without, that is, only outside of the economic struggle. . . . [or] The history of all countries shows that the working class, exclusively by its own effort, is able to develop only trade union consciousness. . . .The theory of Socialism . . . grew out of the philosophical, historical, and economic theories that were elaborated by the educated representatives of the propertied classes, the intellectuals, [or]. . .The spontaneous labour movement is pure and simple unionism. . . .Hence, the task of Social Democracy, is to combat spontaneity, to divert the labour movement, with its spontaneous trade unionist striving, from under the wing of the bourgeoisie, and to bring it under the wing of revolutionary Social Democracy.[17]

Lenin's analysis is probably correct with respect to revolutionary projects, and it was certainly astute--for the theory of socialism as he conceived it, the vanguard party, was necessary. And it was also true that the requisite skill with concepts demanded that theory originate within the bourgeoisie.

Poster points out that in Sartre's fused group, each member has the same project. This may fit the reality of groups rather badly in many cases; certainly both Marx and Engels realized the difficulties of widespread class consciousness among the proletariat, the original class-conscious universal class. As Poster claims and as Lenin recognized, Sartre's fused group seems of rare occurrence; instead, spontaneity among the working class had developed organizations in which varied projects existed, just as Bernstein had alleged.[18]

The vanguard party was more in the nature of the fused group, and it was not a party composed of workers. The danger of the vanguard organization would seem almost inevitable, that the party would also begin to manipulate the workers. There are some indications of this from Lenin: ". . .and that is the whole point--we must *not* regard that which is obsolete for *us* [the Party] as obsolete *for the class*, as obsolete *for the masses.*"[19]

Once such an attitude marks the organizational principle, then manipulation is not long to appear.[20] Laqueur cites the Soviet writer on terrorist groups, Victor Vladimirovich Vityuk (*Under False Flags: Hypocrisy and Self-Deception of Leftwing Terrorism*, Moscow, 1985), that although urban terrorists may not originally hold the masses in contempt, the logic of terrorism "sooner or later induces them to make an about-turn and they come to regard the masses as an object of political manipulation."[21] Vityuk had in mind, specifically, the urban guerrilla phenomenon, but the remark might apply to almost any vanguard-type organization.

Intellectuals in the vanguard designate the proletariat as the universal class with the project of leading society to the post-historical classless society. But the proletariat cannot always live up to the goals and high expectations of their destiny, so that manipulation of them becomes at least tempting. Perhaps the intellectual, versed in dialectical materialism, can hurry the clods on to their destiny. But, it is implicating others unawares to involve them in world historical projects that do not arise spontaneously.

> Capitalism would not be capitalism if the "pure" proletariat were not surrounded by a large number of exceedingly mixed transitional types, from the proletariat to the semi-proletarian (who earns half of his

livelihood by the sale of his labour power), from the semi-proletarian to the small peasant (and petty artisan, handicraft worker and small proprietor in general), from the small peasant to the middle peasant, and so on, and if the proletariat itself were not divided into more or less developed strata, if it were not divided according to territorial origin, trade, sometimes according to religion, and so on. And all this makes it necessary, absolutely neccessary, for the vanguard of the proletariat, its class-conscious section, the Communist Party, to resort to maneuvers, arrangements and compromises with the various groups of proletarians, with the various parties of the workers and small proprietors.[22]

But the projects of the peasantry, a class more backward than the proletariat (indeed Marx denies that the French peasants constitute a class in the *Eighteenth Brumaire of Louis Napoleon*), leads Lenin to refer to them as "the vacillating, unstable peasantry, as the led. . . ."[23] Mao, whose study of the peasantry in 1928 brought him to the revolutionary strategy of organizing the countryside, developed the slogan of land redistribution to the peasants, a chief project among almost all peasantries, but this was not in line with Mao's true project, which was always the system of communes. Communes are not the project of most peasants, of course.

Aidit of Indonesia, also, following Mao's lead, was quite frank about this, referring to the distribution of land as the bourgeois phase of social change.[24] Yet, the vanguard party of the proletariat has frequently implicated the peasants unawares in projects that were not theirs. In France, too, the Mouvement de Defense des Exploitants Familiaux (MODEF), inspired by the Communist party, pursued the line of anticapitalism, defense of small property owners, and opposition to emigration to the cities. These are not quite recognizable Communist policies, but they were shaped to manipulate the audience.[25]

The theoretical problem with the vanguard idea in the context of Marxist theory, is that, as a powerful organizational principle for revolutionaries, it is far more generally applicable than Marxism itself, which predicted the revolution in advanced capitalist societies. But the successful organizational principle may dispense with the theory: Practice obliterates theory here, and the vanguard pursues not the classless society but power only.

One of the most successful vanguard parties was that formed in Vietnam, not a promising locale for a dictatorship of the proletariat. The theoretical spokesperson for the party was Truong Chinh, who, heeding

Lenin's call for "absolute centralization and the strictest discipline of the proletariat,"[26] also called for centralization and control:

> Every cadre must guide the novices who work side by side with him so as to create new cadres. So many active workers and peasants, so many youths fully devoted to the Revolution are ready to accept all sacrifices! Have confidence in them, employ them boldly, guide them patiently, *but do not forget to control them.*[27]

While not deviating from its own project, Truong Chinh recommended Communist alliances with other groups, so long as the Party remained in control:

> In its domestic policy, the Indochinese Communist Party organized the different strata of the people into the National Liberation Front: the Viet Minh Front. The programme of this Front assured the protection of human and civil rights and of property, the respect of private property, the liberty of conscience, as well as equality between nationalities and the sexes with the aim of realising the unity of the whole people against the Japanese and French Fascists. Facing the concrete conditions of the revolution in Indochina, the Indochinese Communist Party, promoter and leader of the Viet Minh Front, left out of its programme the watch word: Agrarian revolution, (deciding for the present, not to confiscate land held by landlords), and this with a view to making a differentiation between types of landlords and winning a number of them over to the anti-imperialist cause, widening the National Front to struggle for independence. This Front should comprise workers, peasants, petty-bourgeoisie of towns, even national bourgeoisie, and include patriotic personalities belonging to the landlord class.[28]

This, of course, is the principle of the United Front, sponsored by the Communist International in the 1930s. There had been an earlier adaptation of the tactic, which certainly drew its principle from Lenin, in March, 1922, and was probably sponsored by Trotsky.[29] This tactic was scrapped by the Third International under Zinoviev in 1924, when the more radical tactic of the "united front from below" was propounded, which meant conflict with the leadership of other groups and appeals to their membership over their heads.[30] This strategy helped disunite the left in Germany, contributing importantly to Hitler's ascent to power and to the disastrous revolt in China recounted in Andre Malraux's *The Conquerors* and *Man's Fate*.

Whereas prior to the United Front of 1935, the Communist parties had generally been quite open about their project in the front from below, in keeping with the injunction in the *Communist Manifesto*, "The Communists disdain to conceal their views and aims," the new tactic contributed to covert maneuvers. In this type of Front, elaborated by Georgi Dimitroff, the Communist parties proposed alliances with any party whose aims might coincide to some degree with those of the Party, while the Communists retained their major project of revolution, their organizational separateness, and the principle of "democratic centralism."[31]

At the same time, Dimitroff made the condition that the party reject "support of one's own bourgeoisie in imperialist war," another fateful error considering world conditions in the 1930s. In any case, while never relinquishing its aim, the party in its United Front adapted conciliatory symbols acceptable to the groups they joined. This was a period in which others were implicated, frequently, unawares, in the projects of the well-organized vanguard parties. It was the heyday of the front organization.

In the United Front tactic, the vanguard party joined with other organized groups and other parties. In a related tactic, it sought to control mass organizations, including trade unions, that were not necessarily organized under other parties. A small, organizationally skilled group, is capable of controlling a much larger organization of like-minded but less organized individuals, a process exemplifying Michels' "Iron Law of Oligarchy."

In such front organizations, the Communists could usually guide and influence the World Youth Congress or the World Peace Council, or other such fronts, in the direction of Soviet policy. Thus, unsuspecting members supported the supergame of Soviet foreign policy without a realization of their own contributions, all the while playing out the subgame that they believed represented the true aims. They were implicated unawares in the projects of others.[32]

This is an effective social tactic for reducing a consciousness to an object. Truong Nhu Tang states that with respect to the Young People's Association in Vietnam within which he worked, and which was organized by the Party, "I was working toward an apparatus of control, a network ready for the manipulation that would come in time."[33]

It is a well-known principle of sociology that topdogs are more easily organized than are underdogs, for the latter simply lack the skills of communication, organizational principles, education, and the resources of the social elite. There are, therefore, strata in society that are more easily taken in by the projects of others. These are the weak, resourceless, and susceptible. For those who might desire to utilize others strictly as objects to facilitate their own projects there is sufficient human material in most societies, even the most industrially and technologically advanced.

And humans are frequently manipulative. Their propensity to manipulativeness is evidenced in their desire to raise animals solely for the purpose of food products: the perfect cattle would be square and stackable in small enclosures. And if mice might be raised solely for the purpose of susceptibility to cancer, why not humans for menial work, as in Aldous Huxley's *Brave New World*?

We have a number of direct expressions of this, in such statements as that of Rabbi Yekuti Azri'eh, leader in Israel of Zikhron Ya'akov, "The Arab nations should not be granted education. If they are allowed to raise their heads and will not be in the condition of hewers of wood and drawers of water, we will have a problem."[34] To be able to think this way is the reason that no ethnic, religious, or racial group should ever be in a position to dictate to another different ethnic, religious, or racial group.

Such forms of manipulation are tools of the political trade. Nor is this a new technique in history: Smollett speaks of polished ruffians, for whom the engrossing game of power was death to others. The reference may have been to Lord Chesterfield's manipulation of the Highland peasantry, whose Revolt in 1740 was supported by Chesterfield, then in opposition to the government that he wanted to bring down. Then, himself in the government, he recommended the execution of these same peasants. They were convenient objects.[35]

Chon Pongjun, to impress his peasant followers, had himself shot with blanks, dropping bullets from his sleeves, convincing many Tonghak adherents that he was supernatural.[36] James Madison, on the basis of his legislative experience, saw legislators exact "base and selfish measures masked by pretexts of the public good," and clever persons duping the public and even other legislators by "veiling . . . and varnishing sophisticated arguments" in order to disguise their real objectives.[37]

But the insight into such machinations is just what is most lacking among the disadvantaged. Politics ought to be the use of power to obtain one's ends while paying regard to the social contract. In moral politics in which others are taken into account, projects may conflict with the projects of others, but the ends are transparent. In manipulatory politics, the end remains latent while some others get taken in supporting manifest ends.

Those who get easily taken in, the manipulable, are often the lower strata, repressed groups (women in many societies), and persons with no firm values of their own, the inauthentic. The peasantry, the proletariat, certain racial or ethnic groups that tend to fall for historical reasons at the lower scale of socio-economic status--low wealth, low education, low prestige--these are the readily maniupulable. Selznick reminds us that "Under conditions of political combat, those who have no firm values of their own become the instrument of the values of others."[38] This is just why an education in the humanities is superior, or ought to be superior, to an education directed too narrowly toward a profession or toward technological specialties.

In Eco's *The Name of the Rose*, the educated monk refers to "the simple," those easily swept up into heresy, unsuspecting, consumed by purposes of which they have no understanding. In the conditions among the masses in the Middle Ages, manipulation must have been both easy and tempting, but conditions in many areas of the world in the 20th century are comparable, far-reaching fanatical projects that implicate others unawares are a mark of the 20th century, even taking in far more sophistical populations.

It must be remembered that there is a vital difference between lying, on the one hand, and implicating others unawares, on the other hand. The former will take people in with regard to our true motives; but the latter technique will induct them as unsuspecting perpetrators of these true motives. The difference is important. The lie will veil our political game, but implication will embrace others into a supergame.

Habermas has defined the true or rational consensus of people in the conditions of his "ideal speech situation." In this interaction, there would be no deception or domination. In the first place, this ideal speech situation depends on the intent of the communicator to be open with regard to intentions. In the second place, the communicated-to has an equal distribution of opportunities (power) "to order and resist orders, to permit and forbid, to make and extract promises, and to be responsible for one's conduct and demand that others are as well." In short, such a worthy society will have enforced no one-sided norms.[39]

In connection with this idea, Martin Buber and Karl Jaspers both advise openness to communications with many other persons. This is just what the dispossessed groups cannot do. And it is effective for ideological movements to seek to close off members' ability to meet other persons outside the movement as person to person, rather than as enemy against enemy.

Morally it is always evil to reduce any group to object status by implicating them unawares in our own projects. This includes that kind of solicitude where one takes over for the other, an implicating concern that deprives the other of "that with which he is to concern himself." Instead, Heidegger recommends that we give care back to the other, helping the other to his "existential potentiality-for-Being."[40] Solicitude of the wrong form is a repressive device. It reduces people unawares to the status of things, which are the "ready-to-hand." People are reduced to clientele for the solicitous reformer. Associated with this attitude are such repressive concepts as the "good wife," the "good worker," "the deserving poor," where good is an indication of their readiness-to-hand, their instrumentality for our projects.

While doing-good to others may be also a moral profession, there is always the problem that by acting in another's stead, that other is robbed of the existential freedom of self-determination.[41] Marx was fully aware of this, writing in his school examination essay, "Dignity. . . can be afforded only by that position in which we do not appear as servile instruments, but where we create independently within our own circle."[42] And it is of just this kind of dignity that we deprive individuals when, for the best of motives, we strive to aid the underdog through quotas, or induct them into higher education unprepared. Those who genuinely succeed at the new profession or academy will be marked, unfairly, with the reputation of being second-rate.

Thus, the correct moral intention of such reforms is not to provide a sense of goodness for the reformer, but to afford individuals the opportunity to become autonomous. This means that the humans affected by reforms of emancipation will actually become emancipated and cease to be a clientele for the social do-gooder. The best reformers, like Robert Owen and Wendell Phillips, have recognized this.

In international affairs, there is also the possibility of too much solicitude for others, the repressive taking over of projects that ought to be theirs. It is difficult to delineate where appropriate intervention and repressive solicitude begin and end, however. On the one hand, the Contra efforts of the United States were a too active intervention into a situation in which opposition to the Nicaraguan Sandinista regime was possible though hazardous. The same is the case in the Panamanian intervention in 1989; the situation might have been left to the indigenous opponents of President-for-life Manual Noriega.

During the intervention in Vietnam in the 1960s, Americans were drafted into the military to serve in combat while numbers of South

Vietnamese evaded the draft or were deferred. The will to fight for a cause was not present among too many South Vietnamese, which was part of the reason why the country collapsed so rapidly when the Americans departed. Under conditions like this, it is unlikely that an intervention from the outside is warranted, regardless of the predictable consequences if intervention is omitted.

It ought not to be overlooked either that some regimes are so rigid and ruthless that although there may exist ample opposition to the government, the opposition is silent and inoperative. No cells of resistance could have been organized against either Hitler or Stalin for long. Jaspers mitigates the guilt of many Germans under Nazism, for the reason that "Once the gates were shut, . . .a prison break from within was no longer possible."[43] Conditions like these, alas, also make intervention from the outside futile.

Again, there are those regimes that elicit the support of many of their society, even though they may be unsupportive in the extreme of human rights. Heinous as the regime may have been to democrats, there is no doubt that the Ayatolla Khomeini had the support of many Iranians. In a situation like this, it is well to leave events to their own course, unless the regime strikes out on foreign adventures.

Finally, there are situations that support intervention morally, but which are fraught with extreme dangers. This was the situation in the infamous winter war inflicted by the Soviet Union against Finland in 1940, where strict justice lay with the Finns, but intervention by the British and French would probably have been a disaster. It was also true of the Hungarian revolt of 1956, a revolt that propaganda from the United States had helped stimulate. It was true of the conquest in 1940 and the half-hearted suppression of independence of the Baltic states in 1991. In these cases, the consequences of intervention appeared to lucid minds too catastrophic to contemplate, so the moral choice at the local level was overridden by the choice that seemed to be moral at another level, namely the level of world politics.

To summarize the purpose of the just society, we ought to agree that "awareness is the first line of defense against degrading manipulation."[44] It means that persons must be enabled to become autonomous. "To resist the manipulation of others, individuals must possess a belief in their own position and a confidence born of experience that they can make their own way."[45] The evidence from studies of internal control have shown consistently that African-Americans and lower social status persons tend toward a belief in an external origin of their acts.[46] Efforts to advance such groups by manipulation of professional or educational standards should be subordinate to the major effort of society, which is to attack the source of much of this vulnerability, namely, the conditions that make some groups dependent and manipulable--lack of wealth, prospects, and education.[47]

Society may stand morally condemned for depriving persons or groups of an opportunity to achieve status and wealth, and in particular for depriving certain persons of the ability to develop autonomous personalities, but a just society cannot be condemned for those persons who renounce their opportunities or choose failure. All this is not to say, of course, that there are any fully just societies extant.

The problem arises whether it is sometimes wrong to deny individuals the freedom to pursue their own projects, in particular when those projects appear to us to be counterproductive. May we under some conditions implicate others in projects that are not theirs in order to save them from themselves? The problem is particularly difficult to answer in foreign affairs, when we presume to see that the projects of certain idealistic others are doomed to fail or to be controlled by some political manipulator. Is it our business to intervene? (This problem will be discussed more fully later.)

Once again, to refer to the social contract theorists, those who take it upon themselves to be in a state of nature against a relatively just society constitute a menace--some of these may be criminals, others corrupt officials, and some may be members of fused groups; almost never would they constitute whole identifiable groups such as African-Americans, women or workers, who most often are lost in their seriality. To repeat, those bent on reducing others to object status must be fought with effective weapons. The danger lies, however, in the ease of rationalizing our manipulations of others who constitute no real danger to social justice. This is the problem of the First Amendment freedom of speech. How far ought we to allow those to go whose principles are to destroy democracy?

The 20th century has witnessed an extreme example of inplicating others unawares in an alien project in the perpetration of the Holocaust by Nazi Germany. In Sartre's *Being and Nothingness* there is a subtle description of a seduction. Seduction was the theme of the Holocaust, and it helps explain why there was very little concerted resistance until the latest stages of the Final Solution, as in the Warsaw Ghetto and Treblinka. The tactics of "implementation in stages" (*Etappensystem*) and time-honored techniques of divide-and-rule deceived the victims.

The system created the illusion that the worst stage had now been reached. Then things became even worse. But still, the illusion remained: What more could possibly happen? So in stages, the Jews and the other victims of the concentration camps were gradually drawn on toward extermination.[48]

When the first restrictions were issued against Germans who were Jews, the fateful blows had already been delivered against elementary justice. Portions of the population had already been declared to be other than human. Groups were eliminated from the social contract. This is the stage at which revolt is warranted, for as John Locke rightly observes in his *Of Civil Government*, ". . . he who attempts to get another man into his absolute power does thereby put himself into a state of war with him"; but who would suspect that worse sequels were to follow, in Germany, in civilized Europe, in the 20th century?

In the camps themselves, living beings were reduced to things, until after death, hair and gold teeth were salvaged from the lifeless corpses. All this for the nihilistic projects of the Third Reich. It was not until later that the Germans themselves, some of whom had already reduced themselves to the impenetrability of stone, were in turn to be regarded as objects by their own regime, as when the German armies were advised to stand firm at Stalingrad.

Toward the last days of his life, predictably, Hitler lamented that the abstraction he had created, his universal class, the Aryan race, had proven itself inferior by losing the war and deserved to be itself eliminated. Those onto whom our projects are foisted had better live up to expectations. Hitler was not an intellectual, lacking the most elementary propensity toward lucidity, but his lifestyle was somewhat representative of that class.

The Holocaust contains a number of lessons. When a group is delegated the status of objects by society, the time has arrived when violent revolt and defense are justified. As some Germans learned, when any group in a society loses its standing in rights and justice, all groups come into jeopardy. The position of the proletariat in the early industrial revolution, likewise, justified revolution, if that could have been brought about by the proletariat; Marx erred by neglecting the possibilities inherent in reform in his own day.

Finally, while there has been moral development historically (as in the transition beyond strictly external values as people pass from *Gemeinschaft* groups to *Gesellschaft* societies), we may take no pride in the present level of morality in the 20th century. Genghis Khan and

Tamerlane would have felt comfortable in our era.

The state, or the institutions of states, are frequently manipulatory. Williams recommends that society, at least, ought to be transparent. That is, its ethical institution ought not to depend on citizens misunderstanding how the institution works.[49] In Marx's terminology, this means that false consciousness ought not to prevail to hold the social fabric together.

Sisela Bok points to the problem of secrecy, which is always required if we are to use others for purposes of our own. She makes the point that the information about the origins and conduct of the war in Vietnam ought never to have been kept secret in the first place. She is discussing the publication of the Pentagon Papers by Strauton Lynd. This was the type of information that ought to have been available to everyone as individual consciousness freely determining projects.[50]

There are complicating problems with this view, however. The United States, which is a relatively democratic society, was faced with a totalitarian opponent. Whereas a good deal of information was reported concerning the war and its vagaries from our side, from the other side we received either very little information or highly biased information. While the Pentagon Papers certainly did not make the American decision apparatus look good, what about the decision apparatus in North Vietnam?

Not until the war was over did Lacouture finally concede, too late to inform his earlier debates, that the Viet Cong had been controlled totally by the government of North Vietnam all along. Morality becomes a very complex issue in imbroglios like the conflict in Vietnam. America erred, in part, by its inability, partly through ignorance, to view the whole fabric of society, with all its people and all its various groups, rather than the government, generally severed from its supposed subjects, alone.

Against a totalitarian regime in the North, willing to sacrifice countless lives for its project (according to General Giap, it does not matter how many people die provided the revolution is successful), the South was unable to draw loyalties toward a semblance of a national will. It is doubtful that any regime would have been able to do so in a short period of time--ultimately, hundreds of thousands fled the united regime, in spite of the toll--perhaps half?--among the boat people. This denoument was probably unavoidable, and outside intervention was ultimately futile without extracting ever more dire human costs.

Related to the problems of the state apparatus, is the project of the planner. There is no necessary relationship between planning and treating people as objects, but the temptation is very great to do so. For one thing, the planner is often better educated than his or her clients. It is not easy to compete among innumerable political projects to win scarce resources and to bring one's own good ends to completion. Obviously, even in a successful project, some opposition will have to be overcome; some projects will suffer defeat; many other projects are denied for one that is implemented.

As in all political choices the project will have to be weighed against competing projects, which always include the null project, or the status quo, on the basis of political feasibility and economic costs. But more important, what does this project do by comparison with others to increase justice and equality, which includes improvements in the quality of life? This criterion is important.

The planner needs to acquainted with those the project affects--will a housing project like this one really increase the quality of life for this neighborhood? It is against moral principle to assume that we always know better what is good than do the people affected, or to assume that regardless of what these people say they want, we know what they really want.[51] George Bernard Shaw put it well in the *Woman's Guide to Socialism* that money was the best antidote to poverty, because it allows the poor to buy what they want, rather than what someone thinks they want. As Parfit says, "we are paternalists when we force someone to act in his own interests."[52] Yet, despite the many pitfalls, there are worthwhile projects of planning, such as the Tennessee Valley Authority.

The problem of morality and the planner occurs not only in the situation of the bureaucrat, but also concerns the social engineer, the advertising person, the behavioral scientist, and the psychologist. It is "an act of violence to force another to be happy in one's own way," declares Kant anticipating modern psychotherapy--he uses the example of the upper classes in dealing with their dependents.[53] Skinner's *Beyond Freedom and Dignity* (see page 168 there) is a forthright project to design culture for our good. In this, it differs not at all from all other projects of power, and the question at issue is whether Skinner's designs are our own, for they have no peculiar scientific merit.

All states espouse an ideology of some sort, which sometimes contributes to social order, at times by keeping groups subjugated, or elevating one group over others, or, possibly, even espousing justice. Mannheim points to the type of ideology that is not a self-delusion, but which is specifically intended to delude others.[54] Sartre refers to the same phenomena as "false totalities," cut off from living totalizing praxis (the give and take, let us say, of real political controversy) which arise in order to legitimate power for the rulers and impotence for the ruled.[55]

Rousseau was well aware of this possibility and the way in which improper conceptions of justice and morality could be deceptive:

> Whoever, renouncing in good faith all the prejudices of human vanity, seriously reflects on all these things, will discover at length that all these grand words of society, of justice, of law, of mutual defense, of help for the weak, of philosophy, and of the progress of reason are only lures invented by clever politicians or by cowardly flatterers to impose themselves on the simple. . . . Justice or morality, as it has developed, is the most fearsome invention of the art of fraud.[56]

For the existentialist all ideologies risk bad faith, which does not mean that one should therefore remain inactive and unmotivated ideologically. On the contrary, one needs a standpoint, a position, from which to criticize political movements that are attacks on human freedom.[57] One ought to criticize any abstraction, or any attempt to set the practico-inert above the projects of the persons the system is supposed to serve.

Moreover, any social ideology that designates a limited section of society or group as the bearers of human destiny is suspect, for this means that the group representing history will most likely, if they succeed in obtaining power, become the new elite, while the non-bearers of history will be spectators or worse.[58]

We find that among the privileged groups,

> The young have been flattered into the belief that they possess a natural birth right of moral and religious truth. And in the same strain, those of riper years are declared to be sunk, petrified, ossified in falsehood. Youth, say these teachers, sees the bright light of dawn: but the older generation lies in the slough and mire of the common day. . . . In all this it is not humility which holds back from the knowledge and study of the truth, but a conviction that we are already in full possession of it. . . . But these hopes are set upon the young, only on the condition that, instead of remaining as they are, they undertake the stern labour of mind.

This conservative debunking of the foibles of the universal class of the 1960s was actually penned by Hegel in an earlier age.[59] Ideologies, although they may implicate others unawares in projects not their own, are at least not secret doctrines--to work, they must be manifest in the world, hence criticizable--nor are they always actual lies; certainly those affirming them often also believe in them.[60]

One technique of ideology, powerful in catching others up unawares in projects, is to designate some words as symbols which come to be accepted unquestioningly by the purveyors and consumers of ideology. Some very significant political controversies are battles over words. Which group can capture the word "democracy" by defining it for others? A favorite symbol is "the people." The people support the people's war; they also support people's democracies; why wouldn't they, for they are the people? Even if we can show that only 15 percent are positively in favor of a people's war, it is still supported by the people. In "Justice and the State,"[61] Sartre uses this catch-all symbol. He comments that the first two volumes of his biography of Flaubert "were bought and read by bourgeois reformists, professors, students, and the like. It was not written by the people or for the people. . . . " That is, some people are not people, but some other people are "The People."

We ought to comment that provided ideology has some praxis to distinguish it strictly from the practico-inert, it will change with time. If it is carried out within the projects of individual people, its consequences may turn out to be changed from one era to another. The ideology of Communism is being caught up in the projects of a new generation since Stalin's death in 1953. The death of such practicioners as Andrei Gromyko in 1989, the participant and often the principal actor in Soviet post-war foreign diplomacy, marks the possibility for a new era in Communist ideology.

While the doctrine of the vanguard party is morally flawed, there is no reason why new men and women, new projects, will not mean new interpretations of this ideological doctrine. It contained in its original Marxian formulations, some constructive aspects in its attacks on exploitation and alienation. Much of the Marxist critique could be directed against the flaws of the people's democratic republics as well as against 19th century capitalist society, and it was sometimes put to such uses as in the Yugoslav review *Praxis*. In the next chapter, we will argue that the past of a doctrine is an important aspect of what it is; and yet, this does not define it once and forever.

A more likely denoument, however, of Marxism is its almost complete eclipse as a major political movement, condemned by its discredited practitioners. Alas, for every Angelica Balabanov, there have been several Ceaucescus. For generations, Communists have extolled Stalinist centralization as the epitome of Communism, and whatever else it might have meant at one time, the collapse of this system has taken Communist ideology with it.

Another technique of implicating others unawares in our projects is the project of the love of mankind, or the love of the people; and the further away these people the better, particularly the wonderful, naïve, spontaneous and authentic people of Bongo Bongo. We all know these persons, living in idyllic simplicity and naturally moral and authentic. They are Rousseau's country elders. Our fellow citizens are a shabby lot of bourgeois hypocrites for the most part, we know them well; the workers I know are mired in bad faith, robbed of their projects by Superbowls and the World Series. But the Angolans . . . !

Thus, we fall into the fallacy of seeing distant others in abstract purity, advocating their cause, we assume, for reasons that we cannot find to advocate the cause of hypocritical others within our own nation. But to reduce distant others to abstract causes, is also to reduce them to objects, to ignore their humanness. If their revolution fails, we are out of the range of their suffering and can move on to a new cause, preferably equally distant.

When their cause, which we took upon ourselves as our own, triumphs and then founders in its turn in oppression and bloodshed, we can easily state that we will now have no more to say about that situation in some distant state. Our project erected upon the fate of distant others has failed, but our defense is silence. We can now wash our hands of the affair. This is all the easier, because our ties were not emotional ties to concrete people at all, but to our concepts of what we wanted to believe these others to be.

This tendency to abstractions also prohibits coming to the aid of others, for there is certainly no people good enough to warrant our help; that is, if we know enough about them. Thus, the Afghan resistance to an oppressive regime that had set about to reform society regardless of consequences, was mired in backwardness and, sometimes, in religious obscurantism. The Kuwaitis invaded by Iraq in 1990 were disgustingly wealthy and tended to be supercilious. The traditional Wahabi Islam of the Saudis oppressed women according to the typical Western view, for which reason, it did not deserve defense against Iraq.

The more we know about concrete others, the easier it is to condemn them for innumerable human foibles. The expectation of prior human perfection and the perfect government in place will preserve us forever from having to intervene in foreign conflicts. To have saved Ethiopia from Italian aggression in 1936 was not to have preserved a perfect government there but rather, a traditional empire.

A final technique of implicating others in our projects is largely unconscious. The project of hedonism or self-destruction leads one, let us say, to abuse drugs. In American society, many drugs are controlled or illegal substances, although some 25 million persons may indulge, and where illegal demands exist, entrepreneurs will flock to fulfill the need. Drug use is the consumer good *par excellence*. The British and French recognized this in the infamous Opium War of the last century. Even the genteel user will be adding to the illicit demand, developing an underground market, sponsoring criminal syndicates, pushers, and murders on the streets as moral nihilists battle for the lucrative opportunities opened up to them.

Finally, users help sponsor the clearing of South American forests, the desertion of subsistence farming by peasants, the establishment of powerful terrorist organizations that control extensive areas of territory overseas. In some countries, it is possible that the drug syndicates are powerful enough to control whole countries, which implies an effect, as in Colombia, on the system of justice and security there. In Panama, Manuel Noriega was buttressed in power by drug money.

The consumers' drug project makes them responsible for all these consequences. The source of the drug problem in the world is the projects of citizens mainly of the United States; at the root of the crime and corruption of the system is the user. The user has set loose the criminal syndicates that supply the drug. The drug user has implicated innumerable others through the ramifications of his or her choice. The world of drug users and suppliers is the world that users brought about.[62] Lucidity reveals beforehand all these potential consequences.

Thus, we ought not, if we regard the minimal demands of morality, to ensnare unsuspecting others in our projects. We ought also to avoid becoming enmeshed in the projects of others. In religious thought, the Devil's mission is that of the great tempter, to ensnare others seeking to realize their own subgames in his great supergame of collecting souls. The Devil is the clever originator of innumerable false images and revelations. The religious person has the duty of determining whether the voices are those of God or the Devil. The choice is a most difficult one; the religious criterion is faith.

To escape the innumerable and devilish political projects that would mire our own freedom, the secular criterion is lucidity. Implicating others unawares in projects not their own, or getting caught in these ourselves, is a moral problem in politics. In the perfect world of translucent communication which will likely never be attained, we would not have to deal with this problem. In the world we exist, we are in the midst of such problems daily.

The highest level of justice possible to real persons may even be a second-rate world, in which everyone is capable of manipulating everyone else; that is, all are potential manipulators because all have the requisite skill, wealth, and education to take in their fellows. It would be a world of equal (manipulative) opportunity. A worse situation is that in which certain groups are always the manipulators, keeping all others in a state of subjugation. Of course, a much better world would be one in which human beings do not seek to dominate one another, but this world is utopian, and it may not be worth the cost to attain it if others must be caught unawares in our present projects to get there.[63]

Notes

1. Joseph Raz, *The Morality of Freedom* (Oxford: The Clarendon Press, 1986), pp. 204-205.
2. See, for example, Popper and Eccles, *The Self and Its Brain*, p. 137. This supports the associated moral view, of course, only if that accords with our free choice, a choice that has been recommended as consonant with the choice of life.
3. Joel Rudinov, "Manipulation," *Ethics*, Vol. 88, No. 4 (July 1978), 347.
4. Bernard Haering, *Ethics of Manipulation: Issues in Medicine, Behavior Control, and Genetics* (New York: The Seabury Press, 1975), 60.
5. Sartre, *Between Existentialism and Marxism*, pp. 252-253.
6. *Ibid.*, p. 244.
7. Machiavelli, *The Prince*, Ch. 18, p. 94.
8. Rothman and Lichter, *Roots of Radicalism*, pp. 361-362.
9. Alvin W. Gouldner, "Revolutionary Intellectuals," *Telos*, No. 26 (Winter 1975-1975), p. 28.
10. Max Nomad, "Master—Old and New," in George B. de Hurzon, ed., *The Intellectuals* (Glencoe: The Free Press, 1960), p. 344. Which is why other classes have an instinctive distrust of intellectuals within their ranks.
11. Lukacs, *History and Class Consciousness*, p. 71.
12. *Ibid.*, p. 51.
13. Arthur M. Melzer, "Rousseau's Moral Realism: Replacing Natural Law with the General Will," *The American Political Science Review*, Vol. 77, No. 3 (September 1983), p. 647.
14. J.H. Huizinga, *Rousseau: The Self-Made Saint* (New York: Grossman Publishers, 1976), p. 160. Huizinga cites the interpretation of I.G. Crocker, who regards Rousseau as a pioneer of manipulation and "human conditioning."
15. Trotsky, "Their Morals and Ours," in Howe, p. 398.
16. Shapiro, *Origins of Marxist*, p. 7.

17. V.I. Lenin, *What Is To Be Done?* (New York: International Publishers, 1943), p. 76, pp. 32-33, p. 41. For Lenin's definition of the vanguard party organization in detail, see p. 116. Lenin's vanguard concept, it seems to me, is derivable from Marx's writings, but nevertheless overemphasizes certain aspects of original Marxism.
18. Poster, *Existential Marxism in Postwar France*, p. 84.
19. V.I. Lenin, *"Left-Wing" Communism, an Infantile Disorder* (New York: International Publishers, 1940), p. 42.
20. Like many intellectuals, Peter Tkachev became impatient at the procrastination of the people: "The [intellectual] minority will impart a considered and rational form to the struggle, leading it toward predetermined goals, directing this coarse material element [the masses] toward ideal principles. In a real revolution the people act like a tempestuous natural force, destroying and ruining everything in its path, always acting without calculation, without consciousness." Albert L. Weeks, *The First Bolshevik, A Political Biography of Peter Tkachev* (New York: New York University Press, 1968), p. 76. And in another statement, "A revolutionary minority is no longer willing to wait but must take upon itself the forcing of consciousness upon the people," p. 77. Lenin was certainly familiar with Tkachev's writings, and cites him in *What Is To Be Done?*; but how influential Tkachev was in influencing Lenin's vanguard concept is the subject of controversy.
21. Walter Laqueur, *The Age of Terrorism* (Boston: Little, Brown, and Co., 1987), p. 272.
22. Lenin, *"Left Wing" Communism*, p. 56. The quotation continues "The whole point lies in *knowing how* to apply these tactics in such a way as to *raise*, and not lower, the *general* level of proletarian class consciousness, revolutionary spirit, and ability to fight and conquer."
23. *Ibid.*, p. 13.
24. For example, D.N. Aidit, *The Indonesian Revolution and the Immediate Tasks of the Communist Party of Indonesia* (Peking: Foreign Languages Press, 1964), pp. 14-15.
25. Henry W. Ehrmann, *Politics: France* (Boston: Little, Brown and Co., 1983), p. 188.
26. Lenin, *"Left-Wing" Communism*, p. 10.
27. Troung Chinh, "The August Revolution," from *Primer for Revolt* (New York: Frederick A. Praeger, 1963), p. 76.
28. *Ibid.*, pp. 21-22. The emphasis is in the original. Truong Nhu Tang quotes a letter to the Saigon Party Committee in 1966 from Le Duan, urging "transitional organizations... under many disguised forms." See his *A Vietcong Memoir* (New York: Harcourt Brace Jovanovich, 1985), p. 104.
29. Philip Selznick, *The Organizational Weapon: A Study of Bolshevik Strategy and Tactics* (Glencoe: The Free Press, 1960), p. 130.

30. Franz Borkenau, *European Communism* (New York: Harper and Brother, 1953), p. 58.
31. Georgi Dimitroff, *United Front Against Fascism: Speeches Delivered at the Seventh World Congress of the Communist International, July 25-August 20, 1935* (New York: New Century Publishers, 1945), pp. 88-89.
32. The World Peace Council is documented in Richard H. Shultz and Roy Godson, *Dezinformatsia: Active Measures in Soviet Strategy* (New York: Pergamon Press, 1984), pp. 114-132.
33. Truong Nhu Tang, with David Chanoff and Doan Van Toai, *A Vietcong Memoir* (San Diego: Harcourt Brace Jovanovich, 1985), p. 107.
34. David Beresford, "In the Compromised Land," *Manchester Guardian*, Vol. 138, No. 10 (March 6, 1988), p. 9.
35. The sources are H. Walpole, *Memoirs*, Vol. I, p. 52, cited by Donald Bruce, *Radical Dr. Smollett* (Boston: Houghton Mifflin, 1965), p. 119.
36. Susan S. Shin, "The Tonghak Movement," *Korean Studies Forum*, No. 5, Winter-Spring, 1978-1979, p. 46.
37. Robert J. Morgan, "Madison's Analysis of the Sources of Political Authority," *The American Political Science Review*, Vol. 75, No. 3 (September 1981), p. 615.
38. Selznick, *The Organizational Weapon*, p. 30.
39. White, "Reason and Authority in Habermas: A Critique of the Critics," *The American Political Science Review*, Vol. 74, No. 4 (December 1980), p. 1009.
40. Heidegger, *Being and Time*, p. 159; see also Robert E. Goodin, *Manipulatory Politics* (New Haven: Yale University Press, 1980), p. 22, footnote.
41. Whiteside, *Merleau-Ponty*, p. 153.
42. Quoted from Marx's "Reflections of a Youth in Choosing a Career," by Eugene Kamenka, *The Ethical Foundations of Marxism* (London: Routledge and Kegan Paul, 1962), p. 29.
43. Karl Jaspers, *The Question of German Guilt* (Westport: Greenwood Press, 1978. Trans. by E.B. Ashton), p. 82.
44. Haering, *Ethics of Manipulation*, p. 59.
45. Phares, *Locus of Control in Personality*, p. 93; Gecas and Schwalbe. "Beyond the Looking-Glass Self," p. 81.
46. Phares, *Locus of Control in Personality*, p. 151.
47. Robert E. Goodin, "Vulnerabilities and Responsibilities: An Ethical Defense of the Welfare State," *The American Political Science Review*, Vol. 79, No. 3 (September 1985), p. 783.
48. See Staub, *The Roots of Evil*, all Chapter 9, "Nazi rule and steps along the continuum of destruction," pp. 116-127.
49. Williams, *Ethics and the Limits of Philosophy*, p. 101.
50. Bok, *Secrets*, p. 208.
51. Olafson, *Principles and Persons*, p. 221.
52. Parfit, *Reasons and Persons*, p. 321.

53. Kant, *Lectures on Ethics* (New York: Harper and Row, 1963, trans. by Louis Infield), p. 51.
54. Karl Mannheim, *Ideology and Utopia* (New York: Harcourt Brace), p. 176.
55. Flynn, *Sartre and Marxist Existentialism*, pp. 132-133.
56. Metzer, "Rousseau's Moral Realism," p. 644.
57. Macquarrie, *Existentialism*, p. 238.
58. Johan Galtung, *The True Worlds* (New York: The Free Press, 1980), p. 396.
59. G.W.F. Hegel, *Logic* (Oxford: At the Clarendon Press, 1975, Trans. by William Wallace), p. 26. This is Part I of the *Encyclopedia of the Philosophical Sciences*.
60. Gouldner, "Revolutionary Intellectuals," p. 33.
61. Sartre, *Life/Situations* (New York: Pantheon Books, 1977, trans. by Paul Auster and Lydia Davis), p. 185.
62. See Tina Rosenberg, "The Kingdom of Cocaine," a review of Gugliotta and Leen's *Kings of Cocaine: Inside the Medellin Cartel*, in *The New Republic*, Vol. 201, No. 22 (November 27, 1989), 26-34.
63. Robert E. Goodin, *Manipulatory Politics* (New Haven: Yale University, 1980), p. 56.

Chapter 13

History

Ethical and moral principles thus far have been applied to the political praxis of the present. The problem of history concerns praxis embedded in the past. Sometimes the past is the source of the practico-inert in which we live, our institutions; in other cases, the only remnants of a past that survive are a few crumbling structures, shards, a tattered papyrus. While we accept morality as fitting others into our schemes as important presences, as living consciousness, there are no longer such living consciousnesses in the past. Their projects have competed in the turbulence of contending empires, but they are now sunk into the long road receding behind us. What, if anything, is morally due these no-longer-consciousnesses, these faded visages that we glimpse fleetingly behind the cracked pillars or speaking inaudibly out of aged manuscripts?

What responsibility is owed the inhabitants of this past? Once they were for-itselves as we now are, contending morally or immorally for their ethical purposes; they are now unrecognizable portions of the in-itself, inert matter. Responsibilities hitherto have been extended to other for-itselves, for the reason that their free projects contribute potentially to the present world, project into contemporary political situations, changing these for better or ill. The past has no more free projects of its own. There is no more potential there--it is set and hardened. It holds only the disappearing tracks of the projects of deceased for-itselves become in-itselves.

So will the present appear as the centuries pass. The inexorable passage of time, the final collapse into the world of objects, is the common condition of humans. As Sartre writes:

> ... [D]eath reduces the for-itself-for-others to the state of simple for-others. Today I am responsible for the being of the dead Pierre, I in my freedom. Those dead who have not been able to be saved and transported to the boundaries of the concrete past of a survivor are not past; they along with their pasts are annihilated.[1]

It is, however, possible and perhaps appropriate that morality and justice can be extended to apply to the past. Certainly, the concept of witnessing would seem applicable to the past as to the present. Witnessing will be one position apparent in our recommendations about history. The past is owed something, partly for the reason that our present quality of life, political and social, our economic progress, much of our knowledge are suffused with projects realized by persons now dead.

Sometimes these persons come to life, in a way, thanks to the historians, who, as Odysseus summoned the shades from Hades, summon the inhabitants of past ages. So, in reading Marx and the Hammonds, we see the children working the coal mines in the early industrial revolution, and the workers toiling in their 14- and 15-hour days at the textile mills. The realization of the oppression of the past, the slavery, the colonial brutalities and the exploitation comes clearly into view. This realization may add some poignancy to our own projects.

If it is our purpose to contribute something to an overall human project, if it is possible to view present projects, in some sense, as a contribution to future mankind, then it must be possible to view past projects in the same light. The suffering of the past is the foundation of our aspirations for the present. The scientific discovery, the bill that has found its way to the legislative committee, a suicide, is someone's commentary on the past.

The projects of the past were either worth something or they were not, and to some extent, projects of the present are a commentary on that worth. Our judgment of the worth of the past is tied to our view of the worth of the present. The very choice of existing, as against non-existence, is a choice that shows regard of the past. To sink into a life of dissipation or to view new objects in the cosmos are a commentary on the human project of history. If there is any worth in the past, it is for-itselves that make that evaluation in the present, through the projects they pursue, and through the position they adopt toward history.

The role of the historian is a peculiar one. Like the scientist, concerned with the in-itself, the historian is concerned with particular aspects of that in-itself, namely, the residue of human projects. The remains of human projects are now in the form of architecture, institutions, old documents, the restored study used by James Madison, and so forth. We may make of the past what we will by way of interpretation, but the historian has selected through his or her role a special duty toward the human past, for, like the scientist, the historian bears a responsibility for lucidity, to try to seek the truth; hence, the role of the historian is to be honest.

This much is owed to the deceased beings who inhabited situations long gone, that we attempt to view them, so far as we can, so far as records are available, as they really were, trying to determine what the motives were that guided these historical personages of the past in their projects. What were their deeds, what were the consequences of these deeds in the destruction or the furtherance of knowledge? As Collingwood holds, we deal in history not so much with events as such, but with actions, i.e., "events brought about by the will and expressing the thought of a free and intelligent agent. . . ."[2] An event, Collingwood reminds us,[3] has not only an outside but an inside as well: Human actions unite the inside and the outside. This is a very difficult task, and many historians understandably hesitate to bring this inside of events into their analyses.

It is past *projects* we are most interested in, with all the complexities these entail. The task of history is unlike science, which observes natural events that are not conscious projects toward future goals. Nature never transcends its present, that is, not consciously. We owe this view of history as transcendence over past realities to past others, because they did act freely in the world and not as objects or laws of nature.

The duty of the historian is to see as deeply and clearly as the records allow, and to try to reconstruct the past as it really was, as a totalization. As in science, objectivity and honesty are the criteria the historian must serve. It is the most we can do for past beings, who count for having once been consciousnesses, but who do not count so much as for-itselves in the present, these who are still aware, whom we affect in an immediate way. The dead can be maligned by historians, or cheated, but they are beyond experiencing injuries.

An object, which since we are still living consciousnesses we are not yet, has no future and can transcend no present situation in projecting purposes.[4] Moreover, an object has no genuine past. For humans, there is a past etched in the walls of this river valley, but it is not there, present, for the river. Indeed, no other living creature within our present knowledge has a sense of time: the lion has no future or past as such. The horse's past, as a series of fossil remains, is not within the horse's ken. But humans have a future, if they have accepted the future to the degree that they have elected to pursue an existence of projects as opposed to ceasing existence.

If the accomplishment of projects is to leave any lasting significance, then those who achieve them must be involved with an attitude toward the past; if the past is to have any significance whatsoever, it is up to persons living to give it that, to draw it a little out of the darkness. Our treatment of the past in our own present, is our recommendation to the future in its treatment of our present. To have a past in this sense, then, is to be somewhat more human. We can choose to close off the past entirely to consciousness, to leave a great blank behind the projects of the present as well. But this choice is not the best one, perhaps, that we might select if we are striving to be human.

The for-itself is "thrown into full 'responsibility' with respect to the dead; it is obliged to decide freely the fate of the dead. . . . "[5] The nihilist, of course, would discard all of the past, including the present to which it has contributed, for the unknowable future.[6] There is also a certain nihilism concerning history in Christianity, in the doctrine of the two cities, in the advice to "let the dead bury their dead." At times, Saint Augustine seems completely future oriented.

The danger to human projects is to be too future or too past oriented. In particular, the political actor must carefully hew a path between the future and the past, avoiding both sacrificing the present to the unknowable, on the one hand, and dragging the practico-inert as empty but heavy baggage, while present concerns are ignored, on the other hand.

Like nihilism, totalitarian attitudes disparage the past, treating the dead as it would the living, as objects to be manipulated for a glorious future. Soviet history, saved to a degree by a few remarkable individuals such as Roy Medvedev, succumbed to the totalitarian view of history under Stalin, when contempt for persons in the present was extended, in a sort of negative equality whereby the past received equal treatment with the present, to the past. There too, the regime could seize and manipulate the person, erasing the founder of the Red Army, Leon Trotsky, from the annals, as if there had been no such individual: indeed, he was completely omitted from editions of the Soviet Encyclopedia.

The regime not only had the means to kill a person and dominate the present and the future, but it had the power, unique to totalitarianism, of bringing the past under its absolute control as well. So, Bukharin, who was tried and executed for treason as the culminating drama of Stalin's great purges in 1938, had his history annihilated and twisted as well, a villain to all believers in the totalitarian future, such as Sartre, who wrote, less excusably in that he had the benefit of hindsight, that Bukharin was a "(rotten) member of a revolutionary community."[7]

In accepting the lie that Bukharin was a traitor to Soviet society, Suhl comments that Sartre would have had to accept, as an apodictic truth, the totalitarian doctrine that Stalin embodied the intent and purpose of the Communist revolution, as Hitler claimed to be the spirit of the Aryan race. Santiago Carrillo, former head of the Spanish Communist Party, saw the past more lucidly:

> On that basis it was possible for the myth that Trotsky was linked with the Nazis and was protected by American imperialism to arise and establish itself, and we youngsters of that period swallowed the official accounts of the October Revolution and of the subsequent civil war, in which Trotsky's role was passed over in silence. [Carrillo refers, then, to the publication of Lenin's texts following the Twentieth Party Congress.] However, that treatment has not materialised. Official historical texts have followed one after another, without giving an inkling of the truth, and they continue to be a biased manipulation of facts, which does not accord with historical reality.[8]

In 1989, following ardent efforts by his widow and other Soviet citizens, Bukharin was rehabilitated, no longer the spy and traitor of the Stalin-Vyshinsky prosecutions, but now an historical figure who can assume a truer position in history. The orthodox attitude to Marshall Tito of the former Yugoslavia also influenced his coverage in Marxist history: William Z. Foster refers to him as a Fascist in his *History of the Three Internationals*, published in 1955 while Tito was still out of favor. But by 1964, R. Palme Dutt could contribute to historical knowledge by omitting any mention of the dramatic events affecting the former USSR and Yugoslavia in 1948.[9]

In accepting the Nobel Prize for Literature, Solzhenitsyn made it clear that the purpose of reconstructing the history of the Gulags was to reassert the rights of the murdered against the totalitarian attitude toward history. Our posture to the history of past others is a projection of our moral attitude toward living others. If past others count for nothing and can be manipulated for whatever purpose we will, then our treatment of our fellow humans in the present will likely exhibit the same attitude.

Our treatment of the past is indicative of our humanity or the lack of it. Collingwood cites Kant as having shown why it is that people should acknowledge a history. As rational beings, the full development of their potentialities requires not just the ephemeral present, but an historical process. Just as we need society and conscious others for a full development of our humanity, so also do we need an historical past to exist fully.[10] It follows from Kant's position, as from ours, that this history must strive toward objectivity, for only this can satisfy lucid beings.

Hitler, the quintessential totalitarian, has it in his *Mein Kampf* that it is the duty of Germans "not to seek out objective truth, in so far as it may be favorable to others, but uninterruptedly to serve one's own truth." In a later presentation of the Nazi program he elaborated on the position that "the National State will look upon science as a means for increasing national pride. Not only world history, but also the history of civilization must be taught from this point of view."[11]

This view does not fit with the ethical projects recommended in this work, for it violates lucidity and is not an authentic stance. The appropriate position on history is clearly presented by Lucian, whose view in his own day was progressive, namely, that the one task of historians is to tell the things as they happened: "For history, I say again, has this and this only for its own; if a man will start upon it, he *must* sacrifice to no God but Truth; he must neglect all else. . . . ,"[12] an injunction repeated by Collingwood, ". . . that [the] prime duty of the historian [is] a willingness to bestow infinite pains on discovering what actually happens."[13]

Akin to the role of the intellectual in general, that of the historian requires lucidity and honesty, responsibilities stemming from the nature of the role the historian has freely chosen. His morality, expressed in giving past others their proper due, is to try to present dead others as they were, in their villainies and their humanity, not as manipulable objects in the projects of the present. It is a strange responsibility for the reason that the dead can no longer assert themselves against consciousnesses of the present. Past others cannot debate their treatment. This is the role that the historian ought to be trusted to honor: To be responsible to both the living and to the deceased, through his or her choice of profession, to honesty.

It is an additional duty for the historian to see the past as fully as possible, to draw out of the past, if possible, not only the projects of the mighty, but some true view of the lives of the less elevated, as well. To implicate others into our projects unawares has counterparts in past usage. In particular, the chroniclers of the past have served the mighty by dishonoring the conquered or allowing the oppressed to sink into oblivion. The Marxist viewpoint, shared from another vantage point by feminists, is an appropriate one, namely, that the ignored of history have also been for-themselves and contributors to the present that we exist in. Marxist historians, therefore, make the effort to illuminate for the present, the life of the slave, the worker, the peasant, all those who as individuals are omitted from the court chronicles.

This admirable, if difficult, endeavor was the project proclaimed by Voltaire, whose mostly unrealized proposal was to create just such a history embracing the common people as well as their monarchs. To attribute the construction of Saint Petersburg to Peter the Great is to ignore a large portion of the historical picture. Of course, the reconstruction of the life of the lowly is hampered by a lack of documentation, for, regarded as less than human and themselves generally illiterate, they were mostly ignored by the historians of their own day. John Lackland's *Piers Plowman* is exceptional in the older English literature in conveying to the present insights about the attitudes of the common people of that day.

There have been many attempts to insert a meaning into history. Historicism would have it that history is a project in which, willy-nilly, all our separate projects are drawn into furthering. Hegel's assumption was that history is in truth not the history of individual projects, clashing, merging, defeating or supporting one another, but the great single project of the Spirit as it develops through time. This is the import of historicism as Popper has defined it.

If historicism were valid, if history were really the progress of Spirit through time, then we would be robbed of the significance of our own individual projects. Not freedom, but unaware implication in the goals of Spirit would be our lot, chess pieces moved by an unseen hand on the historical board.

We contribute a certain sense of historicism to past events whenever we speak in such phrases as "the conquest of the Mediterranean world by Rome," for, as Collingwood reminds us, the reality of this series of events "is only this and that individual Roman" fulfilling his individual project of administration, or warfare. Set forever in the in-itself which is history, however, the long course of events seems to suggest that each Roman acted as though "I am playing my part in a great movement, the conquest of the Mediterranean world by Rome."[14]

Most likely, however, although exceptions no doubt exist, events did not come about quite like that, and no matter how uncoordinated and anarchic individual projects may have been in reality, they always seem to have embodied a single purpose when viewed as fixed in-itself, after everyone's projects have been played out. Thus, there is a compelling temptation to interpret as the purpose of history, whatever happened "in the end."

We are not, however, thrust forward into the future by the past--as Collingwood reminds us, "History terminates not in the future, but in the present."[15] Therefore, and contrary to historicism, the future is still malleable; it is still our future. The past has a hold on it, but that grip can be loosened through free projects. In large portions of the *Critique*, there is more than a hint of historicism. Smith points to Sartre's "idealistically abstract model" of the colonial system, from which he deduces the historically specific necessity of revolution. There is bad faith in this, according to Smith, for it omits the ambiguity of history, its fluidity, those moments when innovation might have altered the entire course of events.[16] McMahon accuses Sartre of creating his own replacement for God, namely history.[17]

It is curious how purpose somehow inhabits the godless physical or material and social world of the historicist. It has always been an intellectual curiosity that, lacking Hegel's Spirit, Marx's historical materialism proposed an advance through historical stages toward a culmination in a classless society. It is a sort of unguided purposeness, a purposeful goal set by no consciousness.

Historicist models implicate us, sometimes unawares, sometimes by misguided choice, in the projects of past others. We are guided in historicism by dead hands. This much deference we do *not* owe to past others. Honesty, yes; lucidity, yes; the sort of historical immortality that honest historians can extend to the hapless dead, yes; but, assuredly, we do not owe the past Daseins control over our projects in the present. We do not have to bend before "waves of history" set in motion by the projects of deceased intellectuals. We pay them heed, as we do the living, although, alas, we realize that they can no longer change, having passed from existence to pure substance. They can no longer engage in the ongoing debates.

We will never know Marx's assessment of the collapse of "Communism" in Poland in the 1980s. We can only guess what he might have thought on the basis of his now petrified commentary now become a totality. Marx had his chance--he cannot grow or launch new projects any longer. The project of Marxism, which he himself sometimes denigrated, has been defined and redefined by Kautsky, Luxemburg, Lenin, Stalin, Gorbachev; it is out of his hands. (Fortunately, for historians and philosophers, however, Marx's and Lenin's works have been preserved meticulously and reverently by the scholars who headed the Institute of Marxism/Leninism in the former Soviet Union, even during the horrible years of the purges. Indeed, at least one head of the Institute was himself slain by Stalin's order. Curious that this should have been so, when so much history was being twisted and destroyed. At least we have a full present view of what these works were.)

Just so, Christianity left the hands of Christ to become the doctrine interpreted by Augustine, Thomas Aquinas, John Hus, Luther, Torquemada, Pascal, Kierkegaard, Maritain, Gilson, Karl Barth, Paul Tillich, and Jimmy Swaggart. (Christian historicism, of course, relies on the Spirit, on the Holy Ghost, which is the power projecting the true doctrine, open to those of faith, into the present, guiding it onto its proper path through the ages. This doctrine, which relies on an omniscient God to supply purposeness makes more sense than other varieties of historicism; but in keeping with our interpretation of history, we must view modern Christianity also as the sum total of the innumerable individual projects pursued in its name.)

We are not, then, bound by past projects, unless we choose to be, and this is among the free choices we might make, but like the projects of our extant contemporaries, we do the past dead the honor of taking their projects seriously and under advisement, of treating them, we hope, with lucidity. Stalin, too, must be extended the honor of lucid exposition. Whatever dignity (we can speak of this, for his course is run and there is no more existence to precede substance, but only substance) he may possess as erstwhile for-itself, as a figure whose projects have also shaped our past, depends on an objective recognition of the collectivization of the rural sector of the USSR in the 1930s, of the killing and starvation of millions, of the judicial killing of Lenin's fellow Bolsheviks, of the Gulags, the Five-year plans, Stalingrad, Trotsky's murder, and his *Lessons of Leninism*.

Like all denizens of the past, Stalin has a right to truthful exposition, provided historians in the present choose an authentic stance toward the past. Historians ought to do him this justice. Thus, justice and equality as it extends back to encompass the past is the extension of lucidity and truth to past others, in so far as this can be accomplished. Lucian, once more, is a spokesmen for this view:

> There stands my model, then: fearless, incorruptible, independent, a believer in frankness and veracity; one that will call a spade a spade, make no concession to likes and dislikes, nor spare any man for pity or respect or propriety; an impartial judge, kind to all, but too kind to none; a literary cosmopolite with neither suzerain nor king, never heeding what this or that man may think, but setting down the thing that befell. Thucydides is our noble legislator. . . . [18]

It is an attitude such as this that makes the historian anathema to totalitarian and dogmatic regimes, or to movements of the same nature.

Sartre has tellingly presented a concept of history, if we can interpret it in that context, in one of his best plays, *Dirty Hands*. The character, Hugo, has been delegated by the Communist party of some unnamed Eastern European polity to assassinate a Communist leader, Hoederer, who is negotiating in violation of the current official Communist policy a united front with recognized enemies of the revolution, a revolution to which Hoederer is committed. The young assassin, Hugo, has mixed emotions concerning Hoederer, whom he comes to admire. Eventually, he carries out his project when he finds Hoederer in a compromising and ambiguous situation with his (Hugo's) wife. Later, the party policy changes, and the project pursued by Hoederer is the new line. The Party cannot now admit that it had once been wrong and dispatched an assassin against one of its own.

Hugo now faces a choice: Either accept the party rationalization that Hoederer was assassinated, not by party orders, but in a young man's temporary fit of passion, an interpretation that would make Hugo acceptable in connection with the new line and save his life, but which would rob Hoederer's project of its meaning, namely, as a courageous decision in the service of the revolution, taken at the risk of his life and in the face of intense party opposition; or stand his ground by refusing to say that the crime was done for personal reasons, a decision that would mean his own execution, but one that would retain the truth of Hoederer's commitment.[19] This interesting drama aptly illustrates the ambiguity and pitfalls of bad faith with which we all confront the past.

We have expressed what we think is an authentic commitment to history. The United States, in part because of the problems covered in Chapter 9, sometimes stints the past in its educational system. The college student pursuing a degree in engineering, business or medicine, who, following four or more years of university training often has no grasp of history, represents social amnesia and alienation from the past. It is the modern person's way of "abandoning the past to the night of facticity," of "depopulating the world."[20] As de Beauvoir cautions,

> ... if the disclosure of being achieved by our ancestors does not at all move us, why be so interested in that which is taking place today. ... To assert the reign of the human is to acknowledge man in the past as well as in the future.

A lack of any attachment to the past is a choice of nihilism in the present. (It is a major shortcoming of phenomenology that it brackets out "men as subjects of history." One of the chief interpreters of the technique underlines this, "... historical problems are not to be handled by the phenomenological method, except in a very limited sense. Most of the historical problems are as remote from phenomenological analysis as death is."[21] But the educational system, indeed the entire culture, in the United States is producing generations that are ignorant of the past; for them there is nothing to bracket out; for them there is the great void behind us.[22] And since the past is empty, the present, as it recedes toward the past, is also empty.

To what degree are past actions open to present reinterpretations, in view of maintaining an authentic historiography based on the principle of lucidity? It is clear, I think, in spite of some existentialist commentary to the contrary, that there *is* a past that partakes of truth, and pasts that are likewise clearly untruthful. For all its devotion to preserving its past, the theory of the Chinese historiographers, who were also interested bureaucrats, was to glorify the present regime and to disparage the preceding dynasty. In particular, the last emperors of a preceding dynasty had to be stigmatized as evil. What does this type of historiography do for the objectivity of our images of Wong Kon (the Good), Kyon Hwon (the Bad) and Kung Ye (the Ugly), actors involved in the formation of the Korean Koryo Dynasty?[23] The historian must try to revise these images in the light of alternative data, not an easy project, sometimes not even a possible one.

Waterhouse accuses Heidegger of spurning historical truth, in the name of the truth of Being, and likens this to Bultmann's refusal to search for the historical Jesus, something Renan made an effort to do, in order to extract the truth embedded in the myth.[24] This attitude of tampering with history, may not be as misguided as one that consigns history to oblivion, but it is nonetheless inauthentic.

And what of hermeneutics, the discipline of critiquing texts? Hans-Georg Godamer has written extensively on this. Godamer's position modifies somewhat the notion of understanding the past as a reconstruction of the original, which would be no more than a recovery of a dead meaning; he holds that "the essential nature of the historical spirit does not consist in the restoration of the past, but in a thoughtful mediation with contemporary life." He has been criticized in this view for abandoning any idea of objective interpretation.[25]

But, in fact, history must really be treated in a number of ways simultaneously. On the one hand, we extend justice to our predecessors by a lucid and honest recounting of the past; on the other hand, historical projects often continue quite viable into the present. For example, interpretation of the Constitution is a project that still exercises legal minds, and some maintain that an appropiate interpretation depends on the original intent. The past is as the past was, but it is never quite dead, for humanity still pursues many of the old projects.

We can follow as a continuous project, for example, the search for justice from Plato to Rawls. Our project can be informed by history, so that objectivity is followed by the integration of the projects of the past into the meanings of the present. Like social institutions, the past does not militate against our freedom, unless we choose to allow it to do so; we may choose freely those elements of the past to pursue or ignore. Such choices are a precarious passage between Scylla and Charybdis.

It is inauthentic to sacrifice lucidity and honesty in our purview of history. It is equally inauthentic to accept the past as *fait accompli*, for, and in this Heidegger is correct, the past is possibilities once realized and capable of being chosen and acted upon again.[26] The question of objectivity is answered well, it seems to me by Sartre, who holds that we do indeed choose the future that we (freely) prefer, but that once chosen, that future will fall into our past, a past we cannot prevent being what it is.

If we want a future, we want its past.[27] This is an authentic interpretation, in my opinion, and it is a very strong argument for truth and objectivity in history. If our future is manifest destiny, and considering the settlement of the United States from the Atlantic to the Pacific, we can hardly deny responsibility for the injustices inflicted on the Indian tribes as part of the real past of America, a past we may choose to continue to affirm. Nietzsche's tendency to believe that "the will to truth is the incapacity to create," is a flippant principle, dangerous to authentic lucidity.[28]

Notes

1. *Being and Nothingness*, p. 112.
2. Robin George Collingwood, *The Idea of History* (New York: Oxford University Press, 1956). Collingwood's interpretation of history sometimes bears a close resemblance to Sartre's. Consider what Olafson has to say: "Sartre, like most existentialists, adheres to the doctrine of ontological individualism according to which all actions are the actions of some individual human being, and the rationale of all actions must be in some sense an internal structure of that individual's life. One major implication of this doctrine is that all the accounts and explanations that historians and social scientists give of apparently collective actions must decompose the latter into an indefinitely large number of individual acts . . . . ", *Principles and Persons*, pp. 146-147.
3. Collingwood, *The Idea of History*, p. 213.
4. Manser, *Sartre, A Philosophical Study*, p. 65.
5. Sartre, *Being and Nothingness*, pp. 542-543.
6. Stanley Rosen, *Nihilism: A Philosophical Essay* (New Haven: Yale University Press, 1969), p. 140.
7. Suhl, *Jean-Paul Sartre*, p. 211. Sartre's comment may be found in his *Saint Genet*.
8. Santiago Carrillo, *Eurocommunism and the State* (Westport: Lawrence Hill, 1976), pp. 117-118.
9. There is a full coverage of the Tito affair in Julius Braunthal, *History of the International: 1943-1968*, Vol. III. (Boulder: Westview Press, 1980. Trans. by Peter Ford and Kenneth Mitchell), p. 389 and footnote 4.
10. Collingwood, *The Idea of History*, pp. 98-99.
11. The quotations are taken from Joad, *Guide to Morals and Politics*, p. 616.
12. *Lucian of Samosata, The Works of*, Vol. II (Oxford: At the Clarendon Press, 1905, trans. by H. W. Fowler and F. G. Fowler), pp. 128-129. The quotation is from "The Way to Write History."
13. Collingwood, *The Idea of History*, p. 55.
14. *Ibid.*, p. 95.
15. *Ibid.*, p. 104.
16. Tony Smith, "Idealism and People's War: Sartre on Algeria," *Political Theory*, Vol. 1, No. 4 (November 1973), p. 433.
17. McMahon, *Humans Being*, p. 211.
18. Lucian, *The Way to Write History*, p. 129. This is a very appealing passage. Thucydides on the Peloponnesian war approaches this ideal and is clearly a model for all time.
19. This is certainly one of Sartre's most playworthy works; see Barnes, *The Literature of Possibility*, p. 264, for a discussion.

20. These felicitous phrases are from de Beauvoir, *The Ethics of Ambiguity*, pp. 92-93.
21. The first quotation is from Husserl, *Ideas*, p. 162; the second is from Farber, *The Aims of Phenomenology*, p. 62. Our interpretation is an existential one; it is, indeed, difficult to see how it could be essentially informed by phenomenology.
22. It is presumptuous to blame the educational system for shortcomings that are the result of the workings of the entire culture. Indeed, it is possible that by the end of the century, reading as a form of garnering knowledge may be largely a thing of the past, with nothing to replace it. Among many such commentaries concerning the lack of contact with the past, see Diane Ravitch and Chester E. Finn, Jr., *What Do Our 17-Year Olds Know?* (New York: Harper and Row, 1987).
23. This curious sample of Korea's interesting past is presented in Cameron G. Hurst, III, "The Good, the Bad and the Ugly: Personalities in the Founding of the Koryo Dynasty," *Korean Studies Forum*, No. 7 (Summer-Fall 1981), pp. 1-27.
24. Waterhouse, *A Heidegger Critique*, p. 213.
25. Quentin Skinner, ed., *The Return of Grand Theory in the Human Sciences* (Cambridge: Cambridge University Press, 1985), pp. 498-499.
26. See Izenberg, *The Existentialist Critique of Freud*, pp. 252-253.
27. Desan, *The Tragic Finale*, p. 112.
28. Olafson, *Principles and Persons*, p. 50.

Chapter 14

The Diplomatic Role

The choice of a role (we are considering professional roles) is freely undertaken in society, although each society presents a limited menu of roles. A role is a form of promise to the society in which the role operates. It is a project the society offers more or less ready-made to make the society functional, at least in terms of that society's definition. By accepting a role, the incumbent promises to fulfill certain expectations that are commonly associated with the role. The idea of a promise presumes that the incumbent of a role has accepted the implications of the social contract, that is, the incumbent belongs to a group to which he or she can accord that degree of trust necessary to enter into the social relation of trust and common cultural understandings.

Implicit in the existence of roles is the social assumption that these are necessary for the goals of the society, but such assumptions are not to be accepted on faith. The nature of existentialism is to place all roles into question, for their existence does not prove either their necessity to society or their constructiveness. Incumbents may, of course, conduct themselves in somewhat eccentric ways, but there are certain limitations beyond which even an innovative role-taker ought not to go, that is, if sociability is to be maintained, and beyond which promises are broken.

Dewey and Tufts suggest that the roles we are dealing with have a representative value; they stand for something beyond themselves. The legislator or diplomat "does not exercise authority as his private possession, but as the representative of relations in which many share. He is an organ of a community of interests and purposes."[1] To the critical mind there will be in all societies roles with which he or she will take issue, roles that might appear superfluous in a well-ordered society, or, at the extreme, certain roles that are downright deleterious. The Communist government of East Germany provided the role of informer, accepted, apparently, by some three million of its people in some form.[2]

It is ethically imperative that the individual make judgments about the acceptability of roles, for the individual at this point will have made a crucial decision for pursuing existence or denying existence; there may be some roles offered in society in which existence is denied. And such roles must not be accepted; projects to abolish certain roles might be undertaken.

But if the national society, *Gesellschaft* though it is, has some degree of moral community binding its members, to accept a professional role is to make a promise to others, in particular to those others comprising the moral community, that one is a doctor, a mathematics professor or an auto mechanic. As a doctor, one accepts, therefore, obligations which society anticipates will be fulfilled--the doctor is the person who will make efforts to relieve the ill, will make every effort to keep current with research in the field of medicine, and so forth. To break the promise made by undertaking a medical career is to sow distrust in society, to contribute to unpredictability and disorder, to make it unnecessarily difficult for people, not themselves doctors, to take for granted what ought to be taken for granted in an ordered society, and so to get on with the important projects of their own lives. To violate the expectations engendered by a choice of a role is to undermine the social contract.

We have indicated that modern nations are far less cohesive than are the tradition-bound societies of the past; this has released the individual, to a great degree, from bondage to the group; it has given rise to such philosophical trends as existentialism. At some point, however, the minimal moral ties that hold the nation together are subject to break down, and, if they do, the nation will disintegrate. One contributes to such disintegration by creating additional suspicion, additional distrust, and additional hatreds.

Thus, accepting a role is an implicit moral charge, for one can choose not to accept a role as well, or else one can pretend to accept a role but not the moral implications of trust that attend it. Hartmann proposes that the value we are discussing be called "reliability," which is closely related to truthfulness.[3]

George Herbert Mead, a sociologist who analyzed roles in society, puts forward a positive view of the role, which he claims advances individuals beyond provinciality, sophisticates a person's life, humanizes persons by forcing them to learn empathy, and expands one's view to include larger communities, politics within the nation, history, and justice. It is also the case that if one declines to accept a common social role, he or she will nevertheless adapt inevitably to some role or another, perhaps to some anti-social role; a project will have been selected even if it is the role of a vagabond.

Of course, if an individual has chosen to deny existence itself, all rules are off and a person is in the position that the social contract theorists regard as "the state of nature" against the society. This is the origin, this denunciation of life itself, of the tyrant, whether dedicated to total annihilation of life, like Hitler, or ostensibly dedicated to the economic construction of the polity, like Stalin; all such tyrants are at root antithetical to existence and dedicated in the final analysis to lifelessness. They have adopted a role antithetical to the well-being of the society.

The destructiveness of a lesser tyrant like Saddam Hussein of Iraq revealed itself in the pointless murders and show trials of his regime, in the ruthless destruction of Iraqis who were Kurds or Shi-ites, in the firing of the oil fields of Kuwait, the release of oil to pollute the Gulf, in the gross betrayal of the military forces that he pretended to lead and left to disaster in 1991. Death trailed in the wake of this man's political path.

This consideration of service within a role indicates our departure from some of the existentialist attitudes. Sartre might admit that to play the part well of the judge, or the soldier, or the professional person might result in some good consequences. He would not likely accept that there is any moral worth for the incumbent in playing the part well.[4]

Indeed, Sartre appeared consistently to denigrate the roles that contribute to the bourgeois society and proposed roles intended to demolish that society; Sartre did not appear to accept the social contract that bound the France of his own time. Indeed, acceptance of the radical Marxist view of society as divided into incompatible classes is a denial of the possibility of any social contract. In fact, all societies have room for critical views that call into question the nature of the social contract when a nation engages to hold onto Algeria, say, against all sense. But, the good role-player ought to be regarded more highly than this, in most instances, for, in the first place, having committed ourselves to a role we have extended a promise to society, the keeping of which is the moral consideration due to others: we treat them as important others whose expectations merit our consideration, particularly if through the choice of role, we have undertaken to meet these expectations.

But beyond this, the assumption of a role ought to be a vital ethical choice, beyond the mere meeting of another's moral expectations, for it also implies the acceptance of a social contract. And here is where certain existentialists have failed to cope with human reality. We have discussed already the responsibilities that follow the declaration of the role of intellectual, one possible social role. But there are a host of other roles available in complex, modern society. One suspects that the typical intellectual tends to view the retailer of clothes, the auto mechanic, the dentist or the police officer, with a degree of Olympian contempt, while relying, nonetheless, on the services these roles provide.

But there need be no stigma to these roles. One can still fulfill them well or badly. To perform a social role effectively is not automatically a sign of inauthenticity. Indeed, the intellectual needs the auto mechanic and the shoe store to function. For the intellectual to spurn the majority of professional roles, which he or she nonetheless makes use of is to be supercilious. It is to operate in bad faith. It is to adopt the same stance of haughty contempt of the commoners exercised by the degenerate and socially useless aristocracy of various *ancien regimes*, an inauthentic stance if there ever was one.

Of course, there are many tasks that may not elicit our highest ethical commitments, so these roles become subordinate to others taken to be more important. No doubt part of the intellectual's contempt has been directed against the bourgeoisie, the result of the low estimation of their professional roles by the intellectual. This is often an ill-considered view. Barnes suggests that existentialism would seem to disqualify anyone from activity in the "serious world."[5]

On the one hand, the existentialists are quite right to focus a very critical eye on society and the role menu it affords; they are quite right to critique the manner in which these roles are played; on the other hand, a society of intellectuals scorning to play functional roles would be unworkable. To recognize the necessity of certain roles if society is to be made workable and to simultaneously denigrate those roles is to take a position that lacks lucidity and authenticity. But the tendency among intellectuals, at least since Plato devised the concept of the guardians, is to pretend to exist in a pristine social vacuum.

Within the confines of almost any role, however, particularly in the professions, there is a latitude for individual interpretation. One can still fulfill society's expectations, maintain trust, and be a lawyer, say, uniquely. One may decide to take on certain less lucrative cases out of a special interest for justice, perhaps defending minorities or specializing in civil rights cases. One can also choose to direct one's career into the most lucrative possible avenues, in which one might still elicit trust, but in which the ends of justice may fall well below one's evaluation of personal wealth.

In any role, there is a degree of compromise, of "forfeiture" to the world. One hands over "Being" to existence.[6] In these compromises the authentic individual will remain aware of what is being compromised, how much is being given up by himself, the social costs. Thrown into the shared world (the Heideggerian *Um-und-Mitwelt*), an authentic individual may refuse certain compromises, even, at the extreme, at the risk of life. But other social compromises may be both bearable and in keeping with the purposes of society embodied in the tacit social contract.

If society offers us enough in return, sociability, a decent quality of life, adequate physical security, a measure of justice with prospects toward improving upon that measure, we ought to be willing to make compromises, always keeping in mind what is being exchanged. The existential outlook, however, places a limit on the degree of compromise. To be entirely self-for-others, as Sartre expresses it, is to avoid the essential quality of authenticity, which requires Being-for-itself as well. Erich Fromm discusses the same issue in terms of the "market personality," a type frequent in advanced capitalist societies.[7] Yet, for all this, there is a degree of courage needed to participate lucidly in the workaday world, as Camus recognized.

In this chapter, the focus will be on the peculiar nature of the role of diplomat. Among many questions, the chief question that exercises us is whether such a role can be chosen authentically. In addition, we will assay the serious problem of whether the diplomat can carry out society's mission while retaining an individual allegiance to morality. Morality is always in question, whatever ethical values we elect to pursue in our projects. It is in question, therefore, if we pursue a career in diplomacy, but the nature of our relationship to moral choices is not fundamentally changed by such a choice, and it is not the case that by acting in the international arena we have elected to discard morality. Of course, we are aware of the clash of values that occurs in this role, about which Cavour admitted to Azeglio, that "if we did for ourselves what we are doing for Italy we should be real scoundrels."[8]

Merleau-Ponty points out that free acts that lack a foundation in "sedimental social structures" can have little or no relevance to history. Society is part of the situation to be accepted, rejected, or modified--to ignore "thrown and acquired structures" would be to play out one's possibilities in futility or pure opportunism.[9] To be purposive, freedom does not have to operate outside the society, although there may be circumstances in which we ought to choose to rebel against custom. Natanson remarks that "it is in the taking of social roles that the elements of anonymity become transposed into the possibilities of transcendence."[10] We can discover aspects of ourselves in the challenges of a role.

In this relation, Hannah Arendt makes an interesting distinction between behavior and acts. Behavior is elicited when an individual is totally immersed within the confines of social routine; in the task of diplomat, we can see the uninnovative role player producing unimaginative memos, excessively careful not to make waves, unvaryingly polite, blandly engaged to any and all situations, and uncritically adhering to whatever political doctrine or goal is ascendent in the department. The office of foreign officer would seem to be particularly susceptible to an incumbency of this nature. But an authentic commitment to diplomacy must not rule out the possibility of *deeds*. Deeds, still keeping to Arendt's distinction, are commitments that transcend mere behavior; while they do not violate the promises made in the acceptance of a role, they affirm the existence in this office, this position, of a person.[11]

An example of a person in the role of diplomat can be found in the memoirs of some former diplomats, for example, Dag Hammarskjold, former UN secretary general until his death in the Congo, or, from time to time, George Kennan. Some roles, of course, may even deny the opportunity for acts as so defined, and if so, then they can hardly represent an authentic choice--one thinks of the doorman at the plush hotel. The opportunity for transcending some social roles may be close to nil, but the functions may be necessary to society. Within such roles, it is possible to try, inevitably with ultimate failure, to make consciousness and the role co-extensive. For consciousness and role to be co-extensive is an obvious example of bad faith, for a human being is ultimately more than any role. Natanson calls bad faith of this form, anonymity.[12]

At times, no doubt, although in a sophisticated person, consciousness will generally extend always a bit beyond the defined confines of the role, bad faith in the form of this anonymity is probably inevitable at some points in the life of the diplomat. In some lesser roles, the sole return to the role holder must be, quite simply, a living. In *Being and Nothingness* (p. 60) there is the famous analysis by Sartre of the waiter:

But if I represent myself as him [a waiter], I am not he; I am separable from him as the object from the subject, separated by *nothing*, but this nothing isolates me from him. I cannot be he, I can only play at being him.
. . .

To reduce the personality solely to the requirements of the role as we glimpse occasionally in the drill sergeant, or the waiter just now, is to seek to be pure being-in-itself, obviously a futile effort in bad faith.

It is just such bad faith in this form that marks Kant's categorical imperative as an exercise in bad faith, for, ideally, one becomes a sort of moral martinet, a drill sergeant of morality, as Schopenhauer noted. But this argument does not put acceptance of a social role, or moral principles, out of bounds for the ethical person; it merely reveals the problems and contradictions faced in assuming roles. Perhaps in our work-a-day role we anticipate little or no opportunity for any form of self expression, and such roles will consume our time but not engage our major commitments.

One recalls Joris Huysmans, hiding his novels in progress in the top drawer of his bureaucrat's desk. The temptation is to posit a society in which only some persons are to be relegated to such menial roles, but this thought is an immoral one that does not take others importantly into account. It is the elitist immorality that assigns oneself and allies to the choice roles in society and hapless others to the menial statuses. Ultimately, such assignments must be enforced by "false consciousness" or violence, for humans, even more that Rossom's Universal Robots, have a way of growing beyond their assignments. It is, nonetheless, a common habit of intellectuals in particular, to delegate obnoxious roles to others, to those convenient persons of iron or bronze.

In the case of the role of diplomat, however, one assumes it is complex enough, challenging enough, to draw both upon the anonymous aspects of the role and the resources of the person. Aspects of the diplomatic task are best got over by behavior, carrying out those functions that are simply routine, leaving time and energy for fulfilling the role as a person beyond its routine demands.

The role of the diplomat is a peculiar one, for it takes its position on the edge of society facing inward and outward at the same time. Inward, the diplomat, like others accepting social roles, is bound into the social contract by ties shared with others within that society. We assume, of course, that the society has the requisite coherence to maintain some form of the social contract, that it has some degree of common culture and understandings that are required for an authentic choice of entering a contract. Thus, granted the foregoing, the diplomat is a member of a community of a relative degree of trust and promises, of expectations and interests that he or she is dedicated to meet and to pursue.

Facing outward, the diplomat does not reside within a social contract, for there is none embracing the international community, such as it is. Here trust and common interests must be accepted only very tentatively and with a high degree of wariness; common language, common history, common expectations, common ethical projects do not prevail to the degree that they might in the contractual community. Of course, there is bound to be some degree of comradeship that develops among even longtime antagonists playing similar roles for their respective societies, an attitude that may be detected in their memoirs. But such feelings, constructive at times for achieving consensus in difficult negotiations, must never override the loyalties that the diplomat owes the society represented. The outward stance, therefore, calls on the diplomat to forego the special relationships that tie him or her to the society. These special ties of the social contract cannot extend outward to embrace other societies.

But there is still the moral stance, that minimum commitment of taking all persons as persons importantly into account. Although it may not be feasible to pursue projects toward the achievement of justice for the peoples of other societies, justice must always be an underlying consideration in dealing with other societies. Moral imperatives still hold in international affairs, if we so choose, and if the basis for those moral imperatives is that which has previously been presented, namely, that others are free consciousnesses.

Perhaps 'the first question that arises if a potentially authentic individual is considering the possibility of assuming the role of diplomat, is whether or not the nation to be represented is worthy of conscientious representation. What good is the security and projects beyond its borders of this particular nation? Some of the elements in answer to this question have been discussed already. In the first place, any nation worthy of representation in good faith must have a prospect for increasing justice, equality, and rights among its own inhabitants. To represent the Stalin regime through the terrible years of the 1930s, as did Maxim Litvinov, is to share responsibility for its internal terrors. But it would be puerile to simply say that Litvinov ought not to have so served: What were his options for improving that society? If Litvinov did not accept his position, did he have more or less leverage for advancing potentially good causes in the world?

The problem of the citizen of a totalitarian country is particularly poignant--no one should leap too quickly to judge another enmeshed in a situation of totalitarianism. Of course, Molotov's is an easier case than Litvinov's: Fully aware and supportive of Stalin's measures, brought into the foreign ministry specifically to negotiate the pact with Nazi Germany, for which Litvinov, as a Jew, was unsuitable, vicious in purging the ranks of the foreign ministry, his responsibility is quite clear: his contributions lent force to totalitarianism.

What of service to a nation in which substantial numbers of persons in the territory of the nation are denied admission to the social contract, the case of the Republic of South Africa? Again, the judgments of cost and benefits, of the present and future prospects for such a society, are not easy to weigh. Justice within the society to be represented by diplomacy is always a relevant criterion to be weighed by the potential diplomat. The role of the diplomat is always a voluntary one, so that morality and justice within the society represented is a consideration for any incumbent.

The existence of some form of moral community is also an essential to warrant efforts on behalf of any society. Despite the centrifugal forces of modern technological society, there ought to be a core, however pallid, as is bound to be the case wherever individuality is possible, of a moral community. By the by, the existence of possibilities in society, whereby we designate individuality, is an indication of justice, but it also touches on aspects of the desirable moral community: Allowances and toleration for individuality is an aspect of the liberal society that binds some people to it. That is, one of the significant ties within the liberal society is the absence of numerous involuntary ties.

One of the causes of the collapse of Communist regimes in 1989 was the difficulty within those societies of exerting enough individual choice; simply the harassment of having to search for food in the shops eroded the time left for personal expression. Trust, of course, is a crucial criterion of a moral society. Where that has broken down in the society as a whole, it may still exist within subsocieties within the polity. Thus, while the moral community of a polity as a whole may be lacking, there still may be significant subcommunities worthy of representation and security. Should the diplomat try to represent these?

Certain polities are in a very shaky position here, including some Third World countries, in which trust has never extended beyond clan or tribe in the past. The United States has problems of another nature, the effect of an advanced industrial society based on individualism and a relatively open immigration policy resulting to some degree in the diminution of social trust. Segments of the country are simply estranged from others. The overemphasis of the capitalist market economy on pure and simple greed does not contribute to bonds of trust. In parts of most cities, law and order verges on nonexistence: The legal system does not always fulfill the minimal duties of the social contract.

Large scale immigration is difficult to assimilate into a minimal moral community, as we have suggested, and the interactions between the black minority and the larger white society still bespeaks a wall of suspicion that separates them. The most apt conclusion, it seems to me, is that, not making one's expectations too utopian, there is still quite enough of a moral community in the United States to draw diplomatic defenders of its security. There are, in addition, also prospects for improvement, because of the nation's political traditions.

The Marxist, of course, cannot be an overt diplomat for bourgeois democracies, although he or she might be able to represent a dictatorship of the proletariat, if there were one. The reason for this is that the Marxist interprets societies and nations as class-divided. They cannot accept the nation as a community at all. As a Marxist, one can only extend sincere civility and trust to the proletariat, which is the furthest extent of pre-Communist "moral community." For the Marxist, then, the bourgeois society does not constitute a community. To represent it diplomatically could not be done in good faith.

It is, according to Heidegger, inauthentic to accept as givens, as national necessities, so to speak, one's social, religious, and national identities. The meaning of these identities must include for the lucid consciousness the sum total of all that they have been in the past. To passively identify with this past, with history, characterizes the (inauthentic) finality that Dasein seeks.[13] It seems the case, however, while keeping a firm hold on the possibilities in the situation, that one can still come to authentic terms with the history of one's nation and society. The preceding chapter proposed the claim that history has on the authentic person.

Remaining open to possibilities, lucid about the nation's past accomplishments, failures, and crimes, not regarding the nation as Spirit or the carrier of destiny for mankind, the aspiring diplomat can still find, perhaps, rootedness in the nation's and his own past sufficient to command loyalty, and he or she may do this without assuming the character of in-itself, embedded in the country's practico-inert.

The Soviet diplomat, even one who may sever loyalty with the oppressive Tsarist and totalitarian past, still had constructive soil on which to plant roots in the remarkable and resilient culture of arts, literature, music, and so forth, that is the heritage of the peoples of the former USSR. There are also acceptable aspects of Marx's doctrine, proclaimed as Marxist humanism, for instance, that might have commanded the authentic loyalty of a Soviet diplomat.

Let us elaborate on this concept of an authentic loyalty to the nation. It includes the retention of a lucid view of the national past, a lucid concept of the possibilities open to that nation in the future, namely as these concern justice and equality, a recognition that by assuming the role of diplomat, we have assumed a station that makes us responsible for the past and future of what that entity did and will do in the world. Thus, we may have to come to terms with our country's imperialism: Is this an inevitable outgrowth of its domestic economy, Lenin's thesis, or is it ameliorable, open to change and reform, Hobson's argument? In the nature of power, it is probable that any superpower is inevitably imperialistic, in one way or another.

Let us clarify a meaning here, accepting Hans Morgenthau's definition of imperialism: It is the expansion of influence and control into new areas, through cultural, economic, and military means. Considered in light of such a definition, imperialism is almost inevitable for a great power. There is also the practico-inert, the totality of imperialisms past, which in the United States includes its westward expansion, in the former Soviet Union the acquisition of Siberia and the conquest of the Baltic states and a number of the peripheral non-Russian republics, such as Georgia. As a diplomat, we need to come to terms with imperialism, accepting it, rejecting it, attempting to modify it. It is part of a lucid view of any country's history, even the history, if lucidly related, of many of the Third World nations. We take on the past, if we take on the role of the diplomat.

These questions, all part of the situation, are of necessity to be grappled with by the aspiring diplomat-to-be. We will assume an authentic decision to take the diplomatic role has been made, as we have shown to be a possibility. What now are the charges to the diplomat--and how can a person authentically remain in that role? The first promise that characterizes the position, is to protect to the best of one's ability, the security of the represented nation. This is of the nature of the position, and it is a trust freely assumed when one accepts the role of diplomat.

Prior suggests that to logically infer "I ought to do X," in the case in point, to protect the security of the nation, from "I have promised to do X," I must hold the ethical principle that "If I extend a promise, I ought to keep that promise."[14] An authentic individual knows that he or she is free to keep or not to keep a promise; furthermore, we have denied deontological moral principles; so why should one keep their word? The ethical project of upholding a categorical imperative by choosing under all conditions to always tell the truth whatever the consequences is certainly not recommendable. The role-commitment is the free one to observe conscious others to whom, all things being equal, a promise is to be kept.

As a diplomat, a pledge has been accepted commensurate with the diplomatic role, to seek security for the nation; to violate this would be an affront to the trust that forms the minimal moral community of the nation, a community a diplomat will want to enhance. . . and because others in that community ought to be considered. In part they ought to be considered for the reason that they are, simply, persons, to whom the individual has chosen to extend moral commitments; but in part, also, they enter into consideration as fellow members of a social contract.

To provide this security to one's own country demands that one keep current with the political situation, perhaps focusing one's view on the relationship between one's own country and the host nation to which the diplomat is assigned as a representative. What is the strength of the political party that would rescind our trade or our bases agreement with that nation? Are they on the path to power, and would loss of these bases reduce one's country's security? It is the diplomat's duty to openly discuss this, to suggest that the decision would injure our security, maybe the security of the host nation (if that is true), and to hint at the possibilities of worsened relations and even certain sanctions that the nation might take in retaliation to an unfriendly act.

Two questions arise immediately: Should a diplomat lie, if it seems effective to do so, and should a country intervene in the domestic affairs of the host country by covert funding, say, of friendly parties? We will deal with these crucial problems later. A further extension of such questions involves spying: In a nation where open sources of information may not exist, should paid informers be maintained to apprise the diplomat of the secret intents of the hosts or the groups that affect his or her nation's interests?

It is interesting that so many moral questions arise in connection with the basic function of working to secure the security of one's own country in view of potential threats against it. This is the time-honored basic duty of the diplomat in the modern world, to quote Ermolao Barbaro,

> the first duty of an ambassador is exactly the same as that of any other servant of a government, that is, to do, say, advise, and think whatever may best serve the preservation and aggrandizement [we will reserve comment on this] of his own state.[15]

Thus, the diplomat maintains the trust of his society and fulfills the diplomatic role by serving the purposes and interests of the sponsoring state. If possible, he or she may contribute as well to the larger interests of international peace. But he or she ought not to bargain away the interest of their state on their own.[16] Harold Nicolson's work on diplomacy is an apt statement of what the good diplomat ought to be, and how one can best work to secure the nation's best interest.[17]

And this, in effect, answers the problem of spying and covert acquisition of information, all of which is a fair gain in the service of one's country, provided that it is obtained in a way that is predictably effective. Data and knowledge can only serve to make decisions more lucid than otherwise; it is also probable that data surreptitiously obtained is as likely to conduce to more peaceful relations as otherwise--it is always possible that some threats are not credible and need not to be taken seriously. The moral problem with spying is the tendencies to which it might give rise, manipulativeness and contempt for persons.

Some further problems of diplomacy will be more appropriately held over to the next chapter. However, it is essential to deal with two major moral questions here--First, we have stated the basic function of the diplomat is to provide security for the sponsoring state. But to what extent should the diplomat pursue higher personal ethical goals through the use of his or her office? May he or she rise above the interests of the nation and the basic functions of the diplomatic role? Finally, does the diplomat require absolution from lying?

From one point-of-view, the best diplomat might well be one of the good founders of Sartre's fictional city of Bouville in *Nausea*, those smug, good citizens, content in their total immersion in the customs, the laws, the traditions of their society, which they know to be a final culmination of the natural order--persons, that is, mired in complete bad faith.[18] While these types are probably representative of types discoverable in any social role, and they live inauthentic lives, our question as to whether a choice of a diplomatic role might be made authentically has already been answered affirmatively: It is possible.

Authentic action is possible within social roles while at the same time retaining social trust. The role

> does not enslave us to norms that are externally imposed, since it takes them over, and lifts them up into a world of meaning that we have thought through and authorized for ourselves.... Acts demanded of me by external norms, which I do not understand, are not mine. I am not the author of them.[19]

To be sure, authentic individuals who fulfill roles are always a potential danger to society in the sense that they know they are free to move beyond self-imposed restraints, but they may also be more insightful and usefully innovative than our good bourgeois, than a mere timeserver.

That said, may a diplomat use the role to insure individual ethical projects that may betray the interests of the represented nation? He or she may, in the sense that they are free; they ought not in the sense of their freely accepted trust. For one thing, under some conditions, violence enters foreign affairs, and state violence may even be the least evil of impending consequences in a political situation. It is a plausible moral decision that might be made by a nation, to conduct a war, to aid guerrillas, to retaliate against terrorists, etc. Under the same type of political situation, however, a pacifist might in good faith sacrifice his or her life rather than resort to violence. But it is never the duty of the diplomatic to sacrifice the life of the state if a war could save it.[20]

In addition, whether the national decision be war or peace, the diplomat must always espouse the fundamental affirmation of existence against non-existence. Thus, never violence for its own sake, but only for the sake of preventing worse conditions: to cite an extreme example, a diplomat might well have supported the invasion of Cambodia by Vietnam as an improvement in the situation of that country, although that invasion was certainly not carried out in order to rescue the Khmer people. The bearers of Khmer culture were in the process of being systematically exterminated by the Pol Pot regime.

There are some very difficult decisions in this regard for the diplomat: What was Andrei Andropov's duty as the representative of the former USSR in Hungary in 1956? Assume that a lucid analysis suggested to him that the defection of Hungary from the Warsaw Pact, under the circumstances a gain for most Hungarians if they had pulled it off, would lead to such unrest throughout eastern Europe that additional turmoil and jeopardy to Soviet security as a state would inevitably result. One might validly fear these consequences even if one denounced the original acquisition of Soviet control over eastern Europe. Should he have called for Soviet intervention? Was Soviet policy wrong and based on a misassessment of the world political structure and the intentions of competing powers? One doubts that Andropov pondered many of these problems from the moral viewpoint, but it would have been an even more difficult decision for him if he had.

The diplomat must always weigh consequences: To intervene in this country, where the people are unjustly oppressed, might bring about a destructive conflict beyond whatever good intervention might do. In 1989, the American decision to intervene in Panama and unseat President-for-life Manuel Noriega, may have brought about somewhat better political conditions in that country; it also cost the lives of hundreds of Panamanean civilians. The ethical purist would scoff at the diplomat who left an immoral enemy a way out of a confrontation, whereby they might save prestige, but the suave consequentialist knows the death and mayhem that would result if the foe were cornered. This is not even a matter of diplomatic bad faith; it is a matter of lucidity alone.

By choosing the role of a diplomat, one has agreed as a representative of a nation that for the most part, the nation is justified in doing what it generally does in foreign affairs.[21] While that subordinate project, morality, considers humans as equal, so that the persons in the host country are as equally entitled to justice as those in the sponsoring nation, the social contract is still a national one and does not yet bind all mankind. The diplomat is a member of a national social contract, and no social contract presently exists to unify the people of the world: Certainly, the United Nations at the present time is not representative of a full-fledged social contract.

For that reason, the diplomat's fundamental duties are to the security of his or her constituents. Without jeopardizing this security, there may be times when the office can be used to further "cosmopolitan ideals of the world." As an authentic individual, a diplomat will take advantage of opportunities to do this, always provided that the represented nation's security remains a foremost consideration.[22] The role of diplomat would not have been taken in good faith, were one to pursue an ethical charitable enterprise in the world, while jeopardizing the security and interests of one's sponsor. (There are international roles that allow us to do good deeds to universal mankind; in good faith, the diplomatic role can always be resigned and another role taken up.)

Rawls' conceptualization of the morality of principles and the morality of association, strongly suggests that diplomats are concerned with the latter, and as a general rule ought to eschew the morality of principles in the conduct of their office.[23] In particular, diplomats must be consequentialists and not deontologists. There must be self-imposed limits on the incumbent's expression of private idealism.[24]

It is not impossible for the diplomat to transcend such a limitation from time-to-time, while not sacrificing his nation's interests, to pursue an ought-to-be; indeed, authenticity would require this. But this is not the definition of the diplomatic role. The worst case of wrongly pursuing the ought-to-be, of course, would occur if the diplomat assumes the position of the bearer of world history. The appropriate role of diplomat is defiled if he or she believe themselves and their nation to be the bearers of world destiny, above all of a unique morality, living in a realm above the mundane where the individual conscience no longer matters. Thus, on the world stage, under a belief of this kind, there would follow inevitable violations of the fundamental moral principle of human equality. Such diplomats represent a danger to the world.[25]

The authentic diplomat ought not take on the task of representing a nation that pursues large, historicist ethical projects in the world, projects of all-embracing imperialism, of a self-righteous civilizing mission, or whatever, because these are the sources of war and destruction; the diplomat is dedicated to a limited pursuit of national security in the world.

It is these very limitations of the diplomatic role and the boundaries placed upon the nation's goals in the world that allow the diplomat to play a moral role on the international stage. On occasion, however, one can transcend the limitations that usually ought to hem in the diplomatic office, and without sacrificing constituents, perform in a supererogatory way: Such an accomplishment was the visit to Jerusalem by Anwar Sadat of Egypt, a truly remarkable event.[26]

In an address to potential foreign service applicants, former Secretary of State Dean Acheson observed, "Generally speaking, morality often imposes upon those who exercise the powers of government standards of conduct quite different from what might seem right to them as private citizens."[27] But this is not correct. Or, better, it is not correct in the sense in which morality has been defined in this work. As we pursue our ethical projects, the moral standards of justice and equality required as our freely-selected subsidiary project, are always problematic.

However, so basic is morality, as we have defined it, and so clearly obvious to us ought to be the standing of all persons having consciousness, that these minimal principles come into consideration at all times. Granted, when we act on the international stage, no social contract facilitates our interaction with others, but morality makes the same claims. We, therefore, consider that taking others importantly into account is a (free) moral requirement for both the diplomat acting on the world stage and for persons acting on the more limited national stage.

In diplomacy, we deal with competing interests outside the sanctions and bonds of the social contract. Sometimes we deal with sworn enemies of our state and a democratic way-of-life. Ryle mentions the case of communication when "talk is guarded," the very case in much diplomacy.[28] This is not the sought-for open society of Habermas, nor is it even a society that maintains minimal standards of justice and equality. Of course, lies must always be weighed, even when we lie to enemies; they always exact a cost.[29] But if we lucidly weigh the consequences, the lie may be the only feasible act within the very imperfect world of international affairs.

The great American myth, proposed by President Wilson and heralded by President Carter, of open covenants openly arrived at, is the communication utopia proposed by Habermas and Sartre elevated to an even less appropriate arena, international affairs. We have not attained any national societies in which this is feasible, and from a consequentialist position, the international society is even further removed from such possibilities of trust. (Neither Wilson nor Carter were able, as they found, to put this errant doctrine into effect. Both had the wisdom not to do so.)

We seem to discuss lies in connection with diplomacy, often, as though the lie were, without further consideration, always the best option. This is false. The truth may often be the better choice, for we often enough want the foe to know for sure where our interests lie. But there will be many cases in the real world, provided we are always aware of the strictures of morality and of meeting these wherever possible, provided we are pursuing the true end of diplomacy, which is a basic, unexaggerated national security, in which lies will serve ends more adequately, always assuming that we hold a correct and limited definition of national security.

On the international arena we will accept some of Machiavelli's principles. Others of his principles we avoid: Especially, diplomats ought not to aim for national glory for its own sake. Hence, *virtu* as an end will be eschewed; indeed, to pursue the goal of national glory on the international stage is an essential evil that violates the limitations that must be accepted if war and destruction are to be avoided: The Napoleonic pursuit was a violation of morality and a gross neglect of considering consequences. Ethically, the Napoleonic wars were anathema to life, although Napoleon may not have so intended them. Thus, international affairs is a field in which morality can be applied; it is not a field intended for all our higher ethical pursuits.

But there are obvious applications of morality in international affairs, situations in which, had moral principles been observed, human costs would have been spared at no expense to the national interest. One such case involved the Kurds of Iraq. In 1991, the Kurds had fled their villages and cities in the area of northern Iraq and were trekking toward Turkey or Iran, many of them dying on the way. This followed an unsuccessful rising against Saddam Hussein, weakened in the wake of the defeat in Kuwait and southern Iraq. However, Saddam Hussein had enough military might spared so that with control of the air through helicopter gunships, the Kurds were crushed. By April, 1991, camps to receive the starving refugees had been established in Iraq by American and British forces, contrary, of course, to international law. Such violations of international custom may well be overlooked. This was not the first debacle suffered by the Kurds, in part through a misunderstanding of larger international games that were being pursued.

Back in 1970, the Kurds had arrived at an agreement with the Ba'ath government of Lieut. General Ahmed Hassan Bakr, although even then Saddam Hussein was probably effectively in power. The agreement was intended to halt nine years of Kurdish unrest directed against the government of Iraq. It offered to let them govern their own territory and elect delegates to the central parliament. Kurdish was to become, with Arabic, an official language. Although the agreement was proclaimed by Bakr as one that "will prevail forever," it was not honored, so that within a few years the Kurdish areas of northern Iraq were in revolt.

The revolt of the Kurds was useful to a number of games that were being pursued in the area, although there was little or no genuine support for any such entity as an independent Kurdistan, which would have embraced, in theory, large portions of Turkey and Iran and small parts of Syria (with, perhaps, a small section of the former USSR). Thus, the United States was drawn into ostensible support of the Kurds largely through the purpose of supporting the Shah of Iran as a buttress of stability in the Middle East. A moral consideration in supporting the Shah was the nature of the Shah's regime, an authoritarian state in which the secret police, SAVAK, was guilty of blatant disregard of human rights.

Both the United States and the British were responsible in some part for the development of human rights abuses under the Shah for the reason that they had collaborated in ousting Premier Mohammed Mossadegh back in the 1950s. The immediate purpose of this ouster was to prevent the Iranian government from taking over a majority control of the considerable Iranian oil supply. From a moral point-of-view, this was not a sufficient reason for undertaking such a coup. Lucidly, it was possible even in 1953 to consider that the outside control of the oil supplies of the Middle East was not going to last much longer, and that future moves to seize these supplies might be made by governments less amicable to progressive political forces than Mossadegh's. Indeed, it was not long before the Shah himself moved to nationalize Iran's oil.

Placing the Shah in power was to unleash, in circumstances that were not themselves so unsettling in 1953 to the West as to require so drastic a solution, the unpredictable train of events that were to lead to worse consequences for Iran and for the Western powers by 1979. None of these future events, however, could have been foreseen. The moral requirement of lucidity does not extend so far. It can only ask whether the events of the present are so dire as to require a coup d'etat. Morality would also have required some consideration of the potential future of the Iranians under Mossadegh on the one hand and the restored Shah on the other.

In his way, the Shah did consider the long range good of the Iranians. He made efforts, partially successful, to modernize the country. In these efforts, he was no doubt encouraged by the Americans, whose major interest was to support Iran as a stabilizing force in the region. Secondarily, the Shah was a major purchaser of American arms, and it was not difficult to rationalize this lucrative policy to the need for a strong and stable power, friendly to the West, in the region.

The interest of the Shah in his support of the Kurd's rebellion against Iraq was to put pressure on Iraq itself. Iran's chief problem with Iraq at the time was the disposition of the border along the Shatt al-Arab, which was in dispute between the two countries. Thus, the Shah became the friend to the Kurd's revolt against Iraq for the purpose of placing pressure on the Iraqi government to negotiate a settlement favorable to Iran. The United States from 1972 supported him in this.

Herein is the crux of the moral problem of this event. The United States and the Iranians had no desire to see the emergence of an independent Kurdish state in the region, the Iranians for fear of unrest, no doubt, among the numerous Kurds in their own country, and the Americans would not likely have any motive to upset their NATO ally, Turkey, which had its own restless Kurdish population. Thus, the Iranians were making use of their aid to the Kurds in order to pressure the Iraqis to negotiate a border settlement.

The implied message to Iraq in this policy by Iran is obvious: we will supply the Kurdish rebellion until these negotiations are consummated-- you can obtain surcease from Iranian aid to the Kurdish rebellion by coming to terms. This policy was supported by the United States for the reason that Iran was to be supported in the region when possible. The goal was regional stability.

The Kurdish leadership might be expected to understand the relationship that they enjoyed with the Shah. It is the business of political leaders to interpret the political situation lucidly when they act politically. The moral responsibility of the Kurdish leadership was to grasp the intricacies of Middle Eastern politics and the history of conflicts and animosities in the region, which would have alerted them to the fragility of the Shah's support. But the United States was another matter, for it was an actor with which they would have had less familiarity, and the United States was a so-called "guarantor" of the Shah's policy of friendship to the Kurds.

While it may be true, as Kissinger claims[30] that the decision to convince the Kurds of the futility of an offensive in October, 1973, (taking advantage of the turmoil resulting from the Winter War against Israel), was based on an accurate assessment of the probability of the failure of such an effort by American intelligence, the fact remains that when the Shah came to an agreement with Iraq over the boundary question, all aid to the Kurds was forthwith terminated, and the Shah advised the Kurds to surrender unconditionally.

Iraq was able to launch a crushing offensive against the Kurds, now bereft of aid from abroad. Thus, the conclusion is inescapable that the relationship with the Kurds was not based on any sympathy to their cause but on the ulterior motives contained within two supergames that were being played: First, Iran was interested in resolving the border dispute; second, the United States was interested in supporting Iran as a stabilizing force in the region at very little cost (in this case).

The Kurds, therefore, were implicated unawares in the projects of the Americans and the Iranians; they were used, that is, as means to the ends of other countries. The policy, in essence, was therefore immoral. In the broad issues of the Middle East, it was a policy that the United States ought to have avoided. By joining in any agreement with the Kurds, however tacit, the United States was bound to contribute to a misinterpretation of the situation to the disadvantage of the Kurds. A moral choice might have been made in this instance by taking the Kurds equally into account. There is some indication that the Kurds once again misinterpreted the intention of the United States in 1991.

There is a final consideration with regard to the Kurds that ought to be mentioned. In the Armenian massacres at the turn of the century, the world played its normal role of nonintervention and futile hand wringing. The Kurds in Turkey took an active part in killing Armenians. They were also implicated in the massacres of Assyrian Christians who inhabited northwest Iraq. Thus, there is the cynical view that affords an escape from responsibility in bad faith, which is that the Kurds, considering their own history, deserved no better. Thus can a person escape from any moral responsibility whatever, for to dig into the history of any people is to find a myriad of reasons why such and such a group deserves no better. To so reason, however, is to adopt a position of bad faith. It is to condemn peoples as marked by the inescapable essence of evil, an unexistential position.

In diplomacy, it is distinctly the rule of individual morality we follow, and the nature of a sponsor nation ought to allow us to do this. Morality is as possible, or as inadequate in some circumstances, in international affairs as it is for domestic pursuits. It is the individual conscience where the dilemma of "dirty hands" is played out and guilt assigned--it is the diplomat's responsibility, and no state authority can exonerate him or her.[31]

Morality is that subsidiary project that calls upon us to regard others as important and to take them into account when conducting diplomatic affairs. To be moral, therefore, is to give due consideration to others, whether others to whom we have made tacit promises, namely, to our fellow nationals, or to others affected by our national security pursuits in the world. That morality and politics need be divorced if actions are to be effective is a mistaken notion.

In Machiavelli, it is the conclusion that follows provided that we have determined upon a personal or national pursuit of glory; but the appropriate diplomatic pursuit should not be glory, but the limited goal of national security. It is within the nation that ethical projects are to be pursued under conditions of justice and equality, and it is to protect these possibilities that diplomacy exists. To adopt as the national purpose the more mundane purpose of security, and, of course, not absolute security, is to be able to maintain moral principles in the world, at least under most political circumstances.

In the *Social Contract*, Rousseau has a farsighted presentation of the clash of projects that we might select. Indeed, he launches into a fine, albeit a brief, discussion of role theory; (is this the first such clear exposition of role theory?): (1) the individual project; (2) the society's project; and (3) the projects of other societies. The diplomat, involved with all of these, must balance them somehow, always with an eye toward morality and consequences. It makes international affairs a most difficult and fascinating moral arena.

Notes

1. John Dewey and James H. Tufts, *Ethics* (New York: Holt, Rinehart and Winston, 1936; a 1932 revision of the book published in 1908), p. 249.
2. See Jonas Bernstein, ""Stalking the Past of a Police State," *Insight*, Vol. 7, No. 3 (January 21, 1991), 8-13.
3. *Ethics*, Vol. II, p. 287.
4. Warnock, "Existentialist Ethics," in Hudson, p. 395.
5. Barnes, *The Literature of Possibility*, p. 169.
6. Marcuse, "Contributions to a Phenomenology of Historical Materialism," p. 14, interpreting Heidegger.
7. See Barnes, *The Literature of Possibility*, p. 309, on this topic; see also Hayim, *The Existential Sociology of Jean-Paul Sartre*, p. 25.
8. Smith, *Cavour*, p. 197.
9. Mallin, *Merleau-Ponty's Philosophy*, p. 271.
10. Natanson, *Phenomenology, Role, and Reason*, p. 77.
11. See Arendt, *The Human Condition*, p. 43.
12. Natanson, *Phenomenology, Role, and Reason*, p. 167.
13. Izenberg, *The Existentialist Critique of Freud*, p. 252.
14. Prior, *Logic and the Basis of Ethics*, p. 22.
15. Garrett Mattingly, *Renaissance Diplomacy* (Boston: Houghton Mifflin, 1955), p. 109.
16. Lefever, *Ethics and United States Foreign Policy*, p. 56-57.
17. Nicolson, *Diplomacy*, pp. 55-67.
18. Marshall Berman, *The Politics of Authenticity: Radical Individualism and the Emergence of Modern Society* (New York: Atheneum, 1970) discusses the relations between Rousseau and his sponsors, the aristocratic Luxembourgs: "These noble lives were governed and circumscribed by a class code of privileges and obligations. The code mediated all their personal relationships, forced their feelings into the fixed forms of 'the duties of society,' and prevented them from

experiencing the equality and mutuality which 'the language of friendship and intimacy' required." Here are those good Bouville burghers in the flesh. (In fairness to these aristocrats, it must be admitted that Rousseau was himself, probably, a pain-in-the-neck.)

19. Wild, "An Authentic Existence," p. 77.
20. Benedetto Croce, *Politics and Morals* (London: George Allen and Unwin, 1946. Trans. by Salvatore J. Castiglione), p. 131.
21. McMahon, *Humans Being*, p. 98, where there is a suggestion of this notion.
22. This discussion occurs in Sterling, *Ethics in a World of Power*, p. 102.
23. Rawls, *The Theory of Justice*, p. 479.
24. John C. Bennett, *Moral Tensions in International Affairs* (New York: The Council on Religion and International Affairs, 1964), p. 15; Parfit, *Reasons and Persons*, p. 98; Nielson, *Ethics Without God*, Chapter 4.
25. See Popper, *The Open Society and Its Enemies*, Vol. II, pp. 67-68. Popper is attacking Hegelianism on these pages.
26. James N. Rosenau, "A Pre-Theory Revisited: World Politics in an Era of Cascading Interdependence," *International Studies Quarterly*, Vol. 28, No. 3 (September 1984), p. 280.
27. Hook, *Philosophy and Public Policy*, p. 57. Hook thinks this view is wrong, and so do I.
28. Ryle, *The Concept of Mind*, p. 184.
29. Bok, *Lying: Moral Choice in Public and Private Life* (New York: Pantheon Books, 1978), Chapter X, "Lying to Enemies," pp. 132-145.
30. See *White House Years* (Boston: Little, Brown and Company, 1979), p. 1265. Additional information on the Kurdish matter have come from such news journals of the period as *Time*, *Newsweek*, *The New Republic*, and *The Village Voice*, February 16, 1976.
31. Michael Waltzer, "Political Action: The Problem of Dirty Hands," *Philosophy and Public Affairs*, p. 177. We disagree with Walzer on this point and accept the formulation of Max Weber, which he criticizes.

Chapter 15

Pursuing the National Interest

Part I. Security

Hobbes was correct in holding that the basis of the social contract was the desire for security. No other rights, particularly that of equality, are viable without a modicum of law and order. If a society has come into being, the assumption is that the members have enough in common to form, even in the loose, or serialized societies of modern industrialized nations, a moral community of sorts. Crimes will, in such communities, be the exception, but a basic predictability based on trust will be the general rule.

Lacking this, the society will not in the long run cohere; it will not be able to articulate any common interests; it will not be able to function lacking some common agreement on due process and civility. Except for those traditional societies that fall into the category of *Gemeinschaft*, no modern, complex, industrial society is capable of functioning without a government which has the final authority to enforce compromises, law and order, and fair contracts among citizens. Anarchism might be an effective system for a small, homogeneous, religious community, but it will not do for a large scale, multiethnic, modern division-of-labor economy.

For anarchy to function properly would seem to require a social cohesion persuasive enough to destroy individuality. Ideally, the state offers a last court-of-appeal to any citizen unable to obtain the equal treatment he or she should receive at the hands of fellow citizens. Again, ideally, this appeal should not have to be made in most instances, since equal treatment should be the norm for a just society.

Since such ideal conditions exist in no extant state, such appeals may be more or less frequent, especially when state and society move to extend justice and equality into groups and regions where these did not operate effectively before. The state ought to be able to surmount occasional breakdowns in the system of security, if the society in which it operates is to remain cohesive. Revolts, civil wars, and revolutions mark the collapse of a state system, sometimes to be replaced by new governments more vigorous in their pursuit of domestic security; sometimes, as in the case of a revolution, by new personnel in command of a new system of rules.

No analogy to the social contract exists in the international world. A society ready for a social contract is one in which most individuals would have concluded,

> I know these people I live among well enough that I am willing to trust them to some degree, provided I can obtain a fair hearing for my interests in some higher, and stronger, court. I am at least at ease with them, for I can predict, generally, that they will react pretty much as I do in similar situations. I can communicate with these people in common understandings; we have similar reactions to concepts and words. Finally, we have a common understanding about due process, about what is fair.

If a moral community exists at all, each member of the community can gain a feeling beyond an abstract reasoning that his or her fellows deserve the same justice as themselves, and that they are fundamentally equal presences in the world. Most societies are far from this ideal, so that while there are social contracts, nations, and moral communities, many of these are quite feeble.

Of course, to review these bases for a moral community is to see just how far most nations are from such an ideal situation. Most nations are closer to (or farther from) a minimal moral community, and some will have to undergo a lengthy process of nation-building before (if successful at all), they can attain the most tenuous moral communities. The social contract theorists were sophisticated enough to realize that such a contract never was overtly proposed and adhered to by any society or national group, although Locke makes an attempt to show what he thinks was such an original agreement among the Indian tribes of America. It is a useful fiction that some modern societies cohere *as though* a social contract had been entered into.

In the international field, containing abstract, sovereign entities called states, there is no social contract. The social contract cannot exist among abstract entities; it must be entered into, if at all, by the source of societies, namely, individual consciousnesses. Therefore, lacking a social contract, no final authority of appeal exists in international affairs, although there are inadequate counterparts, say, to a Supreme Court.

An International Court of Justice exists, and it is useful to the degree that states are willing to submit cases to it and accept its jurisdiction. But in the case of the American ambassadorial hostages imprisoned illegally according to international law by Iran, the Court's injunction that they be freed forthwith was ignored. The United States refused to accept the jurisdiction of the Court, when the Court found against it in the case of the Nicaraguan contras in 1985.

The United Nations itself is a forum for debate--it is not a legislature intended to pass laws binding on members. It has been useful in resolving certain disputes, provided that its members, including the disputants, desired its success. But the United Nations was not intended to be a world government and is further from that status at the end of the 20th century than it once was, becoming, since 1960, more heterogeneous in its membership than it was at its founding. A realist, lucidly viewing the international arena, will make no more of international organization than it can offer.

Hans Morgenthau is severe on what he refers to as "utopianism," "sentimentalism," and the "legalistic-moralistic approach" to international politics. All these are tendencies in modern political thought to substitute for national interest an assumed "supranational standard of action which is generally identified with an international organization." This, he claims, is a figment of the imagination, wishful thinking, the postulation of valid norms for international conduct which are not there.[1] As our discussion has suggested, international institutions do not provide a basis for a social contract, for the requisite civility and shared values are lacking.

The international world has some customs, some laws, treaties among its members, but no sanctioning authority. It tries to provide rules governing the interaction of abstract consciousless entities, namely, states, but states cannot offer an immediate basis for a social contract. It is a mistake to assume that the interactions among separate points of consciousness, the prerequisite for society, can be assumed to exist among abstractions such as states. No present organization purports to offer any state a fair hearing on security against any other state.

The League of Nations collapsed following Japan's intrusion into Manchuria and the eventual war with China, the conquest of Ethiopia by Italy, and the winter war launched by the former USSR against Finland (by which time the League was moribund, in any case). The United Nations has fared somewhat better, but expectations among most political practitioners have never been very high concerning it. At basis, whatever security exists for a state in the world is, to a great degree, the function of its own actions in the world, together with the prevailing system of the distribution of power in the world, over which the single state probably has very slight control. These actions intended to further state interests or maintain state security are based on its own power, or, in some cases, the power of allies, or, in unusual cases, the countervailing power of imperialist rivals. "All serious foreign policy, therefore, begins with maintaining a balance of power--a scope for action, a capacity to affect events and conditions. Without that capacity, a nation is reduced to striking empty poses," according to another realist practitioner.[2]

Thailand, Iran, and Uruguay have preserved independence for historical periods because potential predator states have been too evenly balanced against one another for one or the other to prevail in controlling them. Security is a national matter, that, while making use of whatever international organizations there may be, is still basically a matter of self-help.[3]

The world has seen a number of international systems, distinguished by their different distributions of power, that have appeared throughout history. The *pax Romana* was the accomplishment of an expansive state that ultimately subdued all potential rivals to its state system and achieved hegemony--providing an authoritative structure for all groups. China accomplished the same hegemony from time to time in its own sphere, contending, usually successfully, with threats that could be thwarted on its periphery.

But systems of competing powers may be more usual, historically. The warring state system of ancient China, before the amalgamation of the first empire in 221 B.C., was the classic Oriental example. Kautilya has written about a similar system in ancient India. The Italy Machiavelli described in *The Prince* was another such system. The European system, now grown to embrace the world, has been such a system of competing state entities, at least since the Peace of Westphalia in 1648. The system of competing states, some of which are roughly of the same strength, controlled by no central authority, has given rise to prescriptions of national behavior that are strikingly similar: Nothing in *The Prince* would have surprised Han Fei Tzu, who wrote similar recommendations during the later years of the warring state system in China. Maintaining security in such a system has always been the responsibility of the individual state.[4]

The responsibility of lucidity and the responsibility for foreseeing consequences require that we identify the nature of the system in which nations operate. The realist ought to avoid the error of underestimating the resources the system allows--treaties, tacit agreements, usages; while the idealist ought to avoid the contrary error of overestimating those resources, and in particular of overestimating the authority exercised by international organizations and the compatibility of disparate human projects realized through state behaviors.

Nevertheless, there is for both the realist and the idealist an international system within which diplomats must pursue the interests of their states, and while the system does not determine by a necessary law the behavior of states, since these depend on the decisions of the individuals in charge of policy, the nature of the system nevertheless does affect the predictable consequences that might result from one action rather than another.

The basic task of the diplomat, as we have discussed in the last chapter, is to insure the greatest feasible degree of security for the constituents to whom, as a diplomat, he or she has made promises. How is security to be defined? What place in the world is attainable for a society by rational means, taking seriously moral strictures that take others importantly into account, even if they are not members of our own state? Can morality always or ever be observed in the basic quest for security?

First, and most basic, security is the preservation of the citizens of a nation residing in a territory recognized as sovereign and therefore "protected" by international law from the conquest and depredations of other states into that territory. This is the core interest of a nation. Beyond national borders, security takes in those crucial economic interests, lacking which the nation would have difficulty in surviving. For some nations, oil or coal are such critical resources, although by stringent conservation measures, the quantities of fuels necesary for these states' survival could be greatly reduced.

Alliances come into play in the preservation of these important overseas security concerns. For some nations alliances may be asymmetrical; they are more vital for one member than for its ally. American security does not depend on the American relationship with South Korea, but South Korean security was certainly favored by such a bilateral alliance. Our vital security would be injured in a very limited way if such an ally were destroyed, although our commitments having been exposed as unreliable in such a case might well affect our nation in other areas of more vital concern.

Beyond the core of security interests, and beyond the next rung of important but not absolutely vital interests, lies a more peripheral area, where the nation has interests that do not affect it centrally or even importantly. In areas such as these, to defend the nation's security interests with the same force and determination as in the central core of its security concerns would be irrational--it would probably overstretch the national capabilities as well. To extend alliances into the peripheral area is also dubious, for promises probably cannot and will not be honored there.

Areas of less vital interests are not simply distant from the center geographically, but they may be peripheral according to the kind of interest defined; we would hardly have committed a fleet of ships to the Persian Gulf in order to protect our (and our allies) supply of coffee. (In fact, as a measure designed simply to protect oil supplies, this decision was open to debate--the security interests threatened in the Gulf during the Iran-Iraq War were not well-defined.)

What were these interests when Iraq invaded Kuwait in 1990? The security of the United States was peripherally involved, as a matter of fact, but by extension of the argument based on like events in the past, such as the Italian aggression against Ethiopia in 1936, the prediction was that future events stemming from lack of involvement in the problem of Kuwait would finally involve American interests to a major degree, but, by that time, in conditions far less suitable for intervention. In the case of Kuwait, the analogy to the bystander intervening in a murder in progress makes sense; but for the United States to be the specific power to intervene depended on the addtional argument whether this particular murder contributed to an increasingly murderous world arena. The problem of the superpower is that under many circumstances it will be the only power that could make a difference.   Since the quality of life of a state's citizens is bound up with security, we ought to devote some consideration to this. The measures taken by OPEC since 1974 to increase the price of oil have had a profound effect on the quality of life throughout the world. These measures increased the quality of life beyond what it might have been within some of the oil-rich countries; it reduced the quality of life within many Third World nations, particularly among the resource-poor and those highly dependent on fertilizers; within advanced industrial nations, it stimulated inflation and brought inconveniences.

Fuel is a crucial resource in keeping some nations viable, so that a complete boycott of fuel might force a country to desperate measures. The threatened blockade of Israel in 1968, if it had been gradually increased in severity--Israeli ships were prevented from using the Suez Canal, and the Gulf of Acaba was being closed--would have seriously jeopardized that nation's existence. But in the context of the OPEC measures, the affected nations could shop for lower fuel prices from non-OPEC suppliers, could conserve by various measures (one was the 55 mph speed limit) since some nations are quite wasteful, or could proceed to develop alternative fuels, at high but not prohibitive costs. All these alternatives suggest that negotiations and patience, but not the use of force, were the appropriate palliatives to the situation brought about by OPEC. A crucial resource was affected by the higher prices, but, except for some poor Third World nations, none critically.

Security demands preservation of core interests, which include an abundant life that offers numerous possibilities for the ethical pursuits of a state's citizens. But just how abundant? The first ethical commitment an individual makes is existence or non-existence, choosing which by logical extension the person will be committed to maintaining complexity throughout the in-itself and the hierarchy of living creatures that have emerged from it. Simply, this is a commitment to consider the environment and its components important.

It is possible by unreasonable use of the globe and its resources, to reduce it to a desert, which would be ethically unjustifiable if to exist has been the original choice. Certainly the world's human population can proliferate beyond all reasonable bounds, and containing this is also the business of all humans, particularly those with an ethical view that takes the world into account. Societies can also insist on an unrestricted and profligate use of the world's resources, an unwarranted insistence in light of the moderate demands appropriate to a choice of existence. Diplomats have no ethical or moral right to press the state's resource security demands beyond a certain limit. A decent quality of life is that limit.

To exaggerate the security needs of the state is to (1) reduce the level of resources and environmental quality at the expense of other extant consciousnesses and to mortgage the future of humankind too deeply--

indeed, the nations of the world are running up an immense environmental deficit, much of which will be forever unretirable; and (2) to treat other consciousnesses throughough the world as if they did not count.

No human, no group of people, exist for the benefit of any other group. Hence, in the competition for scarce resources, the demands of the strong ought, for moral reasons, sometimes to be reduced. This is not moralism, which Morgenthau calls "the substitution of what is popularly believed to be moral principles for the rules of politics."[5]

Our prescription of morality is intended to supplement politics and keep the latter limited to genuine interests, defined as those interests conducive to mutual pursuits enhancing existence. Thus, we are not here speaking of extending charity, a topic we will speak to in the next section: We are speaking here of reducing certain demands in an environment of limited resources. This is not easy within the capitalist system, where consumerism is one of the engines that drive productivity. It may also be pointed out that in the United States, there are people as poor as any in the Third World, but the solution to this problem does not call for funneling more foreign resources into the state; rather, this is a problem of the distribution of existing internal resources.

It is not clear how to treat the problem of imperialism. The stronger and more technologically developed nations will always impinge on smaller, technologically backward nations by their very existence in the same international arena. Imperialism has had some regrettable effects in the world. But these must also be weighed against concomitant good effects. That nations are backward in the late 20th century is not mostly the result of imperialism, which may have had some deleterious effects on the potential development of oppressed polities, to be sure, but chiefly the consequence of indigenous problems in those countries.

Economic development and modernization is historically associated with Western Europe, where science and technology first arose as continuing contributors to culture, and that it did not arise in other areas of the world rests on historical reasons that are not the effect of imperialism. If imperialism had never developed in the world, perhaps an unlikely proposition given the unbalanced development that did occur once industrialization began, there would still be a world replete with economically poor and technologically backward societies. Admitting the existence of past colonial inhumanities, the case of neo-colonialism and dependency theory is still a partial and very dubious explanation of economic backwardness.

From the moral view, a nation is bound to reduce some of its demands on the world, particularly those that are not crucial to the maintenance of a decent quality of life. Earlier, the problem of absolute security was bruited. A state in search of an absolute level of security is a danger to the system of states, for it will not cease this search until all threats, real and potential, have been removed from the system. This must mean the subjugation of all surrounding states. Thus, at some level of the attainment of relative security, the search for additional security must relent. Ultimately, a nation may never be fully secure unless it has total hegemony over the world, in the course of achieving which it will produce many dangers to itself and other states.

No leadership has the right to conduct its state along this precarious and destructive path, for to strive for total security requires a vast and destructive effort. The paranoid can achieve a totally secure environment only by killing all those around him or her who constitute a threat, hence everyone, and this must be regarded as morally reprehensible. The need is for the diplomat, the nation, to lucidly assess the nature of the threats to the state in the international system, and to seek to deal with them in the least destructive manner for the long-run.

At times, this will require threats; at other times, wars of a limited nature; at still other times, negotiations may be possible. The choice of means is a very difficult determination to make, weighed together with the intensity of our security interests and those of our close allies. Moreover, threats to security rarely come as an all-at-once event. They are part of a series, a crescendo of events. It is the diplomat, the political leader, who must decide whether this minor threat to peripheral interests is or is not part of a long-term series of ascending levels of threat.

Is it or is it not the policy of a status quo power, or is it the act of a power bent on altering the entire world system? Thus, security is a matter of survival and the retention of a decent quality of life for the citizens of a state. It is not the ideal of a totally benign world, where a single ideology reigns or world government has somehow been established--these goals cannot be achieved realistically as the world is presently constituted.

Thus, it is the minimal national interest, which all states have a right to pursue, with the same reasonable limitations, in the world. It is moral to recognize these mutual national interests, and this constitutes the morality of the individual diplomat, of the political leader, acting within their appropriate roles. They are morally obligated to their citizens, for whom they have undertaken this mission, to seek and maintain state interests, but to also not define these interests in a boundless and unrealistic manner.

A citizenry ought to expect lucidity from its leaders, an ability to weigh realistically the events in the world, and the will to weigh and meet rationally the real threats to the nation. In addition, leaders and diplomats ought to accept moral obligations, implicitly, to other persons in the world who ought also to count, so that this pursuit of their nation's interests will not be an unbounded pursuit, and that they will not hold an unlimited definition of the good life for their own citizens.

To accomplish this, given the lack of a central authority in the world, given hostilities and ideological seekers of hegemony in the world, requires force, power, conflict, threats, and certain Machiavellian techniques, whenever these can be used to reduce conflict and attain limited security ends. What must be morally disavowed is the search for the aggrandizement of the state, that *virtu* or glory recommended by Machiavelli, to seek which leads to instability and unnecessary violence in the system.

It is the nature of states to expand, and to expand in an unlimited fashion if their leaders so determine. But in the end, what is meaningful in the world is the result of individual projects, and not the contentions among states (except as these affect the former). The state exists, therefore, not for itself and not for the furtherance of the march of Spirit through the universe, but to secure the maximum of possibilities for individuals to pursue their ethical projects.

This is the national interest defined for states in the modern world: security to a plausible degree and the establishment of a good life for citizens. The measures to be taken in the world in the name of the national interest so conceived are thus limited. We will not discuss here the nature of nuclear warfare (it is a vast topic beyond the scope of this book), except to say that as a means, nuclear war does not fit with the limited ends envisaged in our concept of national interest. The major argument in favor of nuclear might is the potential nuclear threat that it is supposed to balance and deter. As in all war or conflict, the criterion must be the lucid assessment of gains and losses in lives and destruction: Does this conflict prevent a larger catastrophe? But in the case of a full-scale nuclear exchange, it is difficult to imagine any worse eventuality-- what security is such a war supposed to preserve?

Briefly, it would be appropriate here to discuss the use of the atomic bomb on Japan during World War II. In what way could this use be morally vindicated, or is there no moral consideration whatsoever that might exonerate or condemn the destruction of Hiroshima and Nagasaki? There is little doubt that Nazi aggression was responsible for war on the European front, and that World War II in the Pacific was the result of Japanese expansion. Japanese occupation was ruthless and brutal. As the war in the Pacific neared an end, as Germany entered the final months of defeat, American troops retook Iwo Jima and Okinawa. The first island cost the Americans about 20,000 casualties, including over 4,000 dead; Okinawa cost the Americans 11,260 dead.

In consideration of the fact that the battle to end the war seemed to require the invasion of Japan itself, which the military rulers of Japan seemed bent on defending with the kind of tenacity shown at Okinawa, for the islands had never suffered a successful foreign invasion, and with the knowledge that the order had been given to kill all prisoners held by the Japanese if any foreign invasion of the islands began, the consequences to be weighed included the Allied forces who would die in the final months of such a battle and the Japanese who would die in tenacious defense of their homeland, the decision to use the atomic bomb could be defended morally. Thus, giving all persons their equal due in contemplating the end of World War II, and with the knowledge that the people of Hiroshima were certainly not the central individuals responsible for causing the war, it was still morally defensible after weighing all possible consequences to decide to use the atomic bomb.

It is impossible, of course, to prove that the early capitulation of Japan was caused by the destruction of Hiroshima, but it is more likely that it was this than that it was the result of the Soviet entry into the war in the Pacific that brought about surrender. The Allies in both major theaters of war fought a brutal struggle, but the ultimate result was morally superior to German and Japanese hegemony in the world. There is no need for the Allied powers to beg forgiveness from moral purists for fighting and prevailing in World War II. The decision to drop another atomic bomb on Nagasaki is a more questionable deed, and it is possible that these arguments will not vindicate it. Moreover, it would have been morally reprehensible to inflict bloody reprisals on either the German or Japanese survivors following their defeat, but this was not done.

Security is a limited and fully exonerable goal for a society in the world. Conflict is warranted to protect it, but only so much conflict as is consonant with the magnitude of threat is morally acceptable. Moreoever, the moral use of force, in which other persons are taken importantly into account, requires that the force be meted out, so far as possible, against the threateners only.

In modern war, this is not wholly possible. For example, Tehran might have been threatened with obliteration in retaliation for the death of a hostage held in Lebanon, for Iran probably had leverage with the hostage-takers. But to carry out such a threat would surpass moral boundaries and would not take Iranians importantly into account in weighing the consequence of such a measure. In brief, the nature of conflict is enhanced at the international level, where due process generally does not prevail, but moral considerations are still necessary and possible.

Notes

1. Morgenthau, *Dilemmas of Politics*, p. 73.
2. Henry Kissinger, in *Symposium on President Carter's Stance, Morality and Foreign Policy* (Georgetown University, Washington, D.C.: Ethics and Public Policy Center, 1977), p. 60. This particular statement was reprinted from *The Washington Post*, September 25, 1977.
3. Many of the points that follow are among Mervyn Frost's list of norms in international politics. See his *Towards a Normative Theory of International Relations*, pp. 121-127.
4. The propositions on state activity that apply to the state system we have described are summarized clearly in Morton Kaplan's work as the "balance of power system."
5. Morgenthau, *Dilemmas of Politics*, p. 246.

Chapter 16

Pursuing the National Interest

Part II. Interests Beyond Security

"If the state was a superindividual personality, it must represent all of its components and the whole range of human values."[1] I have argued that the state is not this. However, as leaders guide it, the state can follow many projects beyond security, and these are the subject of this section. First, we must consider what it means to pursue goals in a domestic context, where we pursue goals in a civil environment. If we choose to be moral and regard fellow beings as important, we are greatly aided in this by a structure of institutions, customs, and a semblance of community that prevent our own projects from going too far out of bounds in affecting others.

These are fellow citizens, among whom exists some degree of trust. These are people among whom there is a social contract. Each citizen is committed to, and if not can be forced to observe, a due process that protects these others from competing projects, including those projects developed for doing good to those who may resist it. Efforts at proselytization within the social contract are contained within the bounds of law and decorum. In the international world, there are only contervailing powers that appear to need to be taken into account--the moral community is tenuous or nearly nonexistant; and no authority can protect the rights of others. The international community, therefore, is a potential playground for megalomaniacs.

Typical of the disastrous projects, beyond the needs of any national well-being, bent on amelioration of the world's condition, to be sure, but pressed beyond all rationality, were the conquests of Napoleon. Napoleon has all the characteristics of the Prince bent on glory and national aggrandizement, the type praised by Machiavelli in the Italian context, but the fruits of Napoleon's wars are quite vivid: death and destruction and ultimate futility. Napoleon's career is that of the pursuit of projects that ought not to be pursued in the international arena, projects beyond national security. Napoleon is the most appropriate example of the immorality of pursuing higher ends in world affairs, in fact, partly in that his character was not villainous, like that of Hitler. He appeared to be a rational and constructive being.

An opposing view of projects appropriate to international affairs was voiced by John Quincy Adams: The United States "goes not abroad, in search of monsters to destroy. She is the well wisher to the freedom of all. She is the champion and vindicator only of her Own."[2] Kissinger makes somewhat the same point that ". . . we should never forget that the key to successful foreign policy is a sense of proportion."[3]

While we deal abroad to maintain a limited concept of our national security, we can observe the minimal demands of morality, even in the case of hostilities between nations, where our regard for others advises us to keep the conflict as limited as is necessary to secure our fundamental national interest. Limited not only refers to the resources allocated to the conflict, but refers as well to the length of time the conflict is conducted, which means that there are situations when overwhelming resources might usefully reduce bloodshed. Morality does not require, in cases of conflict, supine submission to the will of foes at the expense of national security.

Indeed, our project in the world is not to be moral (nor immoral, either): The sole rational state project is to gain security and a decent level of life for the state's citizens, while keeping morality in view. A project of morality as such would, as Machiavelli was well aware, be the doom of a polity in a world of competing powers. On the other hand, in Hume's writings one can find the proposition that no nation can attain a goal of greatness--Rome is the object lesson here--if its rulers are limited to the moral behavior expected of private individuals.[4]

True indeed, and for which reason greatness ought not to be an object of a state's international endeavors. According to Sterling, Meinecke's contention was that when *raison d'etat* transcended the stage of mere power deliberations and took on "some kind of spiritual and moral values

...." it would reach its highest potential--but one of those moral values was "an understanding of its own fallibility and limitations...."[5] The understanding of these limitations prevent Meinecke's view from being disastrous.

What ethical projects beyond security ought the state, meaning the leaders thereof, to pursue? Let us first dispose of any project of state glory, by which is usually meant aggrandizement by territorial conquest. Ethical purposes in the world are the projects of transcending the present by a for-itself. The for-itself is the individual consciousness. It is here that projects originate. The state never bends its will to anything. It is a totality, a dead project of past individual consciousnesses or the totalization of present innumerable for-itselves, pursuing transcendence, exercising freedom. As such, the state is a tool, an institution through which individuals, including individuals in concert, can realize certain of their projects.

Now there is one sense of national glory that represents the totality of past projects of individuals who, like as not, took little or no account of the state as instrument. To the state they may owe a cultural heritage, an education, a particular level of economic well-being, but mainly the chance to be left alone to develop their abilities. The state has contributed, but it has not contributed as a tool or extension of these projects.

So, we can speak of the glory of Florence as the wealth of art, literature, histories, that it contributed during its existence as a state entity. This totality, now fallen back into the in-itself where we can view it in museums, can be called a great human achievement. The state of Florence was glorious for the high level of culture and admirable works it bequeathed us. But this was a glory dependent on the projects of individuals, most of whom did not seek Florentine glory through state expansion; yet, Florence attained a national glory greater than many more expansive powers. The proper aim of Florence was the security essential to pursue those remarkable pursuits that built her culture.

The Fascist ideology has it all muddled, placing the location of glory in service to the state, when much of the accouterments of glory, when applied to states of the past, must be attributed to individual achievements undedicated to the state, the very achievements that fascism would restrain. Mussolini sponsored artistic competitions in which artists would submit paintings on set themes, such as "Listening to a Speech by Il Duce." And Mussolini wondered why so few competent artists would compete. The state provides an environment within which the individual consciousness can achieve or not, but it cannot provide the constructive means of projecting personal goals beyond the confines of a single society.

The other aspect of state glory is the aggrandizement of the state itself, the glory of empire building. Here the state itself is the focus, not an individual work of sculpture. This is the glory that springs to mind when we speak of the glory that was Rome. To pursue glory of this nature, the state must relegate the inhabitants to a lesser status, so that only individuals whose project involves increasing the power of the state are honorable: Private projects that do not so contribute are denigrated.

This is the ideal of Fascism: The focus is the state to which individuals are subordinated; consciousnesses with their private projects of transcendence, the for-itselves, are despised, while the in-itself is extolled. The projects of aggrandizement pursued by a few state leaders flourish, while all else stultifies. The state as a unity (although it never quite is this), the ideal Fascist state, is the fused group. This destructive subordination of persons to the non-conscious state (or movement) is an evil project that reduces persons to things. It is the Fascist project, but in another form it may be found in the subordination of art and literature to any political ideology, as in Communism.[6] The Shining Path guerrilla movement of Peru is an example of left-wing Fascism of this sort.

The project of state aggrandizement also produces conflict in the world, where there was none before, making morality moot. It is a project of this nature that makes morality and politics incompatible. It is a misunderstanding to reduce all politics to such a goal and thereby suggest the irrelevance of morality in politics: It is goals such as that of national glory that make politics and morality incompatible, and not political goals in general.

One form of this aggrandizement is the active extension of civilization or enlightenment to others by states or by state leaders. To regard one's nation as the Third Rome or the Middle Kingdom or the source of manifest civilizing destiny is to produce instability in the world and to treat others as subordinate beings, as objects. Culture will spread outward from a powerful source in any case, even if we do not regard the spread of our culture as a destiny for all mankind. Both good and bad features of industrial cultures will penetrate other borders.

The evil here lies in active proselytization, too-activist missionary work that subverts other cultures and judges others self-righteously. Civilizing missions are not given to nations by the heavens--they are self-imposed. It is not easy under any conditions to attain a situation of social contract, and there are numerous states in the past that have not accomplished this. The ancient Khmer culture was probably a Hindu culture of the elite superimposed over a peasant culture that it did not nurture. When the elite disappeared or was overthrown, the more advanced culture was obliterated with them. Nevertheless, groups, tribes, and non-modern states have attained to a degree of cohesion that has sustained a social contract and allowed the formation of a well-knit society.

To work vigorously to introduce new concepts, new ties, new beliefs into such a system, which is the self-imposed task of some world religions, is to destroy the affected society, to tear apart its social bonds, to demoralize it. This is not the duty of any moral individual who takes others into due regard. Insofar as France, then, was following a project of its civilizing mission in the world, a rationalization for its imperialism in Vietnam and elsewhere (but containing, as well, some degree of sincerity), it was a project that violated morality as we define it. In addition, lucidity requires that we recognize the very real economic purposes that often made the "civilizing mission" strictly subordinate.

The pursuit of glory for the state is therefore to be eschewed by all rational people intent on a more peaceful globe and projects of individual transcendence. The consequences of the choice of the state as the vehicle through which to realize our projects of power have littered the human pathway through history with death and destruction. It is projects such as these, associated with the wrong expression of nationalism, that force some to the conclusion that the continued existence of nation-states is archaic in the world, but this follows only if states are the instruments in the pursuit of misguided ends.

But, granted that state aggrandizement is the wrong goal, and a selfish one as well, may the state not become an instrument for helping others in the world? May not the United States contribute to the spread of human rights in the world, and might this not be a worthy project to pursue? This was a major goal of the United States during the Carter administration, and the goal in itself was in some ways commendable. We have recommended this goal, in fact, as a domestic pursuit which intends the extension of equality and justice throughout the society.

But the arena of world affairs does not have the attributes of a single society. The arena of world affairs is not embraced by any social contract. Unfortunately, there was no serious effort in the Carter administration to think through the inevitable conflicts that might arise between human rights as a national project and those equally valid projects, mainly dealing with national security, with which it might come into conflict.[7] The result at times was egregious hypocrisy: silence in the face of dire deprivation of human rights in some countries, futility in the case of hostile states that we could not influence, a meddling officiousness in states dependent on us, and a few commendable effects.

Let us repeat that the business of the nation in international affairs is to preserve itself and its way of life in the face of threats and actual hostilities against it. This may be done with morally acceptable means, which are always applicable in some sense, for other persons, including non-nationals, can always be taken equally into account, even when threats become dire. Suppose we project a new ethical aim onto this necessary but limited aspect of state projects. Now we must balance two goals: security and the expansion of rights for non-national others.

But security ought never to be sacrificed, since, for one good reason, to lose control of our own polity is to lose our ability to act in the world and to forego any other projects as well. There are too many compromises that will have to be made, if one thinks about it: we need to refuel our planes in the Azores in order to resupply an Israel, to whom we have undertaken obligations, under attack by the United Arab Republic. But Portugal, which controlled the Azores, was under a Fascistic regime.

Suppose we had no relationship with that country because we disapproved of its internal politics. When our NATO allies had refused landing privileges (they were afraid of an Arab oil boycott, which, indeed, was brought into play, affecting especially the Netherlands), what choice remained? The security interests would have been sacrificed to the interest of spreading human rights, but in the long term, we would probably not have succeeded in helping the Portuguese much and might have sacrificed our ability to defend rights and our own security interests elsewhere.

In the meantime, our rights program greatly complicated arms control negotiations with the Soviet Union, while we hesitated to criticize the People's Republic of China concerning its innumerable rights violations. Since arms control was a more immediate concern of national security, ought we to have muffled our criticism of the Soviets in favor of possibly facilitating an arms agreement? Ought we to have criticized China for its blatant lack of consideration for its own people as consciousnesses?

The answers are not obvious, but the sum effect of the policy in light of the many compromises that came to be made in favor of national security interests reduced the cause to hypocrisy. In short, the United States has not much power to effect human rights as we perceive them in the world among nations where they do not yet exist. Our attitudes on human rights certainly ought to be made quite public; we should not shun statements regarding our stand on them any more than the Soviet Union or Cuba avoided statements concerning their dedication to Communism.

Where choices arise that we can indeed influence without sacrificing our own security; we may lend our support to human rights; we can attend this trial of a dissident in the Soviet Union or South Korea under Chung Hee Park, seek the release of this poet; we can refrain from bending the knee to China's leaders after their massacre at Tiananmen Square, and so forth. But the chief project of the United States in the world must be always its own national security.

If a nation does not have the power to effect change in another nation, and it frequently will not, a policy of human rights that goes beyond our ability to effect, makes the policy at most a strident and hypocritical pose. It is one thing to witness the truth and to so testify; but it is quite another and far less admirable pose to speak belligerently in a situation that we know we will not try to change. It is the bravado and cheap courage of the brawler in the barroom, who hopes his friends will manage to hold him back.

Kissinger commenting on Carter's doctrine, mentions Walter Lippman's injunction that "as in all other relations, a policy has been formed only when commitments and power have been brought into balance."[8] Kissinger further notes the danger that a highly idealistic policy of human rights is subject to failures in its application in the world, and failure engenders disillusionment and isolationism in the American public.[9] As an indication of the futility of human rights as a major project for the state, Hoffmann notes that if a state desires to deny the rights of their inhabitants, the profitable way to do that and to avoid any sanctions at the same time is to adopt a totalitarian regime.[10]

North Korea has thereby escaped the censure directed at the South--where expectations for change are nil and criticism seems futile; so we end up criticizing allies and sparing enemies. There is another aspect to the policy, however, which Donnelly argues: At times human rights policy can contribute positively to national security. If the Sandinista regime was detrimental to U.S. security interests in Central America -- and it would be to the extent that it became a haven for Cuban and Soviet interests--part of the blame may be placed on the preceding Somoza regime's "feudal style of rule, with its attendant human rights violations."

Our relations with that regime might well have been severed before the radical Sandinista revolt occurred.[11]

If there is a reservation with this argument, it is that it seems to assume that there is always some positive measure the United States can take to insure human rights in a target nation, and this is just not true. The United States could have censured the Marcos regime of the Philippines, but the Philippine's dictatorship was not imposed by the United States. Fallacious doctrines of imperialism would have it that if we have relations with any nation, that we are therefore responsible for the government of that nation. Our control over events in other states is usually far more puny than that.

But should the topic of human rights be therefore downplayed? When Solzhenitzyn was exiled from the Soviet Union, it might have been expected that he would receive an invitation to the White House; he was a well-known writer, perhaps a great one, and a person who had confronted with stubborn courage the Soviet regime in its oppressive era from Stalin to Brezhnev. But no invitation was forthcoming, probably for the reason that it would have irked the Soviets. Although Solzhenitsyn's Gulag volumes are mentioned in Kissinger's *White House Years*, the reason for the snub was not provided. This was a pussilanimous decision.

In fact, while we ought not to project individual ethical goals too prominently into foreign affairs, where security is the chief issue, the country ought to be perceived as having a position on human rights, on justice, on equality. This is the core of our domestic and unrealized ideals, which we ought to speak openly about, just as the Soviets used to speak openly of the virtues of Communism. This should be expected of us, so that under all circumstances our position and meaning are clear. To do this is one aspect of that stance we have called witnessing.

We treated with the Soviets even though they presented their doctrine pretty plainly in speeches and pronouncements, and it should be expected that we will do the same, without hesitation, without embarrassment, without fearing that Russia or China or Ethiopia will refuse to negotiate with us. If negotiations produce results of lasting benefit to both parties, which is why negotiations are conducted, they will proceed apace. We will have made our stand clear, but it will not have to become a crusade to change the internal politics of the majority of nations in the world, which we have not the power to do. Or perhaps, supposing that we did have the power to do this, it would be too bloody a pursuit in any case.

To proclaim human rights as our chief aim in the world suggests a project of actually utilizing our power to accomplish that aim. Inevitable failure will make us look ridiculous. Worse, in at least one case, Iran, the dictatorship of the Shah, in which SAVAK suppressed rights, including the use of torture, was replaced by a reginme under the Ayatollah Khomeini, a fanatic religious fundamentalist, that far surpassed the Shah's in vicious brutalities. Under the then-prevailing conditions in Iran, and given the Shah's physical weakness from cancer, we might not have prevented this reactionary revolution in any case, but the relevant point is that in international affairs efforts to bring about a better situation are always moot and difficult to predict.

While the human rights policy played a limited role in this denouement in Iran, it did enter enough into the equation so that the consequences were, in some part, our responsibility. It may often be the better choice to leave bad enough alone. Haas asks, "Should we sanction a country for its human rights violations, when the alternative may well be a movement that will triumph in that country and institute another regime that violates human rights as much or more?"[12] Where national power and knowledge is lacking, and neither the foreign service nor the CIA were in command of the facts about the Ayatollah and the opposition to the Shah, policies easily lead to unforeseen consequences.

Thus, a sound foreign policy is, in the main, the pursuit of limited national security. Human rights is an area where, from time to time, we can nudge allies and let our enemies know our position: Sometimes, we may place heavy pressure on an ally that is somewhat dependent on us for economic or military backing, in which case we may actually succeed in our aims--but this is a testy problem.

In 1968, verbal accusations were directed against the Soviet Union for its brutal suppression of the Prague Spring under Alexander Dubcek in Czechoslovakia; these rapidly died down. In 1989, the Czechs were still suppressed by the reactionary regime installed under the Brezhnev doctrine. But then, almost spontaneously, the struts of an oppressive Leninist system collapsed, and the Prague Spring was again in view, and miracle of miracles, Alexander Dubchek was again holding a high government position. In such a case, protestations led to little, but the existence of democratic nations outside the Czech nation under Leninism had a persistent effect.

Our major duty on this occasion was to keep our own house in some order, to pursue equality and rights in our own society, to maintain a balance of military power in Europe, and to let events within Czechoslovakia take their course. China after the suppression of the democracy movement in 1989 told its western critics to mind their own business. Had it been our chief policy to assert human rights in China and other countries, the futility of that policy would have been glaring, for there was little of tangible value we could offer the Chinese, in particular, not intervention.

Moral intentions must be weighed by their consequences: Will a human rights policy bring about a better world or will it work to reduce our security and fail to protect human rights in the long run? Do we have the power to put such a policy into effect so that we can actually change the world without destroying it in the process, or is it a policy of futile posturing?

Posturing could be a tempting policy, of course, because it costs little. But it is marked by immorality in this sense: it uses the plight of others cynically to enhance our own esteem. It does not take other persons in their situation importantly into account. In the case of China, witnessing was the best and the only feasible policy (in light of the consequences). In addition, it would have been appropriate for the United States to have been a little less obsequious in our subsequent relations with China.

Should it be the policy of the United States to contribute to charitable projects in the world? On the individual level, we have recommended that ethical projects be pursued: An ethical project is a purpose that fills the world with values--the pursuit of science, of wealth, of fame, are typical ethical projects. In the society in which we pursue our projects, we will make an effort to observe a morality, if we have choosen to be moral persons, and morality is that subordinate project of taking others into account.

Politically, this translates into social equality and justice for our fellows. But social systems are normally unjust, and the distribution of opportunities unfair. If I observe the project of morality, while I am pursuing my ethical goals, I will pay heed to the shortcomings of my society. For some, this becomes a major project.

There are those who make the moral project their chief aim, whose object in life is to succor others. While it is good that there are such people, morality does not require that we pay such a considerable heed to the fate of others, except as our projects may affect them. But if we claim to observe the dictates of morality, even as a subsidiary project it must include contributing to the possibilities of others' freedom. Is there a comparable requirement internationally, if our chief foreign interest must be security, while at the some time observing a fundamental morality?

There are certain decisions, not necessarily directly connected to charity, that ought to be taken as a matter of course by individuals who have selected the project of existence. It follows from this project that other projects pursued ought not to be wasteful of the world's resources. An adequate consideration of life commits us to projects of conservation and the careful exploitation of resources. We owe this much to others in the world and in future worlds, that in a situation of scarcity we ought not use resources profligately. The past history of the United States, of course, is glaringly reprehensible in this respect.

Moreover, capitalism emphasizing consumerism and profit over all other values has no built-in safeguards for preventing waste and destruction of the environment. Citizens must bring these considerations into the economic system from outside the capitalist ideology. By itself, capitalism, as even Marx knew, has some commendable qualities; but there is no rational reason why only a single doctrine or ideology must prevail in a society--better that there are a number of ideologies limiting one another. That is, in a capitalist state, there must be countervailing ideologies to keep capitalism within bounds. Capitalism does not contain a full moral philosophy. It is a partial viewpoint about economics and productivity.

None of these strictures touch on foreign aid, as such; they are what we owe others regardless of any additional consideration. The state has, certainly, no moral obligations, beyond those already mentioned, except to conduct its pursuit of limited and sufficient security while taking others into account. Beyond this, its normal obligations, if any, are best met by individuals, or individuals formed into nongovernmental organizations. Some aid in our pursuit of security might be directed to allies and states with which we want to cultivate better relations. This is not aid to meet any moral requirement; it is aid for the purpose of furthering the national security interest. Other forms of aid might be recommendable from an individual basis; that is, persons located in the State Department or Congress might propose, based on their individual ethical principles, projects of charity that are not deleterious to the national interest.

This aid, provided over and beyond any moral requirements on the United States as a nation are an individual matter; if no great opposition is presented to parting with surplus agricultural products, for instance, and provided democratic processes are observed in such decisions, there is no reason it might not be sent to relieve disasters and endemic starvation in the nations of the Sahel. Thus, American aid to Ethiopia in the 1980s was not conducive one way or another to American security interests, and the plight of Ethiopians was the result of a genuine drought, civil war, and the dogmatic collectivization program of the dictatorial Dergue government, but some lives were probably saved.[13] There is no good reason why such efforts should be discouraged.

The state should also facilitate private or semi-private projects; the Los Banos project in rice genetics is a remarkable contribution to the world's grain output, and it was the project of innumerable agricultural scientists and the Ford Foundation. It is appropriate for the state to not just to allow but to stimulate these projects. It is also appropriate that at a time when the United States was fighting a war in Vietnam, that both China and North Vietnam were provided with these new rice strains.

The Group of 77 in the United Nations have made demands on the developed world to provide aid, up to one percent yearly of GNP (later scaled down to some 0.7 percent) to the less developed nations. The developed countries have no moral obligation to do this, except to the degree that aid is a form of tax that deducts from an ample quality of life and is provided to genuinely increase the quality of life in other countries. The argument that they ought to provide the aid to further national security is a tenuous case. The argument that it has been imperialism that has impoverished the Third World is a moot one; in fact, the strong evidence is against it.

There is no doubt that the project of belonging to the nation also assigns us that nation's past, including its imperialism. In the negative aspects of imperialism, people have been treated as objects. It is morally obligatory on citizens to see that this use of others as objects ceases. The cause of poverty, however, is not primarily imperialism: it is an indigenous structural and historical problem coupled with vast increases in population, an unintended consequence of the improvement of medical technology and facilities. Consider that in spite of the war in Vietnam, that country's population, including North and South, was 30 million in 1954 (as reported in Bernard Fall's *The Two Vietnams*) and 60 million as reported in CIA sources by 1984.

Indeed, without imperialism, little thought would be given to economic development in many of these countries, for economic progress is a modern concept. The industrial revolution was an historical process that occurred first in Europe. It has been extended throughout the world since then, sometimes in the course of violent conquests. But poverty abroad has most of its roots within the less developed nations, many of which have scarcely entered the process of nation-building.

While the ideological explanations of neo-colonialism and dependency theory have some merit, for the structure of the world economy is improvable in certain ways to the advantage of the less developed world, it is doubtful that the developed world is greatly responsible, despite the imperialist past, for the lack of development elsewhere. What gives economic development its present imperative urgency is the vast increase in populations in this century. To aid these countries is mostly a supererogatory act that is not a duty of developed states.[14] Just so, it is not anyone's obligation to spend, say, an hour daily to visit the ill in hospitals (unless they have chosen it as their profession or moral obligation).

When former presidents of Mexico must reside outside that country to enjoy the wealth they have stolen during their incumbency, or, as with the Marcoses in the Philippines, flee, it is unlikely that outside aid will have much impact on the maldistribution of wealth in these less developed polities. Elites will continue to siphon off profits to banks in Switzerland, while the poor will be beguiled by destructive and spurious ideologies. Projects to improve these conditions are best left to individuals, although the state can establish, without much cost, agencies such as the Peace Corps, which facilitate the individual projects of would-be idealists, or A.I.D. which disseminates aid that is closely connected with certain U.S. national interests.

A capitalistic Lebanese shopkeeper may introduce more genuine development, if left alone, in an African polity than grandiose state projects. The latter often prove to be a hoax, while the shopkeeper may spread some real wealth among the indigenous poor. Americans too easily assume that a bit of aid and good will can solve problems and win friends among the less developed countries, but there are some problems that are impervious to these efforts in the short term: Indigenous reform is necessary to build the moral community of a nation, and then some openness to economic imperialism, if you will, to lure industry and investment into the country.

This radical proposal was discovered at long last even by the experts of the International Department of the Central Committee of the CPSU in the 1980s. It is undoubted that without the basic necessities of health, food, clothing, and shelter, human rights become moot. An authoritarian regime that is actually developing its economy and in which maldistribution of goods is not too awry, is at least supportable. The regime of Chung Hee Park of South Korea was an example, although there, the push for expanded human rights should have been begun much earlier.

It is contrary to the international legal doctrine of sovereignty to intervene in the domestic affairs of another state. It is a rule of the United Nations Charter that the international organization may not intervene in any member's domestic affairs (with the *de facto* exception of the Republic of South Africa, in which intervention had the *imprimatur* of the Third World). How should we treat intervention? Let us suppose that we have an official request from Government X to intervene in force to provide military aid, perhaps as a counterbalance to a guerrilla force there.

First, in the case of close alliances, when called upon, intervention to meet obligations would be a matter of national security for us, always assuming that our alliance had been lucidly formed. Second, in the case of non-allied powers, we ought to make an assessment regarding the interests at stake: The intervention in Vietnam was not illegal under international law, although arguments were made that it was. The Geneva agreement on former French Indochina was essentially an agreement to disagree; the document was not signed by any of the subscribing powers, and the United States and South Vietnam did not adhere to it in any case.

Hans Morgenthau's presentation before the Senate Foreign Relations Committee made the point that to have intervened in force was not in the national interest of the United States; furthermore, we were overextended in Southeast Asia, which did not contain any of our major interests, and this dissipated funds that ought to have enhanced our power where it was needed, namely, in Europe. This was, at least, a compelling argument.

What indeed were the security gains to be made in Vietnam, where the center of the conduct of the conflict was in Hanoi, not in Moscow or Beijing? Aid to South Vietnam was at least a debatable option in terms of an expanded containment policy, but the United States ended by taking over the war, which was strategically limited and for this reason fought in an unwinnable manner. South Vietnam, moreover, never developed national loyalties. The Catholic and authoritarian Diem regime remained out-of-touch with its own largely Buddhist population, and succeeding leaderships never were able to consolidate the country.

Defined as a holding action against constant attrition and progressive demoralization among the South Vietnamese and the Americans, the war was bound to be lost against a determined opponent willing to sacrifice large numbers of soldiers and resources to the conflict and able to stay in the field of conflict over a long period of time. The limited national interest of the United States, which was to defend the policy of containment, of dubious application to the situation in Asia, warranted, perhaps, if it were sound at all, limited military aid and advisers.

In this case, the war would have been lost by the early 1960s, but the cost in lives and resources, of both the United States and North and South Vietnam, would have been lower. The war took on the aspect of battling to save the South Vietnamese from a fate that most of them did not perceive, or were unwilling to avert, in too many cases, by personal sacrifices. This was not our business. This, on the whole, was the tenor of arguments against continued intervention made during the period of the 1960s by George Ball, according to his memoirs.

Intervention must be defended mainly on the grounds of the security interests at stake for the United States. To intervene in a situation where a Marxist/Leninist guerrilla campaign is being waged is not our business automatically. If the population of a threatened polity is willing to undertake the necessary defense, which means sacrifices at least measuring up to the motivated guerrilla forces, if an elite is willing to institute necessary defensive reforms, something very rare, for it may entail redistributing wealth, then limited aid may be warranted. In no case ought another power enter actively into a conflict simply in order to save an unheeding population from a cause that lucid analysis indicates is spurious.

If the population is either taken in by false propaganda, or genuinely optimistic about the revolutionary project, or simply neutral, that is the kind of domestic situation which, barring overwhelming security interests, outside powers ought to shun. Regimes like Khomeini's religious fundamentalist and fanatical regime had and retained genuine popular support.

Even considering the economic debacle of the Sandinista government by mid-1989, there was still widespread support for that regime--we cannot conjure up an effective opposition (we did try, in the face of disunity in our own polity, with the Contra forces, some of whom were genuine opponents of the Sandinistas, some possibly interested in reasserting a Somozista form of government from which they might profit), so we ought not to try setting matters aright. In any case, by 1990, the Sandinistas, thanks to a generally open election, were ousted. Whether the Contra efforts played any role in this could be debated, but they probably did.

Where the United States has chosen to intervene in areas of dubious security interests, we run into additional moral problems. In Vietnam, in order to disengage ourselves from what may have been an ill-considered intervention, from a policy that had lost domestic support (beginning around 1968, in particular after the Communist Tet offensive), a policy that had in cost outpaced any potential benefits to the United States, we negotiated a precarious and spurious peace. The concept of "peace with honor" was always a dubious one.

Then, when South Vietnam came again under major attack, the United States, at the urging of Congress, refused additional aid. Thus, former allies were undermined and sacrificed to the inconsistent policy of a larger power. Like the Kurdish case in the 1970s, apparent allies were cut adrift--implicated in the projects of others unawares and left to perish on their own.

This is a positive evil in international relations. Nations should avoid engaging in such dubious projects in the first place, where interests for themselves are slight and domestic support feeble, or in the case of the Kurds, almost irrelevant. In this way, foreign individuals will not be drawn into a cul-de-sac, stranded, and abandoned. Trivial interests of a superpower may be vital interests to those playing the subgame. We do owe others, as a nation, a policy based on our predictable self-interest, one that has generated domestic support. Ragazzo[15] makes the point this way: "Rather, the point is that the moral principles must be of sufficient magnitude to justify the enormity of the sacrifice."

The most difficult problem enters into those situations where an informed and lucid leadership senses threats that are not perceived among the population in a democracy. This was the problem faced by Roosevelt, who tried on several occasions to raise the national consciousness about the threat of Fascism and Nazism. Here, real interests were crucially at stake, but the tenor of democratic opinion was pacifistic, neutralist, and ill-informed. Here the position of trust of the diplomat requires that some might have to sacrifice their careers to the anger of a misguided populace. It is in these situations that some diplomats and leaders determine that they ought to secretly perform what they are required under the Constitution to do openly, temporarily betraying their trust to democracy in the balance with their trust to maintaining the security of the country. And sometimes they are wrong in their own perceptions. Here is where great political risks are involved, and where important moral principles come into conflict.

The principle in individual morality is that it is a positive evil to try to do good to persons who do not want to be done good to in that way. While this principle is an obvious one in domestic politics, it may be less obvious where the affairs of citizens of other states are at stake; no aid to a country simply because we have analyzed their condition and find that the imposition of this revolutionary government would be a disaster to them. The citizens of that nation must make this assessment themselves. The major consideration here must still be national security for ourselves and very close allies. If sizable groups within a threatened nation would do battle against a fused group intent on taking power, even limited national interests may suggest that aid might be extended to them. We might further to some small degree our own security under appropriate conditions such as these even in acting in the peripheral area of our interests. Additionally, the cause of human rights might be enhanced.

There are situations, however, where nothing within reasonable expenditures of resources can be done: This was the case in China in the 1940s, when the government of Chiang Kai-shek toppled from its own corruption and the incompetence and self-centeredness of its elite, and with the help, certainly, of an astute guerrilla strategy of warfare. It was obvious to all but the most misguided that the guerrillas were not, as frequently publicized, "mere agrarian reformers." Granted that the years of Mao's totalitarian rule were a cultural, economic, and social disaster to the Chinese people, there was no call for supererogatory intervention by an outside power, for the potential cost was too massive, the likelihood of success very slight. In this cost must be included the cost to the Chinese people and to the guerrillas themselves. And this was a case in which, given the context of the balance of power of the times, American interests were at least peripherally at stake.

We did, of course, fail to recognize the historical antipathies that were bound to arise between two such chauvinist powers as the former USSR and the People's Republic of China--How could diplomats schooled in history and social relations believe in the possibility of a firm and lasting alliance between the two? But it is not the business of another state to save any government or group from their own stubborn errors and misdeeds. This is what Kissinger meant when he claimed that one of his objectives was "to purge our foreign policy of all sentimentality."[16] Morality, by the way, defined as we have done in this essay, cannot be counted sentimental.

There is another case in which the difficulty of moral judgment is very great, and that is the case presented by the Khmer Rouge government in Cambodia. Here the government, avowedly Marxist/Leninist in a weird and perverted form, undertook the slaughter of its own population and the total extirpation of all Cambodia's previous traditions. Here the intention of persons bent on treating others as manipulable objects produced a hell on earth. In such a case, the United Nations was useless--the government of the People's Republic of China and the United States would probably have prevented through a veto in the Security Council a United Nations' intervention, even if such a project could have been mounted in the General Assembly, a most unlikely event. A situation of this nature did not affect the internal security of the United States, so from the viewpoint of valid national interests, there was nothing at stake.

This kind of a situation calls for witnessing on the part of individuals, for the effect on the Cambodian people as persons to whom we ought to afford moral regard was heinous. It was the case that many persons and groups in the United States and Europe, including religious groups, who had formerly, actively or tacitly, supported the Khmer Rouge, became silent. It was not a stunned silence; it was a voluntary silence that violated all moral principle. The case of Cambodia was so extreme that supererogatory steps seemed to be warranted: The American gain in supporting the Chinese pro-Khmer position was so slight as to pale into insignificance in the face of the consequences.

We ought to have moved vigorously to motivate the United Nations toward collective intervention; failing that we ought to have remained passive when Vietnam intervened and toppled the genocidal Khmer Rouge. The United States had by 1990 a responsibility for the consequences of helping to produce the pressures that have caused the Vietnamese withdrawal. Our supplying of alternative guerrilla and anti-government forces in Cambodia could have dire consequences in the future, for which we will bear responsibility, for the Khmer Rouge are the only forces well-organized and strong enough to profit by our military aid.

These consequences are easy enough to see and have nothing to do with vital American national interests, which makes our policy even more reprehensible. The Khmer Republic is an exceptional case that required exceptional consideration to moral doctrine, that is, if the Cambodian people were to be taken importantly into account. American policy, however, has been far less than supererogatory: It has been short-sighted, unempathetic to the Cambodian people who have been treated only as means related to our weak-kneed treatment of China (which was supplying the Khmer Rouge), and vindictive to no purpose.

This leaves a final consideration to discuss, namely, what duties do we owe to allies? In an alliance, one state has extended certain guarantees to others, to act in predictable ways under certain specific situations.

Assuming a lucid foreign policy, we have extended such promises to other nations for the purpose of protecting our own national interests--if it is in the benefit of our own security, it would be foolish to fail to observe these free commitments. The other nation has entered into such a pact, likewise, to protect their own crucial interests. This is the nature of the NATO pact.

So long as our interests continue to be served by such an alliance, it is in our interest to observe the commitment. There is no moral problem here, although it also follows that when our interests change, it is incumbent on us to revise or end our treaty commitments: the requisite notice to be given of such a change is usually spelled out in the treaty. To opt out of our treaty with the Republic of China was in no way unethical, whatever the arguments concerning the desirability of doing this; it was based on a reassessment of our national interest. The need here is to maintain the level of treaty commitments that are consonant with our security interests, so that when we are called upon to honor a treaty, self-interest will compel us to keep our promises. Self-interest is the only guarantee among states.

But let us make a small reservation here. While self-interest is the major guarantee among states, it is also true that we share a greater community of interest with states that observe human rights and some form of justice than we do with states that do not do so. History has no inevitable culmination or engine of progress built into it. However, at some point in the human experience, there will most likely come about a greater sense of community among peoples of different states than exists at present. All people concern us in the moral sense of taking them into consideration in our decisions. The people of a totalitarian state are living in a most unfortunate condition with respect to their concrete freedom and the possibilities available to them.

At least one Air Force general (General Curtis Lemay) suggested that we might win the conflict in Vietnam by the use of air power, or "bombing them back into the Stone Age," and, in fact, we might have obliterated Hanoi, Haiphong, and so on. To have done so would have been immoral, an action the destructiveness of which, in terms of human life, would have exceeded any rational gain. To destroy the inhabitants of a totalitarian and hostile state is not to save them.

But we are closest to those states, even disregarding our own national interests, that provide some progress toward justice for their own people. We owe these states somewhat more consideration, for the lucid reason that if a moral community gradually makes an appearance in global affairs, it will occur first among like-minded democracies and social democracies. If this view is plausible, it suggests a consideration that somewhat transcends the minimal moral principles and even the principles of strict national interest that have been propounded here. It suggests that there may well be tentative considerations to be taken into account beyond mere security.

To conclude briefly, there are moral considerations in foreign policy, in spite of the fact that a realistic policy is one in which security is the prime value. Morality and politics are not mutually exclusive. The doctrine that they are is most often associated with those ethical doctrines of *virtu* that espouse projects in international relations that no nation ought to undertake, either for its self interest or in the interests of morality. Limited national ends are almost always consonant with morality.

Morality, as defined in this work, is unspectacular and limited. It is one aspect only of the broader field of ethics. But, while ethical goals are generally not to be pursued in the international arena, where they likely will do more ill than good, the inhabitants of other polities, even hostile ones, may be taken into account as persons. This is the stricture of morality, and, in most cases, it does not clash with the limited pursuit of a nation's national interest. Morality and international relations are not mutually exclusive.

Notes

1. Stirling, *Ethics in a World of Power*, p. 135.
2. Quoted in Rubin, *Secrets*, p. 5.
3. Kissinger, *Symposium on President Carter's Stance*, p. 65.
4. Morgan, *Madison's Analysis of the Sources of Political Authority*, p. 619, is the source of this citation.
5. *Ethics in a World of Power*, p. 254.
6. See Mao Tse Tung, *Talks at the Yenan Forum on Art and Literature*.
7. Tucker, *Purpose of American Power*, p. 22.
8. *Symposium on Carter's Stance*, p. 62.
9. *Ibid.*, p. 64.
10. Stanley Hoffmann, *Duties Beyond Borders* (New York: Syracuse University Press, 1981), pp. 134-135.
11. Jack Donnelly, "Human Rights and Foreign Policy," *World Politics*, Vol. XXXIV, No. 4 (July 1982), p. 589.

12. Earnst B. Haas, *Global Evangelism Rides Again: How to Protect Human Rights Without Really Trying* (Berkeley, University of California, Institute of International Studies, Policy Papers in International Affairs, 1978), p. 38.
13. On Ethiopia, see Colburn, "The People's Democratic Republic of Ethiopia: Masking and Unmasking Tragedy."
14. See Lefever, *Ethics and United States Foreign Policy*, p. 130.
15. Robert A. Ragazzo, "Grover Cleveland and Venezuela: The Perils of Moralism," in R. Gordon Hoxie, ed., *The Presidency and National Security Policy* (New York: Center for the Presidency, 1984), p. 113, makes the same point in another foreign policy context.
16. *White House Years* (Boston: Little, Brown, and Company, 1979), p. 191.

Chapter 17

Commentary on Iraq

From 1990 to 1991, there was a war in the Middle East that concerns the moral issues under discussion in this book. In this chapter, an effort will be made to bring these war issues under the rubric of a moral outlook. It is possible that some questions may be easily answered; some questions may be raised but not answered, and the answers to some issues may be very tentative. By now, there should be no doubt that international problems partake of a moral dimension and that political considerations are not to be severed from their moral implications. Morality is pertinent to international politics.

In the ensuing discussion, the morality of the decisions of the United States will be examined. There is also an alternative view, namely, the morality of the situation as viewed from the actions of Iraq. While interesting, this vantage point will not be taken, for the reason that the morality or immorality of one's opponents is to some degree irrelevant in the selection of a nation's own options. That one's opponent may be thoroughly immoral does not prevent one's own actions from being immoral. The appropriate national behavior in the world is not to confront immorality wherever possible but to pursue national security when that is affected, in as moral a way as possible. The wrong way around would be to join conflict out of disinterested moral reasons, to pursue morality, that is, as the prime end.

There is no doubt of the nature of the Iraqi regime under Saddam Hussein. It was a tyranny, a typical Third-World quasi-totalitarian government, although non-communist. Its leader was ruthless, brutal, homicidal, megalomaniac, and highly effective in controlling the government. In the recent past, he has pursued the vision of Iraq as the dominant country in the Middle East, to which end he constructed a powerful military machine, produced chemical weaponry, and was on the way to becoming a nuclear power.[1] Most likely, Iraq would have been a nuclear power by 1991 if not for the fact that Israel, against all conventions of international law, had bombed the Osirak nuclear plant in 1981, which Iraq was building in conjunction with French collaboration. Although a hero to certain dispossessed groups in the Middle East, Saddam Hussein is responsible for killing more Moslems than any other leader in the area--Kurds, Iranians and Iraqi Shiites.

When the revolution in Iran upset the Shah and brought the Ayatollah Khomeini and his medieval version of Islam to power, Saddam Hussein saw an opportunity amid the political chaos of Iran to seize portions of Iranian territory that had in the 1970s been settled by treaty between the governments of Iraq and Iran. Expecting easy gains, Iraqi forces attacked Iran and were initially successful in occupying portions of that country claimed by Iraq. The ensuing Iran-Iraq war that lasted a decade was one of the significant wars since World War II, resulting in large numbers of casualties, particularly on the side of Iran, which, lacking the military equipment of Iraq, resorted to human wave attacks.

Iran at the time was close to the Soviet Union, its chief weapons source, but Iran, after the revolution, had few friendly ties with any other nation. In particular, the United States had no diplomatic relations at the time with Iraq and none with Iran, since the trauma of the crisis that resulted from Iran's seizure of our embassy and personnel in 1979. In principle, Iran was the aggrieved party, patently a victim of aggression, but neither ties of mutual interest nor any American interest compelled our intervention in this conflict. As it turned out, we helped both sides from time to time, but not, generally, with weapons.

The major consideration for American interests in the Middle East was to prevent either side from a clear military triumph. But as Iran, the more populous nation of the two, showed more staying power, the mid-1980s brought about great pressure on Iraq and its desire to bring about a cease-fire. It was clear that its original optimism had been ill-considered and the chances of actually losing the war were becoming apparent. The United States leaned toward Iraq during this time, even renewing diplomatic relations in 1984.

Intervention was unnecessary because both nations seemed capable of holding the conflict to a stalemate, so the question never really arose of intervening to rescue the nation suffering aggression, which, of course, was Iran. A triumphant Iran capable of extending its revolutionary fervor into a new revolutionary government of Iraq was a genuine fear: The repercussions of such an event in the Middle East, the unrest that might be brought about by such a denouement, the dangers to a number of other regimes, such as Jordan, Israel, or Saudi Arabia, caused the United States to conduct its policy, such as it was, with a bias favoring Iraq. Considering the consequences that seemed to threaten from possible conclusions of the Iraqi-Iranian conflict in the Middle East, the American policy was not immoral.

But although the war itself was finally resolved, the United States began a series of associations with Iraq that were part of a policy of appeasement. It is possible that advice to adopt such a policy was conveyed by Hosni Mubarak of Egypt and King Hussein of Jordan. The idea was that Iraq, contained but intact, was necessary as a buttress to Iranian revolutionary aspirations. This policy is somewhat more devious and difficult to defend, considering the nature of the Iraqi government.

Risky loan guarantees worth about half a billion dollars were extended in June, 1984. A Commodity Credit Corporation program that was ultimately worth some $5 billion to Iraq was also underway in the mid-1980s. In March, 1988, Saddam gassed some 2,000 Kurds in Halabja, Iraq, but this did not halt the loans, and the administration tried to avoid sanctions. At this point, the United States and other nations of the world were muted in their objections to Saddam's vile policy toward his own people. As witnesses of political evil, the nations of the world were woefully derelict.[2] Although then-President George Bush was becoming reluctant to extend further U.S. credits by May, 1990, he did not censure Iraq or significantly change the policy of appeasement. And there is no doubt that then-Ambassador April Glaspie ought to have provided a stronger statement to Saddam Hussein than that the United Stated would not take sides in the border dispute between Iraq and Kuwait. It was also true, although impolitic, to remind Iraq that the United States had no "defense-treaty relationship with any gulf country."[3]

At the time, there was most likely no inkling that Iraq had in mind more than pressure against Kuwait in a dispute in which, at least with relation to the slant-drilling into the Rumaila oil field, Kuwait was at fault. In hindsight, it is easy to point out that our statements ought to have been a great deal stronger, which is to say that foreign policy is often not very prescient. At the least, it can be said that this policy was a failure. It did not, as appeasement policies are intended to do, draw Iraq into the body of status quo nations. The consequences of not succeeding at the policy of appeasement were apparent in the Kuwait invasion.

While there was moral shortcoming in the lack of witnessing Saddam Hussein's domestic atrocities, the policy in itself was not immoral. Treating with dictators is not morally reprehensible in itself if the intention is to avoid, as in this case, greater mayhem in the future. In this case, the policy was a complete failure, however. Failure would render the policy immoral, of course, because of the consequences, provided the outcome were predictable. It can plausibly be argued, however, that the invasion of Kuwait was something of a surprise.

It was also a mistake to have provided Iraq with too few clues about the United States' stance in the Middle East, although there were some: The United States had conspicuously chosen to convoy Kuwaiti oil under American protective cover during the Iran-Iraq war, when termination of this supply line was threatened. Nonetheless, the United States ought to have used threats more pointedly in outlining the consequences of an Iraqi invasion of Kuwait; in a policy of containment, this is what threats are for.

But there was no moral turpitude in this policy. Relations with dictators, even those as vicious as Saddam, are often necessary, when, if successful, they cause a nation to be more pacifistic. Following the bloody rise to power of General Franco of Spain, there was reason to be satisfied when he kept Spain from entering World War II on the side of the Axis powers that had helped him to defeat the Republic. It was also worth a try to bring Mussolini over to the side of Britain prior to World War II, another policy that failed badly and may have been carried on too long.

There was vague talk, as there always is in historical events, of a conspiracy to draw Saddam Hussein into just such an attack on Kuwait. There is no evidence of this. On the basis of such an argument, it might be averred that Hitler had been drawn into World War II. Such arguments, lacking evidence, are baseless. Thus, the comment that "It is ironic that Bush chose that particular spot, neighborhood of the Tigris and Euphrates, to start his 'new world order'," suggests that somehow the Americans invented a situation to enhance their prestige.[4] Historically, such manipulation is fantasy. The rationale of appeasement policy is to prevent hostilities from occurring.

Mistaking the new context of international politics, in which the Cold

War was no longer the major feature, Iraq invaded Kuwait on August 2, 1990. Since there is often ambiguity about this, it is worth noting that this is the beginning of the war between Iraq and the states that ultimately drove it from Kuwait. It was this act that placed Iraq in a state of war with other nations of the world. Iraq laid claim to Kuwait for the reason that for a time, both areas, Iraq and Kuwait, had been administered by the Ottoman Empire. However, the claim was tenuous, and Kuwait had a sound argument for distinctiveness. Indeed, since the latter part of the 19th century, it had been quite separate from Iraq.

Perhaps the best way to determine whether one state ought to be incorporated into another is to poll the citizens of that state. This is the way to provide proof that the people in a territory are being treated as ends rather than means only. Under this stipulation, the people of the Falkland Islands certainly would never have voted to join Argentina, which morally obviates the country's claim to the islands.

The citizens of Kuwait certainly had no desire to live under Saddam Hussein. Kuwait had been a semi-autonomous unit in the Ottoman Empire since the early 18th century; that is, it had as much legitimacy under the Sabah family, who rose to ascendency there in 1756, as most nations of the world can claim. In 1899, Shaikh Mubarak, who founded the current ruling line, fearing incursions from several sources, Wahabi, Persian, or Ottoman, negotiated a treaty with the British, which provided independence from the Ottoman Empire; the British maintained control of Kuwait's foreign relations. The borders of Kuwait were secured in 1922--full independence was granted by the British in 1961.

Thus, Kuwait has a history of national existence that dates farther back than that of many other nations of the world. The government of Kuwait was not democratic, since the parliament that might have stimulated more democratic politics had been disbanded by order of the royal family some years before the invasion. The traditional government was not a brutal one, despite the shortcomings of its undemocratic practices.

In general, its distribution of wealth was more fair than that of other Third World states, at least among Kuwaiti citizens. The Kuwaiti citizens also hired innumerable foreigners to do the bulk of their work, to work as servants, for example, and these people had valid objections to their treatment in Kuwait. They did not enjoy the rights of citizens, and citizenship was unavailable for them, even for the Palestinians. Some Kuwaitis were wealthy, and fleeing from the country during the invasion, spent their exile in Egypt and elsewhere in relative opulence.

Still, considering the meager size of their own military compared to Iraq's, the Kuwaitis did not give a bad account of themselves in their hopeless defense, and some pitched battles were fought.[5] In addition to political inequality in Kuwait, there was the Islamic problem of the status of women, who certainly did not enjoy the formal equality that exists in Western nations. This will be a continuing moral problem for Islam, best resolved within the Islamic context, if that is possible.

In sum, the argument was often implied, if not actually stated, that since the Kuwaitis were imperfect people, they had forfeited any right to be liberated from Iraq. This is a stricture that fits all people in all countries, of course, and is in line with the argument that since political society is imperfect and the Kingdom of Ends is very distant, that morality cannot be of any concern--it can only apply when the world is perfected. We have seen this argument advanced at times by Jean-Paul Sartre, for which reason he did not produce his promised text on ethics during his lifetime.

In contrast to this is the idea that any morality that cannot apply to an imperfect world and an imperfect society is useless. A morality too good for the world is an ineffective morality. Critics of the policies that the United States adopted during the Kuwait crisis are on sound ground in criticizing the nature of Kuwaiti society, which did not and does not reflect egalitarianism, but they are irrelevant if they argue that for this reason Kuwait ought to have been left to its fate. To intervene in a political situation, it is not necessary to determine that victims are perfect beings.

Although Iraq made several preposterous claims that it had been called upon to intervene in a revolutionary situation in Kuwait, that claim was patently spurious and soon disappeared from serious argument. Thus, Iraq was quite clearly guilty of aggression against Kuwait--the invasion was a blatant conquest. There can be no question of this.

There was much comment that the United States led the effort against Iraq because oil was at stake. That is to say, the United States was concerned because its own and others' interests were at stake. Rational policy makers might assume that if genuine interests were involved that this ought to have been all the more reason for American involvement, but the tenor of many such arguments was that since vital interests were at stake, the acts of the United States were somehow for that reason rendered immoral.

Such arguments are often based on a version of morality as a pristine intention. A moral act cannot be one in which personal interests are involved: One must act with indifference. Kant develops this notion in his depiction of acts of various kinds. The version of life and activity that this supports, however, is not one accepted in this book. Life is a matter of developing projects, of seeking ends, and morality is one project among many--in an active life, it is unlikely that any act can be undertaken with indifference.

Related to the argument that the motives of the United States were immoral because interests were at stake is the point that intervening in the Kuwaiti situation morally obligated us to intervene in all other situations of aggressive behavior.[6] There are many of these, but all situations exist in a context. Thus, intervention in Cyprus was difficult because Turkey was responding to *enosis* and a situation that could easily have threatened the lives of Turkish inhabitants of Cyprus, who numbered some 20% of the population. It was not Turkey that had originally threatened the status quo situation there. Syria's incursions into Lebanon were at the request of the Arab League, and while the major motivation of Syria's behavior had been the establishment of a Greater Syria, some of its activity also served to dampen the internecine conflicts of that beleaguered country.

When India invaded Goa, it is possible that Goan citizens might not have voted to join India voluntarily, but intervention there would have violated the principle of a measured response; that is, the deaths caused would have far outweighed the moral principle involved. In any case, India was a democratic regime, and the extermination of the Goan population was not an issue.

The complex problem of the West Bank Palestinians was the result of the ill-advised attack on Israel from Jordan in the 1967 war, and the stubborn failure of the Arab states to negotiate with Israel thereafter. All of these situations are different from the Kuwaiti one. Thus, to intervene in one situation does not commit a nation to intervene in all situations, even in those that might be somewhat similar. Nor is it degrading to moral principles that when intervention is selected as a response that national interests also might play a role.

There are two points of significance that should be mentioned in connection with the argument that nations were interested in Kuwait only because of oil. First, the valid criticism that the United States is generally wasteful of resources and probably uses too much of the earth's goods, including oil. Faced with the prospect of diminishing supplies, the United States tends to emphasize searching for new sources of oil rather than emphasizing conservation in use, lower speed limits, and so forth, which would equal a very large reserve of oil.

But that the United States ought to be less wasteful of resources does not make oil any the less important to nations of the world. Second, the point is sometimes overlooked that the invasion of Kuwait made Iraq the possessor of some 40 percent of the world's proven oil reserves, a significant increase in the potential strength of Iraq.[7] It would have made Saddam Hussein a powerful figure in the world economy, not an auspicious situation considering the nature of the man, his regime, and his aims. It would also have altered the balance of power in the Middle East to a significant degree. It would have moved Iraq closer to Saddam Hussein's vision of predominance.

While it is true, therefore, that one reason for intervening in the situation brought about by the invasion of Kuwait was oil, that does not make the reasons for intervention of less merit; rather, it enhances those reasons. Oil was not solely a resource for America,[8] but a source of power for Saddam Hussein. The presumption that a nation ought to be motiveless in the world stems from the moral stance that people ought to have no self-interested projects: that moral questions ought to be decided in a world without goals. As George Weigel puts it, "[A reformed theology of peace] would link concepts of national interest to concepts of national purpose and national responsibility."[9]

By August 6, 1990, Resolution 661 was adopted by the United Nations Security Council, placing an embargo on Iraq. The United Nations served as an agency to put pressure on Saddam Hussein. It is also true, that if the United States had not furnished the impetus for the anti-Iraq policy, nothing ultimately would have occurred to have forced Iraq from Kuwait. Thus, it is probably true that the United States made use of the United Nations for its own purposes, which were also, more or less, the purposes of other nations without the resources or fortitude to have carried such a policy into effect.

Indeed, Britain's resources were stretched thin in combatting Argentina, a truly fourth-rate military power, in the Falklands. There is also some indication that the Executive branch of the United States used the United Nations so effectively in order to by-pass the Congressional branch, which was divided on the use of force.[10] But there is nothing reprehensible with using an agency such as the United Nations to further national interests. Certainly, the invasion of Kuwait was blatant enough that the world of nations was alsmost unanimous in condemnation. Only Yemen and Cuba in the Security Council were reluctant to condemn Iraq. The effort to make the situation one of the "haves" against "have-nots"[11] did not ring true.

While the problem of poverty is a significant problem in the world of nations, it does not apply, except indirectly, in this situation. Iraq, after all, is potentially a well-off country with significant resources, not, by any means, one of the deprived nations of the world. It is due to the mismanagement and waste of its resources in unnecessary conflicts initiated by Iraq that Iraq found itself in economic difficulties. That certain groups found themselves sympathetic to the argument that Iraq was a "have-not" nation may have applied to their own situations, but certainly not to that of Iraq.

The world's poor have been frequently misled by movements in their name but which ultimately benefitted them little. Saddam was clever enough to tap nationalist dissatisfactions and xenophobia, and he aroused a strong response among Palestinians in Jordan and on the West Bank. Egyptian workers, however, many of whom had experience in Iraq were not very responsive. They were familiar with the brutality of the regime.[12] The argument that Iraq's regime was somehow representative of the "have-nots" was quite spurious.

A much more pertinent argument concerned the efficacy of sanctions. Would it not have been better to have allowed economic sanctions to have brought Iraq to withdraw from Kuwait? What need was there for the use of force? There are mixed results from the study of the effects of sanctions. One study done in the early 1970s of over thirty economic sanctions leveled against transgressors of international order, indicated that in only a single case was there any possible change of behavior. Sanctions have, often enough, not worked.

However, in the case of sanctions against Iraq, Fox is correct in pointing out that these were more thorough than most such efforts.[13] The predictability of sanctions is always moot, although in general, it may be stated, that they will not alter the behavior of the target nation. After the war, Iraq showed itself in an even more difficult economic situation to be relatively impervious to sanctions. The result of boycotts after the war indicated that so long as he was able to supply the Republic Guards and maintain military strength, Saddam Hussein was indifferent to his civilian population.

Sanctions would have brought increasing suffering on the civilian population of Iraq, while the military would have most likely continued to be supplied. Goods were still smuggled over the borders--there was no way to have prevented this. Moreover, there was the fear that placing sanctions over a period of lengthening months would gradually have dissipated unity that existed early in the confrontation. In addition, considering the size of the population of Kuwait, Saddam was quite capable of killing or moving Kuwaitis out of the country and repopulating it with Iraqis, a possibility that was open to him under the conditions of sanction.

Sanctions were not costless, either. So long as oil was not allowed to be shipped from either Kuwait or Iraq, the nations of the world would be economically affected, and Third-World nations, "have-nots," most of all. The cost of the war to the United States and its allies was about $60 to $70 billion. But the cost of sanctions could have run this high or higher: 200,000 troops, the number of troops intended for defensive purposes, sitting in the Saudi desert would have been expensive to maintain with the proper supplies. At some point, either sanctions would have been regarded as having failed, too many nations would have fallen away from the consensus, or the cost would have become insupportable after a length of time, or the Iraqis would have been even more difficult to move from their positions in Kuwait.

Indeed, as mentioned before, they might have posed the *fait accompli* that Kuwait no longer existed as a separate entity; there may have been no more Kuwaitis. Should the sanctions have been tried longer? Perhaps, but there was no indication while they were applied that Iraq was showing any sign of relenting. Sanctions are still what they have been in the past, a measure to assure that something is being done in a situation even if they are ineffective--they are of most use as a statement in conditions in which intervention by force is impossible or undesirable.

If sanctions had shown any sign of working to force Saddam's forces from Kuwait, it would have been most moral, perhaps, to have relied on sanctions alone. There would have been problems, however. The withdrawal of Iraqi troops intact with no diminution of military prowess within Iraq, would have meant the necessity of maintaining some military means of future containment in the Middle East, a problem that may still exist, nonetheless, following the partial military victory.

The purported willingness of Iraq to talk about Kuwait provided that other problems in the Middle East were placed on the table for resolution was patently spurious. Iraq did not invade Kuwait to force Israel from the West Bank. The two problems are quite separate. The solution of the one does not depend on the solution of the other. Syrian troops in Lebanon were also a separate issue. Negotiations may be made to go on forever provided these are coupled with additional recalcitrant issues. The United States was quite right to seek to focus solely on the Kuwait situation. To have done otherwise would have been so stupid as to make such negotiations morally suspect. In short, consequences count.

While there is no way to prove that sanctions might not have ultimately worked to force Saddam Hussein from Kuwait, there is every indication that they would not have, certainly not within an acceptable time period. Moreover, as George Weigel points out, sanctions, too, would have done great injury first of all to the ordinary population, affecting the military-political elite of Iraq only after a very lengthy period.[14] At some point, force was the most likely successful resort. War, of course, was the event that occurred August 2, 1990. Iraq had begun the war with its conquest of Kuwait.[15] The decision to oust Iraq from its conquest was within the doctrine of a just war. Since World War II and the Korean War, there has probably not been so clearcut a case of a just war.

Those who argue otherwise can do so only on the principle that no war is just, that is, the principle of complete pacifism. But then the fate of the Kuwaitis and the future disposition of events in the Middle East would have been the consequence brought about by remaining passive in the Kuwaiti case. To decide to oust Iraqi forces from Kuwait by force, however, demanded that all people involved be taken importantly into account, Iraqi civilians, American and allied troops, and Kuwaitis and non-Kuwaitis within Kuwait. In addition, a more extensive group of people would have to be taken into account in predicting the ultimate outcome of a failure to confront Saddam Hussein in Kuwait. The idea that all persons affected by the war must be regarded equally as consciousnesses corollates with the just war doctrine of proportionality.

The Iraqi troops were typical of an unpopular totalitarian regime. Many of them were quite ignorant of the reasons why they were in Kuwait. There were also troops quite loyal to the regime, namely, the Republic Guards, and there were troops that had been mobilized for the purpose of building a large military force. Ill-trained and ill-led, these were often Shiite troops with little positive feeling toward the government. Indeed, some troops were simply left in the lurch by their commanders, who evinced no responsibility whatsoever for the men in their command, and Saddam gave every indication of a leader for whom his troops counted for nothing. The level of leadership in the Iraqi military was often despicably low, beginning, of course, with Saddam himself. Yet, the forces were formidable, and it was difficult to predict the casualties that would result from the effort to oust them from Kuwait.

It is interesting that many who warned that American troops would take casualties from 30,000 to 40,000, later, as the war progressed successfully for the United States and allied forces, would argue that the Iraqis were not, after all, an army. Of course, it is never easy to estimate the number of casualties in a conflict. The purpose of the campaign was to oust the Iraqis from Kuwait, and to accomplish this purpose, first of all, with as few losses of American and allied lives as possible. That must always be a consideration for commanders. In this, the anti-Iraqi forces were almost unprecedentedly successful.

In the case of a just cause such as the ouster of Iraqi troops from Kuwait most certainly was, it is incumbent on the planners to use force in such a way as to diminish casualties. A war of attrition, such as the conflict in Vietnam, was geared to slaughtering, in the long run, in a form of limited war more troops than a full-scale war might have killed. This is the situation with limited wars carried on over a lengthy period; they ultimately may kill more people than would a full-scale conflict. In this, the allies avoided the wishful thinking of William R. Callahan, who desired a long war in the Gulf, ". . . long enough for casualties to be shared and mount for all the nations involved."[16]

Preliminary to a ground conflict, which seemed to be inevitable, considering the recalcitrance of Saddam Hussein, there was an air war to eliminate certain military targets within Iraq. Unfortunately, given the militaristic nature of the Iraqi regime, the national infrastructure was built to support military purposes. In addition, water systems and electricity complexes were targeted. Most of the targets could be defended as militarily pertinent, but there is no doubt that civilian hardships, from contaminated water supplies, for example, led to deaths, perhaps as many as 70,000 after the conflict.

It is impossible to establish how many of these deaths were the result of negligence on part of the Saddam regime, which did not particularly care whether certain civilian groups were inflicted with hardship. Some 2,500 to 3,000 of the civilian deaths were the result of the bombing—while this makes it obvious that civilians were not targeted, there were still ways in which civilians may have been spared. Kenneth Roth suggests that some bombing was carried out during the daytime, when the number of civilians near military targets might have been at a maximum.[17]

Inevitably, there were those cases in which what was purported to be a military target was not, or it was also a civilian: Such was the case in the bombing of an underground bunker in the Amariyah neighborhood of Baghdad, which killed more than 400 people, mostly women and children sheltering there. These collateral casualties were probably too great. While civilian casualties cannot be avoided during war, the numbers of Iraqis who died during the fighting and following the conflict were excessive.

Moreover, and predictably, there were risings of Shiites in southern Iraq, Kurds in the north, which were put down by the surviving Saddam regime with great bloodshed. The Americans had done little or nothing to provide support for these risings; whatever stimulation we provided to them, however, counts morally against us, for there was never any intention of providing aid.

Even the off-handed comment by the President that it was up to the Iraqi people to depose Saddam Hussein was probably better unsaid. Certainly we bear some responsibility for these deaths, since they, too, were among the predictable consequences of the war. They may also have occurred, however, at some point during sanctions, that is, if sanctions were successful.

During the air war and prior to the ground attack, there was a feeler from Saddam conveyed to the White House by Mikhail Gorbachev, on the basis of talks between his envoy Yevgeny M. Primakov and the Iraqi leader. The potential deal was that for a ceasefire on the part of the allies, Saddam would "announce" an "unconditional withdrawal" from Kuwait.[18] Moral principle demands that lesser evils ought to be chosen before greater ones, taking into account all the lives, allied and Iraqi, that were involved. A withdrawal communique from the Revolutionary Command Council on February 15 contained Iraq's usual inflated oratory, accusing the allies and the United States of aggression, which could have been diplomatically ignored, but linking withdrawal with abrogation of all embargo decisions, the withdrawal of all other forces *preliminary* to any move by Iraq, and the withdrawal of Israel from all occupied territories (not a word here on Arab recognition of Israel in return), and conditions on the government of Kuwait.[19] Such a communique was at this late date completely unacceptable and suggests the probable ineffectiveness of sanctions, if these had been the only response to Saddam's aggression through February.

Ought this opportunity to have been seized? The problem with such an offer as that conveyed by the then USSR, is that Saddam Hussein might have announced at any time that he would pull out his troops within X days. To promise a future announcement--when?--in return for a ceasefire, which he obviously needed and might have made use of, not to withdraw but to retrench (making future moves by the allies far more difdicult), was not a plausible offer. Still, the matter is one for debate. The compelling conclusion seems to be that there were no real grounds for dealing with Saddam at this juncture.

In the course of the final days of the war, two gigantic 5,000 pound bombs were delivered to the Air Force with the purpose of demolishing underground defense bunkers. The bombs were directly intended to kill Saddam. Unfortunately, although fulfilling their destructive purpose, they did not accomplish their specific task.[20] The American intelligence agencies are prohibited from seeking to assassinate other world leaders. The reasonf ro this is that assassination puts all leaders at risk. There is also the fear that to assassinate a single ruler would not necessarily affect the intentions or behavior of that nation.

However, there are cases in which a single leader is critical. Without Hitler, there may not have been a Second World War. Without an Idi Amin, the government of Uganda would not have been so bloody. It is not certain that without Saddam, there would not have been an invasion of Kuwait. But to assassinate a leader might be in some cases quite moral, alleviating the necessity for large-scale conflicts and innumerable deaths in some instances. The matter is also a legal one, and it is involved with the morality of following the laws of one's country. In certain historical instances, however, assassination may ahve saved humankind untold suffering.

The number of Iraqi troops killed in the battles may have been some 8,000, which does not seem excessive, in light of the civilian casualties.[21] Considering the nature of the regime and the composition of the armies, it was incumbent on the allies to allow as many surrenders as possible. And, in fact, some 65,000 were captured. The situation of the Iraqi soldiers was unenviable. Once their ground cover was destroyed, and the Iraqi Air Force was early driven from the battle, ultimately many planes finding a haven in Iran, from which they did not re-emerge to fight, the war for the troops was essentially decided. Saddam had gambled and lost.

A responsible leader with some empathy for his troops would have given way to the inevitable at that point: It was time to withdraw. When the order to withdraw was finally given, it was too late to prevent more carnage. The allies certainly did not want the prospect of allowing forces to withdraw and then reforming to inflict casualties on the allied troops. The highway of death from Kuwait City was not so much a scene of carnage, however, as it was one of destruction. After the first vehicles had been hit, most Iraqis seemed to have fled the column, as evidenced by the innumerable trails in the sands.[22]

Another group of people suffered as a result of the war. In their difficult position, the Palestinians within Kuwait were nearly all suspect after the Iraqis were driven out. Where some 400,000 Palestinians lived in Kuwait before the Iraqi invasion, there were only some 50,000 left by 1992. Just after the conflict, there was a violent settling of scores, without a doubt some of this unjustified. Many were expelled from Kuwait; others awaited expulsion. In short, the Palestinian population was probably treated with severity.[23]

The total assessment of the war with Iraq is that it was a moral endeavor, with some important reservations. The high number of civilian deaths before and after the conflict, were probably excessive and might have been reduced. There is a stigma of immorality in this. Moreover, the war was not carried to the conclusion in which Saddam was actually ousted from power. That he remained in power may have increased the numbers of civilian deaths after the ceasefire.

Should the war have been carried to its ultimate conclusion? Having driven the Iraqis from Kuwait, the mission of the United Nations under the resolutions passed by the Security Council was accomplished. In the Korean War, the United States attempted to do more, and was bogged down an additional several years with more destruction and casualties by the entry of China into the conflict. Certainly, a continuation of the conflict against Iraq, at the least, would have meant more deaths of troops and civilians. In particular, the taking of such cities as Basra and Baghdad would not have been easy and may have entailed house-to-house battles. The end of the conflict still allowed some supervision over Iraq's war machine.

During the conflict, there was a debate on how close Iraq was to obtaining a deliverable nuclear device. At one time, the CIA suggested that earlier estimates may have been wrong, and that it would take another decade for Iraq's nuclear weapon. Fox makes use of this argument.[24] However, following the war, inspection of Iraq's progress in nuclear weaponry showed that it was much closer to obtaining a nuclear weapon than had been thought; it was, indeed, a matter of some two years rather than a decade.

It is difficult to assess how much the United States was responsible for *foreseen* difficulties in Iraq after the war. Everything was complicated by the fact that Saddam Hussein contined to be dictator. Most of the Republic Guard divisions remained intact after the war, to be used to brutally put down the Kurds and Shi-ites. The intervention to save the

Kurds from total extermination within Iraq was morally necessary, although belated. The questions of a national homeland for the Kurds is another issue that goes beyond the problems involved in Kuwait. The problems of the Shi-ites is further complicated by the fact that the United States has little attachment or empathy for their cause--we have some slightly more positive feelings about the Kurds, although we have also betrayed them in the past. In these matters, immorality would be to stimulate revolt or to offer any hope of aid whatsoever, for there is little that the United States and other nations desire to do for these people.

Thus, Kuwait has been freed from the Iraqi invaders. The argument presented here is that this was, on the whole, a moral exercise--it was not a crusade, however; the intention was not to make the world a better place than it was before Iraq's invasion, but to make it a better place by undoing Iraq's conquest. But the denouement of the struggle has left the Middle East with innumerable difficulties and problems yet to be resolved. Kuwait reverted quickly to the authoritarian rule it had known in the past. Saddam concentrated on rebuilding his military force. The Palestinian problem of the West Bank is unresolved, although the unity that marked the opposition to Saddam gave the area some impetus toward a beginning of peace talks.

Notes

1. The nature of Saddam Hussein's regime was well-known and is documented in Samir al-Khalil, *Republic of Fear* (New York: Pantheon, 1989) and Judith Miller and Laurie Myloie, *Saddam Hussein and the Crisis in the Gulf* (New York: Times Books, 1990).
2. Simon Tisdall, "Desert Storm Two," *The Guardian Weekly*, May 31, 1992, p. 9.
3. As reported in the *Honolulu Advertiser*, September 24, 1990.
4. Thomas C. Fox, *Iraq: Military Victory, Moral Defeat* (Kansas City: Sheed and Ward, 1991), p. 161. Fox is quite guilty of such unhistorical innuendo: "But Saddam Hussein's threat conveniently erupted almost as if it were choreographed by Pentagon planners," p. 30. But of course, the threat was not so choreographed. Conspiracy theories must accept the preposterous notion that a nation or a group is responsible for events down to the most trivial detail. It is rare than any person or nation has ever had such historical control. The point taken to exaggeration would be that the United States is completely responsible for the events leading to World War II, the Korean War, and so forth. Morally, this robs all other historical actors of any responsibility whatsoever. It robs Saddam Hussein of his responsibility for the Kuwaiti invasion.

5. See, for example, Staff, U.S. News and World Report, *Tripmph Without Victory: The Unreported History of the Persian Gulf War* (New York: Random House, 1992), pp. 12-13.
6. Fox, *Iraq: Military Victory, Moral Defeat*, p. 27, makes this point.
7. Figures differ here. This one, which is also cited elsewhere, is from George Weigel, "Just War After the Gulf War," *American Purpose*, Vol. 6, No. 4 (April 1992), 31.
8. It is well to note, by the way, that the United States obtains only some one to two percent of its oil from this region of the Gulf. Other countries are far more reliant on the Gulf region's oil. See *U.S. Foreign Policy: The Reagan Imprint*, editors of Congressional Quarterly (Washington, D.C.: Congressional Quarterly Inc., 1986), p. 108.
9. James Turner Johnson and George Weigel, *Just War and the Gulf War* (Washington, D.C.: Ethics and Public Policy Center, 1991), p. 87.
10. *Triumph Without Victory*, p. 414. In addition, there was a significant Kuwaiti resistance during the occupation; see Jill Smolowe, "Where Shadows Are Dark," *Time*, Vol. 136, No. 10 (September 3, 1990), 42-43.
11. This point is raised several times by Fox, *Iraq: Military Victory, Moral Defeat*, p. 30, "...the most important overall concept in that editorial was a call to see unfolding events in the context of the growing gap between the rich and poor nations of the world...."
12. James Wilde, reported by, "He Gives Us a Ray of Hope," *Time*, Vol. 136, No. 9 (August 27, 1990), 26-27. And in connection with this phenomenon, see Bernard Lewis, "The Roots of Moslem Rage," *The Atlantic*, Vol. 266, No. 3 (September 1990), pp. 47-60.
13. *Ibid*, p. 44.
14. Johnson and Weigel, *Just War and the Gulf War*, p. 60.
15. Weigel makes the valid point that the war did not begin January 17, 1991, but at the time Iraq invaded Kuwait, *Ibid*, p. 68.
16. An article quoted in *Ibid*, p. 176. The idea conveyed was to diminish the propensity for war on both sides. Considering the nature of this conflict, however, the thought was an immoral one, taking persons into account as means only to a presumably salubrious lesson.
17. Kenneth Roth, "Iraq: Was our war civilized?" *Honolulu Advertiser*, February 5, 1992, p. A12. There were attacks against water-treatment facilities and electric systems that may not have been militarily vital. Considering the deaths following the conflict, these probably ought not to have been attacked.
18. *Triumph Without Victory*, p. 279.
19. The *Honolulu Advertiser*, February 16, 1991.
20. See *Triumph Without Victory*, p. 391.
21. Other estimates run to 25,000, which would indicate a figure that is larger than a measured response ought to have been. It is difficult to assess this, since the Iraqi leadership itself seemed indifferent to its losses.

22. *Ibid*, p. 409.
23. Jean Gueyras, "Kuwait finds new ways to harass its Palestinians," *The Guardian*, January 19, 1992, p. 14.
24. Fox, *Iraq: Military Victory, Moral Defeat*, p. 133.

Appendix

Notes on Free Will

One of the assumptions of this essay is that humans have freedom to choose. This freedom is an ontological freedom. There is also the problem of concrete freedom, namely, that whereas people may have ontological freedom, there are conditions of society or the in-itself that prevent certain choices from being viable. The concrete freedom of the illiterate peasant in the Sahel is so restrictive that ontological freedom at times may appear to be nonexistent.

Concrete freedom is the stuff of politics, of course, but in this brief appendix, ontological freedom will be the issue. The intention is no more than to provide the outline of an argument, since it is beyond the scope of this work to provide all the necessary philosophical foundations for its concepts. Nevertheless, there are political ramifications of ontological freedom, and these deserve to be mentioned.

Intentionality is the essential structure of all consciousness. The object of consciousness (at which intention aims) is outside consciousness (except in the case of reflective consciousness). It is transcendent. Intentionality is the necessity of consciousness to exist as consciousness of something other than itself--a "total fleeing of self."[1] Thus, consciousness is other than its object, but at the same time its whole being is an orientation to its object; it is never "by itself."[2] We do not just view an object; we constitute it, and we may constitute reality in different ways.[3] Intention is the project that underlies reflection. "An intentional action is a change I make in a situation that has been implicitly conceptualized in such a way as to make it call for that change by reason of some feature that it bears."[4]

The viewpoint based on intentionality suggests that "as world-constituting or meaning-giving, Sartrean consciousness is noetically free. Husserl's thesis is that consciousness brings it about that there is a horizon of meanings which we call the world. But consciousness is a world-constituting activity and could constitute the world in its horizon of meanings differently. This is noetic freedom.[5]

Consciousness is always more than its circumstances; it is transcendentally free. It transcends whatever conditions (facticities) may constitute its situation at any given time. A person can imagine because the mind is transcendentally free, that is, not causally determined in the sense that the mind is involved in a chain of material events. "If the universe consisted of a rigid chain of causes and effects and nothing more, there would be no room for minds. For it is of the essence of mind that it involves questionings, doubtings, thoughts of possibility."[6]

It is unlikely that given a universal determination, such possibilities could exist. It is a poignant freedom humans have. As Sartre expresses it, we are condemned to be free. Facticity affects choice, of course. A person may be crippled. Freedom consists in "choosing the manner in which I exist my infirmity . . . ."[7] Such a freedom is the basis of the existentialist ethics that informs the program of this work.[8]

It is possible that Sartre's formulation may be too extreme, that it might require some reservations. For Merleau-Ponty, freedom is limited to those acts which contain an element of personal choice--freedom is not synonymous with existence or subjectivity. Certain biological and practical interests may be actualized spontaneously, that is, without personal choice. So there is no need, in Merleau-Ponty's view, to create and sustain our choices at every moment.

We are free in that we are not bound to essential and determinate ways of experiencing the world, but we are not totally free to create our own world.[9] This is a plausible viewpoint that mitigates some of the absoluteness of Sartre's position. There is a problem in the Sartrean formulation of losing the necessary continuity of personality that is a requisite for moral action, in breaking consciousness into a myriad fragments of potential new beginnings. Merleau-Ponty avoids this problem.

Moreover, Merleau-Ponty's view provides a sounder basis than Sartre's for human freedom in the sense that it seems to correlate better with genetic and biological data. But Sartre's concept of freedom is not one of total indeterminancy either, for it is situational. For Sartre, freedom is not a "capricious, unlawful, gratuitous, and incomprehensible contingency." "To speak of an act without a cause would be to speak of an act which would lack the intentional structure of every act," according to Sartre. The end that we choose operates as a kind of final cause. Indeterminism would be irrelevant to moral decisions, of course--for the agent must be held responsible for acts,[10] a requirement that could hardly hold if events are essentially unpredictable or "causeless."

It is vital to recognize that Sartre understands the situated character of freedom, more so, indeed, in his later writings, and, in fact, partly in response to such critics as Merleau-Ponty. Every true choice is made in a particular empirical situation and with relation to a particular person. ". . . [T]his facticity means a certain restriction with respect to the leeway of the subject as project." Thus, the real world of freedom is distinct from the world of dreams.[11] The world, says Sartre,[12] gives counsel only if we question it, and this implies that we have some end in view. The cause, therefore, far from determining the action, appears only in and through the project of an action.

With Sartre, it may be assumed, then, that existence precedes essence. To say this is not to say that mankind has no essence, but rather to indicate that essence is continuously (at least frequently) surpassed. The for-itself is its essence in the mode of not being it.[13] Humans give themselves essence. They are defined by what they have done. Essence refers to our past, what we have done. And we are even free to "take on the heaviness of stone,"[14] to adopt the pretense, but the pretense only, of existing as in-itself-for-itself. The human is a sort of "hole" in being.[15] Thus, man's essence, his facticity, makes him resemble a thing, but as a self-realizing subject, as freedom, he gives meaning to this essence. Thus, there is not an inescapable "human nature," there is the historical result of the actions of the "for-itself."[16] This freedom is the freedom at the structure of our being. The slave who accepts his chains and the slave who rises with Spartacus both choose within this freedom. Merleau-Ponty might have it that it is only the nature of the choice, in this case the choice of revolt, that constitutes freedom. But this does not seem an appropriate interpretation.

If one is free to choose revolt, it follows that one must also be free not to choose revolt. Merleau-Ponty's point, later adopted by Sartre, to judge from some of his comments, leads to another sense of freedom, namely freedom-as-certain-values. In this new sense one can assess the value of the use to which freedom may be put, suggesting a distinction between these two slaves. It is the passage to freedom in this second sense that requires Sartre's "radical conversion."[17] This gloss on the original idea of freedom, however, is dubious.

There would be little point in presenting a study of the problems of morality in international affairs if humans were fully determined. Without the freedom of choice, moral understanding would be futile. It is necessary, therefore, however briefly, to consider some important objections to our brief presentation.

Determinism requires two theses: (1) There is a way of talking about the world such that every statement describing the world can be represented by it. Such a state-description in this language is a complete description of the world. One form of reductionism might hold that all the events worthy of consideration in the world might be describable by physics. But it is not likely that all events in the world can be so encapsulated. It is more likely that there are many levels of reality in the world, each requiring a different theoretical vocabulary.

(2) There is a theory formulated in this way of talking that is correlated with every variable in the world, so that from a state-description at an antecedent time we could in principle calculate the state description at a future time. Lucas provides Newton's laws of motion and of universal gravitation as such a way of talking.[18] But to revert to an earlier point, would it have been likely for any theory to have predicted in the primordial world a determined course of events leading to life, evolutionary change, and mankind? This is unlikely, and a deterministic view has got to vindicate itself through prediction, not through retroactive analysis.

The view that determinism and moral notions are incompatible obviously will differ from the view that one can hold to determinism and still accept moral responsibity. But it is also possible to accept certain varieties of determination in which free will may still be acceptable. After all, to chose meaningfully is to choose with an eye to consequences, and persons would be unable to assess potential consequences in a fully indeterminate world.[19]

As Ayer suggests, determinism intends to point up factual correlation. It is not the case, insofar as can be ascertained, that one event is "in the power" of another.[20] To say that a person has acted freely in a situation is *not* to say that an action was a chance action, for if this were so, morality and responsibility would be overruled. Determinism requires that an individual's actions should be capable of being explained. Sartre, for instance, provides an intriguing case study of coherent explanation of the origins of anti-Semitism in "The Childhood of a Leader."

From this Sartre could be regarded as a compatibilist,[21] that is, that he considers determinism possible in a world that also harbors free will. Philippa Foot suggests, indeed, that the idea that free will can be "reconciled with the strictest determinism is now very widely accepted."[22] As a matter of fact, it can rationally be argued that determinism is not a standpoint necessary for a science that can make predictions.[23] Predictability is a concept of epistemology, while causal necessity falls into the realm of ontology.

The pertinence of free will to the political descriptions of events is that if there are persons who are not simply "regularly-performing objects," then explanations for their actions must include not only causal antecedents but their reasons for acting as they did. If free will is a factor in history, no complete explanation of actions can avoid reference to the reasons given by the people involved for acting as they did. While the historian might provide these reasons, it might not be possible to say why these reasons were chosen as reasons by the participants, for equally cogent reasons probably existed for acting otherwise.[24]

It would be surmised that the most severe critic of this position would be B. F. Skinner, and this is the case. It would be too far from our central purpose to undertake a complete assessment of the validity of his objections to free will. While these objections are quite pertinent, they are nevertheless surprisingly weak.[25] According to Lucas,[26] there are three conditions to be fulfilled by a threat to a doctrine of freedom: any valid argument that defeats the doctrine of freedom must be infallible; it must be based on some limited range of factors outside an actor's control; it must be completely specific. Certainly, Skinner makes a great effort to fulfill this program of demolition. But, in the first place, there are points of agreement between Sartre himself and the Skinnerian view. Both would disagree with a simple indeterminist position.

But for Skinner, human freedom is a doctrine linked with the traditional dualist view that posits existing side-by-side with the body some immaterial subject, or, disparagingly stated, a "homunculus." Indeed, Sartre's for-itself seems to avoid this criticism, and there is some compatibility between his doctrine and Gilbert Ryle's as presented in *The Concept of Mind*. Both Skinner and Sartre accept that a person is a body with a complex repertoire of behavior. Of course, a person is also a pattern of relations developed by the body-subject over time. The contention lies in the explanation of this coherence. Skinner's view is that of man as only an animal with consciousness superadded.[27]

Skinner presents his outline of a behavioristic analysis as follows:[28] A person is first of all an organism, a member of a species and a subspecies, possessing a genetic endowment of anatomical and physiological characteristics, the product of a process of evolution. The organism becomes a person as it acquires a repertoire of behavior under the contingencies of reinforcement. Behavior at a given moment is under the control of a current setting. We may agree with much of this.

For Skinner, however, the human "begins and remains a biological system, and the behavioristic position is that it is nothing more than that."[29] Of course, the human is also a system of atoms, and it is possible to say that it is nothing more than that, but it is not necessarily useful or meaningful to do so. Such a program of reductionism cannot meet the requirement that it explain behavior at all levels of reality. Dobzhansky is the source of a comment, for instance, that what can be established biologically is not the content of an ethic, but simply "the capacity to ethicize."[30]

Now, Skinner's behaviorism must not be mistaken for stimulus-response psychology. He believes the problems inherent in that are solved by his theory of operant conditioning: accidental traits, arising as mutations, are selected out over time as they contribute to survival, as these are selected out by their reinforcing consequences.[31] What seems purposeful in human genetic endowment is not some antecedent design, but selection by contingencies of survival. Contingencies of reinforcement replace seeming human purposefulness. The causal efficacy of a felt purpose is replaced by reinforcement.[32]

Skinner contrasts this behavioral view with the traditional view, which would have the person perceiving the world around him, selecting features to be perceived, discriminating among them, changing them for the better (or for worse), and being thereby regarded as responsible for his action. The correct view in Skinner's opinion is that the person is a member of a species shaped by evolutionary contingencies of survival, displaying those behavioral processes that bring him under the control of the environment, mainly the social environment. "The direction of the controlling relation is reversed: a person does not act upon the world, the world acts upon him."[33]

This entire macro-situation may be far more subtly handled by Sartre in his *Critique of Dialectical Reason*, where people are indeed affected by the institutions of society, by the practico-inert, but in a dialectical fashion that takes interaction into account. Thus, according to the Skinnerian thesis, we do not change something called perception; we change the relative strengths of responses by differential reinforcement of alternative courses of action. We do not change something called a preference; we change the probability of an act by changing a condition of deprivation or aversive stimulation. We do not change a need; we reinforce behavior in particular ways. We do not give a person a purpose or an intention; we change behavior toward something, not a person's attitude toward it.[34]

In a brief analysis of the malaise of the Roman empire, Skinner claims that "pessimism and a loss of self-confidence, hope, and faith are . . . associated with a lack of strong positive reinforcement."[35] Well, perhaps, but what of the studies of increased belief and hope when prophecies *fail*? Of course, that too can be similarly explained, and herein lies a critical flaw in the program; like many similar positions, it is ultimately not subject to proof, which for a theory of determinism is the ultimate embarrassment.

It can be seen that Skinner's program ends up diametrically opposed to the position in this text.

> [Man's] abolition has long been overdue. Autonomous man is a device used to explain what we cannot explain in any other way. He has been constructed from our ignorance, and as our understanding increases, the very stuff of which he is composed vanishes. Science does not dehumanize man, it de-homunculizes him, and it must do so if it is to prevent the abolition of the human species.

Of course, Skinner has in mind the ability of mankind to harness the destructive powers of technology, but it is moot that his program rather than any other would have that effect. It is also fair to ask what difference would it make if mankind as object went the way of the dinosaurs. We would simply have been determined to disappear. Skinner's program, therefore, is the abolition of a presumably unmanipulable "man." In fact, it is not true that our standpoint rejects manipulability--we can accept that science, chemistry, physics, and the study of human behavior is possible and can provide information to *increase* (or decrease) concrete freedom.[36]

Opposed to the behavioralist program is the other camp. Hazel Barnes recommends that

> We ought to teach people that we are responsible and free, that authenticity and the ethical life are worth striving for. . . . We should help

them to understand their relation to their own emotions, to realize that they are not enslaved to their past and that they will themselves determine the quality of their own future.[37]

So the battle is joined.

Sartre's position that one is never condemned to the given, that one can detach oneself in the sense of imagining a nonexisting state of affairs posed as a future end seems more convincing than Skinner's account of human purposes solely in terms of past conditioning. In this regard, it is fair to require of Skinner that he formulate a uniform set of antecedent conditions which would produce a particular human end.[38] Moreover, if the environment selects our reactions for us, why does it not seem to do this uniformaly for different people, or for the same individual over time?

Skinner himself has suggested that prior to testing a given individual, there is no way to identify a reinforcing stimulus as such.[39] This is rather a glaring weakness in a deterministic program. How could he have predicted on the basis of past conditioning-reinforcement that Mr. Bremer would carry out an attempted assassination of George Wallace? Merleau-Ponty points out the long and difficult learning period needed in a conditioned reflex theory that would ill-explain our sometimes sudden and precocious adaptations.[40] And, as Wilkenson strongly asserts, "The meagerness of behavioral theory, its total inability to make feasible prognoses coupled with a nearly Assyrian contempt for the infinite variety of things in its jurisdiction that need explanation, make arguments in its defense as meaningless as those in condemnation of it. . . ."[41]

Every individual is an N of one, and science typically deals with repetition. Skinner, however, is not reluctant to deal with the essentially unique, and attempts his own analysis of a young man "whose world has suddenly changed." Plunged into a new environment, this youth feels insecure (analysis: "his behavior is weak and inappropriate"), there is nothing he wants to do (analysis: "he is rarely reinforced for doing anything"), and he feels guilty (analysis: "he has previously been punished for idleness").[42]

What enables psychological determinism to attain an aura of plausibility is that it works backward from the action. This is a rather empty accomplishment. What the determinist program has to do to be convincing is to explain with antecedent causes. Skinner's presentation in this case is far too simple.[43] It has characteristics of the bland about it. Finally, it explains nothing. Skinner concludes that a literature of freedom may inspire a sufficiently fanatical opposition to controlling practices to generate a neurotic if not a psychotic response. There are signs of emotional instability in those who have been deeply affected by this literature. [Probably there is some truth to Skinner's point: there has been emotional instability among early Christians, the developing bourgeoisie under feudalism, Marxists, and so forth. Might there not be signs of emotional instability, Skinner himself excepted, among some manipulative behaviorists?] We have no better indication of the plight of the traditional libertarians than the bitterness with which he discusses the possibility of a science and technology of behavior and their use in the intentional design of a culture.[44]

Contrary to this thesis, however, which doubtless, as noted, has some elements of empirical evidence in its support, are studies on locus of control, which suggest that "The internal seems to be a generally more competent individual, with a longer string of past successes. This, of course, creates greater self-confidence, which would also lead the internal to eschew outside support and influence in favor of a reliance on self."[45] That is, for all the evidence Skinner might amass to show the emotional instability of the advocates of human dignity, there is at least equal evidence to the contrary. Some of this evidence, for instance, may be drawn from the accounts of survivors of the extreme conditions of Nazi concentration camps. Skinner has, in short, nor proven his case.

Whereas Skinner proposes the deleterious effects of the belief in freedom, Sydney Hook raises the issue of viewing mankind from the standpoint of hard determinism, the viewpoint of Skinner. Since one cannot do otherwise, it becomes all one what one does, Smerdyakov's formula, as Hook suggests, in *The Brothers Karamazov* that "all things are permissable."[46] Thus, a belief in Skinnerian doctrine or that of the extentialists may make a real difference indeed, but not necessarily in support of Skinner's theses. For reasons argued in the main text, humans must base their actions, whatever their belief system, on a lucid account of the world. If Skinner's were such a lucid account, we would be bound to accept it. But it is unconvincing that a position that regards persons as objects rather than as something more than objects will generate cultural survival, as Skinner would have it. At least some psychologists present cogent arguments in favor of the latter program.[47] Skinner avers that

> The individualist can find no solace in reflecting upon any contribution which will survive him. He has refused to act for the good of others and

is therefore not reinforced by the fact that others whom he has helped will outlive him. He has refused to be concerned for the survival of his culture and is not reinforced by the fact that the culture will long survive him. In the defense of his own freedom and dignity he has denied the contributions of the past and must therefore relinquish all claim upon the future.[48]

I leave this argument to stand and fall with little comment; it appears to be inconceivably weak; none of the conclusions follow from any plausible premises. It is logically incoherent. Cannot the individualist be reinforced by the idea that his culture will survive him? Why ever not? As Perelman asks, "Actually, Skinner undertakes to show us that the methods he advocates could lead mankind towards 'wonderful possibilities.' Why not toward 'frightening possibilities'?"[49] And Perelman goes on to note that in the course of history, "all types of conditioning have been used by the men in power in order to get their subjects to submit." Very true. It all depends, by removing purpose from individuals, who is controlling our environment.

Skinner does offer a program through conditioning. The major intent of the program is to preserve society. Indeed, the chief aim of determined individuals is the preservation of the culture in which they live. But there are political cultures and there are political cultures, and there are some of these that do not deserve to survive, in which conditioning for the purpose of cultural survival would be deleterious to life, taken in the broad sense of Chapter 2. One has only to call attention to the political culture of the Third Reich and the regime of the Khmer Rouge.

But does Skinner's point matter anyway? Since there is no human dignity and no freedom, people will go on being conditioned by whatever political culture they are part of, and Skinner's exhortations seem oddly unnecessary. Why exhort people to do what they are bound to do anyway? Or, if people are determined to follow the route of human dignity and mythical freedom, what difference does this make?

Historically, such polities have done as well or better than others, in view of cultural accomplishments. So, if this is so, and people are so conditioned into Skinnerian false beliefs, this is no great problem for society. The person who has been determined to correctly see that everyone is acting in accordance with determined conditioning has only to view the comedy with amusement. Since we are all effectively conditioned whether we will or no, why exhort us to alter our view, since we cannot choose to do so in any case.

Of course, these arguments are unfair to some degree, since the Skinnerian program is obvious: If we understand that the world is conditioned and that people are determined fully to act as they do, we can put into place a scientific program to condition them toward "good" goals set by the conditioners. Thus, the conditioners of society will undertake a scientifically correct program toward social improvement. They will have become the movers of history, Spirit itself. But, alas, what if the conditioned perceive this?

It is not to be expected that this brief appendix has settled anything, but it has set out a few of the issues and differences between the doctrine of human determinism and that of the freedom of the for-itself. As the argument stands at present, some of the evidence for determinism does not sound convincing, while freedom that takes facticity into account seems a better working hypothesis.

Notes

1. King, *Sartre and the Sacred*, p. 23.
2. *Ibid.*, p. 22.
3. Dagfinn Follesdal, "Sartre on Freedom," in Schilipp, ed., *The Philosophy of Jean-Paul Sartre*, p. 395.
4. Frederick A. Olafson, *Principles and Persons: An Ethical Interpretation of Existentialism* (Baltimore: The Johns Hopkins Press, 1967), pp. 67-68.
5. Flynn, *Sartre and Marxist Existentialism*, p. 5. While it is indeed mankind through which a world comes into being, yet, man is also imprisoned in a world, as Sartre comments in "Materialism and Revolution," *Literary and Philosophical Essays* (London: Rider and Company, 1955, Trans. by Annette Michelson), p. 218. This brilliant essay ought to be read prior to tackling his *Critique of Dialectical Reason*.
6. Anthony Manser, *Sartre, a Philosophical Study* (New York: Oxford University Press, 1966), p. 37.
7. *Ibid.*, p. 88.
8. Kamenka describes Marx's later position as that "everything was a 'moment' in the history of its development toward a final end, it could be understood only in terms of its total situation and the total process of which it was part." According to Kemenka, this forces Marx to "minimize any specific human characteristics and to treat men as no more than a reflection or product of social relations." The products of social relations become mere 'reflections' of them. This point is made in the very useful work by Eugene Kamenka, *The Ethical Foundations of Marxism* (London: Routledge and Kegan Paul, 1962), pp. 130-131. Yet, for Marx, mankind also has a creative essence, realizing through praxis his historically given human potentials.

9. Mallin, *Merleau-Ponty's Philosophy*, pp. 88-89. And see also Warren, *The Emergence of Dialectical Theory*, p. 103, and, of course, Merleau-Ponty's own *Phenomenology of Perception* (London: Routledge and Kegan Paul, 1962), p. 453.

10. Phyllis Sutton Morris, *Sartre's Concept of a Person: An Analytic Approach* (Amherst: University of Massachusetts Press, 1976), p. 110. The quotations are from Sartre's *Being and Nothingness*, p. 453 and pp. 436=437. This position of Sartre's may well jibe with Ayer's notion of free will; see A. J. Ayer, "Freedom and Necessity," in his *Philosophical Essays* (London: Macmillan, 1963), pp. 282-283.

11. Luijpen, *Existential Phenomenology*, pp. 227-228. Thus, Sartre has also solved the famous paradox posed by Chuang Tsu, who wondered whether he was a butterfly dreaming he was a human or truly a human who had dreamed that he was a butterfly.

12. *Being and Nothingness*, p. 448.

13. Fell, *Heidegger and Sartre*, p. 156.

14. King, *Sartre and the Sacred*, p. 171. Morris, *Sartre's Concept of a Person*, p. 84, suggests that the existence precedes essence formulation replaces the traditional empiricist view of the "blank slate." This is not quite so; the blank slate view does not posit freedom. It is even the case that our motivations depend on our aims and not the other way around. See Manser, *Sartre*, p. 119.

15. Luijpen, *Existentialist Phenomenology*, p. 378. And so "human reality is condemned never to coincide with itself, to be a perpetual flight toward selfhood by a being that can never 'be itself,'" Jeanson, *Sartre and the Problem of Morality*, pp. 181-182.

16. Natanson, *Jean-Paul Sartre's Ontology*, p. 79.

17. Jeanson, *Sartre and the Problem of Morality*, p. 191.

18. J. R. Lucas, *The Freedom of the Will* (London: Oxford University Press, 1970), p. 87.

19. Paul Weiss, "Common Sense and Beyond," pp. 232-233, in Sidney Hook, ed., *Determinism and Freedom in the Age of Modern Science* (London: Collier-Macmillan, 1961), suggests another view. Determination is the condition of the past, in which all conditions leading to a situation had to be present and fulfilled. Freedom applies to the present and future, in which new conditions are being created and the consequences have not yet become necessitated. Ayer, in his "Freedom and Necessity," pp. 283-284, touches on this point as he presents absolute determinism in the case of the scientist who can predict the exact future for me. But knowing the future, I can now choose to avert it, even at the cost of my own benefit, if I choose. Or one can choose to believe in fate in the sense that my predicted future, as in *Macbeth*, will come about regardless of my struggles. But this is not determinism. It is fatalism, which is a superstition. For this latter point, see R. E. Hobart, "Free Will as Involving Determinism and as Inconceivable Without It," *Mind*, Vol. 43, No. 169 (January 1934), 16.

20. Ayer, "Freedom and Necessity," pp. 282-283. The point was definitively made by Hume, of course.
21. Morris, *Sartre's Concept of a Person*, p. 65.
22. Philippa Foot, *Virtues and Vices* (Berkeley: University of California Press, 1978), p. 62.
23. Karl R. Popper, *The Open Society and Its Enemies, 2 Hegel and Marx* (Princeton, New Jersey: Princeton University Press, 1966), p. 85. We will not elaborate on this point, except to mention that it is understood by anyone working with social statistics and probabilities.
24. Lucas, *The Freedom of the Will*, p. 171. F.S.C. Northrop, "Causation, Determinism, and the 'Good'," in Hook, *Determinism and Freedom*, p. 211, alludes to experimental evidence that the theory of "trapped universals" (attributed to McCulloch and Pitts) expands our understanding of the operation of the nervous system. It may be the case that symbols ("trapped universals") in the cortex integrate and interpret input stimuli to specify the form of a motor response. If so, scientific knowledge is by no means incompatible with moral responsibility. To show that an event was caused is not the same as to prove that it had to happen. The agent could have altered what he did. See also Alasdair MacIntyre, "The Antecedents of Action," in *Against the Self-Images of the Age* (New York: Schocken Books, 1971), p. 208.
25. A more balanced analysis than ours will be found in Morris, *Sartre's Concept of a Person*, pp. 64-80. Less well-balanced, but well reasoned, is Tibor R. Machan, *The Pseudo-Science of B.F. Skinner* (New Rochelle: Arlington House, 1974). For a competent scientist and an engaging writer, however, Skinner grossly fails to dent the doctrine of free will. His approach is sometimes simplistic, and as Machan shows his logic is frequently faulty.
26. Lucas, *The Freedom of the Will*, p. 32.
27. As Ludwig Feuerbach, *Essence of Christianity* (New York: Harper and Row, 1957), p. 3, fn 1, states it, "... in a being which awakes to consciousness, there takes place a qualitative change, a differentiation of the entire nature."
28. B. F. Skinner, *About Behaviorism* (New York: Alfred A. Knopf, 1974), p. 207.
29. *Ibid.*, p. 44.
30. John Macquarrie, *3 Issues in Ethics* (New York: Harper and Row, 1970), p. 92. Macquarrie is a theologian who makes sense.
31. Skinner, *About Behaviorism*, pp. 113-114.
32. *Ibid*, p. 224.
33. B. F. Skinner, *Beyond Freedom and Dignity* (New York: Alfred A. Knopf, 1971), p. 211.
34. *Ibid.*, pp. 94-94.
35. Skinner, *About Behaviorism*, pp. 146-147.
36. See the discussion in Hampshire, *Freedom of Individuals*.
37. Barnes, *An Existentialist Ethics*, pp. 316-317.

38. Morris, *Sartre's Concept of a Person*, p. 78.
39. *Ibid.*, pp. 75-76. See also Rosen, "Can Behavior Be Predicted?" p. 145.
40. Merleau-Ponty, *The Structure of Behavior* (Boston: Beacon Press, 1963), p. 90.
41. John Wilkinson, "How Good Is Current Behavior Theory?," in Harvey Wheeler, ed., *Beyond the Punitive Society* (San Francisco: W. H. Freeman and Company, 1973), p. 150. The remainder of Wilkinson's criticisms are not so strongly worded. Rosen, p. 147 in the same source, suggests that the language of operant conditioning can, in fact, remain perfectly compatible with the language of "freedom and dignity." He points out that such different levels of explication, which apparently contradict one another, are characteristic of "complex, hierarchically organized systems" like those in biology and the human sciences.
42. Skinner, *Beyond Freedom and Dignity*, pp. 146-147.
43. Operant conditioning does have its uses, undeniably. Whether it works or not, however, does not appear to be relevant to the question of free will. Conditioning has been used for centuries, but it does not rule out cognition, which plays no role in Skinner's program. While it is no refutation of operant conditioning, it is no simple mechanical process akin to the repair of a mechanism, as judged by the relapse rates reported among conditioned homosexuals and alcoholics. Some early behavior modification seemed strikingly successful because the follow-up studies were done after only a few months. See Robert L. Geiser, *Behavior Modification and the Managed Society* (Boston: Beacon Press, 1976), pp. 70-71. Geiser himself concludes that conditioning in humans, "far from being automatic, appears to be cognitively mediated," p. 134.
44. Skinner, *Beyond Freedom and Dignity*, p. 165. It is difficult to imagine that this would make any difference at all in Skinner's deterministic world. Who should care how objects interact?
45. Jerry E. Phares, *Locus of Control in Personality* (Morristown: General Learning Press, 1976), p. 92.
46. Hook, *Determinism and Freedom*, p. 191.
47. Gerald N. Izenberg, *The Existentialist Critique of Freud: The Crisis of Autonomy* (Princeton: Princeton University Press, 1976), p. 278. Note his discussion of Binswanger. His Chapter 6, "Authenticity as an Ethic and as a Concept of Health" is brilliant.
48. Skinner, *Beyond Freedom and Dignity*, p. 210.
49. Chaim Perelman, "Behaviorism's Enlightened Despotism," in Harvey Wheeler, ed., *Beyond the Punitive Society* (San Francisco: W. H. Freeman and Company, 1973), p. 124.